Conversations in Maine

Published in collaboration with the Boggs Center, whose mission is to nurture the transformational leadership capacities of individuals and organizations committed to creating productive, sustainable, ecologically responsible, and just communities.

Conversations in Maine
/ A New Edition /

JAMES BOGGS and GRACE LEE BOGGS

LYMAN PAINE and FREDDY PAINE

Foreword by Shea Howell and Stephen Ward

Introduction by Richard Feldman

Reflections Compiled by Michael Doan

University of Minnesota Press
Minneapolis / London

Published by the University of Minnesota Press
111 Third Avenue South, Suite 290
Minneapolis, MN 55401-2520
http://www.upress.umn.edu

Printed in the United States of America on acid-free paper

The University of Minnesota is an equal-opportunity educator and employer.

25 24 23 22 21 20 19 18   10 9 8 7 6 5 4 3 2 1

LIBRARY OF CONGRESS CATALOGING-IN-PUBLICATION DATA
Names: Boggs, James, author. | Boggs, Grace Lee, author.
Title: Conversations in Maine : a new edition / James Boggs and Grace Lee Boggs, Lyman Paine and Freddy Paine ; foreword by Shea Howell and Stephen Ward; introduction by Richard Feldman ; reflections compiled by Michael Doan.
Description: Minneapolis : University of Minnesota Press, 2018. | Originally published: Boston : South End Press, c1978. | Includes bibliographical references.
Identifiers: LCCN 2018024543 | ISBN 9781517905842 (paperback)
Subjects: LCSH: United States—Civilization—1945– | United States—Social conditions— 1945– | BISAC: POLITICAL SCIENCE / Political Ideologies / Communism & Socialism.
Classification: LCC E169.12 .C587 2018 | DDC 973.92—dc23
LC record available at https://lccn.loc.gov/2018024543

Contents

Foreword

Carry It On

SHEA HOWELL AND STEPHEN WARD

The voices that weave through these conversations are gone now. Each one has fallen silent. Yet the questions they raised a half century ago linger, taking on new meaning for people thinking about the crisis we face today and our uncertain future. These voices challenge us to think anew. They invite us to engage in developing the ideas and actions necessary to create the second American Revolution based on values of caring for one another and the earth that sustains us.

It was the challenge of revolution that first brought these four people together in the middle of the twentieth century and led them to the creative process of asking questions and engaging in conversations that are documented in this book. The conversations are at once the sign and substance of a remarkable comradeship developed over three decades among four people with a shared movement experience and a collectively held commitment to continual reflection as a crucial component of revolutionary theory. As Rich Feldman describes in the book's original introduction, they came from distinct social backgrounds and together cut a magnificent swath through the American society they resolved to transform. Through their conversations, these voices call us to participate in the ongoing struggle to transform our world.

Of the four voices, the most recognizable to today's activists is that of Grace Lee Boggs. Her distinctive cadence and tone are captured in the documentary film *American Revolutionary: The Evolution of Grace Lee Boggs,* and she is easily accessible in interviews and video clips commenting on contemporary issues. In exchanges with Amy Goodman, Bill Moyers, Angela Davis, Vincent Harding, and Immanuel Wallerstein we hear her ask, "What time is it on the clock of the world?" Through her speeches and interactions with community activists, students, and others across the country, Grace encouraged us to do more thinking and less acting; to ask ourselves questions; to consider the philosophy of nonviolence, not just the tactic; to truly contemplate what it means to change ourselves to change our world. In her writings, including the book *The Next American Revolution: Sustainable Activism for the Twenty-First Century*, published in 2011, Grace urged us to be for something, not just against the way things are; not to get stuck in old ideas; to see relationships as essential for ourselves and our communities; and to become the leaders we are looking for.[1] When she passed away at the age of one hundred in October 2015, Grace's enduring call for us to embrace our responsibility to create the world anew had long resonated with various activist communities.[2] Many of the ideas she articulated now flow through the emerging movements of the twenty-first century. You will find them echoed in the closing reflections at the end of this book as people struggle with the ideas and challenges embodied in *Conversations*.

Grace would be the first to say that these ideas are not hers alone. She believed in the power of ideas, and she emphasized that they were not created in isolation, but rather were developed collaboratively, in the context of social movements, political organizations, and local communities. She often quoted James Boggs, her husband and comrade of four decades, who said that we only become "somebody" through our relationship with the "other bodies and many somebodies" in our lives.[3] And the somebodies that mattered most to Grace were those who gathered for Conversations in Maine.

The relationship among the four of them and the history of political struggle they shared began in the 1940s. Grace, Frances "Freddy" Paine, and Lyman Paine developed into revolutionaries during that decade as members of a Marxist political collective in New York, while Jimmy forged his revolutionary commitments as an auto worker, union organizer, and community activist in Detroit. Grace came to Detroit in the early 1950s to work on *Correspondence*, the newspaper of the organization. Jimmy had recently joined the organization, and in 1953 he and Grace began their marital, intellectual, and political partnership. Freddy and Lyman grew to be their closest comrades. The two couples weathered successive organizational splits over the next decade, as they deepened and solidified their personal and political ties. These ties formed the basis of trusted relationships that would later animate their Maine conversations.[4]

Correspondence initially emphasized the revolutionary capacity of rank-and-file industrial workers, but during the late 1950s and early 1960s the group increasingly focused on the rising struggle for Black liberation in the United States. *Correspondence* chronicled the racial consciousness, grassroots insurgency, and local political struggles erupting across the country. For example, in the late 1950s the biweekly paper offered some of the earliest and most comprehensive analysis of Robert and Mabel Williams as they resisted segregation, challenged the moderation of established Black leadership, confronted KKK violence, and organized the Black community to protect and defend itself in Monroe, North Carolina. At the beginning of the 1960s, *Correspondence* highlighted what it described as a "rising tide of Afro-American nationalism," presaging in many ways the emergence of Black Power mid-decade. In January 1963 *Correspondence* asserted that Black people were "the ones best-suited to govern the United States today" in the lead headline of its special Emancipation Proclamation issue. "Anyone who knows the Negro community knows that the greatest emancipation is taking place among those Negroes who are proud of their blackness and separateness," the publication pronounced. "By stressing rejection of the institutions of American society rather than seeking integration into them, these Negroes are achieving an unparalleled freedom and independence of thought."[5] With Grace serving as its editor and Jimmy doing much of the writing in the paper, they used *Correspondence* as a vehicle for both building a network of activists and documenting local struggles.

Indeed, Grace and James became increasingly involved in struggles for Black self-determination in Detroit during the 1960s. Working closely with Detroit activists such as Rev. Albert Cleage (later Jaramogi Abebe Agyeman), who led Central Congregational Church (later named the Shrine of the Black Madonna), and with brothers Richard Henry and Milton Henry (later Imari Obadele and Gaidi Obadele) and their organization, the Group on Advanced Leadership (GOAL), the Boggses fought against segregation, union corruption, and police violence. They organized for community control of schools and for an independent Black political party. They helped organize the massive "Freedom Walk" down Woodward Avenue, where Dr. Martin Luther King gave his first "I Have a Dream" speech in June 1963. That fall they led the effort to hold the Northern Negro Grass Roots Leadership Conference in Detroit, where Malcolm X gave his oft quoted "Message to the Grass Roots" speech. Grace served as its secretary and Jimmy chaired the conference.[6]

The four had faced the killings of Medgar Evers, John Kennedy, and Malcolm X. They had seen the violence of Selma and the bombings of Birmingham. They had seen the uprising in Lyman and Freddy's home city of Los Angeles as Watts exploded. They began to talk about an accelerating revolutionary period and the importance of facing this new reality. They imbued their activity and organizing with a profound respect for ideas and for the capacity of human beings to reflect on their world as a source of deepening their understanding of what needed to be done.

The summer of 1967 marked a turning point in their conception of revolutionary struggle. That July Grace and Jimmy drove to Los Angeles, as they often did, to spend their vacation with Freddy and Lyman. While they were there, the Detroit rebellion erupted: Black residents took to the streets protesting police brutality and long-standing racial oppression. The Detroit rebellion was by most measures the largest and most consequential uprising of the so-called long hot summers. It propelled President Lyndon Johnson to create the National Advisory Commission on Civil Disorders (known as the Kerner Commission), and it exposed as false the image of Detroit as a "model city." Jimmy and Grace had known tensions in the city were reaching a breaking point. In her autobiography, Grace recalls that when they left for Los Angeles Jimmy advised members of an organization they had recently founded to be on guard for an uprising. Jimmy and Grace knew very well that the Detroit rebellion could happen. When it did, however, they found themselves confronting new questions, both practical and theoretical. The Detroit rebellion set in motion a series of important political developments and pushed Grace and Jimmy to a new set of theoretical reflections that would give their gatherings in Maine a unique urgency, significance, and purpose.

By the summer of 1967 Lyman, Freddy, Jimmy, and Grace had already made significant breaks with the dominant thinking in the radical movement. During the 1950s, as anticommunism flourished, they faced an urgent question. Should they continue their work openly and aboveground, or should they move underground? Jimmy and Lyman led the struggle to remain aboveground and advocate for an American Revolution. Lyman, a descendant of Robert Treat Paine, one of the signers of the Declaration of Independence, claimed a revolutionary heritage. Jimmy boldly and frequently said his ancestors had built this land with their blood, sweat, and tears, and he refused to give in to fear. Each of them asserted it was their right and their responsibility to change the country.

The second challenge to their collective thinking was Jimmy's book, *The American Revolution: Pages from a Negro Worker's Notebook*. Published in 1963, it had been originally written as an internal document of the Correspondence organization. Upon reading it for their annual convention, C. L. R. James, the celebrated Marxist theorist and writer, and one of the founding leaders of the group, sent a telegram to the four, saying he was breaking with them personally and politically.

Jimmy had been working in the Chrysler plant for nearly three decades, and in *The American Revolution,* he challenged the Marxist ideas of the working class as the primary social force for change. Reflecting on the dramatic changes in production brought about by automation, Jimmy wrote about the creation of a permanent class of "outsiders" no longer needed to produce goods. It was these outsiders, especially African Americans, who he thought would pose the greatest challenges to capitalism and who held the greatest potential for revolutionary change. Jimmy also argued that the increasing capitalist technologies were producing abundant material goods, so that the American Revolution would not be about what more people would get. It would be the first revolution about what people would give up.

These changing conditions in production, the evolving revolutionary struggles in the colonized world, and the question of material and human relationships caused the four, especially Jimmy, to say that "we must now do for our time what Marx did for his." They believed it was time to reflect on the experiences since World War II, the development of automation, and the emerging social forces to create a new theory of revolution. So in letters, meetings, and conversations the four took up the task of creating new revolutionary theory.

But with the rebellion of 1967, they were stunned to realize they had never really questioned what they meant by the word revolution. They had questioned much of Marx and his theories of change, but they had never asked themselves what they meant by revolution. This question was forced on them as they watched the aftermath of the rebellion unfold in the community. The early feelings of brotherhood, pride, and unity gave way to suspicion, antisocial behaviors, and fear of one another. The Black community was transforming into a dangerous place. Jimmy often said that prior to the rebellion the Black community was the safest place in America. But afterward, people became afraid of one another, locked in a cycle of fear.

In the summer of 1968, a few months after the death of Martin Luther King and a series of uprisings across the country, the four gathered in Maine to ask themselves the hard questions of what they meant by revolution. Was it the same as a rebellion? What was it for? In raising fundamental questions, they began together, from their different lives and experiences, to probe the question of a distinctively American Revolution, rooted not in the experiences of Europe or the theories of change developed in other countries but in the history and development of this country. They argued that the only purpose of a revolution is to advance humankind, to make us more human human beings. They said that revolution is not a universal project, but that it emerges as people choose to confront the specific contradictions and histories of their own time and place.

For nearly a decade they continued to explore ideas of revolution and the future of America. For Grace and Jimmy, the conversations helped focus and expand their thinking, resulting in some of their most influential writings: *Racism and the Class Struggle, Education to Govern, But What about the Workers?, Manifesto for a Black Revolutionary Party,* and *Revolution and Evolution in the Twentieth Century.*

Lyman and Freddy remained their collaborators and conversation partners, but increasingly Lyman's health deteriorated and Freddy spent much of her time caring for him. Their home in Holgate Square became a hub of conversation for young people looking for meaning and political action. "Little Sur" attracted artists, community organizers, neighbors, and old comrades. Freddy engaged in local struggles such as the effort to save Elysian Park from development, and increasingly she worked with young women awakening to a new sense of political power. For Lyman conversations became his primary political action. Especially the young men and women seeking new ways of living brought him new questions, engaging his thinking and rethinking of old ideas. These experiences provided ideas and actions to probe together each summer in the quiet of Sutton Island, Maine.

Jimmy and Grace provided a similar conversation home in Detroit. Field Street, long a hub of radical activity in the city, became a place where young radicals went for new ideas and to discuss strategies and tactics. Emphasizing the pivotal role of Black leadership, Jimmy and Grace moved toward the building of a national Black revolutionary organization. Much of their organizing and ideas evolved around the kitchen table as they gathered with people to talk.

In the summer of 1976 the four had come to believe the movements of the 1960s were over. The country was facing a deep crisis that was not only economic but also spiritual. The radical left was fragmented and drifting from issue to issue. The Black Power and civil rights movements were no longer asking what should be the relationships between human beings, but rather people were moving to advance themselves. Few people were engaged in the serious thinking that needed to be done to create an American Revolution. So with the encouragement and support of many of the young people who had gathered around Grace and Jimmy in Detroit, they decided to release *Conversations in Maine* as a book. South End Press agreed to publish it. They hoped *Conversations* would be an invitation and a challenge to activists to recognize that ideas mattered. They needed to evolve through reflection and talk. There was no blueprint for revolution, but we needed to engage with each other to develop ourselves and our country.

In the summer of 1977, Grace and Jimmy invited Richard Feldman to join them in Maine. As a young activist from the antiwar movement and worker in a Ford plant, Rich would have the task of writing an introduction (included in this volume) to speak to his generation of activists about their responsibilities to think anew about what kind of country we could become.

In the spring of 1978, Lyman died shortly after getting one of the first copies of *Conversations in Maine*. His last words to Grace were, "Carry it on." And so they did. Shea Howell joined them that summer and every summer since for the ongoing conversation.

In 1986 some of the folks working with Jimmy and Grace in

the National Organization for an American Revolution decided it was important to capture on film the three remaining members of the original conversations. West Coast comrade Nancy Vogel organized to bring filmmaker Frances Reid and her crew to Sutton. Freddy somewhat reluctantly agreed. For nearly a week cameras followed the three of them, capturing Grace reading to Freddy as she made cranberry sauce, Jimmy working on his path to the beach, drinks at the boathouse, and Freddy dancing to the theme song of *Fiddler on the Roof*. Working, arguing, eating, and laughing together, Frances also captured conversations with each of the three as they recalled forces, people, and times that shaped their lives.

Every summer in August people came to talk. Roberto Mendoza talked of the role of art and indigenous struggles, ultimately publishing *Look! A Nation Is Coming! Native Americans and the Second American Revolution*; James Jackson, a comrade since the days of the Michigan Freedom Party, shared ideas on organizational struggles. Ossie Davis and Ruby Dee, activists, artists, teachers, young people, comrades, carpenters, and stonemasons were invited to talk. But the Conversations were more than talk. They were a form of political action. Books and articles were selected to guide our thinking; questions were formulated to push us to reflect on practice; and discussions were recorded, transcribed, and shared, often forming the basis for later publications.

In 1991 Jimmy was diagnosed with cancer. The summer of 1992 would prove to be his last in Maine. Vincent and Rosemarie Harding came to spend several days with him. Vincent and Jimmy talked together often, walking slowly through the woods or at the beach. Jimmy had promised the young people of the first Detroit Summer '92 that he would be with them "next year," and he was. Frail, trailing an oxygen tank, he spoke at the opening and closing ceremonies. Freddy and Shea had made arrangements to exchange oxygen tanks along the drive from Detroit to Maine and all prepared for another conversation. But Jimmy died in July. That summer in Maine, the first without him, Grace was inconsolable. Only Micah Feldman, still a child, could get her to talk about Jimmy and the pain of losing him.

It was the young people of Detroit Summer who began to take up the responsibilities for conversations with Grace and Freddy. Sometimes as individuals, sometimes in small groups, they gathered on

Sutton to talk, share ideas, reflect on what we were learning, and what new possibilities were emerging in Detroit. In 1999 Freddy died, leaving the house in Maine to Shea and her friends Dan and Sally Wigutow. For the next ten years, Grace, as the last of the four, continued to come to Sutton, inspiring young people, arguing over ideas, making popovers, and pushing us all to think. In 2003 a group of young Asian American activists, mostly from Detroit, joined Grace for a conversation recorded by the filmmaker Grace Lee. Much of this footage appears in the documentary *American Revolutionary*. Also during this time Scott Kurashige, Emily Lawsin, and their daughter, Tulla, came to Maine as Scott collaborated with Grace on her final book, *The Next American Revolution*. Stephen Ward also came to spend time with her as he prepared for the first of his biographies of Jimmy and Grace, *In Love and Struggle*. Emma Fialka-Feldman, now an educator-activist, began bringing a group of urban educators to hold conversations on the purpose of education.

In October 2015 Grace died at home on Field Street, in the house where so many people had gathered over the years to talk together. In the last months of her life, as people came to play music, read poetry, and offer news of the day, she continued to ask questions.

Today we face questions that challenge our deepest thoughts, hopes, fears, and imaginations. What does democracy look like? What kind of revolution do we need? How do we evolve our spiritual capacities for connection, compassion, and care? What are human beings for? How will we live and make a living in ways that develop whole communities and protect the earth? What kind of people do we want to become?

Conversations in Maine is a book of questions, not answers. It challenges all of us to see that the world is constantly changing and that our ideas must change with it. It affirms that new ideas take time. It invites us to see that in moments of great transitions such as this one, what we do matters. What we think matters. We have the obligation to use our distinctively human capacities to reflect, project, and act to make the kind of future we want for ourselves and our world.

Detroit, Michigan
July 2018

Notes

1. Grace Lee Boggs with Scott Kurashige, *The Next American Revolution: Sustainable Activism for the Twenty-First Century* (Berkeley: University of California Press, 2011). See also Grace Lee Boggs, *Living for Change: An Autobiography* (Minneapolis: University of Minnesota Press, 1998).

2. For an example of this resonance and influence, see Adrienne Maree Brown, *Emergent Strategy: Shaping Change, Changing Worlds* (Chino, Calif.: AK Press, 2017), 20, 27–28, 44, 53, 167–68, 262–63. Brown dedicates the book to Grace's memory and to the memory of Detroit activist Charity Hicks. Of Grace Brown writes, "I dedicate this book to the memory of Grace Lee Boggs, who opened the door to emergence and pushed me through, who taught me to keep listening and learning and having conversations. She said, 'Transform yourself to transform the world.' "

3. Quotation from the videotape of Community Celebration of James and Grace Lee Boggs, May 1990, in both authors' possession. Grace describes this celebration in Boggs, *Living for Change,* 227–28.

4. For a discussion of this period, see Stephen M. Ward, *In Love and Struggle: The Revolutionary Lives of James and Grace Lee Boggs* (Chapel Hill: University of North Carolina Press, 2016), chapters 2, 4, and 5.

5. These quotations are from an editorial titled "Why This Issue?" in the special Emancipation issue, *Correspondence,* January 1963, 2. With this issue, the paper shifted from biweekly to monthly publication.

6. For more on this period, see Boggs, *Living for Change,* chapter 5, and Ward, *In Love and Struggle,* chapter 10 and the Epilogue.

Conversations in Maine

Preface

This preface was written by Marilyn Becker and Fred Miller, who transcribed and edited the original Conversations *for publication by South End Press in 1977.*

We were introduced to these Conversations shortly after having read the book *Revolution and Evolution in the Twentieth Century* by James and Grace Lee Boggs. That book for both of us had represented a leap forward. Suddenly a lot of old questions, like how to apply Marx, Lenin and Mao to America, came into perspective. Many new questions surfaced: What was the American revolution to be about? Who was the class or group that would make that revolution? What were we and other Americans missing in our lives? What was needed to transform ourselves and our country?

The Conversations helped us to deepen our understanding of the complex process we would have to go through in developing a theory of revolution for America. When the opportunity arose to have the Conversations made into a book, we agreed to edit it.

Neither of us are "editors." Rather we are activists—veterans of the antiwar and women's movements.

In editing we have tried to retain the flavor of the Conversations. Although the actual dialogue between participants has been eliminated, the differences in style of speech are evident. We did not try to tone down the statements made during these conversations. We feel that the boldness of the generalizations, drawn from more than forty years spent in struggle as well as in thought, compel us all to rethink our assumptions about revolutionary social change and our own lives.

The Conversations began during a summer vacation in 1968. The first taped discussion in 1970 was only partially recorded and transcribed, and this made for a somewhat compressed section. The discussions in years following (except for 1973) were more fully recorded and transcribed. The book ends with the 1974 conversations, although the conversations have been and still are in process.

We had a hard time deciding how to handle the references to "man" and "mankind" that are so central to the Conversations. It was obvious that the participants' awareness of sexism in language developed over the four years. We wanted the book to reflect that development. The language was therefore left as spoken until the latter part of the book; after their discussion of language and sexism in 1972, we edited to eliminate any remaining sexist references.

Throughout the Conversations particular books, music, artists, and writers are mentioned. The variety of sources used by the participants is a lesson in and of itself. They have not bypassed thinkers and observers because they are not socialists or revolutionaries. A list of the books referred to can be found at the end of this volume.

Transforming the dittoed copies of the Conversations into this book took energy and hard work. We would like to thank the following people for their assistance: Andi Barchas, Ruth Gladstone, David Maki, Betty Thomas Mayen, Laura Siller, Pat Walker, John Willems, and Susan Zaro.

The *Conversations in Maine* are not a finished product; they are not a blueprint for what we must do. For us they were a beginning; they stimulated us to reflect and reexamine the philosophy and positions we had developed. We hope they will stimulate new thinking in everyone about the future of America and the meaning of revolution, that they will be the impetus for thousands of other conversations throughout the country, conversations that will help us all do what we can to make our country a more human place to live.

Detroit, Michigan
December 1977

Introduction

RICHARD FELDMAN

> No radicals are going to get power in this country until we have
> converted a whole lot of people to recognize that they are their
> own jailers; that they take the prison of their own selves with them
> wherever they go; and that they are not going to be free until they
> have decided what they are going to do with their freedom.
> —*Conversations in Maine* (1972)

I read the *Conversations in Maine* during the spring of 1974. It was a critical time in my life. In the four years since I had left the University of Michigan campus I had worked in a factory with the idea of becoming one with the workers and giving them leadership. But I found that only a minimal number of people would involve themselves in militant struggles against health and safety violations, racism, sexism, production speed-up, or union corruption. Those few militants have become the present union leadership in my local. Meanwhile, they and other workers challenged me with questions such as: What is socialism? What will revolution mean to my life? What would revolution mean for my family and neighborhood? They would ask me: "Why are you working in a plant?" and "What is your vision of the future?" Beyond referring rhetorically to China or Vietnam there was little that I was able to say.

During the sixties I was actively involved in the movement against the war in Vietnam. I was in Chicago during the Democratic National Convention in 1968 and at Dupont Circle and the Justice Department in Washington in 1969. My life had been changed by my involvement in support of the black power movement, the women's movement and the struggle against the Reserve Officer Training

Corps (R.O.T.C.) and on-campus military recruiters. I had rebelled against all the standards and expectations that society and my family had projected for me. I had broken with my past goals of becoming a professional and with my past dreams and life-style. I was one of the radicals of the post-war "Pepsi generation," the "rootless generation," the "do-it-now generation" moving around the country, breaking with our families and our communities. While most Americans were looking for individual "get rich quick schemes," we were searching for a fast answer to our problems and the problems of society.

By 1974, the sixties had become history. Many of my friends were either returning to school or joining Marxist-Leninist organizations. Searching for relevant politics and a vision of the future, I went from meeting to meeting. In study groups on the writings of Marx, Lenin, and Mao, I sought an answer to the question: How do we develop a revolutionary struggle in this country, a country where auto workers make $15,000 a year and on their coffee breaks smoke dope, drink beer, play cards, and discuss each other's family problems?

The first thing that struck me about the Conversations was their close relationship to the reality that I was experiencing in the plant and in the community. The daily concerns of people are not limited to their workplace: How does making money six days a week resolve the crisis on the streets where nearly everyone has been either a criminal or a victim of crime? What kind of education can children get in schools where security guards roam the halls, where teachers are "baby sitters," students are "doing time," and parents take no responsibility for their children's education? What is education for? What kind of family relationships should people strive to build? We don't see any point to the work we do; yet instead of talking about *that* we complain to our union representative about grease on the floor or company unfairness. Despite the increased availability of health benefits, the health of most of us is degenerating.

While people often talked about these concerns, their talk was dominated by cynicism and apathy. When I tried to get them involved in a struggle against management, the main argument ran: "What's the use of getting involved!" or "Why should I work if I can hustle my way through life?" As I read the Conversations I began to see that all I had been doing was pointing out the injustices in our society. I had been deepening and increasing the helplessness and victim mentality of people because I had not been encouraging the self-respect they need in order to rise to their potential.

The Conversations brought me face to face with the liberalism of myself and my radical friends. They challenged every premise that I had accepted as being legitimate for all revolutions at all times. The complexity of revolution was being brought home to me at the same time that I was getting new insight into the complex and confusing reality that I was experiencing.

I was struck by how American the Conversations were. Against the traditional concept of politics, they counterposed the need to unite ethics, morals, and politics. Can politics that are not ethical be revolutionary? This question challenges not only the Machiavellian principle that the end justifies the means but also the sixties' concept that to be an outlaw in the eyes of America is the badge of a revolutionary. I could no longer evade this question.

I realized how I had shut out of my life and thoughts the ideas of people who wonder about where our world is going. Until 1974, I rarely read any books which didn't completely concur with the concepts of revolution that I had already accepted and which were based on the realities and development of countries very different from my own.

The Conversations affected me in much the same way as my introduction to the movement of the sixties did. A new perspective was opening up that provided me with a direction from which to evaluate and question the world philosophically. Not that the Conversations were or are a bible; I came to these conclusions only after many months of struggle, discussion, and thinking. My first reaction after reading the Conversations was one of confusion. As I reread them this past summer I relived the turmoil I had undergone during my first reading. The margins in my copy are full of such questions as: What about revolutionary power? What about Marx and Lenin? What about economics?

I would not have read the *Conversations in Maine* had I not come across the Advocator's pamphlet *What about the Workers?* This pamphlet impressed me as describing very accurately the situation in my plant, where we had just finished our national contract struggle in the fall of 1973. It was the first piece of literature I circulated in the plant to which people responded by saying, "I thought the guys who wrote this pamphlet worked in our plant" and "It's definitely telling it like it is." People did not necessarily agree with the pamphlet's goals or its conclusions on the need for fundamental revolutionary change, but they recognized themselves in the descriptions of workers.

I was curious to discuss my questions with the authors, and that is how I got to know James Boggs. Jimmy is different from any radical I have ever met. Before we would start to talk about a particular political issue, he would ask me about my job, my car, my friends, my living situations. He would suggest solutions to various problems and would help fix the plumbing or the car, but only after he thought that I had made an effort myself.

James Boggs is self-educated and can remember the days when he chopped wood for every-day survival. He has developed himself as a philosopher who emphasizes the importance of slowly and patiently building an organization so that every member is critically responsible and able to contribute both theory and practice to the future that we must work to create. Using examples from either his days as a young boy in the rural south or as a Detroit auto-worker, he will develop historically the most complex political questions in simple language and with vivid descriptions. Dedicated to building a *revolutionary* organization of Americans to govern our country, he is also a citizen of his community—sharing with people who do not agree with most of his ideas. He constantly says, "I can live in the same community with people who disagree with me but that does not mean they should be in my organization."

Jimmy was born in Alabama in 1919, lived in the South until his late teens, and rode the rails across the country during the depression. In 1938 he settled in Detroit where he worked at Chrysler twenty-eight years. He was active in the union movement, the radical Marxist movement, and, during the sixties, in the black movement. The years after the 1967 rebellion were a period of travel, writing, and reflection for both James and Grace Lee Boggs. They visited Italy and France during the spring of 1968 and had the opportunity to spend a week with Nkrumah in Conakry, exploring the reasons why the Ghanian masses whom Nkrumah had mobilized against British colonialism later turned against him.

The twenty-five year marriage of the Boggs is intriguing partly because they are so very different. Grace is a Chinese American born in New England and formally educated at Barnard College and at Bryn Mawr, from which she received a doctorate in philosophy in 1940. Throughout her involvement in the Marxist movement in the forties and fifties and in the black movement in the sixties, she has maintained a special interest in questions of education.

What excited me about knowing Grace was her readiness to read and discuss any topic by any author from any period in the history of humanity. Every time I call or visit her, she brings forth new insights to share with me—or says: "We must begin to think about this question in a new way." Or she is typing notes from her reading and ditting copies so others can share in her discoveries. Grace will discuss what was once considered heretical by most radicals—religion, the Gettysburg Address, the family, or morality. Yet no discussion is so important that you don't first have some homemade pie or taste some Chinese delicacy that she has prepared.

Because she had been a serious Marxist-Leninist, and had broken with that tradition, Grace was patient with me as I struggled painfully to break with old ideas. At the same time she made it clear that I had to make a choice; I could no longer straddle both worlds.

This past summer as I was preparing this Introduction I had the opportunity to go to Maine to meet the other two participants in the Conversations. Freddy Paine met me at the Bar Harbor airport. As we drove to the ferry that would take us to the island, she began to share her past with me. She grew up a Jewish orphan with only a third grade education. As a young woman in the late twenties, she lived in New York City near Union Square where she could hear the "commies" on their soap boxes during her lunch break. She became a union activist, organizing in the New York garment district and the anthracite coal mines of West Virginia and Pennsylvania. She also worked with women's support groups during the Auto-lite sit-down strike in Toledo, Ohio, in the thirties. Freddy was clearly the organizer of the foursome.

One evening as we fixed dinner, Freddy and I continued our discussion about her life. The way she talked about her union organizing and political experiences revealed the importance she placed on ethics and moral–political leadership. As she spoke of A. J. Muste and the American Worker's Party of the early 1930s, I was struck again by our need to act and think like Americans if we are to make an American revolution. Freddy has never been a heavy ideologue or "worldly so-phisticated politico." From the beginning, her decisions to affiliate or to split from organizations were based chiefly on the seriousness and the ethics of political leaders. Listening to Freddy talk about herself and her experiences over the past fifty years, I couldn't help wondering just how unique our generation is, and how often we must repeat the mistakes of the past. Her political work and life-style as an activist did not seem so different from some of the experiences and issues of the late sixties and early seventies: Should we live as couples, in a household with other people, or with other couples? What kind of family should we have?

She would take me around Sutton Island every day, walking so fast I could not keep up. I found myself asking this woman of sixty-five to slow down so I could enjoy the scenery. At other times Freddy would say, "Enjoy the island and quit talking so much."

I spent three days at the Paines' house on Sutton Island, one of the Cranberry Isles off Mt. Desert Island. It has no cars and only twenty houses, some of which date back 100 to 150 years. We walked over and around the island hunting mushrooms and berries. One day we picked apples for apple pie, another day at low tide we gathered mussels for an evening snack. The fireplace in one 150-year-old house we visited is ten feet long and had once been used for cooking. Many of the paths are built of stones, carried by people in wheelbarrows. From all this I got a sense not only of living tradition but of the need to move slowly and think carefully in developing new ideas.

The Paine house was once the island schoolhouse, and the school's picture of Ralph Waldo Emerson still hangs in the living room. Lyman's roots are deep in the New England tradition. Robert Treat Paine, one of the signers of the Declaration of Independence, was an early ancestor, and Lyman's father, who lived to be ninety-one, is buried in the tiny island cemetery. One cool night I put on a tweed jacket that Lyman's father had worn on his honeymoon in 1896. This small incident made me aware of the thoughtlessness of throwing something away just because it's old and made me understand the pride in quality work that Lyman is always stressing.

Lyman graduated from Harvard in the early 1920s. He got involved in politics in the WPA (Work Projects Administration) days as an unemployed architect. Today at seventy-six he is a very tall, white-bearded Yankee who says passionately and unreservedly that he is proud of the work he has done, proud to be an American, and proud of his humanity. He questions everything and believes that the most crucial thing in life is for people "to give a damn."

One evening after I had returned from a walk along the rock-lined shore, Lyman asked me what I liked about the island. When I said that I liked the quiet, he asked me in quick succession, "Why is quiet important? How could the national parks be quiet? Should cities be quiet?" Very simple questions, yet each challenged me to ask a chain of questions of myself and others. Lyman not only asked questions but paid close attention to each reply. Although physically weak from emphysema, he never said anything that he didn't mean with every bone in his body. His critical responses toward every word or comment that he considered inaccurate or superficial often bordered on arrogance, yet they clearly stemmed from his challenge to others to be as bold and demanding of themselves as he is of himself. Lyman is the elder statesman in the Conversations.

At night we listened to a jazz album during dinner and to another piece of music before going to bed. On the last evening as we listened to Duke Ellington's *Concert of Sacred Music* the need for each of us to strive to realize our human potential became very real to me. Lyman spoke with feeling about the album and about the way each musician separately and as part of a collective was "perfect" (another favorite word) and proud of his/her skills and creativity. An American citizen and an American patriot, full of love for human potential and anger at human waste: this is Lyman Paine. His respect for people, whether they are involved in political work or not, helped me to appreciate how all kinds of people will help to create a new way of life in this country.

The strength of the Conversations derives in large part from the diversity in background of the participants and their commitment to developing new ideas slowly and patiently, their bold positions on the potential of human beings, and their readiness to criticize themselves and examine unreservedly their own process. The ideas developed in the Conversations are not a blueprint nor are they final answers. They are a beginning. Freddy, Grace, Jimmy, and Lyman are four individuals who have worked together and shared each other's lives for almost forty years. Their passion for life and their sensitivity to human searching have created a basis on which we can create a unifying vision for the future.

During the past three years, I have urged as many people as possible to read *Conversations in Maine*. I am delighted that they will now be available in a more readable and permanent form that will encourage a continuing dialogue in the movement to create a new America.

A few themes come to mind as most important to my personal growth over the past few years. In the past we have struggled to make an abstract or general revolution; now we must work to create an American revolution. We need to understand the uniqueness of our own history—our development as a nation from early colonial days to the present has been radically different from that of European nations.

Rather than accepting a Marxist revolution as the solution to our problems in much the same way as Christians have enshrined Christianity, we need to begin to understand that there is no predetermined scenario and to see revolution as a complex process that is part of the social evolution of humankind.

The Conversations challenge us to open our minds to the ideas and philosophy of people who are not usually seen as revolutionaries— and to expand our thinking to include the writings of people such as Chardin, Mumford, Malraux, Melville, and Schumacher, and the works of artists like Ellington and Dvorak.

In the sixties, we romanticized that revolution was a few years away. The conversations project the need for us to develop a larger view of time and begin to internalize the patient process of changing our thoughts and actions as we attempt to move forward to build a movement of people.

As we and our friends become parents, the year 2050 when our children will be seventy years old becomes less abstract. What kind of human beings are we projecting? What kind of family? What kind of community and nation? What kind of world?

Towards the future.
Fall 1977

Toward a New Man

What is the purpose of revolution?

To give man a new sense of history?
To restore the sense of time?
To compel man to make responsible choices?*
To create a new relationship between necessity and choice?

Can we say any more that man's social being determines his consciousness, his sensibilities, his awareness? Can a worker or a black be exonerated from responsibility because of his class (or underclass)? Are the ideas and contributions of whites and aristocrats to be rejected out of hand because of their class origins? Or are the ideas and actions to be judged on their merits in relation to advancing humanity, regardless of class origins?

In a revolutionary period, the only exit is the revolution. A coup d'etat is not a revolution. A revolution is a specific form of the evolution of man. The only justification for a revolution is that it advances the evolution of man. It is a moment in the evolutionary process, both the result of long preparation and of something profoundly original, new. Without a long period for maturing, no profound change can take place; but every profound change is at the same time a break with the past.

Mankind today needs to redefine appropriate social relations. This can't be done by plebiscite. It must be done by particular kinds of people projecting another way to live and testing it against certain layers, classes, races.

We are at the threshold of a new relationship between necessity and choice. But what does any American know about necessity?

---

*See the Preface for comments from the editors regarding the use of the word "man."

Necessity and choice used to be clearly separate. Today the borders between the two are no longer clear; one can't be defined without the other; necessity can't be defined except in relation to choice. Once you accept the idea that one is free of necessity, then you choose out of possible choices.

A great many people have said, although not all of them mean the same thing by it, that technological man has greatly outstripped moral man. Materialist man had to discover how to keep warm, make fire, grow wheat. Materialist man was compelled to manifest himself; and he then discovered his incredible mental power of invention that enabled him to extend every one of these things. All this has put him in a position where his other developments just don't correspond.

Man has to discover how to give up a whole lot of things before he can again become related to nature. You can't stop pollution without giving up packaging, pesticides and the population explosion. This is a very revolutionary idea which has nothing to do with the revolution as it is customarily projected. Revolution has been thought of as more of everything rather than as making serious choices about what we will give up. Whereas man a few hundred years ago was trying to discover how to do things like tame the Euphrates River, now he has to learn to tame his physical appetites (we will risk sounding like John Calvin) in order to liberate all kinds of powers that he doesn't even know he has or that anyone has.

Most people have an incredibly limited notion of what man is and therefore an incredibly limited notion of who they are.

How do you project advanced ideas to backward but rebellious masses in an advanced country? The average person who feels oppressed in this country is responding as a victim who has been deprived by the oppressor of certain material and political things to which the victim feels entitled. Rebellious blacks and women react to an advanced idea as the idea of someone in a privileged position and don't even consider it. How does one deal with this? How does one project that which is true in a way so that people don't automatically reject it?

Malcolm used to chide the masses. Because he began with the idea of the transformation of people, he could combine attack on the establishment with the chiding of the masses.

The great problem today is to project to people a real notion of the nature of man, something which they have never studied. These notions are not "too advanced"; rather, people don't know anything about them because they have never even thought about them, never studied them. The revolution involves projecting another notion of man, to shake up and displace present notions of man, to project a notion of a new man. How to do this is not a technical question nor is it a question to be dealt with only in terms of property relations. Chardin posed it in its ultimate form: Ultimately man is mind and ultimately the mind of man becomes unified in this incredible thing which is the universe.

Time Dimensions

A few years ago the Bell Telephone Company broadcast some absolutely extraordinary and difficult hours. "What is Time?" Is it a thing? A relationship? Anybody who saw it could never again look at his watch in the same way. The same thing has to be done with What is a revolution? What is humanity? Revolution is not just a change in property relations.

Before we can even think of What is man?, we have to be able to think in terms of duration, the time dimension. From time immemorial individuals, generations, even communities have considered sacrificing themselves for the sake of the species, man. It is not just a question of counting noses, seeking a majority, but of looking at man as a species, a duration, with a history that goes into the past as well as the future. We have thought of species-perpetuation mainly in biological terms up to now, but it should be possible to think of species-perpetuation in psycho-social terms.

What does man have to do to make sure that he doesn't wipe himself out the same way that the dinosaur wiped itself out? The dinosaur was unable to develop so as to continue to exist under new conditions.

We need to develop concepts scientifically and systematically, brick by brick, and to be very careful not to exaggerate or glorify phenomena in the belief that we are thereby confusing the enemy when we are confusing only ourselves.

In 1967 there was a "commotion" in Detroit—to use a politically colorless term. It was a very large-scale commotion which the power structure called a "riot" and which the movement called a rebellion.

Now, three years later, we have to ask ourselves how much did we confuse our own forces by trying to aggrandize the degree of political content in the event.

How you name something is itself an action, especially in light of today's mass media; and we can date what has been happening with young people, and their exaltation of their own spontaneity, with the 1967 "rebellion." We need to give young people particularly a sound foundation conceptually.

Is the youth generation revolutionary or just rebellious? Rebellion springs from specific social conditions but does not go beyond rejection; hence it can degenerate into cultism (sects, separatists, flower people). Revolution must contain a powerful element of political responsibility, a clear concept of what you will do with power. Anyone who speaks of "revolution for the hell of it" or "revolution for the sake of revolution" is not a revolutionary.

Reform and Revolution

You are in a revolutionary period when the antagonisms are such that they cannot be resolved by ordinary means. The first step is to attempt reforms. It is only when the efforts to reform fail that you have to change the whole apparatus. In the old days, we made a sharp distinction between revolutionist and reformist to the point that all reform measures were bad and only revolutionary measures were good; so it has become very difficult to think of reforms, not as tactics, but as social change.

Can one use the word "revolution" in a way that nobody else is using it? Wouldn't dropping the word altogether be an evasion?

If we define social revolution as requiring profound change in man, what revolutions have there been? In the seventeenth and eighteenth centuries in Europe and the United States there were very profound changes in man's conception of himself and his relations with others. Presently, in China particularly, another profound change of this nature is taking place.

"Revolutionary social change" is more descriptive than "profound social change." It is better to begin with the concept of what one is trying to achieve, revolutionary social change, than with "revolution" as an event for which there are so many different and confusing scenarios. It is necessary to counteract the tendency to act out the rebellion scenario as soon as one says "I am a revolutionist." It is necessary to recognize also that the great majority of people have never been for revolution. In this sense, certainly, not all men are equal.

Contradictions

What is the connection between the fact that the founding of the United States involved a revolutionary social change over several decades and the fact that the slaves were not freed and were considered three-fifths of a man? Can the two be reconciled? There can be revolutionary social change without perfection, without resolving every social problem. Following revolutionary social change, there may still be a lot of poor people who say "I'm still poor" or a lot of people still not receiving an education. The American Revolution aspired to so much, and it also exposed its own contradictions not only in its actions but in its initial documents. The contradiction in the American Revolution was structured into the country.

Dialectics requires a tremendous leap forward so that you can see your own limitations, or the duality within the new unity. The American Revolution was a profoundly revolutionary social change; therefore it developed new contradictions. The Civil War was the first serious contest over these contradictions.

You must aim high before you can be revolutionary, but the moment you aim high there are bound to be failures. This is the process we have to look at—instead of expecting that one can design a scenario that can be accomplished without failure. Many people think that a revolution is going to solve everything tomorrow. But the morning after the revolution, there will be more problems.

To bring about revolutionary social change in man, the first transformation begins with those who propose to do the transforming. Not just extending the ideas of Marx or Dewey, but developing a new concept of man.

Crime and Chaos

When it comes to what is most fundamental to people's concerns at this point, it is crime and chaos.

The chaos in the United States today is of a very particular kind; the kind of chaos which people in an advanced country get into. It requires the thinking of thoughts and the making of decisions which nobody has ever had to make before, neither in any other country nor in this country at any previous time. There are probably more people in the establishment who recognize the uniqueness of the chaos than there are in the movement. (See, for example, the discussion in *Needles, Burrs, and Bibliographies* on moral development not keeping pace with economic development.)

How does one bring an end to this chaos? By defining a new way of living and of acting.

The answer obviously is not Billy Graham saying "follow Jesus." Yet the answer has to be a new morality. Revolution isn't just property relations or production relations. We are faced with redefining all sorts of fundamental notions: revolution, human relations, human values. We need to talk less about revolution (an abstraction) and mobilize our dedication and our courage toward these redefinitions.

Those in the establishment who recognize the uniqueness of the chaos cannot lead the blacks, the youth. Nor can they lead the ethnic middle classes and workers who simply want to continue material expansion and repress all who threaten this expansion. The question is how can one set up alternative centers of leadership for blacks and youth who are every year multiplying in numbers and going off in mind-damaging directions, as well as for those who are reflecting on what is happening and those who are threatened by what is happening. Who is going to tell people there is an alternative until we develop and clarify the alternative?

Bandwagon Thinking of Radicals

The Marxists believed that militancy was all that was required because in the masses lay all the answers. This is the theory of "debordement": all you have to do is whet the appetites of the masses, get them into action, and the solution is contained in their momentum and wants.

If you ask kids what they want in schools today, they wouldn't have any answers. You might be able to satisfy or pacify them for a while if you had a swimming pool on the first floor, a McDonald stand on the second, and a rock and roll band on the third.

Those concerned over the chaos usually only think in terms of concessions or repression but have not devoted any thought to fundamental solutions. The idea that the masses implicitly know what's best for themselves because their interests are involved is just not true, and at a certain stage in the movement this myth has to be destroyed or it destroys the movement.

There is a hit album in the black community with a song "Niggers Are Scared of Revolution" which kids sing all day, most of them interpreting it to mean that blacks are scared to fight. But blacks are fighting all over the place. The question is what are they fighting for? In a period of inaction, it is possible to have the illusion that all you need to do is create action and action will create solutions. But in a period of action, such as now, you have to decide whether militancy is the answer. And at this stage, unless you have goals and some conception of how you are going to introduce these goals into the motion of the masses, then you are nothing—a waste—no matter how much you're part of the "action." Many black youth can't think in terms of long-range goals because they are convinced that blacks aren't even going to be allowed to survive in this country. Like the Indian braves of a hundred years ago, all they can think of is that they will go down fighting and take some whites with them (revolutionary suicide). The only demands being put forward in the schools now are "more" demands: "more" counselors, "more" equipment, etc.

New Philosophy

Before you begin to engage yourself with people in motion around schools, you have to get rid of a lot of ideas about education—not only those that the system has implanted in you but those you have picked up from the Summerhillians or Paul Goodmans. You have to have a philosophy of education, which is neither the "education for earning" philosophy of the system nor the "kids know what's best for them" of the progressives. Education must have a purpose, a goal; the educator must not just bring forth but lead forth; he must not only transmit but transform. This is not just a question of methods; it is a question of philosophy. The educator has a responsibility to impart to the young people a vision not only of man's present but of his past and of his future, of his history or duration.

What Is Integrity?

It is impossible to lead a revolution without a sense of integrity, which involves the readiness to examine and project a consciousness of appropriate relations between people. The absence of integrity is the refusal to have and act on a concept of the proper relations between men. Integrity doesn't mean treating all men alike or not struggling against some men, but the absence of integrity means just wanting to win.

Integrity isn't something that "exists." It is something that is constantly being evolved and created. It isn't something that grandpa invented but something that every generation has to invent for itself. It is the outward expression of self-identity; it is personal and it is social. It is the expression in relation to others of one's recognition of man's development and one's willingness to take responsibility for this development.

How should people spend their lives? Is it sufficient to say that capitalism is responsible for the present state of affairs and that we are all its victims? Or is it necessary to develop concepts of appropriate human relations and concrete programs to realize these various spheres of struggles? What is the relation between wants and thoughts? Between masses and revolutionists? Masses have wants; revolutionists must have thoughts, they cannot just rely on the wants and spontaneity of the masses. A revolutionist must absorb and internalize the lives, passions and aspirations of great revolutionary leaders and not just those of the masses.

Leadership has to come from persons in contact with people in movement, but they cannot get their thoughts only from the movement or from the masses. Who will provide this leadership? Will it come out of those making the experiences in struggle? Can we depend upon leadership coming from trial and error in struggle? No.

From Marx to Lenin to Mao to "I Will"

The very great revolutionary leaders projected a revolution that they chose; they did not depend on the masses for their concept of what was necessary. Marx was more a prophet than a revolutionary leader; the development of capitalist production, itself, would lead the working class to fulfill its historic role, to actualize both its moral and technico-economic tasks.

Lenin began to put politics in command in order to organize human consciousness to set the masses in motion and change the society.

Mao has taken this much further to mean organizing a body of thought and organizations to lead masses of people to change society and to change themselves; consciously speeding up the process of physical and spiritual awareness; engaging a whole society in self-change. As Han Suyin has written: "It presumes that man is perfectible and can evolve into a higher form of himself."

Nobody has yet created the ideas worth organizing around in this country. Who will do it? I will. I am the one who has to think it through for today, in relation to today, not limited by past notions, not just improving past notions. It is not enough to say, "a new ideology is needed," as if one is talking about a situation external to oneself.

Each year things have escalated, putting into motion new forces, until what started out as one grievance has opened up a Pandora's box of multiple and complex issues. After World War II there were plenty of problems, but what opened up the Pandora's box was the struggle of blacks in the South. Now the whole country is in a state of constant turmoil, and even though the majority is not directly involved, it is indirectly involved and directly affected. A state of chaos exists in every city of over fifty thousand people.

The people in this country have to acquire a whole set of different attitudes and customs. Workers, on whom Marxists have relied, have reactionary views and values. You can't take them as they are, with the values they have, into the new society. You have to change them. If all they want to do is be boss or to be in control instead of present bosses, they can't build the new society. So it is a question of not just power but values. There are people today who want to change masters but maintain capitalist values.

The various groups in the movement today fall far short of grasping the magnitude of the changes required for the new society. We need much deeper insights into what people have to give up; we need to make choices based on thinking through the results of the choices we make. James Boggs wrote the *Manifesto for a Black Revolutionary Party* in order to show the black movement the type of thoughts they must entertain. The movement had just been thinking of racism; it had not yet begun to think in terms of vision.

Everyone, rich and poor, now lives in fear of personal safety. Yet most people in the movement play as if this means the country is moving towards revolution. Simply condemning or repressing is not the answer. Positions have to lead towards programs.

The wants of people and the capacity of the productive apparatus to satisfy these wants have pushed society to a new point where we can't just encourage wants; people must develop the capacity and readiness and habit of making conscious choices.

Before reaching the stage of power, we need to change people's consciousness of who they are, of what man is. Otherwise we won't reach the stage of power. The average city is in a state of plain barbarism. Shouting "jobs for all" has no content or meaning; working class struggles and demands don't even touch on fundamental social issues, let along tackle or resolve them.

We are agreed that scientific and technological development has outstripped political and moral development. But if we don't deal with the economic system based on private profit, won't we just be going back to childish ideas of what is good and what is bad? Is the structural root "the system," or is it the psychological and moral structure of people? Political and moral underdevelopment permeates all sections of the society, not just the capitalists. What good would it do to put the victims into power? What good would it do if blacks or students or workers abolished the capitalist system if they themselves hadn't been transformed? Doesn't it depend on which students, which blacks, which workers, with what ideology? The question of "who" therefore becomes crucial; it can't just be left to chance or to a particular social stratum. You have to start with yourself, taking the responsibility to develop and embrace an ideology, and to develop others around it.

Black Panthers: A National Experience

Why do those in the movement alienate so many people at this particular stage, rather than try to attract as many people as possible to a new vision of man's future? (Compare what happened to Mao when he was able to appeal to all sections of Chinese society against Japanese imperialism.) Today the movement stops people from thinking more than it stimulates thought. The radicals who give leadership to the movement think entirely in terms of social forces created by oppression. The concepts and scenario which Marx developed in the 19th century (under the influence of the French Revolution and the mechanical materialism of his period) have been applied first to workers, then to blacks, then to the lumpen, and now to women and children. So, from "all power to the workers" we get finally to "all power to the children" or "all power to the criminals." The Black Panther Party has confronted the movement with every contradiction in the ritualistic thinking of Marxism: capitalism creates victims; the only solution is to destroy capitalism; the most victimized are the ones who will do this and build the new society of socialism.

Today we know that moral progress is not automatically a by-product of technological development; that in fact economic overdevelopment exists side by side, dangerously, with political and moral underdevelopment. How can we achieve the political and moral development required to cope with this technological development? Not by more development of economic forces, not by making what already exists available to more people more equitably; not by depending upon the spontaneous development of the oppressed. A conscious struggle, a struggle with conscious values, goals, programs and persons, is required.

The Marxists have relegated morality and consciousness to the realm of the superstructure, so much that radicals are afraid even to acknowledge them as the product of tens of thousands of years of the cultural development and achievements of mankind—developing humanity, advancing humanity.

Are these achievements to be judged by the class from whom their creators came? Were they determined by economic class? And even if they were, are they to be discarded as tainted by virtue of their class origins? Because George Washington held slaves, is his warning of the dangers of a standing army to be disregarded? We have to break out of the mental syndrome of economic determinism whereby everything is judged by its class beginnings.

Mao says, "Man's social being determines his consciousness," but he goes on immediately to add, "Once the correct ideas characteristic of the advanced class are grasped by the masses, these ideas turn into a material force which changes society and the world." He also warns against seeing only matter and not man.

The tremendous historical significance of the Black Panther Party is that they are the first American social force to act out the Marxist scenario on a real historical stage and thus to expose its non-revolutionary character. The Black Panther Party is organized rebellion or rebellion made into system.

Mankind has evolved through the actions and thought of specific men, with a very few pioneering for the great majority. If this particular period requires serious thinking to get at the basic roots of the problem and the basic solutions, then individuals have to take that responsibility. That thoughts have to be put into practice is nothing new; the thought, the idea, has to come first, whether it be a new way of producing things or a new way of living between people. New sets of notions come out of reflection upon experiences, but the reflection is as important if not more important than the experiences.

A Cultural Revolution

Who are the antagonists in the present struggle? We have to recognize that today there exists far more antagonism on questions of social relations than economic relations. This means we should not start out with rigid social and economic classes but rather with posing the issue between those who want to maintain the existing social relations and those who are finished with existing morality and social relations. In the first category there will be mostly workers, middle classes, those who head up the military-industrial complex; and in the second category there will be mainly blacks and young people. But let us start afresh with the conception that men are capable of being transformed. The problem of revolution in this country is the transformation of man, and this is impossible without a radical, revolutionary, inspiring concept of man's essential spirituality, of his capacity to pioneer in creating new social relations.

In this struggle it is important not to be paralyzed by fear of fascism or repression. One must think realistically about the dangers, but in thinking about the counter-revolution in relation to the future, one must be convinced that it is a "paper tiger."

Revolutionists have been able to think of a revolution in every sphere except in man's concept of himself. Revolutionary struggle consists of a series of illuminations—not simply plodding or leaping from peak to peak. Revolution should be to discover and create where we should be tomorrow, not merely to correct past injustices or put to rights past grievances. Mankind is obviously at a threshold, a border, a frontier. Precisely because of the growing counter-revolutionary danger, it is necessary to utilize the wealth of human resources in this country, including ethnic diversity. The conflicts are not just between rich and poor, or between generations, but between two different concepts of what a human being is.

Man is his own worst enemy. The contradictions are within man, internal, not without. They are in his biology as well as in his psychology. Because he has crossed the threshold of reflection and because each man is an individual, there are thousands of choices each man can make, including how and where and when he would like to live with his fellow man, and how he will think about himself, about society, about mankind.

Year by year we are in the process of revolutionizing our concepts of revolution, of man, of ourselves, so that we can organize a nucleus and prepare the programs by which to mobilize social forces.

1970

Changing Ourselves

What Politics Has Been

Last year we drew a clear distinction between rebellion and revolution. A revolution does not just deal with past injustices. A revolution must involve a new stage in the evolution of mankind, the creation of a "new man."* If, for example, you spend the rest of your life worrying about what happened to blacks during slavery, you will never be able to make the leap into the future which a revolution demands. Particularly today in the U.S.A. a revolution is not just a struggle between the rich and the poor, between the haves and the have-nots. A revolution must deal with the contradictions within man himself. We cannot look at a revolution inside an advanced country like the U.S.A. within the confines of "class struggle." A revolution within the U.S.A. involves a struggle between people with different sets of values, and decisions within people to live by one set of values rather than another. What are the new values, the new standards by which people should live today, in this epoch? A revolutionist has to take responsibility for developing a new vision of man and for projecting this new vision of man. The creation of a "new man" is a process; we can't expect the "new man" to blossom suddenly one morning; we can't look at revolution with a D-Day mentality.

In all these ways we have broken completely with what has become Marxist dogma. It was only after many years of practical and theoretical struggles that we acquired the courage necessary to reassert the distinctive character of human beings—not only to work but to have thoughts (to be had by thoughts), to make choices, and to live purposefully. We have yet to explore all this in terms of its full political significance, but it is important to see that we were able to arrive even

---

*See the Preface for comments from the editors regarding the use of the word "man."

at this stage only through (1) struggles within and between ourselves and (2) participation in and reflection upon the historical developments of the sixties. Without this we would not be able to recognize how we were previously controlled, dominated, possessed by another way of thinking—a way which conceives of revolution in terms of necessity rather than choice, in terms of material wants rather than purposeful actions, and in terms of victims and villains rather than in terms of human purpose and the creation of a "new man."

It was hard to break away from the old way of thinking because it governed our actions and participation in the Movement; and because it is the way of thinking that prevails in our society today:

1. among the various liberation groups and the constituencies with which they identify;
2. among sociologists, liberals and Marxist radicals whose minds are still in the nineteenth century, who are motivated chiefly by guilt for their own privileges and by sympathy for the masses as victims, and who look to the spontaneous rebellions of these victims to make "*the* revolution" out of their grievances;
3. among defenders of the status quo who only see revolution as a threat coming from those whom they have victimized.

It is not easy to break away from the way of thinking characteristic of all these groups—or, having made the break, to keep from slipping back into that way of thinking.

THE CHALLENGE WE NOW FACE

On the one hand, we have to grapple with philosophical concepts, to explore the philosophical question of what it means to possess ideas and to be possessed by ideas, to understand in what sense they are not something you possess externally like clothes or things that you can buy over the counter. On the other hand, we have to explore the *political* relevance of this new way of thinking, i.e., what it means to an American revolution.

Last year we dealt philosophically with the nature of man. We talked about necessity and choice. We used terms like "responsibility," "purpose"—all of which are very general. We have to become more clear about what we think philosophically, but we should also start to explore the relation of these philosophical concepts to the historical process by which those various elements within the population who are rejecting the present society can begin to create a new society.

In the United States today most of the liberationist groups are separatist in their thinking: centrifugally minded. Is it possible to pose the question of the American revolution as the creation of a "new nation" or rather of a new national unity on the basis both of repudiating the present *and* of recognizing and building on what has been achieved in the way of human knowledge, experience and power over the centuries—rather than to return to a new Golden Age or some form of primitivism? (We have to be careful not to use the word "nation" so freely: today people talk about "Black Nation," "Woodstock Nation" without any sense of what is historically necessary to the creation of a nation.)

Can we inspire and challenge those millions of Americans who have rejected the present society on the basis of its injustices, its inequities, with a vision, a perspective that is centripetal, i.e., that poses a common goal for all the diverse groups, that projects a vision of a new unity that will embody and encourage their diversities?

WHAT IS POLITICS?

What does it mean, for example, when former Chief Justice Warren says, as he did recently at the Fifth International World Peace Through Law Conference in Yugoslavia, that "we have grown up in the comfortable sense that politics is the art of the possible. Few of us have faced the fact that science has transformed politics into the art of the indispensable."

Everyone uses the term "politics" as if he or she knows what it means, but maybe what we need today is an entirely new notion of politics. It would appear that politics includes much more today than it has ever included before. If you decide that you don't want nuclear power plants, for example, that is politics.

Most people think of politics as a "thing." Perhaps the first thing to understand is that *politics is a process,* a method of social action and decision-making that involves the organization of society and of the institutions responsible for the organization of society.

First we have to review what politics has been; then find out what it can be. We do not have to be governed by what politics has been;

rather we should explore what it should be in order to accomplish what it must accomplish—without at the same time being in a rush to arrive at the last word in the definition of politics.

If we are going to talk about a new revolution, we have to talk about a new man. The concept of a new man requires not only new concepts of the relationships between people but new concepts of relationships between government and people. These new relationships have to spring not from institutions but from new attitudes in people themselves. New institutions cannot be created without new concepts; only human beings can create new concepts.

ECONOMICS AND POLITICS

In the eighteenth and nineteenth centuries, Western political economists drew a sharp distinction between economics (civil society) and politics (the super-structure) and claimed that the latter should be subordinated to the former. Thus the physiocrats and Adam Smith fought for freedom of trade and laissez-faire for the bourgeoisie versus the intervention of the State as the best way to achieve the harmonious development of society. Marx's nineteenth century vision of the "withering away of the state" and of Communism as a new form of civil society in which each receives "according to his needs" and gives "according to his abilities" was in the anti-political tradition of the eighteenth century.

On the other hand, when we think of politics today, we have to think in terms of the mutual responsibilities of government and people, and not just in terms of relations between individuals within the civil society.

Most radicals still have a concept of politics that flows from the Marxist concept of "economics in command." If a militant worker says nothing about politics, that has been considered profoundly political because his actions presumably expressed the instinctive drive of the working class to reorganize society on socialist foundations.

For most radicals, revolutionary politics is little more than being "on the right side," the side of the oppressed masses. Yet often (although it takes courage to say so), you can learn more about the modern crisis of Western civilization from people who have been thinking seriously about the dilemma of modern man but who are not on the "right side" in terms of class.

Not until Lenin does a Western revolutionary attack economism and seek instead to put "politics in command." Lenin understood that workers in production were concerned chiefly with their economic needs and that a political party was required to raise them to political consciousness. After the Russian Revolution he developed the concept of "politics in command," warning that if the Bolsheviks allowed economics to command, the workers' state would turn into state capitalism. After Lenin's death the Bolshevik Party under Stalin gave priority to the development of the productive forces, i.e., they put economics in command.

Coming to the Chinese Communist Revolution, politics clearly takes command, both because the Chinese were able to learn from the Russian experience and because the Chinese tradition is based upon politics in command (Confucius).

In our technologically advanced societies, where so many social decisions need to be made about what should and should not be produced and in what quantities, we are going to find it very hard to distinguish between economics and politics, or between economic and political decisions. Politics is taking on new and wider dimensions. It must be redefined to take in much more than has ordinarily been considered political activity. Politics involves making choices and choosing directions, not only for oneself or for one's own intimate group, but for the whole society.

POLITICS AND ETHICS

In the West, particularly since Machiavelli, a distinction has been drawn between ethics and politics. Now we must ask ourselves, "is it possible to create new politics without new ethics?" This country is lousy with politics without the slightest trace of ethics. In the recent past people always determined their ethics by politics—if it didn't pay, you changed your ethics. We have to think in exactly the reverse today: if it is bad ethics, it isn't good politics.

When the Italian city-states fought one another in the fifteenth century, what did they care about ethics? Ethics was completely subservient to politics; Machiavelli said that you can't confuse ethics and politics; politics is a science, value-free: a politician can't be ethical.

Now that we have lived through five hundred years of this kind of separation, we should begin to realize that one of the reasons we are in the dilemma we are in is that ethics has for so long been subservient to politics. It is impossible to project a revolution without ethical concepts, or without concepts of the appropriate role and relationships between people.

In the new era we are entering, we must reject any pretense of value-free politics or of politics independent of ethics. No politics can be anything but self-defeating unless they are ethical. The big problem that remains is to decide what is ethical.

Politics involves citizenship—relationship and responsibility to a particular polity, the creation of governing structures, of plans, of laws, of leadership—whereas ethics deals with one's social relationships with friends and associates, irrespective of citizenship. One can engage in politics and have no ethics; one can be ethical and not engage in politics. At least that has been the situation up to now.

Most people think of "going into politics." Is politics an activity that everybody should be engaged in, that is, not appropriated by an elite or assigned to an elite? Why shouldn't everyone take positions on issues not just with regard to his friends or his intimate circle but with regard to a constituency to which he belongs, which includes a lot of people he doesn't know?

You have to have conflict before you can have politics. But you have to have an idea before you can have conflict over it. Politics involves taking sides. It means proposing or supporting particular plans, programs, perspectives for your community which you believe are right. Most people in the U.S. don't want to be "involved in politics." Politics is "dirty" or it means dictatorship or "elitism." But doesn't their attitude to politics stem actually from the fact that politics means taking sides over issues and conflicting with people over issues—something that they would rather not do? They cherish the illusion that things develop automatically without the need for political decision-making, that the best government is the one which governs least. Yet many of these same people are the ones who are today demanding a strong government to "establish law and order."

Up to now they have thought of government chiefly in terms of the administration of social services, a welfare state that takes care of sanitation, prisons, old age pensioners, Social Security, and the lights on the corner. Jacques Ellul in *The Political Illusion* criticizes the readiness of the modern citizen to leave all these decisions to someone else, as if they were value-free or made by God in heaven, or purely technical questions which did not involve actual choices or principled decisions. In fact, we are beginning to realize that political decisions are involved in all matters and that people are going to have to take responsibility for making these decisions—not only in terms of paying taxes but by debating what should be done and what shouldn't be done.

Will some people have to move out of Washington if the Potomac River is ever again to yield a pure water supply? Does the birthrate have to be cut? Should Americans reduce their standard of living? What keeps the average Russian from saying, "You have an automobile, why can't I have one?" When the rulers of Russia say, "We are not going to get into the automobile business," is that an ethical or a political response? We haven't faced these questions. People have to arrive at the appropriate answers to these questions out of a different set of basic values. Who is going to give up what? Is that a political question or an ethical question? Could we say that the general statement: "People are going to have to give up things in order to have a decent society," is an ethical statement; while the process of deciding who is going to give up what, and the actual making of decisions in a particular polity and for a particular polity, is a political question? Can we say that ethics deals with principles, while politics deals with the actual decisions, the choices—that the governing principles are the ethics, while the decisions on how to govern, made on the basis of ethics, flowing from ethical judgments, are the politics?

We are trying to reestablish the concept of politics as based upon principle and not only on power. Modern man has been dominated by the concept of means rather than the concept of ends, by the question of *how* to do things rather than *why,* by the concept of politics as a value-free science. Modern societies manipulate the minds and actions of people through propaganda so that it is difficult for the average person to proceed from principles. The fault is not with the propagandists alone; it is with the basic concept of value-free politics which is shared by both propagandist and propagandized. Modern man tends to rely upon external forces (the state or the economy) to resolve problems rather than accept the responsibility of people to resolve problems. Many Frenchmen (like Ellul) who have had experience with European Communism have a kind of anti-political bias, in the sense that they distrust the tendency in modern masses to rely upon the centralized state to resolve all problems. They want to reestablish responsibility within the people—but this cannot be done by turning your back on politics.

NEW POLITICS?

For many years we thought we had the answers to how this country should be run because we were on the side of the workers, and the workers were the ones destined to reorganize society on new foundations. This was called "our politics" (as opposed to other people's politics). Now, through an arduous process, we have begun to examine and explore what principles should govern the relations between people and what is the nature of man in this day and age? Meanwhile the country's politics have been going to rack and ruin. So we are now challenged to begin to relate the principles we have been developing to the political sphere in a more concrete way.

Up to now we have thought that politics existed only if you had a clash between classes. Today we can see that what must be involved in the American revolution is a clash over values. As Revel says in *Without Marx or Jesus*, it is not a question of redividing the cake but how to put together a whole new cake. There is a tremendous clash over what values should be involved in creating this whole new cake. This is a politics with which few people are familiar, since redistribution of property has been at the root of previous politics.

In the past ten years various liberation movements have come into being. Many of these are still concerned chiefly with the question of redistribution of the cake, how blacks or chicanos or women or young people should share in it. Others claim that their values should be the values of the entire society. Few, if any, of these groups think at all in terms of their commitment to the whole. *A kind of absenteeism has developed.* Liberation has come to mean separation. All that each group is concerned about is itself. Each one has a conception only of its own rights, although some claim superiority of their life-styles above all the others. So as Revel says, they have added to the rights of man, two other rights, the right to walk away and the right to be internally contradictory. "Do your own thing" is the most prevalent tendency within the liberation movements.

Revel does not deplore this because he thinks the only alternative is a police-state; and in fact to bring these groups together at this point would require a dictatorship. But Revel has little idea of how all these groups which are formed on a biological basis (race, sex, age) can degenerate. There is nothing beautiful about youth or women or blacks in themselves, and people who do not recognize this are bound to degenerate. Womanhood, ethnic origins, age are the ground on which individuals, cast adrift by a disintegrating society, can come together on the basis of what they have in common, to begin to explore and develop through struggle and conflict and through criticism and self-criticism. If they are unable to develop a more historical identity, they are bound to degenerate.

If you create a collective or a commune with the idea that you are going to develop ethical standards among yourselves but the hell with everybody else, you are not being ethical. Yet this is happening. One group will steal from another on the basis that its members come from those most oppressed in the society.

If a doctor believes in the right of women to abortion, he could just walk away from the law and say he is going to give abortions. On the other hand, there are doctors who perform abortions as test cases in order to bring about abortion reform. They walk into establishing something for society; they don't just walk away. They act for the sake of a new positive.

Revel claims that, through this catalog of various groups organizing on the basis of race, sex, age, and life-style, and with this new view of the rights of man, a new kind of politics is emerging. Yet isn't it obvious that these groups are going to have to get together at many different levels before we can achieve anything like a revolution in the U.S.? But what will they have in common? Up to now they have been unified chiefly by anti-imperialism or their common opposition to the war in Vietnam. As long as these groups think of their grievances only in terms of their own interests and do not reflect on these interests as they relate to the whole, there isn't much of a basis for their ever arriving at the point of being part of an overall movement to advance the whole—which is the only basis for a revolution. All you will have is constant disintegration and a continuation of the present chaos.

Obvious? It is not obvious to them. And extremely unclear, and yet to be explored, are the principles on which they will be brought together. To what end will they be brought together? Unless somebody begins to think about the principle or principles on which these disparate groups can discover a new unity, we will not have a revolution or a new society. In their anti-ness today, each sees itself as better than everyone else, as having the key. In their separateness they can only degenerate, whether they are black or women or gay. By their excesses and their "couldn't-care-lessness" about what has been achieved by mankind over the ages, they provoke middle America into counter-revolutionary positions.

We have to shift what unifies these groups (anti-Vietnam War, anti-racism) away from just rejection to projection, from just denunciation to annunciation. We need to develop projections that contain both unity and diversity.

Up to now, the tendency has been for each group to view itself in the same way that Marxists have traditionally viewed the working class—as the class with the solution to all social problems. Blacks were only interested if you were talking about blacks; they could not see anything in the past as related to them unless it was black. Women's liberation groups have substituted the sex of women for the class of workers or the race of blacks. None of these groups seems to have thought about how all of this is to come together or converge at any point. This is a period of the disintegration or fragmentation of the social structure. But, unless the dividing lines within our society are projected on different bases than those on which each of these groups started, each group is going to become increasingly negative, and the possibility of bringing them together on any basis is going to become harder.

Are these groups open to another vision? They have each had perspectives but they have been limited and negative ones. Last November (1970) the Black Panther Party made an effort to unite these groups at its "Constitutional Convention" in Philadelphia. The result demonstrated what can happen if you begin from abstractions. Huey Newton drew up the theory of "inter-communalism." Instead of nations—or communities with a common history or language or habitation struggling to transform themselves and their institutions—people were going to set up voluntary communities, based on whatever they had in common, racially, sexually, etc. These then would come together and create the new society by relating to one another instead of to any government. Under the aegis of the Black Panther Party, all kinds of groups actually came together to write a "constitution" in which the rights of each would be protected. It was really a very naive conception, yet a lot of fairly sophisticated people bought it.

If you are thinking abstractly, or if you are so guilt-ridden that you have suspended thinking altogether, it is easy to arrive at this kind of conclusion. Not only did the Black Panther Party call this convention, but all sorts of really "heavy" people attended. Huey went around to universities and gave long lectures on "inter-communalism." All sorts of people listened while he held forth. It indicates how impatient people are for something that will pull together all these liberation groups.

For the same reason, they look to the Vietnamese for leadership. There is a hunger for somebody to come along, some individual, who will provide the focal point for unity.

Can we begin the search for a basis for unity by saying that the U.S. revolution is going to be the revolution of the last quarter of the twentieth century—or of the twenty-first century? Since this country's technological development already makes it possible for everyone to have according to his needs, the U.S. revolution is not going to be around the issue of the distribution of goods and property, but around values, around the further development of the human personality. In this country, there is an enormous variety and enormous scope for variety—by comparison with other countries. The whole concept of what man can be, of human potential, of humanhood, goes far beyond anything imaginable elsewhere. This tremendous diversity and variety would have to be an element of the new unity, as well as of the new concept of revolution. Up to now, revolution has always been conceived by socialists to be "following our program." Maybe, today, it is possible to move toward revolution with a whole lot of programs.

Forming the Vision: The Politician as Artist

By what vision can these various groupings begin to see themselves as moving in the same direction but along their own particular lifelines? One of the most important reasons why we are so far from achieving that vision is that no works of art have been produced which represent a unifying vision. None of the psychedelic stuff, the Woodstock Nation stuff, or the Black Arts creations (LeRoi Jones, etc.) really presents or projects a new vision for this period.

It should be emphasized that we are not asking artists to be politicians. Rather we, as politicians, are wondering how we can discover in art the manifestations of what we are seeking to discover. If anything, rather than asking artists to be politicians, *we are asking politicians to be artists*—to put it in an exaggerated form. We are demanding of revolutionary politicians that they expand their horizons, their vision of humanity, that they enrich these visions with the illuminations of the artist, that they be constantly receptive to the human potential that the artist opens up to view.

Up to this time, most of the stuff coming out of the Movement is pure protest politics, guerilla art. All of it is very narrowly political. The painters of 1890–1940 demonstrated an amazing ability to break with the past while maintaining a continuity with the manifestations of man which artists for thousands of years have been trying to accomplish. The music of Duke Ellington, of Louis Armstrong recalls the relationship of art to mankind, not just to the man who is playing or blowing. But in the last decades we have entered into a period of self-expression where people who know or care nothing about the past or the future of mankind only express their own emotions, their own angers, their own frustrations. Are Ornette Coleman, Archie Shepp playing music or only their passionate rejection of the horrors of modern life?

How does one become historically angry, futuristically angry, philosophically angry, wondering about tomorrow as well as angry about yesterday and today? Artistically angry because one feels so deeply that man is so much more than he is manifesting himself to be today. An artist must project, not just express a personal response.

You can go to a film like Truffaut's *Wild Child* and in an hour and a half get a feeling for duration, i.e., for how long it has taken man to get to the state he has reached and how far he still has to go. How many guys could have put that feeling into an hour and a half of film: any white man? Any black man? Any Marxist? It takes very special people to develop and project a vision, just as it takes very special people to become revolutionists at the beginning. And we are just at the beginning. We have to accept this exceptionalism. In a column in the *New York Times* this summer William Shannon describes:

> The children of the television age see politics as a happening, a demonstration, a dramatic confrontation. They do not realize

how much time and effort are needed to alter the character and direction of a large, mature, complex society like the United States. . . . Their despair, like the apathy of the hippy and the alienation of many middle-aged people, is a response to a world of undirected technology and unnecessary speed.

Resenting death, we murdered time. Now, time vanquished, we lie exhausted alongside our victims. Almost too late, we see that what we have slain is not time but our sense of ourselves as human. Left alone with our machines, we know not how to wait, to prepare, to discipline, and deny ourselves. Therefore, we know not the rejoicing which comes when we have reaped and consummated and brought to fulfillment, all in good time.

To reject the past is to deprive today of its meaning tomorrow. To evade the limits and significance of time is to empty life of its limits and significance. It is that meaninglessness which pervades this age of instant gratification and instant results and permanent dissatisfaction.

In the same issue of the *Times*, William Serrin writes in an article describing the rising murder rate in Detroit since the 1967 rebellion, "It's terrible that life can be so cheap." In many of these killings, the victims and murders are desperate young people with no sense either of the past or of the future.

We need a new sense of time as duration rather than as units ticking away mechanically on a clock. More than any other art form, the film can give people a sense of time. It can do this because it compresses events into a process that develops in time. People who view a film can identify with this process. *Wild Child* gave those who saw it—people who, like most human beings today, feel as if they are just flotsam and jetsam with no solid relationships—a tremendous sense that human beings have come from somewhere.

What does one say to a thousand black kids in Detroit who say, "so let's buy a gun and make it?" What do you say to them about time and about the past?

You might tell them, "After the Russian Revolution, the Russians claimed that they had invented practically everything. That was natural, but it was also false. Today, among black people in particular, there is a lot of talk about art and culture—meaning principally African art and culture—and big claims that long before anybody did anything,

Africans had done it. Blacks are making these claims to justify their being, their rejection of the white man's superiority. This too is part of man's development, of the process of learning."

You might say, "Black youth and white youth are both saying that they don't have time for the past, that they are only interested in Now, right now! Yet how did you get here? It is obvious that if it were not for your mother and father, you would not be here. Or are you just accidental people? Because if you are just accidental people, we don't have anything to discuss at all. You didn't just get here by accident. Undoubtedly there was a process for you even getting here.

"Now, suddenly, you are saying that you are going to change this whole world, *today, right now,* as if the very process by which the whole world got to this point never even happened. Take this room, for example. Where there is now an air conditioner, there used to be an orange crate. So somebody had to develop an air conditioner.

"Now suppose I entrust my future to you—which is what I have to do really. But you have no concept at all of process, neither of the process by which your very present is dependent upon the past, which in turn was brought into being by men and women from a still further past—nor of the future which has to be created from this present. It isn't enough to want to tear up a house because it is old and rotten and the door doesn't fit. You have to have some vision of what kind of house you are going to put in its place. Very few of you have any idea even of how the present structure functions. You are mad at how it affects *you*; you are concerned with *your* feelings, *your* pains, with what *you* don't like. Society is always made up of people with all different kinds of feelings. You are not the first young people in the world nor the first people to have felt frustration. The people who organized the Boston Tea Party were youngsters, teen-agers. The founding fathers were mostly young people in their 30s. As a matter of fact, at that time few folks got to be very old."

We have to make a further penetration into the revolutionist's relationship to art. There are films today that tell us more about man and the revolution than anybody on a soapbox. People who went to Shakespeare's plays saw and heard things they had never heard before: They had never seen a black man make love to a white woman, or gotten so close to the intrigues of nobles. Shakespeare's notion of what was real was incredible; people learned about it with joy. Antonioni's *Red Desert* is an extraordinary film. Every frame in that film is a painting. Antonioni did it very deliberately, to tell you how incredibly beautiful everything could be—an amazing demonstration that life is not as simple as you think it is. Art and revolution are fantastically intertwined. Obviously not all art—but art, the notion of art, is absolutely fundamental to the notion of mankind. If we are going to get out of this, art is one of our most revolutionary weapons.

WHAT IS VISION?

Vision is not a portrayal. That is exactly what it is not. A vision is what might be portrayed, but never has been. A portrayal of something is a painting or a likeness of what has been. A vision raises your sights, gives you a feeling of what might be. For example, life in America as a "land of milk and honey" was the vision perhaps of a Sicilian who might be coming here in steerage. Vision is not a description or portrayal of anything that is or was. It is insight or foresight. Within a vision there can be the envisioning of certain sets of social relationships. The vision suggests or projects what might be.

We must search for an enlarged notion of how one contributes to the revolutionary process. It is so easy to imagine that the revolution has nothing to do with art, that art is a "bourgeois luxury." Suppose it is true that, in the past, only the rich had the leisure to create art. Would that mean that the art they produced does not represent man? Or would it mean, rather, that their art represents what other men and women could do if they had the time? Actually, of course, throughout the long history of man—long before there was a bourgeois or privileged class—a great deal of art was produced by other than the rich. Dance was the first language. The people who made utensils for use also carved them. We must thoroughly rid ourselves of the idea that art is a "bourgeois luxury," that "art is a product of slave labor." Art is perhaps the most profound expression of man's humanity. Therefore we have to use art again particularly in this materialistic age—after a hundred years of deeming art a bourgeois luxury—as a revolutionary weapon. If we don't, we are going to fail in the totality of our approach to man's desires and man's humanity. Revolutionaries who do not incorporate what artists are trying to say in their vision of revolution don't know anything about man's future. They have a materialist concept of revolution, rather than a humanist concept of revolution.

We have the opportunity today to put forward a new idea of man. The idea of man as purely producer, as purely rational, as knowing only in the scientific sense and therefore reducing reality to what can be measured and machined (a concept which is about two hundred years old, a very short time in the history of mankind) has now demonstrated both its enormous power and its enormous limitations. The latest moon shot is the best example of this—both in its fantastic technological perfection and in its equally fantastic fragmentation and reduction of human beings to instruments of the computer.

A new idea has little power over man unless an old tradition has exhausted itself. Today we have the opportunity to unleash our own vision of the tomorrow for which mankind is striving.

As you listen to jazz, you realize that here in America, humanity, in the form of black people mainly, has achieved a form of self-awareness and a kind of spontaneity which is combined with discipline and control—all of which represents an extraordinary achievement in the evolution of humanity. It is a combination that is uniquely American. There is in jazz a kind of wisdom and a kind of mellowness which comes from the awareness of human development as a process, involving time past, time present and time future. These are all attitudes which are extremely important for the next stage in human development so that human beings can organize themselves and their relationships to one another and to their natural environment in a different way.

American jazz expresses something of America which is unique. It is crucial to understanding America. America isn't just technology. American technology itself is the product of incredible diversity, of scientific knowledge and sensitivity. American jazz came out of America because this was the only country with this diversity. America is the result of these different strands, something qualitatively different from any other country.

Western man has a kind of self-awareness and a spontaneity that is precious and worth preserving. This comes through in jazz and blues. There is a sense of human hopes, of the infinite potential of the human spirit.

Jazz was created by black men in this country because their experience in this country was one of suffering *and* hope. They had heard white folks play; they had heard the drum from Africa. Then, out of the liberation which blacks felt after World War I, came jazz. Jazz built on the spiritual which had been created in the South out of the music from Europe and that from Africa. Due to the African experience, blacks had a unique notion of rhythm and timing that nobody else in the world had, of physical freedom and buoyancy. Also nowhere in the world is the drum so much an expression of *being* as in Africa. They added to this the experiences of both joy and suffering which they found in their situation. (Note: Bach's music stemmed from joyous attitudes which he had to his God and his church. All the greatest music Bach wrote was in relation to his religious experiences.)

Something in the American experience drew jazz out of the blacks; and the response of so many other Americans to jazz suggests that everybody in this country is in certain sense like a black in relationship to society. Everybody is enslaved in his own way by U.S. society. Of all the popular musical forms which express the contradiction between man's aspirations and his enslavement, jazz remains the greatest liberator. Nobody knows why.

Jazz is a form of music which devotes itself to the exploration of equality, of freedom, of humanity. Beethoven, Bach made statements. Jazz explores the content of man's aspirations and hopes (partly because it has vocals). Jazz asks everything; and gives some notion of tomorrow. And suddenly it became the music of the whole world (except the East), the music of liberation, the music that says you can be different from what you were yesterday. Jazz is an attitude expressed musically, which is why it is never written. It is invariably improvised. It cannot be "programmed." It epitomizes creative freedom. It is one of the least contaminated and least full of bullshit of any art form.

Jazz suggests new forms in which man can express his attitude to his own nature—and therefore his attitude to man's nature, and to the changing, developing character of truths (versus, for example, Plato). It is an exploration of that which is not yet. Jazz is not trying to discover fixity or correctness. Jazz is the expression of an attitude.

Revolution is improvisation or creativity just as jazz is. Nobody knows what the revolution is going to be and who is going to do what. Nobody. Just as in the jazz form, nobody ever told the other man exactly what he should play. Jazz is an expression where a bunch of people (not like one guy writing a novel or a song) say, "We agree on what moves us, this is the general idea. We are going to do this rather than that. We will start off this way." After that it is left to improvisation. The American revolution will be exactly the same kind of thing. Something is going to start after enough people have agreed on the general idea, but it will be improvisation. If somebody writes a scenario, it isn't a revolution. That does not mean that a revolution just happens, spontaneously, and that no preparation is necessary. Quite the contrary.

Why is politics an art rather than a practice? Because practice in itself does not imply the element of creativity which is essential to politics. Politics must involve political leadership; political leadership must be creative. Leadership requires responsibility and the capacity to think grandly.

Changing Basic Notions: Truth, Equality, Personality, Freedom

2,500 YEARS OF PLATONISM

You are in trouble the moment you accept notions of absolute good and absolute evil, the same as if you were to accept notions of absolute truth and absolute falseness. Confucius and Plato both lived at approximately the same time. But they had completely opposite attitudes to good and truth. Confucius understood that man is part of the universe. He said that people need principles by which to organize themselves and society, and these principles should be the same as the ones that are at work in the universe. Plato, on the other hand, said that there are absolute truths by which societies should be organized, and that man should strive to know these truths: only those divorced from the confusion of "change" and "becoming" can know them; and knowing them, people become good. The Western world comes from this other (Platonic) conception of truth. This is 2,500 years that we are coming to grips with.

What is meant by principles in harmony with the universe? These are three kinds of unity which we must achieve: unity within ourselves, with other human beings, and with the universe. At the very beginning, when he talked about truth, Plato set up a separation between one's material and one's mental being. The further away you got from the confusion of matter, the higher you climbed on the ladder of truth. Plato created this dichotomy within the concept of the human being from the beginning.

What is interesting is that this dichotomy applied in thinking about man is much worse than the Confucian concept which accepted the difference in the role between peasants and intellectuals, but which said that there should be a harmonious mutuality between them. Each should contribute what it has to the whole, and both must relate and be responsive to the other, because this is the way of the universe. If you deny something that is actually real, then you build a whole series of conclusions that eventually crack up or crack you up. The Chinese said that there are two sets of people—not equal but unequal—the peasants who till the land, and the intellectuals who do the work of the mind and advise the rulers. If those who do the work of the mind and advise the rulers don't do right, then the peasants have a right to rebel. This is your unequivocal right, to rebel against misrule. That is much better than saying you are equal when you are not equal—so that you are forced to prove your inequality before you can justify your rebellion.

For two thousand years, at every critical stage in the development of Western man, leaders have come forward with new interpretations of the concept that all men are equal. For Jesus Christ it was all men being equal in the sight of God. For Rousseau, the French revolutionary thinkers and the American revolutionary leaders, it was all men being equal politically. Obviously this concept of the equality of men goes very deep in the history of the Western world. Yet men are in fact obviously not equal, so it is bound to lead to all kinds of contradictions. You can't keep building your world on a conviction that is so manifestly not a fact. We must realize that individuals are very different; that there is a very wide range of individuality. We must start from the fact that all important truths change over given periods of time: there are no fixed truths. We have to recognize that the only ideas that matter are ideas created by human beings, that are, therefore, changeable and relative.

Let us for now abandon the word "truth" in order to get rid of the Platonic idea of truth as fixed ideas, and in order to internalize the concepts of principles and convictions that are held and created by human beings. This will help us to appreciate that ideas, like human beings, have changeable characters, improvable characters, complicated characters. If we use the words "principles" and "convictions," then we will be able to see that important ideas are the ones that move us to act, and we will have something that is much closer to the Chinese idea than to the Western idea. The Western concept of idea is of something "out there" that you catch onto, a thing, something that you contemplate and to which you have a passive relationship. It doesn't have to move you. The idea of a principle, on the other hand, is that it is no damn good unless it moves you to act. It was enormously difficult for Western man to accept the idea of evolution of the species. Now we are trying to get him to accept the concept of ideas as evolving. Most people think that the evolution of man as well as the evolution of ideas have come to an end. We are saying they haven't. Marxists have not grappled with the Western concept of ideas. They have concentrated their attack on the class character of particular ideas.

We haven't even begun to try to create the new ideas for our age. We are still working on the shattering of the old shackles of fixed ideas—of materialism and rationalism. Marxists have always had a class objection to Plato. The class critique is easy—"class-angling." But it does not deal with the concept of ideas at all. All evil is on the other side, not in you. This is the attitude of the liberationist groups. Now, however, we are saying that if Plato thought that way, we must also be thinking that way until we substitute another way of thinking—because Plato is one of the first creators of Western thought, and we are Western thinkers. Liberationist groups have simply taken their specific biological state of being—sex, race, age—and substituted it for class. They have the same ideas about race, sex, age, and so forth as Marx had about class—that all the evil is on the other side. They have the illusion that since those whom they oppose are the ones who rule, "our" ideas can't be "their" ideas.

Take, for example, the question of law. We are convinced that a society based on law is the best society; yet the concept of model (emulation) is much richer than the concept of law. When we look at what is happening in the courts today, it should become clear that we are going to have to devise another way for people to govern their interactions than by means of law. Otherwise all it amounts to is reforming the courts. What is happening in the courts is not accidental. It is based on the idea that human behavior can be regulated by laws.

"The Chinese had no power to legislate directly, no power of taxation, no voting right. But they had at all times the right of rebellion" (Riencourt, *The Soul of China*). The right of rebellion stemmed from a conviction about the appropriate roles that different sections of society should play rather than from any concept of legal right or inalienable right.

What are inalienable rights? What are legal rights? The concept of legality is not prized in China. Over two thousand years ago, in the midst of tremendous chaos and conflict, a group of legalists emerged. They simply established a kind of equality and justice in order to get some sort of unified order. It lasted only about fifty years, and thereafter it came to be recognized that law and order are not sufficient foundations for a society. So the Chinese then said that order must come from within rather than from without, and they began to establish an ethical basis for people to live together. "A civilization can establish itself only on an ethical basis, and the cynical realism of the Legalists, useful to bring about the necessary revolution and unification of the civilized world by fire and blood, had to be discarded as soon as its limited purpose has been fulfilled" (Riencourt). Hence the ensuing Confucianist revival.

As soon as you begin upsetting one part of a structure, you have to begin rethinking all its parts. You can't just discard the foundations or one corner. That is what puts such an awesome responsibility upon a revolutionist. You can't just talk about getting rid of the evil bastards. We have said that this is the greatest crisis that Western civilization has ever faced.

In the *Critique of the Gotha Program,* Marx says that if you deal with the concept of rights, you are already dealing with a deprived society organized on some negative basis. We have always dealt with rights as if they were great positives, rather than seeing rights as a way to limit the infringement by some men on other men. There is a punitive quality written into them, an assumption that you can't trust people to behave in a civilized fashion with one another. You can add the word "inalienable" to make it sound nice, but the concept of rights is still restrictive.

NO THOUGHT IS "MERE"

In Western thought, absolute truth has come to us as a positive goal to be striven toward, while relative truths have come down as "merely relative," mean, material, and negative. This started with Plato (whose class bias was unmistakable). It was extended by Christianity (to save the souls of the meek and humble). Then science gave it new life. At each of these critical stages of Western development, the idea of absolute truth became more deeply entrenched. Therefore, it is hard to impress upon people the idea that truths are constantly being created and that this creative process is in fact the greatest achievement of man. We tend to speak of ideas as "merely relative," implying that what is relative doesn't matter too much because it is not fixed, as if only fixed truths were important.

It is self-evident that science has discovered many facts about physical realities that are repeated again and again and are relatively unchanging for millions of years. Yet some day, someone is going to discover that something even in these spheres, e.g., in the speed of light—by which everything is measured—is, in an Einsteinian sense, relative; and then all things will have to be reevaluated.

The concept that all truths (because they deal with the nature of man) are relative and not absolute is indispensable to revolutionists. In order to make a revolution, you have to discard the notion that anything one has previously known as true is necessarily true. Revolution is an effort to discover or to create truth, not to prove that something is true. It is hard to persuade most radicals of this. You shatter their personalities if you question what they live by. For them being a revolutionist is living by certain truths, rather than discovering or creating new truths. The New Left—as distinguished from the Old Left—started out by trying to discover rather than prove. But they were empirical and pragmatic to an extreme. The Old Left has a body of ideas which the masses of people are supposed to prove for them. So they are happy, gratified, satisfied whenever the masses do something to prove what they already believe. All this has nothing to do with revolution.

A revolution is to create new truths about man and society. That is why a revolution is such a challenging, dangerous enterprise. In a revolution you sail out on uncharted seas. There is no proof really that the road you are taking is the "true" one. You have to make it true. Revolution is becoming, creating. Revolution creates new bases of tensions—new unities which will split again into other dualities.

Man's concepts are in constant evolution. God was a concept. Man created the first gods. The first gods that man created were closer to nature because man was closer to nature at that time. As man progressively departed from the dominance of nature, beginning to master nature for the first time in the last few hundred years, he created other, more complex gods. As man was enhanced in one direction, he was dulled in another. This is the contradiction, the duality in man. When man crossed the threshold of reflection, he began to discover things about his own developing nature. Man thinks he has discovered the final truths about himself, and therefore he knows what he is. But he doesn't; we don't. The nature of man, not just the future nature of man but even the present nature of man, is infinitely more complicated than we have permitted ourselves to recognize or to express.

Maybe we have to discard the concept of truth because it is more confusing than revealing: "the truth, and nothing but the truth—so help me God!" Perhaps in China there are no such words as "the truth" since this concept (of fixed truth) began with Plato's idea of truth, of a heaven in which perfect truth resided which imperfect men were always striving to reach. When we think of the limited class character of the society from which all our basic concepts spring, it is incredible that we have clung to them for so long. Plato thought you reached truth by removing yourself from every kind of confusion and material involvement. It is almost impossible for us to use the phrase "a truth." We always say "the truth." It is so difficult to think of truth as human, as evolving. But the words "truths" or "convictions" would be much more accurate. Then one could always dispute, struggle over ideas with the clear understanding that we were talking about convictions held by actual people. "Truth," on the other hand, implies independence from human beings, like the law of gravity. Under the umbrella of the word "truth," we have subsumed both facts and convictions. Now we want to make a separation between them. By using "truth" to refer to hard facts, we have given facts a human value they don't possess. Conversely, by using the word "truth" to refer to convictions, we have given convictions a permanence and an independence of historical and human relations that they don't possess.

A revolutionist does not believe in absolute truth, but he does have strong convictions—thoughts that move him. How does one relate thoughts and convictions to reality? How can you have strong convictions that possess and move you, and yet develop them in relation to struggle, to practice, and to unfolding reality? The highest form of being human is the continual developing and advancing of your vision. This is the dialectical process of thinking.

Vision is more than thought. Vision brings to the rational process of thought all the instincts, intuitions, untapped qualities in man. That is why vision is indescribable, why it can't be analyzed the way thought can be. A vision isn't just a thought. You don't consciously think up a vision, it occurs to you.

Just as we recognize that truth is not absolute and that ideas are not permanent in the sense in which Plato conceived them, we understand that we cannot change the ideas that people invest with truth merely by arguing with them. Ideas cannot be changed through argument. We are not seeking to discover new ideas but rather to create new attitudes in ourselves and others with regard to ideas.

EQUALITY

Certain attitudes and convictions that Americans have concerning equality, abstract freedom, personality, truth exist nowhere else in the world. Many of these attitudes and convictions must be modified; some should receive opportunity for enlargement.

In many respects the idea of equality is ridiculous. People are not equal. Yet in some respects people should be equal. Many equalities should be taken for granted, e.g., equal access to medical care. In the realm of capacities we are all unequal; yet we are all equal in our ability to recognize inequality. There are spheres in which people are equal and should be equal. There are others in which they are manifestly unequal.

Revolutionary politics has been mixed up with liberal humanitarian notions, stemming from Rousseau's idea that everybody was a "noble savage" until he got messed up by civilization. Everybody is not equal, but people feel queasy about making such an absolute statement. Men, women and children are all equal in the sense that they all need to eat, they all need to be born. But essentially all these equal qualities are mere generalizations, least common denominators. No one fights over these. The equalities that people fight about are the ones that matter, the ones that need to be investigated.

The United States, by creating political democracy in accordance with an abstract ideal of equality, also made it a process that excludes political development.

Not to recognize that in the realm of politics everybody is not equally dedicated or equally capable, and that there has to be a dialectical inter-relationship, a process of mutual education, between leaders and led, is to make nonsense of politics. If in a democracy, everybody is equally entitled to vote, then it is naive to think that the equal voters are actually deciding which way society is going. It is as naive as the idea of having a national plebiscite every night on TV with everyone watching and punching a button. As if any society could decide important questions on the quantitative basis of which side gets more of the equal votes. You make nonsense of important matters when you make equality central to these matters.

Equality is only applicable in spheres which are no longer relevant to the organization of power.

> The existence of the hierarchy of power has been largely neglected by humanistic thinkers because it does not conform to their ideal of man. But an ordered society can admit the equality of men only in fields other than those which determine the hierarchy of power at any particular time. The establishment of religious equality was only possible at the Reformation because political power had replaced religious power, and the various sections of the community had accepted their place in the new political hierarchy. Similarly, political equality could be realized during the nineteenth century in communities where financial and economic elements already effectively determined the hierarchy of power. The overthrowing of an old social system from within is possible only by those who can call to their aid a new principle for the organization of power. Humanitarian socialism failed to achieve power because it offered no alternative to the economic hierarchy, and totalitarian national socialism succeeded, temporarily, because it transferred power to the hierarchy of technicians of total war. (Whyte, *The Next Development in Man*, 132)

Before the modern age, religious equality was the ideal. Everybody should be able to go to God. Then came political equality—everybody should be able to go to the polls. In the Western democracies, everybody has an equal right to go to the polls only because the organization of power is not in the ballot box at all. It is taking place through industry, through the Pentagon, and so on. We are all equal in helplessness.

What we have not faced is the need to have a principle for organizing power in terms of new principles. We begin to face it with the idea of a "prophetic voice"—with the need for people with prophetic voices to reach out to some other people—not to everybody at once, but to those who are searching for new principles. Those in turn have a mission with regard to others. Thus there is an actual hierarchy in the sense of political leadership according to political conviction and dedication.

In the new society, there should be a tremendous amount of equality in terms of economics. Clearly the realm in which equality does not exist is that of political responsibility. The aim of the society will be to develop general, universal, political responsibility. Precisely because this will be recognized as so precious, so valuable, so crucial to society's and humanity's development, there will be no illusion that everybody is equally responsible. But if you tried seriously to build your society on illusion, you would be building nothing but disillusionment.

There should obviously be equality in many spheres of human life where there is terrible inequality today. But the idea that all men are equal is an illusion that destroys the possibility of the leadership—not just political but also ethical and aesthetic—which special individuals can give and which is especially needed by us all in times of very great crisis.

If all men were really equal, then all motion would stop—unless all men could change simultaneously, which is obviously ridiculous. This is why those who believe all men are equal also believe that all big changes take place with a kind of spontaneity. As in a school of fish, all change direction at one time, because of instinct presumably.

Totalitarianism took this mass of Western man—like a school of fish who had no ideas in their heads, except of themselves as equal and a lot of other abstract notions—and handled them as masses. Lancelot Whyte wrote *The Next Development in Man* in light of the reality of fascism. A very advanced Western man himself, he asked why fascism had come to the West. He concluded that if there were no great ideas to move Western man, then the contemporary technical apparatus of propaganda could be used by those with the most distorted ideas to influence Western man.

If we believe that it is necessary for man to create a closer harmony with nature, with his own nature and with others, would the development of these harmonies also bring a higher form of equality in most spheres? Is it equality we are aiming at—or is it greater harmony in these spheres? What does harmony have to do with equality anyway, except in the minds of certain people who feel uncomfortable if they don't see equality all around them?

Do modern tensions come from lack of equality or from frustration over our powerlessness to do anything about what has occurred or is occurring? Or from neither? Are people in the U.S. concerned with powerlessness at all? For example, a lot of people felt tense during the Cuban missile confrontation, but they didn't want to get in on the conference between Kennedy and Khrushchev.

Society, or the organization of a new society, depends upon how one relates the spheres in which people are equal to the ones in which they are unequal. We are constantly confusing the two spheres. As long as we keep yapping away about equality, we are not going to penetrate into the nature of man. Part of having a human nature is the ability to recognize the differences between people: some are men, some are women, some are hunters, some musicians, some witchdoctors, some educators. Out of a conglomeration of Christianity, liberalism and Marxism, we have screwed up the whole notion of human quality to the point where we can't evaluate the quality of human beings or project to human beings the diversity of their own qualities or the vision of a new unity based upon this diversity. The idea of equality was projected originally against a rigid feudal inequality. There was a very good reason for it; it was a fantastically revolutionary conviction at the time. That is why every black man in the U.S. is still under tremendous pressure to insist upon equality, to think in terms only of equality. Yet one of the most revolutionary things we can do today, in 1971, is to advance the notion of the *inequality of people.*

The concepts of equality and inequality are different from the concepts of sameness and difference. Equality implies parity in relationship to some standard. Inequality implies some concept of hierarchy, the recognition of real unevenness within the particular sphere—and therefore a need for hierarchy. For example, the notion of the "new man" is meaningless if everybody says "I am the new man." If everybody's claim to be the "new man" is equally valid, then you can't move; everything and everybody is on dead center.

Fifteen years ago in *Facing Reality* we wrote:

> There is no mystery about what is happening to our society. If so many find it easier to accept total destruction of human society rather than see that a new society is all around them, a society based on cooperative labor, it is not merely because of greed, desire to retain privilege, original sin. It is because, arising out of these material privileges and reinforcing them, is a habit of mind, a way of viewing the world, a philosophy of life still so powerful because by means of it man has conquered nature. It has governed the world for over four hundred years and now it has come to an end. . . .

> I think, therefore I am, said Descartes, and the world rejoiced at the perspective of the expansion of individual personality and human powers through the liberation of the intellect. The resting of self-certainty on man's own thought and man's thought alone was a revolutionary defiance of the medieval dogma which had derived certainty of self from God or the Church. Rationalism encouraged and developed an elite, the organizers of ideas, the organizers of industry, the discoverers in science. At that stage of human development they were needed. They cultivated the individual personality. It followed that they looked upon the masses of men as passive unthinking servants of the active organizing elite. Rationalism saw each human being as an individual, the natural leaders being the most able, the most energetic, the most far-seeing individuals. . . .

> Today the tasks envisaged by Descartes, the great men of the sixteenth century, and their followers in the seventeenth and eighteenth centuries are accomplished. The pressing need of society is no longer to conquer nature. The great and pressing need is to control, order and reduce to human usefulness the mass of wealth and knowledge which has accumulated over the last four centuries. In human, social terms, the problem of mankind has gone beyond the association of men in a natural environment to achieve control over nature. Today mankind is sharply divided into two camps within the social environ-

ment of production, the elite and the mass. But the trained, educated elite no longer represent the liberation of mankind. Its primary function is to suppress the social community which has developed inside the process of production. . . . This antagonistic relation between an administrative elite calculating and administering the needs of others, and people in a social community determining their own needs, this new world, our world, is a world which Descartes never knew or guessed at. . . . Two philosophies, the philosophy of man's mastery over men and the philosophy of man's mastery over things, have met face to face.

It sounds beautiful, it is a tremendously challenging passage, but why is it so wrong? Why did it seem so simple at the time? We were trying to release man's mastery over nature as contrasted with man's mastery over other men. We had no sense of the need to discover in contemporary human nature its tremendous complexities and capacities. We had an answer, a solution: "Man needs to plan and administer 'things'; the proletariat must do this administering rather than the elite or bureaucrat." We had a dogma and we were trying to prove it. We were not trying to discover new truths. The same man was to shift his emphasis from mastering "men" to mastering "things." We didn't wonder whether the same man could do it or whether mastery was what was required. We assumed that Stalin was wrong because he didn't follow what Marx said. The "way" had already been laid out by Marx but Stalin had departed from it; if he had only followed it, he would have gotten the right result. As if that result were already predetermined, as if there were no question of what man should be striving to achieve. There was no sense of any development, any evolution, taking place in man himself.

Socialism as we saw it was simply the administration of things, the cooperative, organized, rational administration and reduction to order of the tremendous abundance that could be produced by the development of the production forces. To this day, that is what most people think of as socialism, and it is the ultimate of what they strive for. People talk and write about the administration of things very glibly because they consider that this is what Marx conceived of as the goal, generally speaking. Three, four generations of socialists have accepted this as the goal of modern society. Yet even Marx did not stop at socialism. He went on to the idea of communism, the classless society, in which each would receive according to his needs and give according to his abilities. Today we are not only beyond simple planning, but even beyond the concepts of "to each" and "from each." We are at the stage of discovering and creating a new human nature.

For over a hundred years, radicals have accepted that if the proletariat were to administer the developing productive forces, the contradictions between people and within the human being would be resolved. How could they think this? How could we have thought this? *There has been no contemplation of the complexities of man's nature at all.* Man's whole being has been determined by his relationship to the productive forces. Why?

Any revolutionary breakthrough has to be considered in light of the stage of historical awareness at the time the breakthrough took place. Thus, Western self-awareness of the individual came two thousand or more years ago with Socrates and Jesus. The reason why the concepts of individualism and self have remained so narrow is that they were born at a time when the individual who was looking within himself and becoming aware of himself was a limited individual, i.e., limited in relation—not to his time but in comparison to where we are today. Thus, anybody who is a dogmatic Christian is automatically limited. We don't say this because we are anti-Christian, but because we realize that Christ lived so long ago—when man, and therefore man's concept of the self, was so undeveloped. Similarly, if the various racial and sexual groupings now seeking liberation were actually developed, whole people, then out of their liberation might emerge a whole and developed society. But they have become self-centered and are seeking their identity on a very narrow basis. Therefore, if they try to make a principle for the whole society out of their identities, it is bound to be nonsense.

PERSONALITY

China never had the individualism that we have in the West. This helps to explain Chinese history and its present and future. But it doesn't change the fact that the concept of individual personality that emerged in the West is now part of the evolution of humanity. The question becomes, how do we keep these individual personalities from remaining narrow individuals who are only expressing themselves?

The Chinese and the U.S. revolutions could not possibly be the same. Unlike the West, China never had a period of Christianity—a period when what was most important was the immortality of the individual. In China, human continuity was achieved through the family; it was not personal or individual. The Chinese never had an individualism based upon freedom of enterprise, tremendous mobility, and all the other features of a country like the U.S. Even if in the U.S. there is a tremendous egotism and concern for one's "precious personality" which has to be modified, individuality, as a human achievement, still has to be respected. Otherwise you do violence to the developments of two thousand years. In *Moby Dick,* Ahab and Ishmael are very individualistic and self-destructive types, but the "noble savages," Queequeg, Tashtego, and Daggoo, are no longer possible in the U.S. And who wants to be a Starbuck or a Stubb who just goes along? Individuals known for their achievement are very few in the history of China and India, but in the history of Western civilization there are thousands of such individuals.

What is a whole man? Harmony with nature is essential to a whole man; so is a relationship to work (as distinguished from labor) and a relationship to time (i.e., to the past and future as well as to the present).

Mankind today has three great needs:

1. somehow to integrate his ideas, feelings, skills and actions without the rigid separation which leads to sentimentality, technocracy, and abstraction;
2. somehow to create some kind of collectivity that will allow diversity, because it is the rampant individuality of the U.S. that has led to mass-man;
3. somehow to develop an organic relationship to nature, in place of the aggressive, exploitative, relationship to the environment, which by destroying nature is also jeopardizing man's survival.

Wherever man is not separate from nature, you do not have a concept of individual personality, of equality, of freedom, or abstract value-free truths. Hence the difference between China and the West. (We are using China here as a contrast to help us understand our own society better.) Western man has to move beyond where he is, to acquire some of the serenity that resides in a certain kind of relationship between man and nature. His relationship can't be a Confucian one. But when you ask the average guy, "How long can we continue to deplete and pollute the earth without a plague?" he isn't concerned because he thinks it is a question of fifty years or more, not the next year or two. So it is "not in my time." The phrase "not in my time" is as obscene as the concept "doing my own thing."

On the one hand, we say individuality is wonderful, that to reduce everybody to nothing but a part of the whole would be reactionary. Yet we know that individuality also has within it the contradiction of the "cult of personality." Great creative individuals have had a scope in the West of a kind that they have not had elsewhere. And yet we cannot but deplore the self-centeredness which sees everything in terms of the self, e.g., the "cult of personality," "what about me?" or the "leader" to whom everybody always looks for salvation. People who are only concerned with their own precious personalities are pretty horrible people. Yet personality *is* something previous, to be neither wasted or eliminated.

What do we want? Or what we think man should be wanting? We have to know what we want before we can go out and tell others. That is why it takes such a long time, why it is necessary to be patient. We cannot approach what we want as we did in the past because we now have to examine the nature of man, the nature of technology, and the nature of nature. What we want is tied up with all of these. It is obvious, for example, that unbridled technology is catastrophic to man's future. Yet it is equally obvious that what man has learned about the uses of technology should not, cannot ever be lost. We can never return to the Garden of Eden.

CONCEPTS OF FREEDOM

What do we mean by freedom? We will have great difficulty in defining this—more even than with equality, truth, personality—all of which could in some way be pinned down to a particular historical period, a group of thinkers, a series of events. We are in very deep water indeed.

The Civil Rights movement asked for (given) specific rights. These specific rights were what it meant by "freedom." What did people mean by "Freedom Now"? Freedom from white domination. But you can be dominated in five hundred ways. Which domination? When we talk about a specific historical movement like the Uhuru movement in Africa, we are in a sense in less difficulty because Africans clearly mean self-government by "Uhuru." They have in mind a historical image of national independence. (They refer to George Washington, Thomas Jefferson, Patrick Henry.) Even in the U.S. the early movement for "Freedom Now" was very concrete—for the civil rights of blacks to be able to move about as freely as whites were moving about. They were not talking about the concept of freedom in the elusive sense in which we are pursuing it now.

Again, using China as a contrast, the idea of freedom does not exist in Asia. Not even in Russia. Chiefly because in these countries the idea of a subjective, individual will separate and apart from the will of the community, from the order of the society, from the external pressures of the environment, or institutions, or objective world does not exist in Asia. Thus a historical, philosophical concept of freedom (apart from a specific movement) has never existed. The abstract concept of freedom could not, in fact, exist separate and apart from the concept of separate individuals each with a will of his own. Precisely because this concept of separate, individual wills emerged in the West at a time when the individual had a very limited concept of the world and of historical development, it has turned out to be a very arbitrary, capricious type of freedom.

For example, if a child says "I'm free," he could then begin to do all kinds of capricious things because his freedom has no internal limits. This helps to explain the Movement in the late sixties. When the human nature that you are trying to express is limited, while the concept that you are projecting is very vast, there is bound to be contradiction in your actions.

In what sense should man be free? We certainly don't think he should be un-free. Man should think of himself, perhaps, as free in the same sense as a bird is free. A bird is in total relationship to its environment. It knows that there are cats around that limit its freedom, that would like to eat it up, so it organizes itself accordingly. A man is free when he is confident of his relationship to the world he lives in and is not fearful of it. He is also free when he is confident of his relationship to other men and women. Freedom is above all a relationship. It comes from recognition of the dialectical inter-relationship between oneself and one's social and physical environment. There are all kinds of extensions of these inter-relationships, but no notion of freedom which frees one from inter-relationships is a valid notion. Freedom is not a thing that you get or you gain or you accomplish or you buy.

Few people talk about freedom in terms of the freedom to move and to act with people in a certain relationship. They usually mean being able to do what you please—the freedom of the individual. They are dissociating the individual from any necessity, from any relatedness, because to Western man any relatedness is a kind of restriction.

This is the concept of freedom that we have to attack. Lancelot Whyte talks about Europeans never having been able to accept external conditions as necessary for integrity and life; of their fear that as part of the general order of nature, they would lose the reality of freedom, and their precious sense of individual freedom. By treasuring this individuality, they have actually destroyed the integrity, the wholeness of the individual which can only come from inter-relationships. Since their concept of freedom was asserted in independence from reality, it never has had any basis in reality.

Western man has had this concept that he was free in himself, that the individual is not dependent upon the conditions of society, that he has his own "blithe, free spirit" within himself, to be nurtured and to be respected by others. That sense of individual freedom, precisely because it was so unreal, unrealizable and illusory, has haunted us all, because we are all part of the West. It was expressed in *Facing Reality*: "The free development of the individual personality, the right of the meanest intelligence to wander through the strangest seas of thought, alone if need be, this freedom has been established as a universal principle, however limited it might be by the actual conditions of existence at any particular time or place. It is now an ineradicable part of the human personality." All the present liberation groups are permeated by this definition because they too are part of this tradition.

In the U.S. there was a more objective basis for this sort of individual freedom than anywhere else in the world; hence this concept became more entrenched. All the liberation groups—blacks first, women and others later—still share this concept. They see themselves as part of some sphere of freedom which does not in fact exist at all. Hence the concept of "doing your own thing." Because Americans have lived in a land where it was more feasible to think about freedom this way, it has also permitted them to believe that they are the defenders of freedom throughout the world—a kind of "chosen people." What is most objectionable in U.S. foreign policy is derived from the notion that we know what freedom is and nobody else does. Therefore we are going to give some of it to the world. Actually, you can be against U.S. policy in Vietnam and still be biocidal at home, because you still haven't grappled with and uprooted this illusion of individual freedom.

Freedom, equality, truth—none of these has ever been seen as a relationship. Each has been seen as a thing. There are relationships which permit freedom and relationships which don't. Freedom is not a concept that one is free to define for oneself. It is utterly impossible for man to transcend nature because he is part of it. If there is no such thing as freedom, we can only talk about freedom from what, for what, to what.

Should people be free at all times to say just what they feel? There are a lot of illusions about that. This idea of the unlimited right to speak—proceeding from the preciousness of this internal sense of freedom—has to be abandoned. It is not easy to abandon. Even after agreement that this or that specific freedom—e.g., the right to yell "fire" in a theatre—should not be preserved, there is still that urge to preserve the internal sense of freedom as precious. All of us are under enormous pressure as revolutionists to defend the freedom of people. When do you not defend a person? Where do you draw the line? What is appropriate? In the name of an abstraction like freedom, we are destroying other values and relationships of incalculable importance.

People who have lived in other societies are more likely to think first and not be so cocky about their freedom. They have some recognition of realities, of relationships, of limitations. But because Americans have had more of an objective basis for their concepts of individual freedom, they have extended it to every sphere. We have reached the point where millions of people regard it as a God-given right to do what they please. All the "free" movements that have developed in the last three/four years are manifestations of this. The implication in all of them is that human beings don't have to make choices. They thereby represent a very narrow, backward view of man.

How does one project a new notion of freedom to those who have rejected this society? What freedoms can we discover; what freedoms do we want after we have freed ourselves from erroneous concepts of freedom?

Because Western man's concept of freedom was erroneous or too narrow does not mean that it did not, in the past, enable enormous contributions to be made to the advancement of man. However, the new notion of freedom must be a *social* one, which is the greatest freedom there is.

SMASHING OLD IDOLS

Truth, personality, equality all have to be concretized and clarified in order to create new harmonious relationships; but we seriously question whether the concept of freedom can be corrected. It is too individualistic, too antagonistic to community.

What we are trying to discover are new relationships which are not based on old concepts, e.g., the old individualistic notion of freedom or the old abstract concept of freedom. If we could project and create the appropriate set of relationships, we might discover that we were approaching freedom. We block ourselves from discovering new relationships by holding on to old concepts.

> The dissociated idealist is unable to understand this experience of necessity as freedom. He looks for the fundamental conflict which he is convinced must always exist between the compromises of social life and the standards of the individual conscience. This is just the trouble with the idealist: the conflict does exist for him, he cannot escape the antithesis of the real and the ideal which reflects his inner dissociation. . . . The idealist seeks the security of the static harmony, and therefore considers every tension evil. Unitary man recognizes tension as an essential feature of the formative process operating in man. Man creates in resolving tensions, but never brings them to an end. The contrasts of past, present and future forms provide an inexhaustible source of tension. In every society, there is a wide scattering of individuals at all stages of development, just as the tradition comprises *ancient myths, contemporary platitudes, and prophetic vistas.* The individual who can understand and accept the long-term development of his community may have to stand alone. (Whyte, 274–75; emphasis added)

Chinese man could understand this, but Western man is such a fragile creation of his own concepts. If we want to make a revolution, we have to smash these concepts. It means smashing a great many of the idols on which Western man is presumably built. Our job is to make the notion of freedom a derivative of real relationships, not of old abstract concepts. Where man once created God in his own image, he has now created himself in the image of God.

There is tremendous release in thinking about all the other things we will discuss in this way, in the sense of smashing old idols. We must try very hard to project a sense of new relationships—aesthetic, ethical and organic—out of which will come a new notion of freedom.

If our society, and we ourselves, are made up of "ancient myths, contemporary platitudes and prophetic vistas," we will need some conception of these myths and also of the platitudinous character of many of our own notions in order to move ahead.

Ideas Shape Man's Becoming

How do people begin to move in their minds? How do you move people in their minds? How can we help them to penetrate through the ancient myths and contemporary platitudes, particularly myths and platitudes of equality, absolute truth and abstract freedom?

Last year we called our conversations "Toward a New Man." Essentially what we tried to do was get clear in our minds the difference between a revolution and a rebellion (in which the oppressed rise up in protest) or a revolt or an insurrection (in which there is simply a change of power). A revolution—we made clear to ourselves then and have been trying to make clear to others since—must involve both a drastic change in direction and a leap forward, an advance, in the evolution of mankind.

This year we are trying to move towards new concepts of ourselves and of humanity. We now understand much more clearly how ideas have been the instruments by which human societies are organized and integrated. Over the years we have been afraid that it was "idealistic" to think this way—that societies are organized only by the division of labor. Paradoxically, the most important lesson for us in the Chinese Revolution is the crucial role of ideas in shaping man's becoming. The philosophy that "once the ideas characteristic of the most advanced class are grasped by the masses, they become a material force capable of changing society and the world" (Mao) is a fantastically liberating philosophy. It stands on its head the thesis that contemporary radicals have taken from Marx to justify their mindless militancy: "Philosophers have only contemplated the world. The thing is to change it."

These notions have not only shaped Western man, they have shaped us, in this room. They shape the great "silent majority" of Americans as well as those who presumably have repudiated or are antagonistic to the views of the great silent majority. Our becoming has been shaped by these notions. We must destroy, smash, change these notions, if we are to advance new notions.

WHY CHANGE OURSELVES?

Why would Americans change their concepts? Perhaps we should distinguish between cause and reason. Causes are what push us from behind; reasons are positive goals that attract or pull us forward. What are the reasons that would mobilize the American people's will to go ahead? We are exploring new attitudes because we are convinced that unless we can persuade other people similarly to change attitudes, none of us can do anything more than continue to accumulate goods, pollution and war. But what reasons would motivate the average person in the U.S.?

What about some kind of therapeutic reasons? For example, someone discovers that he is getting nervous, losing or gaining too much weight, working too damn hard to make too little money. The best possible way for him to get rid of all these problems is to try to do something different, acquire new relationships. As some guy who has enjoyed smoking all his life might suddenly wake up and say, "I think it would make sense to stop. I would like the results of not smoking better than I have liked smoking." Is this too limited an analogy?

At crucial periods in history very rare people come forth with prophetic convictions. "Such voices appeal because they convey a sense of resolution of earlier tensions within a new harmonious rhythm" (Whyte, *The Next Development in Man*, 247). That is very general and philosophical, but if we could discover the way to project it, it could be very specific and personal to anybody and everybody. Damn near everybody in the U.S. would admit that he is aware and conscious of tensions. Most people would also realize that there is such a thing as "harmonious rhythm," that it is desirable—although no one knows how it could be created. Many people go on dope because that seems the most accessible release from tensions.

When we, in this country, think of harmony with nature, we think of going on a vacation—we never think of continuous harmony. What we then get is the invasion, congestion and destruction of vacation sites. When people think of seeking harmony only as a respite or as a temporary measure, then soon it can no longer be achieved even temporarily. The generation to which we belong is still struggling, bumper to bumper, to get to a tree, but the next generation might not even know that there are trees, and so won't struggle to get to them. They will only struggle to get from one motel to the next. Anything in between won't exist for them.

It goes back to something characteristic of Americans: when Americans reject what exists, they tend to take off in some way. This is the Pilgrim—the Roger Williams—the Brook Farm syndrome. The difference is that people used to go off to new geographical frontiers. (This is still happening with some hippies—off to New Mexico.) They leave one area behind and go on to another, not caring about what happens to the area they leave behind. This "new frontiers" mentality has been an obstacle to the development of U.S. civilization, because people tended to abandon problems when the "auspicious beginnings" didn't pan out (*Five Easy Pieces*). The challenge is to make a human environment by reconstructing and reorganizing where you are. When you take off, you not only leave behind used-up buildings, but you leave behind half-built cultures.

One of the most important results of our discussion this summer is that we have been able to appreciate ideas in relationship to human process and to human development and to human history. This doesn't in any sense mean we are seeking to abolish ideas or to abolish intellectuals. We are rather affirming the crucial importance of ideas precisely because of this historical, relative character.

Many young people in the New Left are also convinced that you can't have fixed ideas and that you can't change yourself just by changing ideas. They believe that you have to develop ideas in practice and that through the life style, the life process by which you live together and develop a new style and new relationships, you are advancing the revolution. Many of them are very serious about this. But they have not really confronted the basic ideas that they must reject before this process of creation can develop something new. Ideas cannot develop without practice, but if you don't grapple with your theories, your ideas, you are simply practicing inside the limits of your shackles. If you try to create something new without having made a profound critique of old ideas, then all you are going to do is capitulate to the existing ideas.

The ideas that you start with delimit or circumscribe the ideas that you can arrive at. In order to achieve the freedom to create something new, you have to be sure that you are not imprisoned in what you think you believe. The revolutionist must acquire the freedom to think without being limited by generations of Platonic thinking.

The people in these collectives have never come to grips with the Western ideas of truth, equality, freedom, personality. Being purely pragmatic and empirical, they are bound by existing ideas. They fall into lots of traps; they have all kinds of illusions about equality; they are antagonistic to any kind of leadership; they are open to all kinds of influences because they have no basis on which to judge things in this society. Hence they are collective subjectivities, aggregates of individual self-expression.

Do we just wait while they try to find their way? True, they have to arrive at new ideas through their own experiences. We are not saying they have to arrive at our ideas. But we can question the way they are trying to arrive at their new ideas, the way they limit themselves to ephemeral, subjective, insignificant agitation. Many young people haven't the vaguest idea what they are for, only what they are subjectively against. How demanding should we be on youth, rather than just understanding? Must everyone have a long experience before they can have a base from which to advance? Or can people learn from other people's experiences? If everyone had to go through the same experiences, the world would be in pretty bad shape.

People who are merely resentful can't give leadership. They are too obsessed with their resentment, with themselves. If you are going to lead, you have to be deeply concerned with more than yourself. You need a great "generosity of spirit." Most of the volunteer armies of liberation in the U.S. are made up of people with resentments. The task of the leader is to project goals in such a way that they become more than that. If you become a leader who expresses only resentment, then you are in reality a follower, not a leader. Whoever accomplishes any great change must first stop feeling sorry for themselves, blaming society and others for doing things to them. Rebels and reformers both project tomorrow in terms of today—a little better than today—or a lot better than today. They don't raise the question of the new man of tomorrow who will want entirely different things.

How do we go about persuading people that the advancement of mankind comes through changing what man wants? What do you do while you are struggling to develop new appropriate ideas?

Ideas are not developed full-blown. You can't get them completely clear from the get-go. They don't come out like a blueprint so that you can say that these are the ideas by which mankind will be governed for the next period. You begin to move in your mind away from certain kinds of thinking and towards others; and then the energy that comes from working with these new ideas and with people who have been looking for new ideas by which to think and live begins to give a new strength to these ideas. "Thoughts are born of failure." About the time your new ideas are firmed-up, they are ready to be thrown out and replaced by another set of ideas. Western civilization has never understood this because it started out with Plato and his concept of fixed ideas. It took Western civilization until the time of Hegel to begin to understand the process of developing ideas. That is the importance of Hegel.

Maybe we are doomed in the sense that the speed with which we develop the new ideas that are necessary can't match the speed of technological change. Or perhaps with the aid of the artist and the mass media, and with the hunger for ideas that may emerge as people begin to realize that they are jumping up and down in the same place, we can begin to develop ideas quickly enough—yet not so quickly that they become only "experiences" and not ideas in the process of development.

We are fortunate to live at this point in history. If the Chinese Cultural Revolution had not taken place, it would have been difficult for us to recognize the tremendous role of ideas in the shaping *of* man's becoming. People could have argued about their importance, but it takes a tremendous revolution like the Chinese Revolution to help us feel it in our guts. This does not mean that we expect the

Chinese Revolution to be all smooth sailing. But it is a demonstration of the importance of ideas, of thinking. The Little Red Book is a symbol of this. Thus observers like Barry Richman (*Industrial Society in Communist China*) noted the tremendous amount of discussion and debate taking place among people at their work. Felix Greene has called the Chinese Revolution a revolution of "perpetual discussion." The Chinese people discuss and debate ideas because they believe in the importance of ideas.

IDEAS MATTER

The Chinese had to adopt Marxism at a certain stage in their development as the only way to internalize the notion of rapid economic development and to break up the rigid social structure. But having done that, they are now calling on many ideas from the humanistic philosophies of the past. (The Russians did not have such philosophies to fall back on.) Having stayed at a low level of economic development for thousands of years, the Chinese are now in a position, historically, to learn from what has happened as a result of the rapid economic development in the West.

Until this century, Western man's concept of his own importance, his determination to impose his ideas upon reality, his use of his intellect to conquer nature was still piddling in scope. No massive technological development had taken place, no creation of mass political parties dedicated to "increased prosperity." No charismatic individual had at his disposal either tremendous armaments or the mass media to create real threats to all humanity out of his conviction that he has all the right answers. In the last hundred years ideas have begun to reach great masses of people. They now have tremendous social and technological force behind them. That is why incorrect ideas are now so dangerous.

As long as ideas were in the province mainly of philosophers, and the masses of man just went plodding along trying to survive from one year to the next, ideas couldn't matter too much. Now, however, people with wrong ideas can acquire enormous power.

Great masses of people have been mobilized behind the ideas of Marxism. America in the name of "freedom" feels it has the right to police the entire world. It is a very different situation from freedom being just an idea in people's heads. Ideas move people internally, emotionally—and multi-million dollar media organizations exist to spread ideas.

The only way to get rid of Platonism is not to be impatient for certainty, but to develop a profound feeling for the continual "becoming" of ideas. Marx had a concept of historical development, but at a certain stage he began to fall short in his own conviction, trying for a final answer and using his mind to organize the world and human history in terms of fixed categories. That was when he became dogmatic rather than dialectical. New sets of contradictions are constantly emerging. There is no end to them, no "final conflict." "In their calmer moments Marx and Engels knew that their doctrine was not a universal conception of man or of history, but an interpretation of one phase only in the development of a particular civilization" (Whyte, 231). Analogously, the Russian Revolution was one phase in the development of revolution. To regard either Marxism or Leninism as ultimate is to betray the concept of dialectics, the concept of the continuing evolution of ideas. Marxists treat as permanently dominant such transitorily dominant concepts as class. In the same way that Hegel rushed too quickly to impose an idealistic absolute, Marx rushed too quickly to impose a materialistic absolute. Freud fell into the same trap with the "unconscious."

Marx's "passionate sense of justice led him to identify his entire being with the struggle of the poor" and thereby to a "fixing" of reality into a rigid duality of good and evil, victims and villains. The same thing has happened with many white liberals today. Otherwise how could anybody in his or her right mind believe that Eldridge Cleaver was going to lead society into the future?

Music critic Ellen Willis says in the *New Yorker* (August 14, 1971) that Janis Joplin wanted to adopt the blues form without the blues sensibility. That is, in classical blues you can feel the determination of blacks to survive abuse; Janis Joplin is crying out the pain and wanting instant relief. Revolutionaries must have the conviction that there is going to be a continuing development of mankind. They must recognize continuing struggle, conflict and tensions as the reality of historical process. Reality is not something that can become ideal like "a shot out of a pistol" or "without the labor, patience and suffering of the negative" (Hegel versus Schelling). To believe that it can is "now" thinking. When you repudiate "now" thinking, it doesn't mean that you just sit and wait for change to come. But neither do you just sit and complain. You develop perspectives and programs based on your belief in the tremendous resilience of human beings, the strength of the human spirit.

Mao knew that the bitterness in the Chinese peasants had to come out, but he also knew that bitterness was not enough to create the new society. He realized that a new unity had to be created (which would, in time, be split again); that the rebellions had to be focused on a new society, not just militate against the old. Women were encouraged to struggle against their husbands, but they also realized that if they married someone of their own choice, they had a duty to try to make the union work; they just couldn't go on being resentful of men. Because Mao was close to the peasants, it was impossible for him to idealize them, to believe in their perfection, to regard them as "noble savages." So the peasants were made to realize that they would have to transform themselves in the course of struggling against their oppressors. Otherwise why would they rule? In the U.S., few people think of changing themselves. Each group finds it easy to adopt the concept of its being the "chosen people."

There is a great temptation for the gifted person to see himself as alone, as knowing everything, as bearing the entire burden of the special contribution. There is a great need to guard against arrogance and conceit. Special people are necessary, else everything would be homogenized. Mao walks around looking like any other soldier in the Chinese Army; but at the same time the special qualities that he had to contribute were recognized by his associates. In China the intellectuals have always had a special role to play. The Chinese would not be scornful of the intellect, but they would be scornful of intellectuals who have no concern for the masses, i.e., of pure intellectuals.

Many more difficult periods of struggle are going to emerge. Many more ideas will have to be developed in the course of these struggles, stage by stage, until we develop unifying direction. The change in people has to be fundamental. We can't set a timetable for it. In this particular period, as a part of and not separate from our ongoing activities, we are taking advantage of what is taking place and reflecting on it and on ideas, trying to go beyond the present frame of ideas that most people operate in. Our aim is to create a new vision for the next period in man's history. Today contradictions develop much more rapidly into conflict than in the past. The U.S. Revolution is not going to be a final revolution; it is going to be another revolution in the evolution of man, the most highly advanced revolution of all up to now—or it will not take place at all.

Note that every critical stage of the Chinese Revolution was prepared for by a philosophical document by Mao: "Correcting Mistaken Ideas in the Party" (1929); "On Practice" and "On Contradiction" (1937); "The Struggle Between Two Lines" (1949); "On the Correct Handling of Contradictions" (1957); "Where Do Correct Ideas Come From?" (1964).

Now, in 1970–71, a tremendous philosophical battle is going on in China—in their own words—a "momentous struggle on the question of the identity of thought and being." They are insisting that "peasants can certainly learn to study and apply philosophy."

We have to talk about leaps forward in our own thinking, not in the Chinese thinking. What leaps in thought have Western revolutionaries made to match the tremendous leaps that have taken place in man's material development? Most radicals have been saying, "Let workers control the means of production instead of the bourgeoisie!"

In fact, now, with rapid technological change, ideas will have very short life spans unless those who project them constantly develop, revise, and explore their ideas on the basis of the realities that have been created (in part) by these ideas. Historically, the tendency has been that those who take people to a certain plateau are unable to take them to the next, because they become the guardians and protectors of ideas which once served to stimulate but no longer fill that function.

Anarchy, disintegration, tensions are going to increase. People usually come out with absolute ideas because they want to resolve the tensions; they want to unify what is breaking apart. We have to find ways of developing unifying conceptions without becoming imprisoned in rigid, fixed ideas. The increasing chaos is not itself revolutionary, but it is going to increase; it would be very deceptive if it did not.

THE UNITY OF DIVERSITY

The Western mind tries to resolve things one way or the other—excising the other which is an essential element—and believing that we have gotten rid *of* it. This is murderous. We have to develop instead a concept of duality in process. We must feel within ourselves the ability to live with and use the challenge of duality as a basis for movement. Chinese philosophy is based on the acceptance of opposites. Westerners (Montesquieu) believe you can create unity by imposing the ideal on the real. (The United States Constitution comes from that conception.) This leads to a society based on laws rather than on men. Today the reactionary calls for more and more laws to create order. The revolutionary should be able to conceive of struggling for a society which is based more on the wisdom of men and women than on laws. Fighting for more laws is like fighting for better jails. We believe in prison reform, but those who concentrate their energies on struggling for prison reform are not revolutionaries. They have no vision of a new society in which we will need fewer jails. Today, the more you try to reform institutions rather than to change people, the worse things become. All you are doing is increasing human dependence upon institutions; you are multiplying bureaucracies and diverting human energies and attention from the changes that people have to make in themselves. Methadone is becoming the next big welfare institution. It's the old pill treatment, the quick remedies approach—instead of demanding that people face themselves, grapple with their problems. The result is that more and more people are unable to confront themselves and their reality. Welfare and methadone have built into them their own perpetuation. You don't have to join Reagan to recognize that the more people go on welfare, the more corruption takes place in people.

What is the alternative? Everybody is always asking for *one* solution—free heroin, or methadone, or Synanon. There is no one solution. More important than methadone for reducing drug addiction would be the refusal of the ordinary householder to buy hot stuff. Today the ordinary guy is buying a hot TV sold to him by a drug addict, knowing damn well that it was stolen from one of his neighbors, and that next week it will be re-stolen from him by the same or another addict. It is not only the addicts who refuse to face their own reality; the ordinary guy refuses to. He complains all the time about crime in the streets, but he continues to subsidize it by buying hot stuff.

Most people today have been demolished by their materialistic idea of themselves. Very few people are obsessed with the grandeur or the magnificence of man—as Renaissance men were. Most people think of themselves and of other people as mean and grubby—as imperialist or bureaucrat. They think of man, the proletarian, or man, the revolutionist, in terms of only one segment of man's total being. The awesome challenge of the American revolution is to project to Americans the grandeur of man. Americans think less about the grandeur of man than practically anyone else in the world. All an American is thinking of is himself. How do we persuade Americans to make a revolution because of the grandeur of man and not because of the necessities of this or that?

All the great ideas of the last two thousand years have revolved around mankind—not Jewish man or Arab man or Western man or Black man or Proletarian man—but just man. The American revolution is going to be made by people who are thinking in the same sense about man. We have to recapture the glory and the grandeur of man. Nothing else will enable us to transcend the fragmentation and the segmentation and the sectarianism. We have to start from a basis that is utterly different from class struggle.

The national liberation struggles of the post–World War II period have narrowed our view of revolution. Ignoring the fact that undeveloped countries make undeveloped revolutions, we have failed to realize that the scope and depth of a revolution cannot be separated from the size and complexity of the nation which is involved. A really great revolution puts man at the center of its perspective, of its proclamations. We had the Declaration of the Rights of Man, the Declaration of Independence, and to a lesser extent the Russian Revolution. The Bolsheviks talked about the "workers of the world"; they saw the Russian Revolution as the world revolution of the epoch. Very soon after the Chinese Revolution, Mao talked about the "new man." Not Chinese man or Guatemalan man, but man. In that sense every great revolution, as distinguished from a rebellion or a national liberation struggle, is one that projects a new concept of man, a concept of a new man. The liberal idealist has very little concept of this because his understanding is limited to the vague idealism of moral virtue, sympathies and altruism.

It is impossible that there be an American revolution which does not incorporate into itself everything that has happened for the last forty to fifty years to everybody. How can there be an American revolution which does not encompass what has been added in Mao's China to the concept of man? If the American revolution is not a revolution to advance the nature of man and the struggle of man to create a new nature, it will be just a seizure of power by a different group of people that happened to take place in the U.S. If it is just an American revolution, it won't be a revolution, and it won't even take place. Philosophically, an American revolution must take all of mankind beyond the stage that mankind has reached.

What does unite Americans or what could unite Americans? Until there is some agreement on this, we are not going to be able to set up any kind of new government. We have to discover a new basis for American nationhood, an absolutely new basis for American nationhood. It has nothing to do with who came over on the Mayflower. What does a Chinese who came over in 1889 or an Italian who came over in 1910 or a Pole who came over in 1929 care about the Declaration of Independence? They just came over here because it was impossible over there, that's all.

When we ask what is the nature of man, we are asking about the nature of man for this time and in this country. Therefore, What is a Man? is not a general philosophical problem or question. What is an American in the last quarter of the twentieth century? When you give nationhood to the concept of man, you add a political dimension to your concept of man.

You can't have a great revolution if only one section of the particular nation feels itself involved in the struggle for revolutionary social change. The entire people must feel that the future of humanity is involved, that they are fighting against the past and for the future of humanity. As Marx put it (*German Ideology*), "Each new class which puts itself in the place of one ruling before it, is compelled, merely in order to carry through its aim, to represent its interest as the common interest of all members of society, put in an ideal form; it will give its ideas the form of universality and represent them as the only rational, universally valid ones."

Can we take advantage of the plurality which still exists to some degree in the U.S.—although what the situation will be in another generation we don't know—to encourage the formation of identity groupings based on ethnic origins? We encourage their formation not for the sake of demanding special privileges or for the sake of separation but in order that they may learn through the recapitulation of the concretely lived time which is their history, the social weaknesses as well as the social strengths in that history. This can begin to give them a method by which to discover how they can become more human, discovering themselves not through biological identities but rather through historical identities.

Ethnic groups are essentially historical, particularly in the U.S. When you come together with those of the same ethnic group, all the excuses that you use with other people no longer work—and you no longer can be liberal with yourself. You begin to recover a sense of development in relationship to cultures which still have their history, which have not yet become homogenized. Before too long, if the U.S. continues to become McDonaldized and the world continues to become Coca-Cola-ized, the average person will have great difficulty discovering and recovering history. Only the elite may be able to use languages from the past. This is a very crucial period in history—as it is in the history of the environment, or of nature. *How much can you wipe out of the past and still be human,* still have a sense of time, a sense of the value of human life?

Developing identity groups in this sense may be a means of using diversity as a principle of unity.

It is easy to fall into the trap of thinking that to discover the nature of man is to discover a thing instead of discovering that in the nature of man there is a diversity analogous to the diversity in nature. It works beautifully in nature. If lions did not eat the sick and crippled antelopes, antelopes would die out. The survivors are the healthy ones.

The development of man implies not a lessening but an increase of diversity. The further development of man requires him to be able to accept more diversity as a way to discover ever-widening horizons for man-ness. We are in favor of increasing diversity—provided that it is not competing diversity.

Unitary thought permits the inclusion of everything. It doesn't require the banishment of certain thoughts. The American revolution is for the purpose of discovering how a hundred different types of cultures can all live together in enormous enjoyment and enriched by the fact that you live next to a guy who differs with and from you. Writing in the 1940s, Lancelot Whyte *(The Next Development in Man)* saw a grandeur in Russia measured against what was happening in the rest of the world. But he had no idea of the complexity, the plurality, the diversity of the U.S. Nor had the Chinese Revolution (with its concept of the transformation of man) taken place. We are able to contribute much more about diversity, give more meaning to diversity from where we are today—in the United States and since the Chinese Revolution. Yet we must be careful not to base our idea of diversity just on the U.S., the actual situation here, but on the need for diversity as part of the developing nature of man. We are not discovering a *thing*, we are creating man. We are human beings in the process of becoming, and you cannot have a concept of development or of becoming unless you have a concept of diversity.

No revolution has ever taken place without affecting the entire world. When Revel talks about the American revolution (*Without Marx or Jesus*), he is talking too limitedly about America. But an American revolution can't be an American revolution if it is just a lot of Americans trying to solve something within the confines of this country, thinking solely about American problems. We have to incorporate into our thinking everything that man is thinking everywhere—or else it is just a little sectarian thing. The American revolution of the twentieth or twenty-first century must be a world-wide revolution, even more than that of the eighteenth century.

The greatness of the U.S. results from the diversity which it has embodied. All the arts of people from all over the world came in and contributed to what the U.S. is. But the concepts of equality on the basis of which this diversity was brought together are now creating disunity, fragmentation, alienation rather than unity.

We are not just talking about diversity that existed in the past. We are saying that diversity is absolutely crucial in a conception of the future; that if one, in the slightest sense, renounces or demolishes the value, the beauty, of diversity in order to obtain monolithic or monotheistic power, one has crippled the definition of the nature of man and therefore the definition of the nature of revolution. This is not a question of liberating slaves or getting Jews out of Egypt. Rebellions are made by people with resentment; revolutions are explosions of man's nature in order to further expand what his nature is. There can be all kinds of revolutions, but each differs from the other according to what one intends by trying to make that revolution. This is one of the weaknesses of Fanon. He wasn't talking about revolution but about the liberation of a colonial people.

The Chinese have at the back of their thinking the Taoist idea that as history progresses, there is differentiation, a constant evolving of diversity, and consequently a movement away from unity—which poses a problem of how you are going to keep the whole thing from being fragmented. You always require a combination of unity and diversity—otherwise everything just goes up in smoke. There always has to be a unifying principle which, however, is constantly being altered. It is by no means absolute—otherwise the whole thing stagnates. Unifying principles must themselves develop. That is what Stalin didn't understand and Mao did. Stalin thought that having reached one stage, you could stop and entrench—whereas you must always have at the back of your mind the interplay of unity and diversity. You must understand that they complement one another, that you must not get stuck in one, that your present unifying principle is not the end; it is rather a description of the envelope within which all the diversities continue to expand and develop in tension with one another. Unity is the relationship between diversities—not the creation of unity by smashing diversities. That is totalitarianism.

Whenever you hear someone talking about "betrayal," it is usually because they are referring to some kind of fixed concept in their minds which has been outmoded in the course of developing history. Thus, when radicals talk about the betrayal of the rank and file worker by the bureaucrats, they imply that the workers are united and revolutionary (according to their concept of workers), but that the bureaucrats have created disunity and non-revolutionary individualism between them.

WOMEN

Precisely because the division of labor between men and women has been so long-lasting, women's groups need a profound philosophical concept of what a human being is. Otherwise in the absence of knowing what they want, they are likely to adopt the most limited conceptions of a human being. All radical groups—not really knowing what they want—adopt all these easy superficial responses: "I want to be free, etc." Why should all women think the same thing? Why shouldn't there be diversity among women? Women want equality with men but the equality of women and men is a little ridiculous in a lot of spheres. Men want superiority to women, which is equally ridiculous. But it is difficult to talk to U.S. women today about diversity.

When you are oppressed, it is difficult not to think that your thoughts, your reasoning, are imbued with correctness simply because you are a woman or a black who is oppressed. We are not just quarreling with the tactics of the various liberation groups; we are saying that none of them really knows what they are striving for. Therefore they are shackled with the same concepts of the nature of man as their oppressors.

That is why we have had to deal with equality, freedom, abstract truth, diversity, and all these basic concepts.

What makes the problem of women so difficult is that women have been oppressed by men for so long, and men have for so long controlled society and felt themselves superior to women. Up to now, all revolutionists, including ourselves, have thought that in order to support revolution, you not only listened to but also received the truth from those who were oppressed. One of the things we have been striving for is the courage and the clarity to understand why that is exactly *not* true. It is a denigration of women's liberation and all these liberation groups to believe that they can't stand being challenged. They don't amount to anything if nobody can ask them some hard questions. The average radical is afraid to ask them any questions because he will be assumed to be a liberal, or a counter-revolutionary, or a member of the oppressing group. We are convinced that this is a form of destruction of revolutionary advancement.

Whyte says that the ultimate role of women is to preserve unity and continuity in the chain of life; that women are of special importance to dissociated Western man: "She can heal him from a tradition absorbed too earnestly." Is the concept of yin and yang in Chinese philosophy expressive of a "male chauvinist" attitude?

The first, fundamental diversity is between men and women. Because moderns start by class-angling history, we usually assume that it was the male of the species who set into motion the division of labor. Couldn't it have been a common understanding at the beginning?— which does not mean that it should continue or endure. But, by and large, we have taken for granted the class approach without wondering whether there might be other reasons why such relationships exist. How much of the division of labor was inevitable? How much natural? Every time we think about equality, these are the sort of questions we are raising.

Do we need to discover a new word for "mankind"? To make clear that "man" does not stand only for male but for the human species, for homo sapiens? Not for the sake of the women's liberation movement but for the sake of our own concept of revolution as an advancement of humanity? If we said, "All men and all women are created equal," would we have solved anything? Does the use of the word "mankind" imply a monolithic or static concept when we should be recognizing diversity and development? We should first try to think about the relationships differently—and then think about the word. We should not prejudge the question by saying "the word doesn't matter" or by just using another word.

Because there is difference between men and women does not mean that there is therefore inferiority or superiority. We have to recognize that there has been domination of women by men; but at the same time we have to recognize that there is a natural difference between men and women—which does not mean that we accept domination. The tendency today is *to believe that the only way to escape domination is to deny difference.*

We must be careful not to be looking for some kind of fixed truth about the relations between men and women, when in fact whatever we discover about it is going to be created and not found. Precisely because this question is so complex, it is important not to have any concept of absolute truth, let alone, absolute equality. The only important thing is that we undertake a search for a new relationship between men and women, having rejected the idea of the superiority of men to women. Rejecting the concept of superiority, repudiating oppression and domination is the only absolute truth we need to start with. From then on, we try to discover a new relationship, not an absolute truth, a relationship that is based upon diversity which is complementary and non-antagonistic, rather than equal or dominating.

We emphasize that we are *not discovering identities but creating identities.* We are searching for new ideas as the means for creating new appropriate relationships.

Maybe the less we know about the origin of the family, the freer we are to create new appropriate relationships. A great many scientists have assumed that they know everything and therefore they know the conclusions they are coming to. Then suddenly someone discovers that the molecule or the atom isn't the final unit they thought it was.

So everything gets altered. We don't need the myth of a golden age in the past—when women were either equal to men or dominated men—in order to believe that there should be equality or domination in the future.

The past does not have to control the present or the future. In the "Correct Handling of Contradictions" Mao makes clear that there are antagonistic contradictions and there are non-antagonistic contradictions. When reactionaries put you into a corner, then you have to fight them (although not at every moment); but all other contradictions must be seen as non-antagonistic, to be resolved by discussion, not by power relationships. Most women in the women's liberation movement have a women's power concept.

The fight for the right to abortion is not a question of women versus men. This is a question of women versus reactionaries, whether they be white, or black, or men, or women. It is a political question in which the Church, which has been defended most by women, is against abortion. Women who have children in order to hold men are reactionaries. They shouldn't be supported because they are women.

At this stage the women's movement is still at the stage of gripes, getting things out of their system. It is progressive for groups to get together on their own because on their own they can't blame others for interfering with their struggle to clarify their direction. But oppressed groups feel terribly touchy about any question. They are unsure of where they are going. The cadre does not deny the need to organize separate groups, but it has the responsibility not to be limited by them. Why should the women's movement have to go through all the stages of the black movement? Obviously women feel much the same way as blacks do about their movement, but what is advancement if one group can't learn from another group's experience?

Learning presupposes inequality between people. If there is no inequality, then nobody can learn anything from anybody else. Everybody can't always be starting from scratch. Advancement means that sometimes you start from a place that somebody else has reached.

Blacks have talked about identity as if it were some *place* in Africa or in a book by Du Bois, when actually they are struggling to create a new identity in the last quarter of the twentieth century. Because they got bogged down in the idea that it already exists, they have not been able to create a new identity. Women have to create an identity which is appropriate to the new situation in the world, the new stage of civilization. They have to make use of the past in the sense of understanding as much of the past as possible, of what women have done as an indication of what women can do. But we should not be burdened by the past. The great problem today is how to relate to the past without being burdened by it. Marx got bogged down because he tried to imagine a primitive communism as the basis for a new communism, and therefore his thinking about the new communism was limited by the kinds of relationships which he dreamed back into the past.

People with particular things in common come together to see how, by virtue of their particular past and their particular characteristics, they can contribute to the creation of a new identity with diversity. One of the most important developments from women's liberation is that it has led men to explore what their identity should be; thus not to take for granted that, being men, they can move immediately from the past, without any examination of the past, into a new identity as human beings.

Could a woman have written the *New World Symphony*? No, because women never had that sense of tremendous vitality and triumph in relation to the creation of a new nation. This is a role which men assumed, adopted, carried. It is not a question of "you sons of bitches, you didn't let us do it." Rather we have to recognize that women did not take that role, and therefore society assumed a certain form—grand but also limited. To walk around feeling guilty about it is just plain ridiculous. One has to relate to a past in order to create a future, not to be burdened down by it, not to feel guilty for it, but to understand the limitations and mistakes—in order not to repeat them.

Why should the battle between the sexes be one in which one side wins over the other? Once you stop thinking in terms of equality, then you not only recognize that each person makes a different contribution, but you also recognize that not everybody makes a contribution at a particular time. This is difficult to appreciate in our idealized egalitarian society where everything is judged in terms of the moment or the instant. For twenty years China said practically nothing to the nations of the West, and now she begins to speak. What she begins to say now has an enormous importance. China didn't have to say something every time an issue arose. Maybe not saying anything for a long time was the most important thing to do, since not saying something is also saying something. *Developments take place over a long period of time.* To get this concept in your mind is very difficult. The women's movement is important because it includes every woman in the world—but maybe we don't have to debate with men today over whose vision is correct. The contributions of women can be so fantastically diverse from those of men that one has to think when does one try to make this contribution. Until women have gotten over their tremendous sense of inferiority and self-hate, until they begin to develop a much surer sense of who they are and what they can contribute, those qualities which women are best able to contribute will not be contributed. Most women today in the women's movement are full of resentment. Without generosity you can't create revolution. Without generosity you can't accept diversity. *Generosity is not the same as liberalism; it is a revolutionary trait.*

ONLY IN AMERICA

Strange how long it takes to catch up with ancient wisdoms if you haven't been thinking historically and philosophically. U.S. revolutionaries haven't been thinking in terms of history and philosophy at all. The Industrial Revolution set up a "doing" mentality which reached its ultimate in the U.S. At least in Europe the Industrial Revolution was related to a *thought process*—the Renaissance and the Reformation. In the U.S. it wasn't related to anything at all—except what some guy brought over from Europe. The U.S. sent its dynamism back to Europe and the rest of the world. *No thoughts.*

We have to understand that a generation is now being created which has not experienced the last thirty years in relation to the last one hundred. *Our generation is the tie that binds, the link in the chain.* Very few of the post–World War II generation have any sense of what it is like to have lived through the pre–World War II period, the twenties, the thirties, the forties—each decade very different from that which preceded and that which succeeded it. Living through them gave you some sense of human history, of time as history. The postwar generation has been born like test-tube babies. They don't even know what a past is. The generation which is sixty-seventy has lived through two world wars.

Many writers like Lewis Mumford and Lancelot Whyte have made a critique of the last two thousand years and have understood the role of Marx in relationship to these two thousand years. What is our relationship to them? They, writing from outside the Movement, seem to be writing as humanists from the pre-Marxist period. We are not. We are part of the American Movement from rebellion to revolution. So that the time it has taken to get us to the "long view"— the history that we have made—is important. We are not going to last much longer. There aren't very many of us. Someone who hasn't participated in the Marxist movements and the liberation movements might as well be back in ancient Greece. Our ideas are very special because they have been arrived at through a very special kind of historical experience, a particular historical process, a coincidence in time and place. The four of us—a black worker, a descendant of Robert Treat Paine, a Chinese woman, a Jewish woman who has been a labor organizer—*could only have come together this way in America*. It happened this way because we were all in the Marxist movement, to begin with. Otherwise we would have been all in our separate milieux. Black and white, Chinese and Jew, we were first brought together by a very Europeanized West Indian, a Marxist who was convinced that the American revolution would be the first, most perfect, manifestation of Marxist theory but who paid more attention to the American revolution than any American Marxists had ever done. Breaking with his theories, *but still intent on discovering and making the American revolution,* we began to discover our diversities and our special contribution.

Without the consciousness of particular people, there is no consciousness at all. There is no consciousness "in general," no "abstract man," no "abstract consciousness." In one sense we have the same ideas as Mumford and Whyte; in another, very important sense, we do not. Their ideas come from one experience while those we have come from another. We can have genuine dialogue but it is still a dialogue, an interaction between their ideas and ours, even though we may use the same words. Otherwise we are thinking of ideas as things—which they are not.

We have to understand that Whyte and Mumford have made tremendous intellectual criticisms which are of extraordinary value to us. But they have not been members of the movement of Marxism, have not been active in the Movement, the labor movement, the black movement, as we have. Therefore we can give a reality to their ideas which they couldn't possibly give them. The whole thing goes back to the question of diversity. The relationship between people should never be competitive. The average revolutionist, however, thinks his job is to be competitive; he is going to win and others are going to lose. Most people don't understand complementary relationships which involve process and mutual interaction and change. The complementary relationship between diversities is a revolutionary relationship. There is a kind of individualism in the radical movement which demands that their group know "the truth" and that they owe nothing to anybody except Marx, Lenin, Stalin or Mao. If those were the only ones we owed anything to, we wouldn't know very much—certainly about America. In a sense men like Mumford and Whyte are more important to us than Mao because they have made a critique of the West from inside.

Most radicals do not have the courage or confidence in their ideas to use people like Whyte and Mumford as a resource, to expand their minds, to enrich their thinking. We don't look to them to tell us how to organize or how to work in different types of organizations with people. We know a lot more about that than they do. We have had a lot of experience in how to listen and how not to listen. We have made a lot of mistakes and therefore we have some idea of how not to make these same mistakes. So we do not ask them for programs, for tactics.

ACCUMULATION OF CULTURAL CAPITAL

How much tradition and knowledge have to be accumulated in order for a house to become more than a shelter? The Marxist sectarian thinks only of money capital, when in fact the greatest capital of man is the accumulation of everything else besides money. *The cultural development of society is the capital we have to preserve.* Hitler and Stalin both paid no attention to the historical accumulation of cultural capital. They were going to create another society right off the bat, like minting a new silver dollar. How are we going to rediscover the incredible cultural capital which has been piled up by innumerable generations of all kinds of people: Bushmen, Eskimos, Japanese, Prussians, Englishmen? Who is responsible in this country for perpetuating the past? In other civilizations, the very history itself perpetuated; there were no special people, no special institutions picked out to do it. The fact that these things had taken place and moved so many people stimulated so many rebellions and revolutions—that history was the perpetuator. But in the U.S. there is no history, there are no perpetuators. In Detroit there is nothing that gives you a sense of the past. You wouldn't know that Detroit was the crossing point for the Underground Railroad unless you went downtown looking for a plaque. In the ancient days, when there was nothing but continuity to the development of civilization or culture, people were aware of *process*. Now—over the last two hundred years—in this technological society, we have lost all notion of *process*. The criterion for deciding whether one is civilized is a computer or a snowmobile. The notion of continuity, of the relationship of the present to the past to the future, has been completely and totally lost. That is why today's music—rock and roll—has absolutely no past whatsoever. It is just saying *"I am."* It is a subjective expression of anger and frustration: alienated, angry, isolated men seeking togetherness (which a fascist cell can also provide).

How do you help a kid understand the basis of human civilized living?

Outward Bound is a program sponsored by people who believe that if you want to teach kids something about nature, you put them in relationship to nature. Those who have enough courage to embark on this program are turned loose like primitive man to grapple with the necessities of nature. They learn that you don't play politics with nature, you don't maneuver nature; there is absolutely no manipulation possible. You suddenly realize that you are in a position where you don't control things with a computer. You learn the most profound lesson of all, that man is a child of nature. What do most people know today about how people have lived for tens of thousands of years, and the external necessities that nine-tenths of the world still live under? How you get along with other people depends on how you relate to nature. If you understand nature, you begin to understand where your relationship to another man begins.

Indians couldn't conceive of living unless they trusted their own people. Without this they couldn't even send out a scout. The trust that grew out of these relatively simple actions was the cornerstone of existence of early societies and must be the cornerstone of modern society. You can't live by chicanery, by cleverness, by double-dealing.

To trust your neighbor is a very human concept, not revolutionary at all. It's a sign of the horribly degraded state of our society that one can think that to believe in these elementary human values means you are revolutionary. Yet we have practically reached the stage where to have *any* values means you are a revolutionist. (Yevtushenko: "How fantastic to think I was a man of courage when I was simply a man.") To begin to realize that the basis of trust between one man and another is an extraordinarily delicate yet definable thing! If he's a liar, you can't trust him. The basis of human relationships is so simple, and yet it is so incredibly difficult to get at the expression of this basis.

How do you get a kid to realize this? First, you try to be an example of these values. You don't cheat, you don't lie, you don't gossip behind people's backs just because you don't like them. Then you tell the kid that any time you live in a situation where you can't live by these elementary human values, there is something wrong with it, and he or she should look into what is wrong with it with the aim of doing something about it.

If he wants to do that as a Republican or a Democrat or a revolutionary, that's his business. But if you don't start that way, you're a gangster. A Weatherman who teaches his kid only Weatherman values will find his kid growing up to be a Weatherman gangster rather than another kind of gangster. Somewhere we got lost in this business of "their" morals and "ours" on the assumption that we, the self-proclaimed revolutionists, were the only ones with morals and also the only ones with the definition of morals. The other guys were enemies, less than human. This way of looking at the world has come back to plague us: everybody now says it. Sectarianism lies in believing that only revolutionists are right, and anyone who calls himself a revolutionist is therefore right.

Because of the chaos in the schools, and because schools are a normal place for shaping people's minds, we think of using the schools to shape people's minds with values. But schools should not be used to give revolutionary training. You can't believe in the revolution until you have some values. Don't think you can make the revolution and then somehow get some values.

You can't just *teach* ethics, you don't *instill* ethics. You help kids to discover the human values which man has created over thousands of years. Tell them what man has tried to do—from the time of the caveman to the day before yesterday in Greenland. You can't get to politics until you have investigated ethics, and the particular politics you arrive at will be an expression of your ethics, although ethical people will not necessarily have the same politics. With Marxists, politics determined ethics. We are saying that politics must spring from ethics.

It is impossible to be a revolutionist unless you have a concept of new, positive human values; but having such concepts does not make you a revolutionist. Not only revolutionists have a concept of new positive human values.

In the situation we are in today, it is impossible to establish human values unless you are revolutionary, i.e., seeking to bring about a drastic change in man's direction and in the society. You have to discover the standards first, and then, having discovered them, discover the need for revolution, for fundamental social change. To be a revolutionist, one begins by wanting to create ever higher forms of human values; ever more mutually respecting relations between people. So that if this could be done in an evolutionary, not a revolutionary way, you would nevertheless still be for it.

To teach anybody to be a revolutionist is impossible. A teacher can illuminate for youngsters the history of man, so that out of their own volition and their own responses, they may or may not decide to be revolutionists rather than reactionaries. But you cannot teach anyone to be a revolutionist rather than a reactionary. There is only one basis for being a revolutionist—that is to care deeply for human values, like honesty, long before you talk about the complexities of being revolutionary or reactionary. You can't be a revolutionist by just wanting to jump stages. You have to go through stages of discovering what it is to be a human being.

Last year we distinguished between rebellion and revolution. This year we have penetrated some distance into what is revolution. It is not an assertion; it is a relationship which springs from such a powerful sense of human values that you feel you want to change things. It doesn't start from anger; it starts from notions of human values which are being denigrated, defamed, denied. Revolution is the product. It is not the producer. A person with elementary human values is not necessarily a revolutionist; but at the other extreme neither is an angry rebel who is determined just to get rid of what is.

No person who is seriously thinking about the advancement of man should stand still; but it is important not to jump stages of thought before you finalize each stage. *It is a process that takes time.*

It is easy to think of a new thought every day, but if you do this without internalizing each stage, then after a while you can't make any judgments. Discovering that making a revolution in the U.S. is infinitely more difficult than it was thought to be is itself an important discovery.

Nobody has the final word or completes the entire job. You complete what you have put into the process. Hitler was a type that has existed before in history. In his bunker he probably said, "Well, I didn't make it, but if I had, the world would be completely different." He wasn't thinking of himself as part of a process at all. He was it. His destiny was the world's destiny.

We are discovering that for years we used the phrase "world revolution" without knowing what we meant by it. We are now not even talking about making revolution; we are still talking about extensions of awarenesses, which will permit us to talk about making revolution tomorrow. If one pushes too fast, not only is one making a mistake, but one blockades oneself from internalizing what is already known.

One of the incredible things is that after the Russian Revolution, almost every revolutionist was restricted in his thoughts and imagination about revolution, in the sense that he felt compelled to think that the Russians had made the revolution—that it was the end of revolutionary creativity. And in a strange and horrifying sense that was true until Mao came on the scene. Until then, the revolution was there, to be grasped, to be accepted, to be rejected. We went through thirty years of the most incredible diminution of man's revolutionary creativity and imagination. We were so paralyzed by the pattern that we were unable to understand that the revolution isn't limited that way. It isn't a *thing*. What we have been trying to do is liberate thinking about revolution. We are not trying to make the revolution in these discussions. We are trying to think about what would make the making of revolution possible.

ENGAGING OTHERS

When you begin projecting ideas to people, they want to go out and organize to change the system. It is very difficult to get them to understand that their first task is to organize in such a way as to disseminate the ideas, and to become witnesses themselves to the ideas in their practice and process. That concept of projection, of propaganda, of process, is what has to become clear—that you are engaged in a process of evolving ideas, disseminating them and developing people who become disseminators and witnesses to the ideas, models. People usually say "Now we have had a good discussion; what do we do?" as if the discussion had been only a burdensome preliminary to militant actions which no longer involve any ideas.

We are not talking about getting involved with the mass media. The American media would destroy Castro in ten minutes. He would talk himself out without having a chance to develop his ideas in a process of interaction. The Chinese say that if they had had television in China, their revolution would have taken many times as long as it did.

We are just at the beginning of opening up our minds and those of others to the realization that we are *creating the ideas for the next historical moment in history.* The Chinese Revolution was the last of the revolutions which began three hundred years ago. It may be some time before we discover the form of the next series of revolutions. Maybe if, from this year to the next, we challenge one hundred people to think differently, that will be an important step to what happens in the year 2000. What happens in 2000 will not happen because that year the ideas suddenly emerged. They have been developing all along the way—from today—and attempts will be made, all along the way, to implement some of them, eventually bringing qualitative leaps in the ideas themselves.

The next revolution can't take place in America if there is nobody in England, Africa or Asia who has the faintest idea what people in America are thinking about. There are going to be persons in other countries thinking "that's right." But they can't think that unless there are some persons here developing and disseminating ideas. We should see ourselves as raising the aspirations of mankind all over the world. Otherwise there will be no American revolution.

1971

New Questions for an American Revolution

Turning Point in History

In our 1970 Conversations, "Toward a New Man," we emphasized the difference between rebellion and revolution.* We determined that a revolution is not just to deal with past injustices. A revolution begins a new stage in the evolution of mankind.

In our 1971 Conversations, "Changing Ourselves," we began to realize how much we have to change our own thinking in regard to such basic concepts as politics, truth, freedom, and equality. We need to develop a new notion of politics as creative human activity to supplant the one that most radicals have of politics as "superstructure," and the one that most Americans have of politics as "dirty" or at least less worthy of human endeavor and pursuit than economics or private happiness. We made distinctions between truths of fact and truths of conviction. We contrasted the freedom that relates people to one another with the inner, subjective freedom that an individual feels. We emphasized the importance of recognizing the diversity between individuals in contrast to perceiving everybody in terms of some abstract concept of equality, which thereby reduces to a least common denominator. Note: we are grappling with these fundamental concepts as people who have come out of and are part of the revolutionary Movement, and who recognize the need to make radical changes in our own thinking if we are to help bring about radical changes in society.

This year we have to go deeper and wonder about the nature of man, not from the outside as an anthropologist does, but from within, in terms of how man conceives of himself.

---

*See the Preface for comments from the editors regarding the use of the word "man."

Men and women have been exemplifying this nature for fifty thousand years, but most people today know little about those fifty thousand years, and therefore know very little about the nature of man except as illustrated by their father and mother, their brothers and sisters, and themselves. If you ask someone "What do you want?" he or she is always going to answer in terms of yesterday or the immediate past, never in terms of tomorrow—until they have a notion of tomorrow. Our job is to project the concept that there is a tomorrow, and that the revolution is not an expression of the past or the present; it is an expression of this desire for tomorrow.

Have there ever before been so many people saying "We are in the struggle," without any common notion of what the struggle is for? The Crusaders knew they were out to convert everyone to Christians. Today people in the movement have no unifying idea of what kind of "whole new person" will create, or will be created, in the process of revolution. And yet precisely because in the U.S. there is such a deep cult of the individual and because people have so many different points of reference, we need a unifying view as to what kind of more human, human being will create, and will be created in, the course of revolutionary struggles.

SINCE THE REBELLIONS

In the Russian Revolution it wasn't so necessary for people to have a concept of the nature of man, of what man has done down through the ages. In the past, acting out of material necessity and with standards and traditions still remaining from the past, people could move almost reactively and by their reactive actions advance society. They were pursuing a course of history whose direction was already to some degree set by the pursuit of economic necessity and which they were only in a sense improving.

In the past we never asked workers whether they were for a revolution. The very fact that they rebelled against present conditions, that they thought of themselves as "us" versus "them," was enough for us to be sure that they were for the new society. In a sense it was not until the United States experienced an extended period of continuing rebellion as over the past ten years—reaching the point where rebellious masses feel that because of the despicableness of the present society, they have the right to do anything—that we were able to arrive at a really serious evaluation of the difference between rebellion and revolution.

Unless we are willing to make this evaluation now, we can only wind up making excuses, rationalizing why we didn't succeed—which is what radicals generally do—*if* we had only reached more people," or "*if* we had only gone deeper" etc., etc. What we have to reexamine is our major premise, which has been that "the masses are ready" and all we had to do was get to them and stir them into motion. Their momentum would then bring out the instinctive and elemental drive to reconstruct society, which was already within them. Hence the typical radical emphasis on "militancy" as the measure of how revolutionary an individual or the masses are.

Blacks took this assumption even further, particularly after the rebellions of the late sixties. They assumed that all blacks were really for revolution, or that all blacks are beautiful, which is another way of saying that all blacks are the same: "All blacks are oppressed; therefore all blacks are beautiful." Yet, precisely at this point of greatest apparent unity among blacks, or of greatest black identity, of greatest assumption of the sameness of blacks or of the possibility of uniting all blacks in the wake of the rebellions, all the differences that are within blacks were beginning to come out.

It is impossible to overemphasize the significance of difference. For example, if you ask one black guy "How would you like to live?," he might say, "I would like to live like Adam Clayton Powell with a mistress, a house in the Bahamas, and a guaranteed salary from Congress." Another guy might answer, "I want a Cadillac and a million dollars in the bank, and I am ready to push dope to get these." Another: "I'd like to live like Martin Luther King." Or: "I want to live like Eldridge Cleaver because he is a revolutionist and Martin Luther King was just a Christian liberal." Each is describing the difference that resides within him; also, of course, the differences socially inculcated by his father and mother, what schools he went to, or whom he met or didn't meet, but essentially the differing answers to these questions spring from within the nature of the individual. Richard Wright was Richard Wright, and the only one from his family and community who emerged. The rest were submerged by their oppression. There was in Richard Wright something that said, "I am not going to be oppressed; I am not going to be shaped by my conditions."

Revolutionary thinkers, revolutionary theorists and leaders, or revolutionary individuals who can give leadership —we are not talking about revolutionary masses because there aren't any such things in the U.S. at this point—are made up of people who are different in that sense. We can't begin to move until it is clear that that is where we are moving from.

"THINGS FALL APART"

What is the despicableness of our society today? In the thirties you could start out with pure economics; even as late as 1969, it was possible to believe that you could make a radical change in the social, economic, and political fiber of this country within the old framework of economics. Today you would have to start by talking about the "quality of life." Everything is breaking down. Why? People find it easy to blame the moon program or the war in Vietnam. We are against both—but we also are convinced that not going to the moon or ending the war will not stop the breakdown as long as there has been no serious thought given to alternatives. That is why the question "Whom would you like to live like?" is such a revealing one. Or "Who do you think is moral?" We have to reveal people to themselves—and also to discover the people who are different, who are not shaped by their conditions, who are determined not to be shaped by them.

We can say that certain things are not worrying the American people as a whole. For example, "inequality" bothers specific groups but not the American people as a whole; and it bothers specific groups chiefly because they "want in." "Quality of life" is too depersonalized a term to describe what is bothering people. It is the kind of discursive word used mostly by professional intellectuals in order to talk *about* the prevailing disintegration. The average person experiences this breakdown, this deterioration, this disintegration, in far more basic human terms.

People feel that this "falling apart" syndrome is contrary to the nature of a society, that a society should be "a coming-together" rather than "a falling-apart," that centripetal forces rather than centrifugal forces should be at work. They feel that the whole situation is beyond human control, that nobody is controlling anything and that it is wrong for things to be going in all directions with nobody at the helm. If you probe, you find that what bothers people most is the purposelessness, the meaninglessness of existence. "Why am I doing what I am doing? Why does anybody do anything?" Today the only answer people can give you or themselves for what they do is "why not?" If we once begin to see that this is what is really bothering people, we might be able to arrive at some fundamental concept about what people need and the absolutely crucial role that the search for meaning plays in human life.

If we take European history alone, not even considering Oriental or African history, we would discover the fantastic things that happened during the past two thousand years; for example, the Crusades, the dance mania, the French Revolution—literally hundreds of expressions of man's strivings to discover and create meaning in human life. But by and large, as a people we are ignorant of human beings having striven for anything beyond the material—and of what human beings needed to make their lives meaningful throughout human history. The only way we judge anything today is by looking at what is happening in Northern Ireland, or Detroit, or Los Angeles. We don't have enough awareness of the incredible, the indomitable power of man's search. The average person doesn't have any idea that anybody ever did anything.

We have to look at the U.S. today in fundamental terms—not just in terms of economics, e.g., high prices. In this connection, it is not so much the actual highness of prices that bothers people so much. It is rather that there seems to be no end to the price rise. The whole thing seems so senseless and irrational. In the U.S. prices never go down, no matter how much is produced or how quickly more is produced. It is the irrationality of this that is so destructive, because unit costs should go down as more is produced more efficiently. What is so disconcerting is the apparent impenetrability, the meaninglessness, the senselessness of the whole situation. We live in a Kafka-like world in which what is happening seems to be brought about by nameless shadows.

We are trying to discover something new about man. Until we begin to learn more about this, it is impossible to have programs—because any program would just be based on what we have already determined, i.e., on the past. The past paralyzes all of us. A vision enables you to escape paralysis.

THE TECHNOLOGICAL REVOLUTION

Seventy-five years of technological revolution have created a completely new situation. The Industrial Revolution—two, three hundred years ago—did one thing: it completely shattered the world of its time, because prior to that things had been practically the same for thousands of years.

Now all of a sudden, the technological revolution has burst upon us and has done something else: it permits us to create material values without limit. It permits us to pollute our planet. It permits us to do a thousand things. And it also compels us, for the first time in history, to wonder where man wants to go. Up to now, man has known where he wants to go, but where does he want to go now? Suddenly you can have Cadillacs and food. What the technological revolution does is require man to ask himself some questions that in the past were asked only by very particular individuals. Now all of a sudden, man-in-general is being asked, "Where do you want to go now?" Who is going to help man-in-general decide this?

The technological revolution is so totally embracing, the powers that have burst upon man so great, that man suddenly has to discover what does he want to do with those powers. He has never been asked the question before that way—imperiously! What does man want to do with these powers? He has to discover, "Are we going to have morality? Or are we only going to have greed?" The answers that Marx gave to the questions of his epoch are no longer adequate to the issues of this epoch.

We are not trying to deny Marx, but there is no question that Marxism is limited by the historical determinism that has become Marxist thinking. Most Marxists have believed that if you could only sneak up on the masses, prod them into motion around their grievances, then, as a result of their objective social condition in production, they would keep moving in such a way as to create a socialist society.

Everything that has happened in the past fifty to one hundred years has demonstrated that this is not true. We have to repudiate this concept that the consciousness of the masses doesn't matter; that they don't need advanced ideas; that their physical energies and their objective situation in production are all that matter; that the self-interest of workers (or of any social group, per se) objectively and automatically coincides with the advancement of the human race.

Essentially the people who are relying on Marx for theoretical and political guidance are still trying to communicate on the basis of a vision from the past, when in fact the task of the revolutionist is always to communicate on the basis of a vision of the future, a vision as yet unthought of.

The important thing today is not to wonder about what one doesn't like but to wonder about what one does like, about how one wants to live. "How would you like to live otherwise?" That is the question. Is the new society going to be an air-conditioned society? Are we all going to live in cities under plastic domes, with everything in the environment, including climate, controlled?

The vision we project can't be a purely physical vision, although obviously it will have to achieve physical embodiment. Essentially it must be of a certain kind of human being, the way he or she lives in relation to nature, to other people, past, present, and future; the things for which he or she has reverence. That is what philosophy is: a way of thinking about man's nature, his relationships to the cosmos, to others, to human history, and to human destiny. That is why philosophy becomes so important in periods of great historical transition.

GETTING RID OF DETERMINISM

We cannot repeat too often that we have a responsibility to discover and to project new concepts of man that will be appropriate for this period, this specific stage of human development. Seventy-five years of technological revolution have outmoded the concepts by which man has lived, struggled and cared in the past. The technological revolution has totally and completely changed the historical situation just as the Renaissance destroyed the Middle Ages. The technological revolution is the contemporary equivalent of the Renaissance.

At this conjuncture, as at every great historical conjuncture, man has to bring about a great change in his concept of necessity, in his assessment of his power to shape his destiny. At the beginning of the Industrial Revolution, man was able to abandon his previous concept of religious determinism. He was able to recognize that man had created the gods. Now, what man has to get rid of are the concepts of economic determinism and historical determinism. He has to stop thinking about man as completely shaped by his circumstances. He must begin to think and to project to others the idea that man *can* change his circumstances, and that, in fact, man's circumstances were made by man himself. Just as through technology, man has practically remade the world, so man can remake himself. The system is man-made, just as technology is man-made, just as the gods were and just as the church was. What man is going to be, what society is going to be, is going to be determined by man. But he can't do this until he stops seeing himself in the role of creature and sees himself in the role of creator, stops seeing himself in the role of victim and recognizes himself as truly self-determining.

Modern American man has lost the notion that he is the determiner of anything. If the degradation around us is the act of man, then man can come to the conclusion that it isn't right, that it isn't necessary and that he is going to change it. We have to reaffirm that nothing exists on this planet except as man makes it so.

One of the reasons why the radicals have failed is that they think of the revolution as a struggle to reach an end, a closed system—to prove a theory—rather than to make another beginning. They have not been able to project notions of and for tomorrow. Tomorrow's ideas depend on our recognizing that what we have been trying to achieve is no longer right: that we have to aim for something new and that this process never ends.

LANGUAGE

A similar process of unending creation is involved in language.

For about one hundred years there have been two ideas about language among linguists. One school believes that we are not really different from animals, that we only have more of the qualities that they have. They have mouths and larynxes, their speech organs are shaped like ours. Nobody has been able to find any difference in their frontal lobes. They can make noises and tools, e.g., put sticks together. So this school of linguists, who have been dominant in the U.S., believe that we are only quantitatively greater apes.

On the other hand, Noam Chomsky believes that we are qualitatively different from animals because we have genetically inherent in us, first of all, a generalized capacity to symbol—which is a creative capacity expressed in language as well as in ritual and in art. You can't have the idea of sin or of the flag, for example, without an idea of symbol. Helen Keller describes in her life story how she felt repentance and sorrow for the first time on the day she learned about symbols. One morning she had broken a doll in a fit of temper. She had been playing with it, and then in anger smashed and kicked it aside. Later that same day she learned about "water" and had gone around touching "tree," "grass," "ground," "mother," "father," "teacher," and had burst into a storm of tears, overcome with emotion because she could communicate. When they took her back into the house, she saw the doll and, as she says, "I felt great repentance in my heart. I felt an emotion I had never felt before, and I knew what I had done." She "crossed the threshold of reflection," in Chardin's phrase, that day.

Chomsky also believes that somewhere in our brains are implanted certain particular ways to form grammar. He thinks that all the languages are related, that they are not just learned, that there is something about grammar which is inherent in the human mind— innate forms of associating and separating concepts, of constructing syntax.

Among Chomsky's highly technical theories, one part is fairly simple—his idea that talking involves a kind of segmenting process. A sentence is made up of words, but words are made up of sounds; so you have a box within a box, and you can't have human communication without this one-inside-the-other relationship. Apes can only have the whole sound by itself; it is the whole thing to them. We have words (e.g., "water") which are made up of several phonemes and we have sentences that are made up of blocks (words in some languages, phrases in others). All human symbolization consists of these two parts, regardless of language.

Without this innate capacity to segment, we could not learn to speak. We do learn to speak quite automatically; children create sentences very early that they have never heard before. These sentences are usually incorrect grammatically, but the children are creating. Every sentence is a creation that is being said for the first time. Speech is absolutely open-ended; and the same construct of words can mean something completely different, depending on how you accent each word. For example, "He is leaving tomorrow," means something completely different each time you accent a different one of the four words in the sentence.

Emily Dickinson caught this when she said, "A word is dead, some say. I say / It just begins to live that day." The whole notion of its being said leads to something else being said, to the expression of other reflections. "In the beginning was the Word."

At the same time there is a basic contradiction to language: Once you have taken something concrete, with all its uniqueness and individuality, and fixed it by putting a word to it, you have to keep in mind always that what you pinned down, fixed with a word, still goes on living and moving and changing and growing. It is difficult to keep this in mind unless you begin with the concept of the fundamental contradiction in the use of words. Lao Tze recognized this when he said, "The Tao [way] that can be thought of is not the eternal Tao." So did Hegel when he fought against the "fixed concepts" of the understanding.

This contradiction becomes especially important when you are dealing with something as overpowering, as crying out for thought and analysis, and which sets such a fine example for future development as a great revolution: the French Revolution or the Russian, Vietnamese, or Chinese Revolutions. When the Russian Revolution took place, progressive people all over the world grasped and embraced it as an advance in the evolution of mankind.

Radicals and intellectuals are inclined to believe that they know what a revolution is, when, in fact, every revolution is unique, happening for the first time. When we struggle for a revolution, we are not struggling for something fixed or general but for something that is "open-ended." We don't know the answers—otherwise it wouldn't be a revolution.

THE DYNAMIC ROLE OF MAN

Objective thinking about human beings has been relatively recent. Perhaps it comes out of the rationalism of the past few hundred years and the transference of the concepts of causality and Newtonian physics to the social sciences (especially by scholars and intellectuals). Also in bureaucratic societies like ours, our daily lives are to a large extent determined. In past ages, what they couldn't do anything about they attributed to gods or to magic; yet they did think in terms of a large area of choice. Shakespeare expresses the two opposing attitudes: "As flies to wanton boys are we to the gods / They kill us for their sport." This is the victim speaking, the attitude of the determinist. And then the other side: "Men at some times are masters of their fate. The fault, dear Brutus, is not in our stars but in ourselves that we are underlings." Shakespeare was writing at the beginning of the revolution in England, and he saw these two attitudes and created in his plays those who thought they were masters of their fate, and others who thought of themselves as victims. Marx combined the two attitudes: man creates his own destiny, but he doesn't create it just as he chooses.

Whether we like it or not, or whether or not we know what we are doing, we do create our own destinies, just as we keep speaking sentences that have never been spoken before. We also create the s.o.b.'s who tell us what to do.

Most people living before the Industrial Revolution thought that God determined a great deal of what happened and that there were certain things you couldn't do much about. At the same time they believed that "God helps those who help themselves." Every society has known that gods don't determine everything, that magic doesn't work unless you do the gardening. Yet there has been a fatalistic element in relation to things you couldn't control—like when the rains came or the sun shone. It is when we get to the era of science that people come along with the idea that everything is determined. Some, like Marx, replaced God with natural law or objective conditions, but they also knew about choice and that you continually took both into account. Marx was not a determinist the way Marxists have been. Perhaps we can say that determinism has ruled thought to the degree that people have been of small mind, without much hope or perspective. On the other hand, everybody who has been revolutionary in the sense of carrying on real struggles for the involvement of great masses of people in making large scale changes, has thought in what has been called "voluntaristic" terms—in terms of the capacity of man to shape his destiny. (The *Peking Review* is full of articles on philosophy, which always begin by emphasizing the "dynamic role of man.")

Rigid determinism is relatively recent. It seems to have appeared at roughly the same time in both the U.S.S.R. and the U.S., when both were becoming heavily machine-oriented and bureaucratized—in the thirties, forties and fifties. This is still the dominant trend of thought in U.S. social science, although it is being challenged. It is not only a question of social sciences however; the masses also tend to think of themselves chiefly as victims. So that whenever you talk to people about what they need to do, they say, "*They* do such and such, what can *we* do?" Determinism becomes a very real enemy the moment you begin any kind of practical political work among the masses. You are immediately challenged to break through the concept of victimization. Determinism is a very real question of revolutionary politics. It is not an abstract philosophical question. This is why the Chinese place so much emphasis on workers, peasants and soldiers studying philosophy (in order to appreciate "the subjective, dynamic role of man"), and also why they are so much harder on their Western-trained social scientists than on Western-trained physical scientists (Richman, *Industrial Society in Communist China*, 219).

MAN CREATED THE GODS

Determinism is the negative of revolutionism: "I have been determined; I can't do anything." If somebody says he can't do anything, he isn't going to do anything. To do anything, you have to believe that man can do things.

In the beginning man created gods. That is why "religion is the opium of the masses" is a very bad formulation. It puts man in the role of victim. On the other hand, we must understand that man created the gods; therefore he can create anything, including himself. (If you're hooked, you hooked yourself.) If you don't think this way, you're not going to do anything. It is easy, and in a sense comforting, to believe that you are determined by objective social forces beyond your control. Most Marxists encourage the masses to think this way and thereby encourage the passivity of the masses. The responsibility of a revolutionary leader is to encourage just the opposite; the self-concept of the self-determining, creative individual, capable of choice. Marxists think that they are encouraging the masses, but the very use of the word "system" imprisons people, drowns them under a heavy load of something they can't get out from under.

It is also dangerous to give people the impression that they already have the ability, the capacity to do anything, an illusion that's reinforced every day by push-button technology. If, side by side with a deadening determinism, you have a kind of naive reformism, the illusion that you can change anything, do anything just by pushing a button, this contradiction explodes in a kind of rebellious anarchism: i.e., the assumption that you can create a revolution by running out in the middle of the street, or by saying things on TV, or by planting bombs.

Whatever the risks, we have to believe that man *can*; that it is the fantastic capacity of man to do anything he sets his mind to; that the objective social forces are his own creation—so that the destruction of the objective social forces is also his own creation.

First, modern man has to have a philosophy, a conviction. We have to be evangelists to persuade or project to modern man this philosophy: "You can do it. It isn't going to be easy. But first you have to believe you can do it. Then you can discover how to do it."

Why don't people do very much? Because they don't believe that they made the gods; they don't believe that they made this society. They don't believe that they are responsible for the objective social forces that are oppressing them.

Obviously we are not asking blacks to believe that they created the white man who brought them into slavery—because they didn't do anything of the kind. But now that they are here, blacks have to be able to shatter the notion that "the man" controls everything they can think or do about revolution (we are not talking about making money or running a grocery store). *As long as blacks think this, they will never be anything but protesters.* Our job as revolutionists is to persuade every man and woman: "You are the master, nobody else—not the capitalist, not the boss, not the white man. Man is not a victim except as he creates himself as a victim." Only then can people say, "Yes, the problems are enormous; they are formidable, but we can solve them. We can change the way it is." Because if people don't think that they can, they are not going to try, and all we are going to get are sporadic rebellions or bomb-throwing.

Man's Continuing Search for Self

In the past century we have become accustomed to thinking of man as a toolmaker. Mumford says in *The Myth of the Machine* that nothing could be more incorrect. Twenty-five thousand years ago man painted the cave, invented dance and gesture, and then invented language— his greatest creation. If five thousand years ago he was still ploughing with a crooked stick, isn't it obvious that he was not chiefly concerned with perfecting his tools, but rather with discovering himself? Inseparable from whatever man has done to survive down through the ages have been his rituals, art forms and value systems. It is modern social science which has split man up into so many parts, which has made the concept of his survival separate from his art, his artistic endeavor and his concepts of human destiny. Man himself has not made this separation. In whatever he has done, he has always expressed his essence.

The understanding of this process of man's continuing search for self and for identity is absolutely crucial to understanding the humanity we are talking about. Humanity isn't what we have been thinking it was for the past hundred years. Humanity is an incredibly creative expression. It isn't just a search for well-being or material goods. Man's symbols go back thousands and thousands of years. They illustrate what he has been thinking about, what has been on his mind. When man called the moon the "lunar goddess," he wasn't filled with moon madness. He was busy creating another symbol, something that sprang out of himself, not from fear but from within himself. Man's symbols don't express outward things imposed on him by voodoo doctors and the like. They are an expression of what man thinks of himself. The symbols are infinitely more important than the words. Jung in *Man and His Symbols* illustrates what man has been doing with symbols. A lot of modern painting is symbols; it isn't language. Without imagination, man wouldn't be a man; he would just be another animal.

How should man live? We have to be enormously imaginative and creative in dealing with this question. Most people don't have any idea of what their imagination is. Some think that by taking LSD they stimulate their imaginations. Jesus and various medieval saints imaged quite specifically. They didn't have psychedelic dreams. They imagined a new world, a new set of relations for their time. They knew what it was; they could tell you. We can't tell anybody for our time— yet. Jules Verne had incredible imagination: he imagined trips to the moon and under the sea. But now that we have been to the moon, what will we imagine?

Most people don't have any idea of their creative capacities because they don't know anything about man's past, about Angkor Wat, Versailles, Shakespeare, Bach's music. They have no idea what man was capable of, let alone, *is* capable of today.

All we can be sure of at this moment are some visions of tomorrow that we don't want to waste time struggling for because they are based upon the past. E. G. Bellamy's air-conditioned world, or the nineteenth century socialists' "planned production" as contrasted to anarchic production. Our problem is not production at all. Similarly with the communist vision of "to each according to his needs, from each according to his abilities." Not that we are against planned production or against each having according to his needs and giving according to his abilities. But the concept of man that is embodied in these slogans is just much too narrow in relationship to his potential at this stage in history. "To each according to his needs" was a vision for a society just beginning to sense the possibilities of abundance. It is based on scarcity-thinking.

ABSTRACT OR CONCRETE

Which "human being" is abstract, and which is concrete? Most people will say "I am a human being" or "I am"—meaning living and breathing, eating and sleeping. This is really an abstract or superficial concept of a human being, in that it reduces humanness to its lowest common denominator.

People who think of a human being in this way haven't given any thought, any imagination, to what it means to be human. They haven't wondered what a human being is. Man started some fifty thousand years ago to become somebody. That historical process is as concrete as anything can possibly be.

We can't make a Chinese Revolution or a Cuban Revolution in the U.S. We are going to make a completely new revolution, the revolution of tomorrow, the revolution of an advanced industrial country. Nobody has done that yet. The only way we can do it is to shatter yesterday's generalizations about revolution. We have to create completely new aspects of revolution. Mao did that in China—but China is an agricultural country. And also the Chinese people are very different from the motley crew which inhabits the U.S. We are trying to do something incredibly difficult, which requires a much deeper penetration than anybody has yet given to the problem. Which is why "put human beings above material things" isn't a very deep penetration. It isn't right because it isn't enough—we can't persuade people to make revolution just on that concept. And we have yet to discover the concept which will inspire people toward revolution; or rather inspire people to become the kind of people who will make the revolution. We want to illuminate the incredible, the unique grandeur of man, to recognize that when man crossed the threshold of reflection, he became something.

Most people haven't the faintest idea that they have crossed the threshold of reflection. They haven't any idea that they are unique. They just keep on living as if they were earthworms. Man has never lived like an earthworm. But most people don't know that.

A BETTER WAY TO LIVE?

Is there anything which unifies the American people today?—apart from individuals like Henry Kissinger who is really a nonperson in the sense that he doesn't care what the historic (human) goals are. He is just doing a job; you tell him what you want—to present Nixon as a great man or bring the U.S. out on top in the current negotiations with Hanoi—and he comes back with a worked-out plan of how to achieve short-range goals. In this sense Kissinger is not a modern American. More typically, a modern American is someone who somehow feels that there should be a better way for people to live—as when John Updike's Rabbit says, "There should be a better way for a man to live than demonstrating some gadget in a variety store and coming home to find his wife drunk." Most people are on the verge of asking themselves some very basic questions. What we need to do is discover some fundamental concept of the way to live that would unify Americans, regardless of race, sex, national origin, social status, or what-have-you. Then, having given everybody an adequate opportunity to see what is involved, we unify with those who are prepared to struggle along the lines of this concept and to fight only against those who oppose the concepts.

But first we have to discover what unites us all as human beings in this new epoch, without worrying about the sensibilities of any particular group—and in confidence that we have reached the point where modern man is searching for that which is new. At this stage we have to discover what is right—and not be tied down by the concept that one group of people is automatically right, that its interests and grievances automatically coincide with the interests of all humanity. We must first discover what is right and what is wrong, rather than who is right and who is wrong. Then we can judge people not based on their birth or conditions beyond their control, but by their convictions, by the truths they are prepared to exemplify in their lives.

How ready are we to decide on a set of values? Don't we first have to get into people's heads that they can determine which set of values they want to fight for? Modern man is not yet aware that he creates values; he thinks values are things. At the same time we must not underestimate the new situation that has been created by the Movement of the sixties. It is true that people have by no means arrived at the conclusion that they can shape the future. But when a group of whites gets mad at blacks for upsetting the status quo and even talks about those "damn blacks," there is more chance for movement than in their just getting mad at capitalism. Capitalism is so anonymous. How can you get mad at it? Martin Luther King and Malcolm X were human beings, and if human beings can mess things up, then maybe some other human beings can also mess things up—or put them right. In other words, the whole situation has been brought down (or up) to human scale.

In this country it is very important that human political energies be set into motion—which is what the sixties achieved. It is better for people in Pontiac, Michigan, to begin organizing against busing than it is for them to sit at home believing that their destinies are being shaped by economic development or by Rockefeller.

The unshakable confidence that men and women are capable of shaping their own destiny is a vision that is part and parcel of any great revolutionary leader or organization. No revolutionary leader has ever been able to touch the masses of people without this vision. Fidel gave the Cubans the confidence that they could change Cuba; but he could make a four-hour speech in Union Square and it wouldn't make a bit of difference to the people of this country. What is our vision for the United States of America? In the United States no revolutionary leader has been able to pose the vision of "everyman or everywoman can." Yet even a bourgeois like Robert Kennedy sensed the need for a vision when he said, "I look at the problems of man. Most people ask 'why'? I ask, 'why not'?" We must never forget also that common denominator of the people who make up the U.S.—which emerges when we as revolutionists come among them and say, "you can fight City Hall" and they look at you and say "but look at the other people who tried," or "I am ready, but what about the other guy?"

When a worker or a black or anybody complains about the war or about work or about discrimination, the average radical tells them that they ought to join the movement or the organization to oppose capitalism because the capitalists are screwing up society. What do we tell them? We have to tell them that nobody is going to shatter capitalism until they want to live differently. And we have to get them to begin wondering, "What do we mean by living differently?"

IDEAS MOVE PEOPLE

Modern man isn't going to change anything, he isn't going to struggle to change society just because he wants more things. Difficult as it may be for the average radical to understand this, it represents an advance in revolutionary struggle. "Peace" (stop the misery of war), "bread and land" were a bunch of things in Russia. On the other hand, as Hannah Arendt points out, the American Revolution was the only revolution made on ideas. However, the ideas we have to project today are so extraordinarily more difficult, more profound, than the classical ones of 1776 or of 1848. That is why we are having so much trouble and must take enough time to develop them. We have spent thousands of hours of thought and effort searching, and we still haven't gotten there. We would like to get there sooner. But if we are in a hurry, we block ourselves from getting there.

This is a moment in history—like that in Lorenzo's court. But while they were trying to place ancient classical history in relationship to the development of Italian civilization, we in the United States, at a different moment in history, are trying to figure out the relationship of technology to the future of man, of humankind. People like us must do something comparable to the way Italians started the Italian Renaissance.

AMERICANS AND THE WAR IN VIETNAM

Einstein said that when man split the atom, he changed everything but the human mind.

Can we say that when the atom was split, the mind of man was changing, only not in the West but in China and Vietnam, the countries receiving the full brunt of Western technology? That in these countries, alternatives were being created which were in fact inventions of the human spirit: great unselfishness, new relations between men and women, a great sense of international solidarity, whole new ways of looking at the relations between people, both inside and between countries? So that in China and Vietnam, people were not just making "third world" revolutions aspiring to where the West is. Can we say, therefore, that since, dialectically, mankind is one and we are all tied together, the mind of man has been changing?

Nobody can become a human being who is not totally and absolutely opposed to the war in Vietnam, to what the U.S. is doing in Vietnam. If you can't recognize that, you can't think anything human at all. But to go on from there and say "therefore the primary task of Americans is to end the Vietnam War" is to go from a judgment to an action, which doesn't necessarily follow. Unless there is a revolution in the U.S., the U.S. isn't safe for the world. But the Vietnamese can't make the U.S. revolution.

Americans have to make it. In that sense the revolutionary struggle in the U.S. takes priority over all other struggles.

To talk about our ending the Vietnam War because the war should be ended is an abstraction. The Vietnam War expresses the fact that we, Americans, still don't know how to be human. How else could the Vietnamese War go on? It is being waged by this country because this country is made up of a bunch of people who are damaged human beings. Nixon is trying to end the war before the elections; but if he does, that will not change the way that the American people think about anything. Being against the Vietnam War doesn't mean that you have any notion of a new way in which human beings should live together. If Nixon ends the war, it won't change any American by a hairsbreadth. We change ourselves; Nixon doesn't. The only way that one approaches the question of genocide is by dealing with how to change the people who tolerate genocide.

Americans have to solve the problems of the world in this country—precisely because every problem facing man is focused here. We have a melting pot which didn't melt; we have thoughts which nobody else has; we have a kind of materialism which nobody else has. We are facing every problem man has right here. That is why the American revolution is the most important revolution in the world.

We must remember also that, if Nixon ends the Vietnam War, it will be chiefly because the Vietnamese people defeated the U.S. by revolutionary struggle—not because the people in the U.S. changed. An important part of the Vietnamese revolutionary struggle was to undermine the morale of the U.S. in the most fundamental sense of the word. The Vietnamese carried on a moral struggle, and as a result, this itsy-bitsy nation was able to defeat the most powerful country in the world. The Vietnamese people are telling the Western world "don't talk about civilization until you can talk about morality." We have reached the stage in revolutionary struggle, in revolutionary thought, when it is impossible just to talk about facts. We are forced to wonder about morality. Who has what morality? What is morality? That is what this war means: whether Nixon ends it or not doesn't mean a thing except in the politics of being re-elected.

The Triple Revolution

The technological revolution poses three areas of problems that have to be surmounted; and they can be surmounted only by creating something new: First, there is the technology of production; automation and cybernation pose totally new problems of *work*. Second, there is military technology. This poses the end of the nation-state and war. They just don't make sense any more; and they are so dangerous, as we pointed out ten years ago in *The Decline of the State and the Coming of World Society*. The third problem area is the technology of reproduction, of maternity and of child care. This poses a whole new set of challenges that underlie the women's movement. The pill, the fact that we are getting close to overpopulation and can't go on having all these children, that children live longer because they are not carried off by childhood diseases, that abortion is simple and safe—all this means that unless women find a new role for themselves, they will stagnate. This challenges us to change the old relationship between men and women and poses the possibility of the simultaneous development of men and women. These are not "women's" questions any more than the question of work is a question only of the working class.

Thus, the technological revolution has created critical questions in three spheres: work, the state, the family, economics, politics, and social relations. Up to now we have tended to think of these as distinct categories, with economics as the foundation and everything else as superstructure. Now we can see how they are interrelated, and we can think about them more concretely in relation to the daily lives and the search for human identity of people.

We are facing all three questions at once, and they are interrelated. They pose the possibility of our moving again to the evolution of humankind—as before the rise of the state; the possibility of both men and women contributing equally as they have not been able to do for the last five thousand years—in ways that have been possible before.

We must never forget that the state is only a moment in the evolution of humankind. It only emerged five thousand years ago, and already it is outmoded. Before that, ninety-nine percent of human development had already taken place, including the rise of Homo sapiens, let alone those who preceded him. So the period in which men have been dominant hasn't been very long—although it is still with us and therefore dominates our thinking (and our language). Hence if we are referring to historical development over the last five thousand years, we cannot lightly substitute a non-masculine word for "man" or we will be misrepresenting what actually has taken place historically. We have to be careful not to be looking at these questions only from the point of view of the woman's question. Obviously it is ridiculous to denigrate women. It is also obviously impossible to discover what a *human*, human being is at this moment by discussing whether God took Eve out of Adam's rib or vice-versa. What we are talking about is the creation that people, humankind, men and women, make of themselves.

For the average person the idea of five thousand years is difficult to imagine—it is like a million dollars. At the same time we must realize that the momentum, the tempo, the pace of development has been speeding up. During the first half million years, the pace was so slow that it seemed nothing was happening. Yet human beings were probably busy inventing language and the family! If you look at what was happening in terms of the size of communities or level of politics or technology, it was very poor. In the last five thousand years, the more we have moved, the faster we have moved. Almost everything we use in the Western world was developed in the last hundred years.

Chardin said that man will probably live for another seventy-five million years. Which is why, in one sense, five thousand years are insignificant; but in another sense, it is urgent for us to think about another direction now. Einstein said that when man split the atom, he changed everything but the human mind. How are we going to make the tremendous leap to that kind of expansion of the human mind?

The reason we seem to be going back to this question repeatedly in these conversations is because it isn't easy to grasp the magnitude of the leap in human thinking which is required, the kind of leap that we need to make in order to expand the human mind in this direction. How do you make such a leap? How do you get your mind to break out of old patterns? The only thing we can be sure of is that when you reach a threshold like this, you can't make the necessary leap just by brooding over your grievances, by thinking like a victim—by arguing, polemicizing, defending your own position and stating your disagreements with others.

That is why it is necessary not to be impatient; not to be in a hurry to do something when we are not at all sure where we are headed. Modern man has not even asked, let alone answered the question, "Where should man be going?" Man knew the answers to this in the past; he doesn't know them now, especially in the U.S. That is why the U.S. is such a fantastically important place. We can have everything we want—and then discover that this isn't what we want. What *do* we want?

We are at a turning point in history. We are not just trying to deal with topical issues, topical grievances, e.g., we are not trying to prevent corruption in the New York Police Department. The problems of the new epoch are not just a continuation of the problems of the old epoch—food, survival, a roof over one's head. Obviously we are talking about the U.S.—not about India—although the solutions we come to here are going to affect the entire rest of the world. For example, every country in Africa looks at what is happening to the U.S.

The Word "Man"

Last year we raised the question of discovering another word for mankind to make clear that "man" does not stand for "male" but for human species, for Homo sapiens. We said that we would not prejudge the question by saying "the word doesn't matter" nor would we just adopt another word.

We have been very conscious this year of the importance of language and of formulations. Earlier we discussed how when we use the word "man" or "mankind" we clearly refer to the historical developments of man or the advances human beings have made since they crossed the threshold of reflection. "Human beings," on the other hand, suggests zoological or anthropological species who made the transition from apes to humans. Also the word "man" by being singular conveys the notion of the individual and hence the uniqueness of every individual member of the species.

When we write and speak these days, are we going to talk about the evolution of man or mankind, or are we going to talk about the evolution of humanity and humankind? Are we going to hesitate to use the word "man" for fear that we are accepting a male chauvinist interpretation of history? At what point does one retard one's own and other people's understanding of the overall Movement by being overly sensitive to a particular movement's grievances and its (often transitory) insistence upon the use of a particular word, e.g., black rather than Negro? Is it possible to get so bogged down in the particular that we can't look at the general?

Note on the cover of *Mariners, Renegades and Castaways* the quote from Melville reads:

> If, then, to meanest mariners, and renegades and castaways, I shall hereafter ascribe high qualities, though dark; weave round them tragic graces; if even the most mournful, perchance the most abused, among them all, shall at times lift himself to the exalted mounts; if I shall touch that workman's arm with some ethereal light; if I shall spread a rainbow over his disastrous set of sun; then against all mortal critics bear me out of it, thou just Spirit of Equality, which hast spread one royal mantle of humanity over all my kind.

Most people understand the last word as "mankind." But Melville said "my kind," which is quite another thing.

Obviously only a patriarchal society could have created the myth of woman coming out of the rib of man. Equally obviously, the idea that one existed before the other is a myth. But, at the same time, isn't it true that the dominant political-cultural forms of the last ten thousand years since the rise of the state, the years which we refer to when we speak of the history of civilization, have been created by men? For example, if the world had been run by women for the last ten thousand years, would the state have emerged independently seven times as it has? Or, again, what great symphonies have been written by women up to this time?

Language is very meaningful. For example, in China today, instead of using the old phrases for husband and wife, both are referred to as "ai-ren," meaning "loved one." But the Chinese do not talk about the past as if the husband-wife relationship has always been based on equality or on love. They don't try to extrapolate from the present to the past. They recognize that there was a different reality in the past. Similarly, if we begin talking about the evolution of humankind in relation to the past, we are implying that we can disregard what has happened in the past and remake the past in terms of the present or future.

Almost all the early inventions, especially in the passage from hunting to horticulture, were certainly created by women. This includes almost every important craft: pottery, basketry, cooking and storing food, spinning and weaving, sewing, housebuilding, all the equipment for tending babies, medicine. The situation is less clear in relation to fine arts; e.g., men did paintings of the hunting of animals. Almost everything except killing animals, fighting other men, and boat-building, seem to have been done by women. There is no question but that women invented horticulture and agriculture. In early times women were the ones with the spatial stability and the leisure which are both necessary to create new art forms, new technology, new thoughts.

It is only after you get to advanced horticultural and horticultural-pastoral societies—when populations become concentrated on valuable land, and around irrigation sites, and other property that was scarce and fought over—that the military arts become important and men come to the fore. Also you began to have full-time specialization. In the early period of part-time specialization, spinning, weaving, pottery, etc. were done by women in addition to cooking and caring for babies. But once you get to metallurgy, it is complex and time-consuming enough that you have to have people doing it full-time—so it becomes an inherited craft. You get men doing it because women do not have the time. They have too many other things to do. So you get the conditions for the rise of the state. And from then on, men become the advancers of civilization while women become more the conservers, the links, the peacemakers sometimes, and the traditionalists.

It seems obvious that in the earlier stage women played a tremendous role in advancing society. Then at a certain stage, men took over. It is not a question of whether it was good or bad. It happened. But now we are at a technological stage where we are free to wonder what is the appropriate relationship between men and women? Who does what? We don't need men for protection in the sense in which we used to. What is the problem we face now? The issue is not whether women preceded men or Adam preceded Eve. What do we need to do to advance humankind?

Confronting Ourselves

Why is man/woman's mind lagging so far behind? The splitting of the atom was the culmination of a method of thought, the scientific method, which had been developing and had been achieving wonders for nearly four hundred years. This method of thought, while concentrated and achieving its highest professional development in people like Einstein, also shaped the thinking of most everybody else in the Western world.

But now all kinds of questions are being asked, precisely by those who, like Einstein and the atomic scientists, achieved the breakthrough of splitting the atom. Einstein recognized that those who were the culmination of this kind of thinking probably would not be the ones to break loose from it with a new kind of thinking and provide the answers.

How can we expand our minds? How can we expand the mind of modern man? How can we help people in the modern world to break out of old patterns of thinking? Individuals have to confront themselves. Nothing could be more important. Anthropologists, sociologists talk about the nature of man/woman as if it were a matter of looking at somebody else. But it is a question of looking at ourselves. Until we have stimulated enough people to think about themselves, to confront their selves, we won't be able to wonder about new human relations.

In 1970 we talked about a new man rather externally. In 1971 we talked about changing ourselves. This year we're beginning to discuss how we can bring people to confront themselves as a step towards creating their new selves.

How does one bring about confrontation? By creating a sense of duality, of conscious polarization between the negative and the positive. What kinds of confrontation are we trying to stimulate in the U.S. today? Between bourgeois and socialist attitudes? Between the subjective and the social?

All socialists up to now have conceived of man/woman as either subjective, selfish, bourgeois or as a communist who didn't have any sense of self except in relation to the communal. This has been proven to be nonsense. Mao isn't trying to create a new man/woman who doesn't have individuality or subjectivity. He is trying to advance the idea that new men and women in their subjectivity can recognize community. Mao is trying to create an opportunity for people to be individual and subjective without being anti-communal—because being communal satisfies their subjectivity. He has refused to accept the duality of subjective and objective—the basis of so much Western thought which hampers our minds and our communication with people so that we can't appeal to the creative and dynamic energies within them. We can't rule out the subjective because each individual is a subject. We have to appeal to and arouse the subjective will.

What is a socialist? We have used the word for a hundred years, and yet nobody really knows what a socialist is. We are not going to get anywhere until we have put together a bunch of people each one of whom decides individually, subjectively, what kind of a person he/she wants to be and what kind of society he/she wants to see and what he/she is willing to do for it. Each one has to do it. Talking about "socialist man/woman" in general is an evasion of individual responsibility. It is easy to join a socialist party, but you haven't done anything by signing the card until you have internalized something. People have talked about being socialists without any personal definitions being involved.

It is always a person, an individual who decides. But he/she has to decide with regard to the transition from one kind of person to another and to understand that these two kinds of persons are in opposition to one another. There has to be a concept of historical transition, you must feel that you are part of it, and that your decision to be one kind of person rather than another kind is not only a personal but a historical decision. But it has to be someone with a concept of self-worth who makes the decision.

We have to transcend the traditional Western dualism between the subjective and the objective. Of course, it is possible to be subjective in the sense of not being objective—looking at things only from your personal point of view. This is what we mean when we accuse a person of being subjective. But a man/woman is automatically subjective. How he/she uses his/her subjectivity, responsibly or irresponsibly, grandly or meanly, is another question. What we have to do is recognize and welcome subjectivity and to insist that people take responsibility for their "I"—not slough it off. We are rejecting the old dualism between the personal and the political.

"CHOOSING"

In medieval Europe people built Gothic cathedrals—the most fantastic things that people have ever built. The incredible thing about them is that nobody knows who designed them; there weren't any known architects or engineers. In a sense every stone in the Gothic cathedral is different from every other. They were not mass-produced, and there are hundreds of thousands of them. The cathedrals were built by the people of the area. Maybe it took a hundred years to build, but they did it. Nobody stood around with whips, but for some reason these people contributed their knowledge, their skills. They felt something for their creation. This is an aspect of role rather than rights. These folks *wanted* to do it. They *chose* it.

We have to find reasons for people today in the U.S. to want in this way—at a time when apparently nobody wants to do anything. Whereas people in the past wanted to do such things as build cathedrals under very difficult conditions, today under far better conditions people don't want to do a damn thing. We face the awesome challenge of discovering how to give people the will to build when there are constraints in society which do not allow you the freedom even to go into the country and cut down a tree to build a cottage.

Suppose we said to some folks on welfare, "Instead of demanding more welfare, why don't we take over all the chores that have to be done in the community, including getting rid of dilapidated buildings, cleaning up lots and building playgrounds in them, carrying out community campaigns for birth control, administering to the sick and the old, setting up small scale community clinics? And, wherever these activities conflict with activities already categorized as paid jobs, let that conflict be recognized as one that we will have to work out in order to establish new relations."

This might be a form of expressing the same creativity that people used in building the cathedrals. These people didn't live in cities; they lived in small towns of 1000–2000 people. Sometimes it took them a hundred years—but they had a goal of some kind. Maybe it was to praise God or the Virgin Mary, but it was a goal that expressed their humanity as they understood it.

Can people on welfare do what we outlined above? It depends upon whether they feel they want to do it as an expression of their own humanity, their selves. You can't ask anybody to go out and clean up a lot and build a park out of it if all he/she is thinking is "Why should I? I am not going to get paid for it. I can sit home and do nothing and get the same amount of money." Or who says, "My brother is a park worker. If I do that, I will put him out of a job" (even though he knows his brother won't do it because there isn't any money to pay him at the rate he is accustomed to).

FOR ONE'S OWN SAKE

Workers, as well as those on welfare, need to examine their attitude towards work. Take, for example, a garbage collector who doesn't give a damn because he/she has the nastiest job. So he/she spills half the stuff in the gutter and doesn't bother to pick it up. He/she doesn't think of or care about the rats that will have a chance to feed and breed as a result of carelessness. A person who has that attitude to a job, no matter what job, can't possibly build a socialist society. A person with an attitude like that isn't an asset to any society.

Does it do any good to accuse a person like this of "not thinking about society"? Wouldn't it create more movement, more movement of self if we were to say, "You are permitting yourself to do a lousy job, and you don't give a damn; that is a helluva way for a person to live." Then, when he or she replies, "Why should I give a damn? I'm being exploited. All I care about is my eight hours," we say, "For your own sake you should give a damn." What Mao seems to be saying, and what we are still trying to discover how to say in this country, is "I'm sorry, you are not a member of the working class or of any advanced class, if you behave this way. You are not standing for anything, neither for yourself nor for society." This is the kind of thing that is involved in confronting one's self.

The question is legitimate whether we should continue to use the words "bourgeois" and "socialist" to distinguish between the "don't give a damn, I'm only concerned with my eight hours" attitude, and the opposite attitude which cares about one's self and society. In favor of its continuing use (although not for a broad mass audience) is the responsibility to tradition and to define ourselves in relation to that tradition—in order to make clear what is being preserved and what is being changed and why. We have to make the definitions. We don't just throw out words and start afresh (as with the use of the word "man") because we recognize that the words came from somewhere. So, through an enormous amount of effort, we arrive at what we mean and don't mean by "socialist," and thereby we also help those with whom we are working to understand that nothing remains the same, and how and why changes take place in concepts along with changes in society. Hence we should clearly establish our definitions of socialism, boldly accepting our responsibility for redefining it because of the differences between nineteenth century Europe and twentieth century America, making absolutely clear what we mean and what we don't mean by socialism, bourgeois society, etc.

So we say to a person who is doing a lousy job, "Your attitude to work is the attitude of this lousy society which you have accepted. You are thinking only about your own lousy self and not about your job in relation to other people or to yourself as a creative human being. Therefore, you are defining your self as mean and petty. Just because this society defines human activity in terms of exchange value doesn't mean that you have to accept that definition. There is another attitude to work which each of us has to do and can discover for our own dignity, our own selves—our own concept of self."

Radicals who are still talking to workers (including women workers) of revolutionary struggle in terms of going on strike completely misunderstand the present stage of society and human development. Going on strike is what workers had to do in the nineteenth century or as late as the 1930s in order to get recognition as human beings. Today, going on strike is what particular groups of workers do to "get theirs"—without giving a damn about other human beings, with no concern for anybody but themselves. Therefore for revolutionaries today to talk to workers in an advanced country like the U.S. in terms of going on strike shows absolutely no understanding of the way the human personality is being torn apart these days because of the lack of perspective for the whole society, or of what is involved in the development of a whole new person.

TOWARDS A NEW WORK ETHIC

The Puritan work ethic contained within it a certain rationality. There was not only the discipline from without but an intrinsic rationality about what was involved. It is perfectly legitimate to say to everyone that he/she has to contribute to society. What you do contribute may be subject to a great deal of choice or differentiation as the society develops; but, for your own sake, you have to accept the fact that, if you want to live, you have to do something besides just be—like a vegetable. This is also part of confronting one's self. Those radicals who believe that the Puritan work ethic is completely outmoded by the technological revolution are thinking like the slaves in all societies who begin to fantasize the new society in terms of the leisure and uselessness they envy in their masters. It is dehumanizing to inculcate in anybody the idea that they can live without working. We have to recognize that, despite the technological revolution and indeed as a result of it, there are a million new things that can be called work.

There is no job, no activity, in which you are not relating to somebody, *if only to yourself.* If you become sloppy in your work you become sloppy in everything else. You can't divide yourself. You become a sloppy person. Just as you become a criminal if you do criminal acts—even if your crimes are against your oppressors.

Today, as a result of the rebellions and the identification of work with slavery and white oppression, blacks have developed an antagonism to work which has to be fought in a revolutionary way, by insisting that the socialist attitude to work involves working well. Anyone who says, "I am a victim of bourgeois society, of white oppression, and therefore whatever attitude I have towards work is legitimate, whether it be leeching or stealing" is accepting the dehumanization of bourgeois society or of white oppression. Most people who are just rebelling against the old society think that under the new society they won't have to work. That is why the notion of the relationship of work to human creativity and the very nature of man/woman is so important. Note: We are *not* saying that "if you don't work, you starve." We are saying that if you don't work, you don't express yourself as a human being and if you don't work well, you are a lousy human being.

This is another way of saying that anybody who accepts the victimization of society is not going to change that society. All he/she is going to do is remain a victim and perpetuate the society. The socialist work ethic involves tremendous creativity, tremendous self-reliance, rather than reliance on others to do things for you.

The Movement in the U.S. today does not exist, and will not exist until some very fundamental ideas of the new kind of human being we are striving to become have been developed and propagated. There is nobody else in the U.S. today except ourselves who is systematically trying to develop these new ideas and with a real relationship to the victims. When slaves develop or grasp advanced ideas, they have a contribution to make which is different from that of "free men" like Lewis Mumford or Lancelot Whyte. When Martin Luther King was ready to give leadership in 1962, practically everybody who was progressive (although not the radicals) was ready to follow him. Today the search for direction is in much wider sections of society—not only among "progressives" but even among the Rabbits (hence the importance of Updike). As we seek to develop these ideas of polarization and confrontation, we should recognize that we are doing so for large sections of society.

WHY PHILOSOPHY?

We have been discussing the "bourgeois work ethic" versus the "socialist work ethic." Neither exists. The Puritan work ethic did exist. The question today is "What is your ethic?" The Biblical saying, "Do unto others what you would have them do unto you" sounds fine until one asks, "Well, what would you have them do unto you?" Then it is obviously only another way of defining what you want to do unto them. This is not an abstraction. What to do unto others? Ethics is always specific. Ethics is not a *thing* to be discovered. It is created over and over again down through history by individuals discovering and defining and redefining what they mean. It is a subjective relationship to necessity and responsibility and to one's capacities and desires.

There is no abstract "ethics;" but there is a need in people in periods of great historical transition to discover the human reasons for their actions—"rites of passage" for humankind analogous to rites of passage for individuals and groups—valid reasons for the human race, through which they can establish their bond with humankind, past, present and future. When one set of human reasons goes into decline, people feel the need to find another. That is why philosophy itself was born of crisis at approximately the same time in both the East and the West and why people create new philosophies in times of crisis.

In the past, especially in the village, life depended on what each individual did. As long as a tremendous amount of cooperation was so necessary to survival, a work ethic did not have to be so consciously worked out. The Puritan work ethic evolved out of a situation in which the external necessities for working together, in towns, were not so pressing. Now, once again, we are in a major transition, brought about by the technological revolution, which demands that we establish the human reasons why people should work. Men and women have to arrive at these reasons consciously and philosophically and not wait until material conditions compel them to move or think in a specific direction, which they must then follow—after the fact.

This is why the Biblical saying, "Do unto others etc." is meaningless until one has decided what one wants to do unto one's self. What does one owe one's self as a human being, as a person with bonds or ties that bind one to humankind, past, present and future? At the present time our society is drifting without a philosophy, without a work ethic. People either repeat the ethic of the past, "*They* ought to go to work" (which is no longer a bond and is, in fact, a statement of division: "they" versus "us"); or they see no ethic possible at all—it is everybody for him/herself.

Why does a Richter work his ears off to learn to play the piano, or a Henry Moore to sculpt? Why do they work that way? Not just to earn money nor to increase the totality of goods and services but because they feel that their work expresses the human personality. (This is why the phrase "socialist work ethic" is too abstract; it still suggests a society trying to overcome scarcity and economic under-development.) Creative work cannot be restricted to work that can be quantitatively measured. The reasons for work will have to come from within. So to the kids who say, "I don't have to work, the machine will do it all," all we can say is "if you are going to sit around and enjoy the fruits of other people's work, if you can't think of any work you want to do for your community, for other people, for your self, then you are destroying your self." At the same time we realize that it is not going to be easy to start the multitude thinking this new way, when they have been used to thinking of work only as being enslaved.

THE NATURE OF WORK

Marx opened up the contradiction within the work process at the very beginning of *Capital* when he drew the sharp distinction between use-value and exchange-value, between concrete labor and abstract labor. The concept of the human nature of work is even clearer in his *Economic and Philosophic Manuscripts.* Hannah Arendt points out in *The Human Condition,* "Every European language has two etymologically distinct words for what we have come to think of as the same activity, and retains them in the face of their persistent synonymous usage." Thus, the Germans distinguish between *werken* and *arbeiten*; the French between *ouvrer* and *travailler.* In each case, one word suggests a form of human creativity; while the other suggests pain and travail.

Nothing is more demeaning than to go into a workplace and be told to do this and that, and not have any idea of the connection of what you are doing with the rest of society. You can't be creative under such circumstances. In an agricultural society, people had more opportunity to be creative because at least they had a picture of the relationship of what they were doing, e.g., sowing, harvesting, to the whole process and to nature. If it didn't rain, you had no crops. But the moment you are into an industrial society, that link to nature is gone. For example, Chrysler concentrates its production in the heart of winter when the weather makes it most difficult to get parts from all over the country. Nature, in an industrial society, is no longer the deterrent or directly helpful factor that it was in agriculture—so the average person doesn't think about nature. We can't go back to what was, but we do have to wonder about what new forms we will have to create for human beings to live creatively and in harmony with nature today, and we will have to struggle to be free to be creative.

In the past work was to a large degree governed by the whip, either in terms of actual, undisguised force (slavery) or in terms of wages. Obviously we must get rid of this completely. Already, as a result of an economy of abundance and welfare, this kind of necessity is no longer with us in the same sense, although a lot of people are still thinking in these terms. We can't move one step until we recognize that exploitation is actually decreasing, although the human condition of people is worsening. What are the new necessities for living like a *human*, human being under these new conditions? How do we resolve this new, unprecedented contradiction?

In the past people could see what they were doing as socially beneficial, even if it was for wages or if it was dirty or menial work. The scale of what they were doing was small enough to be comprehensible by the human eye, e.g., cleaning away trash from railroad tracks provided safety for trains. Today the huge scale of operations, the destructiveness or wastefulness of so much that is produced, all make it difficult to see one's activity as part of a meaningful whole.

So, generally speaking, we can say that work is necessary to the development, the creation of one's humanity. But that is not saying enough. We have to be specific about which fundamental ingredients should be incorporated and which eliminated to enable people to develop, to express their humanity through participation in work. It is clear that one has to have some purposes—not necessarily directly utilitarian—but as some kind of contribution to society, to humankind. There has to be an element of self-determination in relation to purpose. One must also be able to see the relevance of the methods one uses to the goals or purposes one is seeking to achieve. There has to be some sense of process—that doing things takes time—and of the logical and temporal relationship between the various steps of the activity, some coming before and some after others. And there has to be a sense of workmanship, that the excellence of the results depends upon the effort.

THE WELFARE STATE

In the past there were people who did chiefly creative work: artists, musicians, and others who did utilitarian work, who still tried to the best of their ability to put into this work some of their humanity even though the chief motivation for it was social necessity. We have come now to the point where a lot of folks feel that social necessity in the old sense no longer holds.

How did we in the U.S. get so many people on welfare? Welfare is one of the most degenerating, destructive institutions in this country today. Welfare came out of struggles for reform—but now it is a permanent fixture which is destroying human beings. We have reached the point where all the reformist thinks about is more welfare. What do we think?

We have to see first that the concept of society's responsibility for taking care of people outside of institutions is an extraordinarily recent phenomenon. Before this, poor people went to the poorhouse or a madhouse. Now suddenly, we are facing the fact that what we have created—through caring more for and about people—stinks! Even though what we have created is a fantastic innovation over what existed historically. What would be better than welfare? We must be prepared to deal with this question, recognizing clearly that the folks on welfare aren't at this point ready to deal with it themselves. Originally people on welfare were those in dire need. Then came the Depression, and there were lots of people in dire need, and WPA and welfare were created. WPA was a transmission belt back to work. When, after the Depression we cut out WPA, everybody went directly to welfare with no transmission belt back to work. Since that time there has been developing a welfare culture in this society. People began thinking, "If I can be on welfare and make $350 a month, why should I work at a job paying only $550?" People became choosey about whether they would take a job or not. It is going on in millions of cases all over the country. People are into the whole victimization complex to justify being on welfare and being parasites. Now, as a result of the coincidence of the technological revolution and the culmination (in blacks) of the long, hard struggles against the compulsion to labor, people have lost sight of the human reasons for work: to develop, to express and to create the human personality.

How can we persuade people on welfare to want to rediscover their humanity? Because they are the ones we have to persuade. They are the ones who are in most urgent need to find a new, enlarged human identity, enlarged concept of themselves as human. When you accept the parasite's role in a society, you are destroying your humanity and destroying society at the same time. We are accustomed to thinking that people only lose their humanity when they commit a crime. But we have to realize that people on welfare are losing their own humanity in a very deep sense. Welfare has become a crutch for not participating in society. It has become a right, like the right to speak your mind; it has acquired the status of a universal, of a philosophy.

Note: We are not talking about objecting to welfare. We are

talking about how one frees oneself from being so wound up with and imprisoned in the past that one can't think about the future, about a new way to live, a new way to care.

What do we tell somebody on welfare? We can't just say, "Make a revolution, and you won't need welfare." That is just an evasion. We have reforms today that Marx couldn't possibly have envisaged, because they didn't exist in his day any more than television or satellites or trips to the moon. We have no doubt that Marx could have encompassed these changes—if he were alive today. Our job is to try to do what he might have done. The Marxists have failed because they weren't ready to recognize the tremendous changes that have taken place since Marx.

It is all connected. You can't persuade anybody to be a socialist just by yelling about socialism. You have to persuade people that something of their human identity is embodied in the concept of socialism. The new work ethic involves trying to persuade somebody, not that they should take a dirty job and keep their mouths shut, but that unless they have a job and do the best they possibly can do in that job, they are demolishing both their selves and society.

How does one explain to somebody that we are asking, almost imploring, them to join us in understanding that human life does not go on in the way they now think it does—by living on welfare; that people have to work, even though their definitions of work may be very different from those of the past.

The average person might say about a guy like Richter or Louis Armstrong, "That guy isn't working; he is playing music, he is having fun." Our job is to persuade that person that everybody who is trying to be creative in any possible way, whether by playing music the best he/she can or by picking up the garbage he/she drops, is working.

But since some people just make garbage and others see their whole lives as picking up the garbage that others throw out the window, it is almost impossible to persuade anyone to do the best possible job in their work. The people who have been working at picking up garbage then begin to lose some of their humanity too. So it has to be related to a whole lot of other things.

A few years ago we were saying, "all we need is the socialist revolution and everybody will enjoy working for the communal good." Now we know that isn't so. Unless we persuade people to think differently about work in relation to their selves, all we would end up with would be somebody ordering others to do what has to be done. What we are trying to discover now is how to persuade people that we are going to be ordered about unless we are willing to reconsider which responsibilities to ourselves and to others we are willing to accept. This is why the whole question of the work ethic is so important. If you say "the hell with work," you get totalitarianism, not socialism. In Marx's time, there was the need to work in order to produce goods and to achieve direct utilitarian results. Now the need to produce no longer exists in the same direct way. This is the dilemma of the U.S. Under capitalism today, it is possible for vast numbers of people to say "the hell with work," and society still goes on. There are enough people on welfare today who accept the way things are, not to want to change a bloody thing. They will be a barrier in the road toward any fundamental change unless they first begin thinking about themselves in completely new ways. What we have to realize is that anybody who accepts welfare as a way of life isn't going to be for any kind of new society. He/she is helping to demolish society as well as him/herself.

Methods

When one is dealing with kids, does one have to start with concrete problems, in order to give them a sense of time in relation to human development? Our friends in Muskegon were first able to give their kids an enlarged conception of their humanity in relation to getting or not getting a snowmobile to take the groceries up the hill. The issue was discussed not as one of economics but of human development. The parents explained to the kids that if they bought the snowmobile today, they would end up buying Cadillacs tomorrow—that they would be ruled by things. So they all sat down together and began to examine what they were trying to achieve, apart from the immediate question: what kind of people they wanted to be, what kind of household they wanted to achieve, how to live, work together as a household in order to develop into the kind of people they wanted to become. In other words, the solution of the immediate, utilitarian problem, was placed within a human context. The solving of the technical problem was not separated from the problem of human self-becoming.

Effective as this may have been in dealing with children in a household, how does one address the multitude of people in today's society who think their problem is "more things"? How does one start them in another direction?

First, we have to ask them to begin to look at themselves, and wonder whether in the present expression of their selves, they consider themselves to be human.

Next, we have to ask them to look at the forms in which people have expressed their humanity through the ages. We have to ask them to look around for people who may not even have as much in material things as they have, but who have rejected just seeking material things, who exhibit their human abilities in their work, their lives and their communities—people who by not just sitting around and waiting for their checks are keeping themselves part of the mainstream of mankind.

We have to bring about a polarization in people's thinking, a duality, asking them whether they think they are worse or better than these people. Do they have a sense of integrity, of wholeness, of pride, and in a sense, joy in what they are doing now? Or don't they? It isn't a matter of making a revolution around these people, but of getting them to look at themselves.

On the other hand, since there are so few people who are exhibiting human abilities in their lives today, doesn't this sound unrealistic? Don't we have to approach the question in terms of actual problems, making clear at the same time that these are not problems to be solved immediately but that they pose the kinds of human beings we want to become, the kind of society we want—as in the case of the snowmobile?

NOT "PROBLEM SOLVING"

There is a danger of being too concrete, of taking too much of a problem-solving approach. We want people to open up their minds, to help them to see that there are other ways of resolving issues than the particular track they have been on, that other ways existed in the past and can be created in the present.

In the August *Intellectual Digest,* there is an excerpt of a letter from architect Lawrence Halprin to Mayor Teddy Kollek of Jerusalem. Halprin tells Kollek, "You people in Jerusalem embody almost everything most important in all religions and in different peoples.

But in your plans to extend the city, what you are thinking is one hundred percent wrong. Because you don't even look around to see how, for hundreds of years, people in your area, in villages and small communities, have discovered solutions. Why can't you think that way? Why do you in Jerusalem have to look for solutions from Detroit or in the latest issue of *Architectural Forum* or from Corbusier? How can you persuade people to think that way if they haven't ever conceived of community except as an auto traffic community?"

How do we get people to want to get off welfare? The Muslims, for instance, don't believe any of their people should be on welfare, but they have given them the "work ethic" of the small business person—which, when put into practice only turns into a hustle—to get people to buy the little things one makes or grows. Perhaps we should suggest that everybody on welfare go to work in some way that will benefit the community. In other words, we could begin to project a concept of work as self-determined human activity and not just as labor.

RIGHTS VERSUS ROLES

We said earlier that welfare was originally a question of need and that it has now turned into a culture of rights. It is a way of life which has now acquired a mystique. To get yourself on welfare and get more welfare is considered part of the struggle to advance humanity, something to be proud of. So what we have to do is not only explain to people how welfare destroys their humanity, but also to put another concept in place of rights, which is only a way of degrading people at this stage in contrast to what it was a hundred years ago. We have to get into people's minds the concept of roles, in every relationship—whether it is welfare or sex.

The concept of rights is based upon a quantitative comparison of what a particular individual or group enjoys, in contrast with what other individuals or groups enjoy. Hence it contains within it the potential not only of struggles for equality, but also of envy and competition. The conception of roles, on the other hand, involves appropriate social *relations* between individuals or groups.

All previous societies have had a concept of roles rather than rights. Only bourgeois society has developed a concept of rights, and nowhere has it been more developed to the extreme than in the U.S. Because nowhere have people been so concerned with equality—

everyone on the same level—and nowhere have people been so conscious that certain groups are deprived of equality.

How can people in this society develop a concept of roles? Maybe we need to have an idea of what, let's say, a Chinese person thought two thousand years ago about roles; otherwise our concept of roles is a product of this society, not of the previous development of man/woman during whose evolution the idea of roles was elaborated.

From there we can begin to explore the need to develop a concept of roles as a further enlargement of the concept of appropriate social relations, and as a fundamental advance over previous societies in which roles were fixed by birth or assignment, where individuals had no part in determining their roles and no possibility of a variety of roles, as we have today.

We today can conceive of a new society in which people understand, determine and accept roles through democratic decision making, conscious of the tremendous opportunities now available for virtuosity in roles and at the same time of the actual differences that exist between people. Thus we move from the question of democratic rights (a concept of bourgeois society) to the concept of democratic decision-making which is organic to the new society. We must bear in mind also that in any society people must conceive their roles in relation to contemporaries as well as to the past and future of humankind.

We have to be wary of the problem-solving approach. People who are solving problems communally begin to learn that the problems are communal—which is an enormous advance. But if we approach solutions to problems without having any idea of how people have solved them before, the likelihood is that we are going to solve them incorrectly. In modern society almost all problems are "solved," but they are solved incorrectly. That isn't bourgeois particularly. It is just that people haven't enlarged themselves to solve problems in ways other than they have solved them heretofore: so to get more people into a given space, they build skyscrapers. Or to get more traffic moving, they build expressways. People only think fundamentally in relation to where they are now; they have not freed their minds to think differently. In *Focus and Diversions,* Lancelot Whyte says that at a certain point Einstein couldn't think freely because his mind remained in the classical framework. People have to struggle, yes, but just struggling doesn't necessarily mean you arrive at the right answers. You can be struggling over real problems and be struggling incorrectly, "treading water" and not making any real advance.

"CHIDING"

It is necessary to struggle with one's self. But it is impossible to arrive at some confrontation with yourself if you haven't the slightest idea of your heritage, if you don't know that man/woman has lived a million years, or that humankind has "crossed the threshold of reflection," or if you think that the way you are is the only way man/woman has been or can be. Individuals can try, but they can't really struggle with themselves unless they are aided by having some idea that their struggle is infinitely richer than they think it is, infinitely larger than their present selves.

We have to "chide" people, telling them things about their selves, making them face their selves as they are. (Malcolm X was a master at this kind of chiding.) Because they don't believe anything is now happening to them, they don't believe anything can touch them. We have to combine this "chiding" with illumination of where they have come from, because they don't know what they are doing to their selves until they put their present selves in relation to where man/woman has come from. Otherwise they can't really have any idea of the self they are destroying: It is a whole lot bigger than they think it is.

We might say, "So this is happening to you. You can't do this and you don't have that. Now let me tell you something else that human beings have been doing down through the ages." We lay out a panoramic picture to them. Then we bring them back to reality, to today, to what they are doing, and we tell them, "If you keep on like this, it represents such and such."

We are searching for the process by which to relate people to their selves. This is what we are getting closer to this year. Last year we were examining concepts. Now we can see that a lot of people *think* they are getting their rights: equality, their freedom, by being as they are, e.g., on welfare. That is what freedom, equality, rights mean to them. We have seen how these concepts, which were once the basis for concrete progressive struggles, have become abstractions that enable people to see themselves as *victims rather than masters, as creatures rather than creators, as products rather than makers*; and we are clear now that at this stage, victims, as such, do not contribute to the advance of society.

SELF-DEVELOPING MOVEMENT

Thus, we see that we must have (1) a historical concept which relates to the past; (2) a conception of negation and polarization—of struggle and confrontation between different concepts of what advances a human being, e.g., between rights and roles; and (3) a process of chiding or confronting people in relation to their own selves on fundamental questions like work. If we just seize on issues and try to exploit them to mobilize people, we can't develop within people the new concept of self that is necessary for any self-developing movement. Moreover the projects we mobilize them for will inevitably turn out to be failures, and we end up demoralizing people and immobilizing them even more than they are now.

To give people a reason why they should care about their selves is incredibly difficult. People have so little conception at this point of the potentiality of human beings, of what they have in their selves, of where they have come from and where they can go.

Aspects of human society are fragile, but human society itself is not. It has lived a million years inventing language, etc. Among the things we have to project to people is an incredible pride in being a member of the human species. If one wants to be a human being, one has to exhibit and maintain some of that incredible pride and indomitable spirit that the race has previously exhibited. "Are you just going to sit around on welfare and say that you are a human being? It is an outrage not only to yourself but to the human species!"

We are not trying to persuade all people on welfare of this possibility. We are rather projecting the idea that this kind of project is possible. We are asking them to consider: "You are getting paid, you have a certain amount of free time. Would you care to use it in a community effort without worrying about union scale—and with the understanding that you are going to have to struggle with people who consider this their turf—in the course of getting such a thing under way?"

UNIONS TODAY

All of us know, but few of us want to face that the union is also part of our entrapment today. We can't forever evade the fact that unions, which were formed in the era when exploitation was getting worse, have (in this era when exploitation is decreasing but dehumanization is increasing) become one of the instruments of our dehumanization. They are able to do this, not only because of their physical power but because of the concepts of work and of class on which they are based. One of the important things a revolutionist is going to have to do in the next period is confront the attitudes that unions represent. Because unions, in the most fundamental sense, represent the attitude "get ours" regardless. Unions also represent the attitude of "don't work, because by working you increase profits," without consideration of what the process of work, the nature of work, means to human rationality. What the unions are doing also gives the impression, creates the attitude, that somebody else, the system, can do things for you. The radicals, in criticizing union bureaucracy, reinforce this attitude by giving the impression that somebody else beside you, the protester, is to be held responsible for important decisions.

In all these ways that affect the very essence of the self-concept of people in daily life, unions represent all the worst attitudes. It is very difficult to accept, when so many struggles have gone into their organization, that unions today are the culmination of reformism, and that we have reached the point in history in the U.S. where the more you reform, the worse things get. *It has never been so before.* In the past, it was inconceivable that struggles for higher wages could act to destroy human rationality. Such struggles were revolutionary in the past in the sense that the changes they engendered advanced everybody in society. But look at the constitutions of most of the unions, particularly the AFL unions. They read like a combination of Karl Marx and the Declaration of Independence. The concepts behind them are all pre-technological revolution.

Unions are not the only examples of this kind of destruction of human rationality, but they are an important example. We are not advocating an attack on unions; we are discussing understanding, internalizing, recognizing that we are at the stage in the U.S. today where the changes which have to be undertaken are not going to be undertaken by reformists, or by people who are thinking about how to "get ours." They can be undertaken only by people who know *what* they want to change.

One of the things we are attempting to clarify is that the only basis on which the next development of the human race can take place is through identification with the human race through establishing your human identity—not as a restrictive class, race, or sex identity. At this stage unions restrict not only people who are not working but those who have a human attitude to work. This is part of their function in this society. Therefore they are an obstacle to developing the new forms of identification with the human race that are now needed.

If you plan your struggle on the basis of a false duality, a false opposition, or an opposition which was once concrete but is now abstract, then you are part of something which is both incorrect and a barrier, and may actually be destructive. The basic struggle today is between the people with the philosophy or attitude of "get ours" or "get mine," and those who identify with the whole human race. The attitude of "get mine" or of rights in the sense in which we have discussed it is the absolute final culmination of bourgeois society. It existed in no previous society, it permeates everybody in this society, and now it is particularly imbedded in those at the bottom even more than those at the top.

As an end-result of bourgeois society, the victims of bourgeois society now have the bourgeois attitude more than anybody else. The attitudes of bourgeois society are not necessarily the attitude only of the bourgeoisie. What we have to do is establish the attitude of identification with the human race as the socialist attitude: that is the new struggle which we have to introduce. It is the struggle which must take place in everybody, in every person, in every race, in every group. Whether or not we call it a class struggle is not so important as recognizing the need to develop and create a polarization between everything that the present society represents in terms of attitudes and the new attitudes which are necessary to create a new society and which a new society will represent. It is a political struggle which must take place in each person. Class or past is no excuse for evading this choice.

A Too-Hasty Attempt to Come Up with Answers

What does it mean to live humanly? In a speech at Cleveland State University last spring, "The American Revolution and the Evolution of Humanity," a premature attempt was made to answer this question. The intent was to proceed methodically, from an anti-determinist *philosophy,* to *principles,* and then to *program.*

Out of the Movement of the sixties, certain principles were selected:

1. Put human beings first, rather than material goods or profits.
2. Put the interests of the collective, of the cooperative, first over selfish, individual, egotistical interests.
3. Develop creativity; resist becoming a cog in the machine.
4. Live by your convictions; don't be a hypocrite.
5. Develop control from below, from within the community. Be self-reliant; don't depend on government or others to do everything for you.
6. Finally, everyone, regardless of race, sex, age, or educational and class background must be encouraged and have the opportunity (in principle as well as through practical arrangements) to participate in the daily continuing struggle to transform humanity and society in accordance with the preceding principles. The old way, in which it was natural, normal and possible, for those of one race, class, sex, or age to use those of another race, class, sex, or age as adjuncts or stepping stones for their own advancement, cannot be allowed to continue. Moreover, every nation which has benefited by the exploitation of other nations, with the U.S. at the head, has a responsibility to those other nations, the nature of which responsibility is to be decided by those nations who have been systematically exploited.

What can we learn from this attempt? Essentially it was a too-hasty effort to make the philosophy operational without deepening the ideas sufficiently. The result was a flip-flop, a standing on the head, of one kind of determination (economic) for another (moralistic)—a kind of Sunday School preaching.

What does it mean to put human beings first? Nobody can disagree with this the way it is put. That is what's wrong with it. The New Left has been saying this for the last ten years so that it has become a cliche. The formulation "put human beings first" doesn't enlarge or extend our concept of what it means to be human.

Most people haven't the faintest idea of what it is to be a human being. What is a human being? Is it just any living person who survived at birth? Some people are more human than other people. This is our dilemma. Our job is to create within human beings the sense of what it is to be a human being. Our evangelism is to help man/woman understand what a human being not only is but has been—that he/she hasn't just lived organically, but that he/she has been differentiated by creations of a thousand kinds. A human being isn't just a living organism called "human." A human being is someone, past, present, and future, who has expressed his/her capacities, his/her creative human powers, and still strives to express them. So that everybody defined as "human" by anthropologists or compilers of dictionaries is not a truly human being.

There is no point in going out and asking anybody if he/she thinks people are "more important than things," because he/she is going to say "yes" and we won't have enlarged his/her conception at all. Furthermore, we won't teach ourselves anything either, if we base ourselves on the notion "people are more important than things" as such. *What* people are more important than *what* things?

The six principles cited were too general. They would do for anywhere—India, Cuba, China. They have been put into practice successfully in China, but they do not come to grips with the peculiar dynamics of the United States. They are like Sunday School maxims. Maybe Sunday School maxims are all right in China—with its Confucian tradition, and, even more important, its ongoing revolutionary struggle with millions of people—but they do not give any hint of the tremendous transition or transcendence that man/woman has to undergo in this country in order to reach truths of conviction.

An important ingredient for revolutionary struggle is confrontation. You have to struggle for your convictions, but you can't have confrontation without convictions. There isn't enough real jamming up in this list of principles. They assume the penetration which we still have to discover. When Martin Luther walked up to the door of the castle church and pounded some nails into it to affix his theses, he was saying, "I believe this." Maybe nobody agreed with him, but at least there was something to talk about.

This notion of confrontation, of polarization, should be extracted from traditional ideas of class and retained. We are getting rid of the old sociological ideas of class. First, we have seen the limitations of the philosophic method adopted by the social sciences. Then we can also see that the most oppressed in this society are more likely to think in the old terms of "more" or of getting "a piece of the action" even than those who are privileged. Living in the second half of the twentieth century, we have seen this happen with the labor movement; we have seen it happen with the black movement. So we are trying to shatter a particular kind of thinking. This is especially important in the U.S. where there is such tremendous abundance. Not only do those on welfare often have as much as people who are working, but with the mass media reaching all strata indiscriminately, everyone, except a very few people, thinks of progress in terms of the dominant ideology of this society—in terms of "more." This is a very different society from nineteenth-century Europe, or from Chinese society. Class can't possibly have the same definitions today.

We can see the tremendous changes that have taken place in the concept of class from Marx to Mao: In Mao it has nothing to do with social origin. It is a concept, an advanced idea, which enables you to evaluate how you actually think and act, not how Marx or your parents thought: Do you think and act in terms of your social responsibilities, or in terms of your own personal advancement?

In the past, class consciousness was construed to conform almost automatically to your role in the production process. Now we are saying that each person decides what class he/she is going to be in; and when he/she decides this, he/she is also deciding what epoch he/she is going to live in.

THE NEW DUALITY

At the same time we have to have a sense of duality in relation to this personal decision or commitment. In social issues we don't just pose a perspective of each person saying "I" in relation to an infinite number of options. At a certain point you are confronted with a choice between roads. At a certain stage of transition, you can only decide what kind of person you are in terms of a choice.

Thus, instead of a system—organized distinction or duality (you are a worker, therefore you are automatically a member of the progressive class; you are rich, therefore you are automatically a member of the reactionary class) we reach a stage where each individual has choices between polarities in relation to important questions at critical points. The concept of polarity and duality is preserved, *but the concept of system-organized duality is abandoned*; that is, there are two sides to these important questions, and only one side is right. And no matter what class, color, sex you are, you can be on the wrong side or you can be on the right side. You can be the most oppressed victim from every possible angle (e.g., a young, black lesbian) but if you are a dope pusher, you are on the wrong side.

GETTING RID OF LIBERALISM

By confronting people we help them to deal with questions seriously. We set up positions so people can grapple with fundamental issues. We state our positions sharply enough so that people can't evade what is involved for the human race. Not that we expect them to make up their minds immediately. We take positions in order to help the person discover what is his attitude to him/herself. The only way to help a person towards understanding is by jamming him/her. For example: "If you don't care about anybody else, why should they care about you? Maybe you ought to starve to death." We have to confront people very sharply so that they discover some of their own humanity before they destroy themselves.

When you take positions on fundamental issues, you have moved beyond the abstract discussion of the nature of man/woman. By taking a position, you reveal to people their attitude towards humanity and how this attitude must change if they want to be human. You remove this liberalism which cripples them. Positions are a means whereby we get individuals to confront themselves, to begin to define their humanity; by which we force them, through ideas, to act rather than complain. In other words, we establish a framework within which they can grapple with themselves. We are not pushing them up against a wall but compelling them to face the question of what their human identity is. We decide which issues are fundamental at this time in terms of where people are and where society is, and we make the polarization. *We* choose the issues. For example, we have chosen the issue of work because of this historical conjuncture and because work involved something intrinsically human that has developed down through the ages.

Logically, one can say that you arrive at the particular (the issue of work) through the general (your notion of man/woman); and that is the way we arrive at it, in part. But, historically, it becomes necessary for those who take the responsibility for bringing about a confrontation of man/woman with him/herself, to take the issue which agitates people—which is the point of real controversy—and help people arrive at definitions of man/woman or of the universal. Work is not the only vehicle through which we can ask man/woman to discover him/herself; but there is a crucial polarization actually developing around it at the present time. We are asking the question in such a way so as to enable people to start thinking for themselves, and become conscious of how they think.

Right now the polarizations are taking place between blacks and whites, between employed and unemployed. We deliberately turn this into a different polarization; not between *groups,* but between the different attitudes on the basis of which people take sides. It is true that blacks feel that they will never be in the work process as whites have been. Some people say, "Why should they, considering what whites have been doing to black folks over the years?" A lot of young whites are developing a similar attitude, only their attack is directed against their parents. We don't jump into this; we start with a position on work that will enable people to begin to think about it.

During the next period there will be a significant number of young people re-evaluating the sixties. Why didn't it offer anything but activism and separatism? Why didn't it take positions on the fundamental issues which affect the totality of society and are so basic to it? We are creating these positions so that in the future some of these young people can find a direction and a focus for their thoughts.

Positions enable you to begin discussing with people who have questions on their mind and who are not just blaming others but can make choices. By taking a position on the question of work, we are able to help people clarify their relation to society. At first we may not be able to reach people who have made their whole life and culture one of victimization. But people who are already wondering, who already have a healthy attitude to work, are able to become advocates or proselytizers for something bigger than their own selves. People will begin to understand that a work ethic isn't just a personal thing, that it relates to something much larger—the advancement of humankind. The most alienated elements are not going to grasp this early. But the controversy has to begin so that they will not be allowed to go unchecked in their disintegration and in order to help those who already have some inclination in the new direction to take the offensive on a more positive basis. The "radlibs" are the worst obstacles to revolutionary struggle because they make it unnecessary for people to confront themselves. Liberalism is the opiate of the people.

We are looking for a process that will give people an opportunity to make some evaluation of themselves. We cannot begin just by asking them questions—like a Gallup pollster. And we cannot start by consensus. We have to start by going way beyond the radicals who are perpetuating myths about victims and therefore encouraging thinking in terms of past concepts—inalienable rights, etc.

A revolutionary must have an incredible belief in the capacity *of* humankind. People are incredible. They aren't mean, even though they are acting mean. They are capable of sensitivity, heroism. But most people in the U.S. have so diminished themselves that they haven't the faintest idea that men and women are not the s.o.b.'s they are acting out. People are capable of extraordinary dedication, commitment, creativity. But we can't just exhort them. Our way is confrontation, not exhortation. We do not just open up to them a vision of the positive; we force them to confront their own negativity.

The people of the U.S. are damaged people. We have to bring about a confrontation between their damaged character and their potential character.

There have been societies in the past in which people have worked together, conscious of their goals and playing their roles in relation to the whole. These have usually been societies on a very small physical scale. Today people don't even believe that this kind of social relationship is possible. As a result of only a few hundred years of bourgeois society, folks now believe that everybody is just an individual pursuing his/her own hustle. This self-concept has become a barrier to our thinking about our selves as capable of grandeur.

By talking about primitive communism, Marx thought that workers, liberated from oppression by the bourgeoisie, would behave like primitive communists, with additional social qualities produced by the organization and discipline of modern industry. We are saying that bourgeois society has transformed the most oppressed into the most individualistic, and that the individualism of bourgeois society is now deeply rooted in the character structure of the most oppressed. The individuals who are oppressed have to confront their own nature before they can even begin to realize the human nature that they are capable of. This is how we differ from Marx.

What Do People Really Want?

Last year we emphasized the historical relativity of truth, of convictions. It is necessary always to keep in mind historical origins of social concepts and recognize that what was true or meaningful at one time is not necessarily true or meaningful at another. Sometimes we must give new content to old concepts and at other times we must give up concepts altogether, recognizing that it is very hard to put new wine into old bottles.

The most difficult and most crucial thing we have to do is somehow to project to people that what they really want is not quantitative, not things or status, but the quality of their humanity, the quality of human achievement. That is one reason why Kenneth Clark's TV series "Civilization" was so important. Clark projected an historical vision of man/woman as creative, not as greedy, or starving, or autocratic or dominating.

What does man/woman really want today? People have the sense of something wrong but can't define it because it is unconscious. It takes the form of depression, a sense of vacuity, of vague purposelessness even when you know what you are planning to do, a kind of flabbiness of relations, a tension in relationships, an irritability, a self-questioning. "Why am I so tense? Is everybody so irritable?" The unconscious isn't the unknown. It is something actual which is within man/woman, which is active, and which is tremendously, incredibly important. Imagination and vision are explosions of the unconscious—because you don't consciously imagine anything. Therefore it becomes our job to persuade men and women that they are fifty times grander than they think they are. They don't really know who they are. They haven't taken the time to envisage, to imagine who they are.

Our job is to enable men and women to understand that what they really want is something entirely different from what they think they want. People today, especially in the U.S., want yachts and homes in suburbia. They don't give a damn about the cities; they have no notion of the culture that cities represent historically, that cities were created by people because they wanted to live where they could meet with other people on the streets. That was what a city was. That is why in Europe the rich lived in the center of the city. In the United States the rich live in the suburbs. That is another way of saying America is infinitely less rich than it thinks it is.

The average person scoffs at the idea of spiritual wants. Yet we know that city dwellers don't have any relationships with their neighbors a few doors down the streets; that they are afraid to lie down in their own homes without locking all the doors and windows. We know that there is something wrong with all this. We also know, although we may not say so, that if exploitation is not worse than it ever was, in the human sense society is much worse than it ever was.

Why do people feel so unhappy, so unfulfilled? Because of these wants that they don't know anything about. They have never formulated them, but because people are human beings they are within people. You talk to people about "human relations" and all they can think of is being sympathetic or emotional. The concept has no thickness, no grandeur, no vision in it for them. Their concept of being a "human being" is related to what their father or mother thought ten or twenty years ago. It has no relationship to the nature of man/woman or to any concept of humankind as it has been expanded through the qualitative achievements of man/woman over the centuries.

One is reminded of the conversation between the Indian and the guy who was trying to get him to go to work. "For what?" asked the Indian, and the guy replied, "To make some money." "For what?" the Indian asked again, and the guy answered, "To build a big house and have in it everything you want." "For what?" the Indian persisted, to which the guy replied, "So you can retire and go back to the country." At which point the Indian said, "I am in the country already."

For the past fifty to one hundred-fifty years in the U.S. most people have thought that their purpose in life was to accumulate enough to assure them a roof over their heads and to send their kids to school so that they could go on to have a better house and a few more material things. If they accomplished this, they felt they had fulfilled themselves as human beings. Now they face the question, "Is that enough?" How do we think a human being should live today? We don't have to go back to the Indians, but we do have to relate to nature in the context of where we are, within our technology. We can't resolve this fundamental question by simply sending our children out into the country to play in nature. We have to resolve it according to a concept of the uniqueness, the limitlessness, the open-ended capacity of man/woman to go beyond where he/she is.

The moral authority that comes from providing and projecting a new concept of humanity or of human nature is the only basis for gaining revolutionary authority. Most radicals want power in order to create this moral authority. Whereas, in fact, until they have created this authority, they can't create anything. No radicals are going to get power in this country until we have converted a whole lot of people to recognize that they are their own jailers; that they take the prison of their own selves with them wherever they go; and that they are not going to be free until they have decided what they are going to do with their freedom.

WHY ARE WE SO FRUSTRATED?

How do you change what a man/woman thinks he/she wants? The Russians didn't do it. The Chinese are trying to. How do you do that anywhere else? How do we change what Western man/woman thinks he/she wants—Cadillacs, snowmobiles—to something else? Human beings are in this mess, in mental hospitals, drinking themselves to death, not because they lack material things, but because they haven't brought their concept of self to a level of correspondence between their consciousness and their needs. This is what drives us up the wall. Why are we so frustrated? Because we know that people in other periods lived in harmony with themselves and with nature, were creative and achieved things of qualitative grandeur. In the nineteenth century Marx pointed out to European industrializing man/woman that primitive communism had existed, in order to demonstrate to people that they had the capacity to cooperate, to live without class antagonisms, to build, to love, to excel, to be artistic. We too have to reveal to people today that they have these qualities within them, whether they are fifteen thousand, fifteen million or fifteen billion people. The fundamental nature of human beings—that they have crossed the threshold of reflection and have the capacity for self-determination and self-enlarging—remains. True, it was much easier in an agricultural society to express this. But humankind remains the same organism.

THE QUESTIONS WOMEN ASK

Men and women have never really faced the question of their relations before. Today women are saying, "Look, let's stop and face it." In this is a clue to facing all other human relationships, not only between men and women but between adults and children, brothers and sisters, patients and doctors, and between every aspect of our human nature—biological and psychological, economic and political, all of which have been dealt with separately up to now.

It is not a question of the many specific grievances that women have. About these there could be bargaining, with each getting a little more or a little less. What is involved is the evolution of humankind.

We could ask, "Why didn't women start raising this question in this way at the very beginning? Why did they wait so damn long, until the last half of the twentieth century?" Because originally, there was a natural, biological division of labor between men who did the work of hunting and killing the animals, and women who bore and raised the children, who gathered, and grew and prepared the bulk of the food. It wasn't the choice of men that they should not have children or of women that they should. It was a natural division. A division established maybe a million years ago and which crystallized with the rise of the State. It didn't change earlier because it has taken all these decades to develop the technology which has made the State anachronistic and which makes it possible for men and women to share more equally. Therefore men and women are now searching for what the new relationship should be.

In this search for new relations between men and women, we have an illustration of the search for a new relationship between people.

The women's struggle illustrates the complex relationship between the particular and the universal. When you discuss something, you have to talk about the universal, i.e., something more general than the circumstances that have just taken place. On the other hand, in any continuing relationship with anyone, you have to struggle over particulars. You can't just store up the particulars and struggle over them in some universal way unless you are able to pose a new universal. Most women have been storing up their particular grievances for years, mulling them over and now exploding with them. But when they do this, it is not just the sum of the particulars that they have exploded over but a universal for which they haven't yet found the concept. And when they are asked what they really *want*, they can't give an answer.

The fact is that during the last hundred years, and particularly the last twenty-five, the division of roles between the sexes has lost its basis, and women and men have not yet found the new universal to correspond to the new stage.

There are certain roles that won't be changed, e.g., women's bearing of children. We can't start by saying that men and women should bear children equally, or that since only women can bear children women should only be child-bearers. In fact not bearing children for ten years might be just the opportunity that young women need in order to explore and enlarge their humanity.

It is not easy for society to accept a proposition like this. People are still responding with the attitudes of a hundred years ago when every kid you could bear was needed to till the land. The previous role of women, continuous child-bearing, has created prejudices in people, not only in men but in everyone, including women.

If young women didn't have children for ten years, what an opportunity it would give them—to consider what they would like to do, what they would like to become! That is what is happening through the postponement of marriage in China. Young Chinese women now have the opportunity during these important years of vitality, curiosity and creativity, to develop and explore their selves. For hundreds of thousands of years, in most societies, these most vital years have been spent by women in the social responsibility of bearing children.

What kind of meaningful choices can a girl or a woman make if she has a lot of kids running around after her, whom she has to feed, diaper, etc.? In the old days women didn't have postnatal neuroses because there was a social reason for their bearing and rearing children. Today, with the social reasons very much modified, many young women have a nervous breakdown after they have children.

A lot of women go about saying they are imprisoned by being mothers during these crucial years, and they blame men for knocking them up. Others, in order to evade the problem, say they should have sexual relations with women instead of men. They are seeing themselves as victims rather than thinking about and choosing a whole different way in which society and they themselves could be developed. Why don't women take a pill or use a diaphragm or rubber or even douche? Not because these means or this knowledge are unavailable. Until we have persuaded people to think differently, as they have done in China, the women's question will be seen only as a question of the *rights* of which men are depriving women, instead of as the need for women to develop themselves.

These ten years could be crucial years to develop new relations between males and females of a type, a qualitatively new character, whose scope we cannot even imagine at this moment. Women would have an opportunity to develop themselves intellectually, technically, politically, artistically, giving them a purpose other than getting back at men.

Why can't a young woman or girl say, "I don't want to be a mother until I am thirty because I want a chance to think." She can decide that right now. First she has to internalize the idea that she is self-determining, that she decides whether she has to be a mother or a sexpot in order to achieve her human identity. With the knowledge that society perpetuates and reinforces this concept of woman as brood mare and sexpot, she can still free herself, become independent of this concept.

For example, we who are in Advocators are thinking of issuing a "We Can Change the Way It Is" statement to young girls, along the lines of the crime statement. We want to address ourselves to the growing number of teenagers who can't think of anything else but having children and who are therefore in their early and middle teens settling their futures as ADC and welfare mothers. How can we get these kids, who have barely begun to live, to develop a self-concept which will not allow them to settle for this kind of future? How can we enable them to see themselves creating another kind of future? They are the victims of past concepts. We are not blaming them, but we do want to get them to think differently about themselves.

"Aren't you married yet? Don't you have any children?" Young women are faced with these questions all the time. They need very different concepts of their selves in order to stand up against such questions. But just because society imposes upon women these questions, doesn't mean that one can expect society to free women. They have to solve it themselves—by wanting something very different. Those who are burdened by the past have to develop and/or appropriate for themselves a new outlook, a new vision, a new perspective. They can't expect society to appropriate it for them.

Looking at these young girls, we see how far we have to project the concept of a self-determining, self-enlarging human identity, as well as how hard the most oppressed masses always have to work in order to grasp and make their own these advanced concepts. But the determination to achieve this advanced state of human identity is what always gives momentum to the struggles of the most oppressed masses when they begin to reject being shaped by the past.

TOWARDS FEMALE SELF-DETERMINATION

These young girls now think of themselves as nothing but biological test tubes; it is difficult to go much lower than this in your concept of self. Many of them don't exist in their own minds as people unless at fifteen they have slept with a man or been knocked up. This is their self-concept. They don't see themselves except as bedmates or brood mares. They think they have achieved something if they have had a child by a football star or a rock musician.

For a woman today to feel that these are the only realms in which she can achieve identity is self-denial, not self-determination. Because she is human, she has the capacity to envisage a thousand other ways to be creative, but nobody has projected these to her or permitted her to enlarge her self-concept.

We are not trying to inform these kids about how not to get pregnant, although obviously we believe that such information should be made available to them. We are trying to change their thoughts about themselves in order that they will want to live differently. If they haven't any idea of how to live differently, they are going to get pregnant. They don't have any other purpose in life or any idea of another way to live.

That is why it is so important to give every child a historical conception of where we came from and how humankind has been developing since our evolution from the ape. Only when one begins to reflect about this, can a person understand the views he/she has about women. Most people have never been introduced into manhood/womanhood except in petty little ways. In early societies there were rituals (rites of passage) to connect the individual's development to the development of the human race. Today we tend to think of society only in contemporary terms, not in temporal terms. To think only of the immediate, the contemporaneous, is not human. Human beings need a concept of history, of the past and of the future of the human race. Otherwise you screw on a bolt and you launch a whole lifetime for a person and for society, without ever having thought about what you really wanted for yourself or for society.

NEW SELF-CONCEPTS

If you haven't begun to think of revolutionizing relations between men and women, it is absurd to talk about changing relations between classes or races. The women's movement is potentially the most revolutionary of all movements because it is asking the most profound of all questions, the question which underlies all other movements, the question of the relations between people. Without dealing with this question, we are not going to solve any other questions except superficially—which is what all the other radical movements are doing. Only in China, and possibly in Cuba, have they tried to insist that you can only solve the problems of society by solving the problems of human relationships—not economic relations but human ones.

As long as we only talk about day care centers or women getting jobs or men helping women with the housework—all of which are progressive—we are still talking only about *reforms*. We are not talking about *revolutions* until we begin to talk about women thinking of their selves in different ways, or until women can say, concretely, "I do not want to be tied down to the biological role that women have played in the past."

In order to break down the many manifestations of male domination, men should not only respect this but should themselves recognize that they have been part of the pressure to tie women down. Part of the problem is to persuade men that *this demand is equally in the interest of men.*

Red Blossoms, made in China a few years ago, is an exciting film about a young woman who is elected head of the sheep-raising commune of a minority group. Her difficulties in assuming this responsibility, her husband's efforts to make her think about their home and not the commune, make a fascinating film. In color, with horses, chases, and so on, it illustrates how the great dramas of critical transition periods in the past dealt with the fundamental contradictions involved in creating new relations between men and women, man and man, woman and woman, parents and children, rulers and ruled.

To say that men shouldn't look at women as sexual objects isn't very realistic. They are going to look at them as sex objects but they shouldn't look at them as sex objects only. In this country most people think that the only way a man and a woman can relate is sexually. It is impossible for a girl to talk with a boy without everybody thinking that they are having an affair. On the other hand, we are told that in Japan, for example, when boy and girl students talk together, the assumption is that they are talking about their studies.

A woman has first of all to look at herself as a person. Our whole society is sex-oriented. Sex is looked at materialistically: "I want an orgasm" or "I want to prove I am not chicken" or "I scored with him or her." This is characteristic of a society which hasn't altered its values to correspond to the new stage of human development. "I can make any chick on the block," says the guy. "I can be as tough as any boy on the block," says the girl. Both mean that they haven't arrived at any discrimination in their hearts or heads, in relation to their own selves.

This kind of behavior is not acting like an animal, as some people say. It is acting like an s.o.b. human being. There is a big element of choice in this situation: there is a lot of consciousness. Foxes don't play chicken.

We are not taking a moralistic position about whether or not people should have sex. We are talking about human behavior of a very dehumanized kind. For people to say, as many do, that man/woman is acting like an animal because we came from animals, is a complete evasion of the real question as to what we should do now that we have crossed the threshold of reflection. We now have responsibilities to our selves as non-animals, as human beings. Humankind has been carrying on an incredible search for human identity for tens of thousands of years. We have to keep carrying on the same search with the utmost effort, the utmost passion, the utmost imagination. It doesn't come automatically. You don't just go to high school and come out a human being.

People are behaving this way according to a concept they have of themselves—a self-degrading, dehumanizing concept, but they are still behaving according to a concept! The horrible thing is that the concept is so degrading. We are not only referring to population growth, or the absence of need for so many small children today. *What concerns us is the dehumanization of self which mushrooms when a new self-concept is not created to correspond to the new stage of human development.* It is as if these kids cannot think of anything in life worth striving for. So they flit from this to that.

ILLEGITIMATE REASONS

The concept of love has changed a great deal over the ages, as we know. In previous periods families played an important role in production and reproduction and therefore sexuality automatically had a social importance. Today what one does for personal reasons or for personal pleasure has no other concept associated with it. So you need a much more profound concept of what you are doing, in order that what you do for pleasure becomes more meaningful rather than solely dependent upon your caprice, your whims, your personal feelings at the moment.

We are not saying that sex was invented or created by the economic system. Sexuality developed out of a whole lot of things, but it *did* have economic purposes, it did have a social framework. Infant mortality being what it was (and still is in some parts of the world) only two of a whole bunch of kids might survive to take care of their parents in their old age. But that isn't the case in the U.S.

Just because biologically you can have kids doesn't mean you have to have them—in order to prove your existence. That is why a lot of men and women, and kids too, have children today. They have them for illegitimate, sick reasons. We are not talking about illegitimate children (many of these people are "married") but about the illegitimate reasons why people have children. A revolutionary change would be one which enabled people to think that there are other ways in which they can express their selves. Now they don't know any other way. Nobody has illuminated it for them. They don't see it around them or in the society. We have to project to them that this is not the way; that there is another way.

The woman suffragettes were advanced in relation to other women and to the men of their time; yet they merely wanted to participate in the man's world, i.e., to vote. Women's liberationists today are saying, "I don't want to participate in the man's world; I want to discover what is the proper world." That is why this is such an extraordinarily important movement. When the workers took over the plants in Russia, Lenin said, "This is socialism." He thought that if you could change the relationships in production, you would change people. If you change relationships in production, you begin a process, but you don't change people. You have only begun a process.

We have to have confidence in man/woman's mind. He/she doesn't use it most of the time, but he/she does have a mind. We are arriving at the stage where we have to change what people think as well as their relationships in production. Because what they think will shape the changes they want to make in all their relationships, in production, with the opposite sex, with children, with other men and women. A lot of the things that made it impossible or difficult in the past for the human mind to progress no longer exist. This means people are even more capable than they were yesterday. For fifty thousand years man/woman has had a mind and has been trying to discover how to use it—in language, in astronomy, in art, in architecture. He/she has had a mind all this time that was a human mind, not an animal mind, and he/she has been using it and striving like hell to use it.

PHILOSOPHY FOR EVERYBODY

Then all of a sudden this mind has gotten bogged down. As during the Middle Ages it got bogged down in theology and religious determinism, now it has gotten bogged down in materialism and economic determinism. It is preoccupied with making more and newer machines, having more things. Men and women have stopped thinking about their relationships to other people, to the cosmos, to their selves as human beings. Yet they have this fantastic mind. Now they have to rediscover it. This is what philosophy is.

It is obvious that the teenager in the black ghetto can't begin doing differently until he/she thinks differently about his/her relations to people and to him/herself. But you can't change until you have a will to change, a reason to change.

We are not just trying to improve the relations between men and women. We are trying to develop in everybody in the society a different concept of his/her potential as a human being, which will in turn give them a different concept of their relationships with one another. It is so easy to want the wrong things or the things that will defeat the revolution right off the bat. It is so easy to defeat creativity by coming up with too-hasty solutions.

How do you get people *to want to live in time,* to have a sense of the importance of time for growth, development, of the need for ups-and-downs, of non-homogenized development? Almost all great artists in the past were first of all apprentices. They went to school with the masters of the time and knew everything that these masters knew before they began to discover what was new about themselves. They not only accepted this, but enjoyed it; they expected to undergo a kind of recapitulation of the past in order to gather the momentum to leap into the future. It is so vital to get that concept of the relation between the past and the future—not to see apprenticeship as subordination of yourself or humiliation or a deprivation of equal rights, but as the natural logic of growth and advance. This is very rare in the U.S. It is practically impossible to develop a great artist or a great leader because anybody with talent is plunged into stardom the moment he/she exhibits talents. A revolution in the U.S. is only going to be led and made by people with some sense of the thickness of time, of time as duration, of time as heterogeneous, of development through contradiction, not in a straight line. Before any child learns the three R's he/she needs some sense of the development of humankind. Wanting your name in the history books is very different from having a sense of historical development.

RELATING TO REAL PEOPLE

In this country in the past, special interest groups have been used by politicians to advance themselves. Sectional interests, ethnic interests, each thinking only of what it wants for itself, have been built by politicians into coalitions. The success of the politician depended on his/her ability to promise and his/her ability to produce in relation to promises. Hence the concept of politics as who gets what and how. These groups and coalitions have always been used by politicians because they wanted to be promised certain things for themselves.

Now we have to begin relating again to real groups of people. But instead of relating to them just in terms of their wants and their demands to "get ours," we need to relate to people in such a way that they can begin learning about themselves in an expanded sense and to develop some sort of direction for themselves and for society through how we relate to them.

In the U.S. today there are tens of millions of people who for the first time are in no material want but who are extremely unhappy, frustrated, alienated, running away (like Updike's Rabbit) from reality, because the reality they face is so unsatisfying. But they are discovering that no matter how far they run, they still take their jailers with them. Somehow we must enable people to grapple with the reality of their alienation. They are extremely unhappy because they haven't any idea of what to confront; they don't realize that what they have to face is the nature of man/woman. How does a man/woman relate to nature, to other people, to affection, to virtue? All these years they have related exclusively to material things, to quantitative values, so that they don't know anything about these other things. The only nonquantitative things they have any idea of are the ones they heard about from some Baptist preacher, involving going to heaven, disembodied spirits, etc.

A person has to know what he/she thinks about him/herself before he/she knows how to relate to other people. He/she has to start subjectively. He/she, the subject, is doing the thinking. What one thinks one's relations should be to other people, including people one doesn't like, depends upon one's concept of oneself.

Note: It has taken us nearly ten years to discover how to confront our own ideas. If we are in too much of a hurry to ask people to confront themselves and to come to decisions, we are going to end up like Billy Graham, getting people who don't know anything about themselves or about the process of discovery they have to undergo, to "pledge themselves to Jesus." If you ask Updike's Rabbit to think about himself, he has relatively little to think about. We want people to ask themselves questions they have never asked before—and not to be in a hurry to come up with answers.

You can't possibly know who you are unless you have some idea of where you came from. You can't possibly discover who you are just by looking into your self. You can't ask somebody like Rabbit to confront himself when nobody has helped him to wonder what he is confronting. Is he just somebody with two legs and a pecker, or is he the result of thousands of years of struggles, of history, of defeats and victories, of creations and achievements? If he is only the former, he can only confront himself in relationship to a chick, "Do I exist in your mind, lovely girl?" If she says, "Yes," then he is to some degree satisfied. If she says, "No," he is completely disrupted. That is a hell of a way to confront yourself. But there are a lot of Rabbits. Even Michael in *The Godfather* had other criteria, based on some past traditions. Now we are trying to discover the criteria which produce the new revolutionist.

Why is it easier to address young women of fifteen and sixteen than it is to address the Rabbits? Because these teenagers haven't even begun to try to do something with their lives, while Rabbit has achieved something, i.e., in basketball he had some success. On the one hand, precisely because Americans have arrived at this stage where the question of material wants has been solved, it should be easy to face them with the question of the relationships of people to people. On the other hand, it might be more difficult to do this because they have acquired so much without caring about such relationships.

Alienation, disgust, confusion, purposelessness is evident in every sphere of U.S. life. Mao's "new man" doesn't oppress himself because there is a correspondence between what he does and what he thinks a human being should do. In the U.S. people do things because they can't see any reason why not to. "Why-not"ism prevails. How do we give them a sense of "Why"?

There are fifty million Rabbits in this country who don't want to change anything. They are barriers, but they are not dangerous. Barriers are just things to be overcome. At this time there is little point in going to the Rabbits. On the other hand, after we have been able to develop momentum among certain types of people, people who begin to throw their energies into redefining themselves as human beings and who exhibit what human beings can achieve with purpose in their lives, then people like Rabbit will take on more character.

We have to go by degrees. For example, the French Revolution was first of all a creation in the mind of whole flocks of intellectuals with new ideas of freedom, equality and "the people." It drifted down to magistrates and civil servants, and finally got to the masses in Paris who said, "That's right; let's stop talking and do something." The masses didn't invent the French Revolution.

The Rabbits are barriers; the Godfather types are dangerous. They will shoot you, they are just out for themselves and don't care about the rest of society. The Godfathers are successful, they are making it so why should they listen at all? The Rabbits would listen. They might not understand, but they would listen. There are people like Rabbit in every class. You are not going to persuade them in an hour and a half's conversation, but they will listen. They are looking for a better reason to live than just changing diapers or demonstrating a Magi-Peeler in the "5 & 10." They are trying somehow to explain themselves to themselves.

WHOM DO WE APPROACH?

Once we don't accept that any group (workers or blacks or women) is in itself revolutionary, we must begin to discover new criteria for deciding who is revolutionary. Whom does one approach? We can't just appeal to multitudes to begin with. Who are some of the people we might start with? It is important to think of several different types in order to have a concept of diversity rather than a narrow homogenized concept. Who is more revolutionary, a person with a bomb in his/her pocket or one with a crusade in his/her heart?

After the McGovern campaign, there will be lots of young people looking for some direction. They won't be militants particularly, but rather seekers after perspective and direction.

Then there are people in particular communities, e.g., the black community, who also are seeking for meaning in their lives but who are at the same time worried about specific issues, like the crime right on their streets, their children—the grandchildren who are being dumped on them and the godfather types who are making them.

NOT FACELESS MASSES

The important thing is to have in mind different types of people, not just homogeneous or faceless masses or sociological categories. The radical's working class was faceless; therefore the radicals didn't have to ask workers to be much more than warm bodies. On the other hand, when you begin looking at people as people, you can begin asking them questions that are in their hearts. You can't change what people are unless they are at least wanting something and not just going along.

In projecting Rabbit, Updike was making clear that nice thoughts are not enough. What is enough? If you want to get an idea of what is happening in the U.S., you have to have an idea of what is happening with the Rabbits and realize that they are beautiful in a way. At least Rabbit was wondering about something. He is so capable, finds it so easy to move about and to achieve—so that he can see the emptiness of his achievements. But that is not enough. What is enough?

The types we are least interested in are those who are just looking for issues in which to get involved, i.e., militants. We are not seeking them out at all because we realize that those who are just looking for issues don't have time to think about anything but the issue and about strategies and tactics. Those who get involved in issues all the time think they already have answers for what are still questions.

The number of people who matter to us, i.e., whom we are interested in approaching at this time, is very small. They are just handfuls. That has always been the case when great transitions are just beginning. We have to keep clearly in mind that there is a difference between people. We can't just go out on the street corner and go by what people want. *To advance is probably the most difficult thing that human beings ever try to do.* We are trying to advance against an enormous current of thoughts from the past: Marxist determinism, liberalism, and people who are searching for power without any knowledge of what they are going to do with power.

This is a historical transition of which we are a part. For centuries people thought of utopias in religious terms. Then came the Industrial Revolution, and people began thinking of utopias in economic terms. We have gone through the religious utopias, then the economic ones. Now we are trying to discover what is the next stage in human development, not the final stage but the next one. The American revolution is going to take place in relation to this new stage.

Looking back at the old socialists, the Old Left, we can see that they had a historical vision, the vision of a planned economy, which was very narrow and really not relevant to the U.S. Then the New Left came along, without any vision and without any historical perspective. All they had was their activism and their good intentions and good deeds. Now this has fallen apart. What we are talking about now is a historical vision that is relevant to the present age and yet relates to the historical past.

Since 1970 the Chinese have been distinguishing between the struggles for independence, liberation and revolution: "Countries want independence, nations want liberation, people want revolution." Almost every speech by the Chinese since their entry into the UN has centered around this phrase. In emphasizing this, the Chinese are showing a recognition that globally people have moved beyond the stage of a class struggle of poor against rich. These struggles are, of course, still going on and will continue for some time. But the epoch of poor countries struggling versus the metropolises of the world, which characterized the world scene after World War II, is coming to an end. The new trend in today's world is "People want revolution," and this is what we must address ourselves to, especially in the U.S. One of the reasons why Lin Biao is out could very well be his identification with the "countryside versus metropolis" concept, a concept with which many radicals in the West, who have never seriously applied themselves to the question of revolution in an advanced country, still identify.

EVERY REVOLUTION IS UNIQUE

What is meant by "People want revolution"? There are all kinds of people and all kinds of revolutions—i.e., a great diversity can be imagined now that we have witnessed so many revolutions since World War II. "People" is also a very different category from "class." It is a category that allows for many distinctions, diversities, many selves.

Among a growing number of people there is now an understanding that the Russian Revolution was a revolution in which power came first and the attempt to transform people came afterwards—and that is precisely why it degenerated. In the Chinese Revolution on the other hand, power came only after a long period of protracted struggle to "Fan Shen" (meaning "to transform"). Thus the Chinese and Russian Revolutions represent two entirely different concepts of revolution.

We are very fortunate to be living in a period when two such different revolutions as the Russian and the Chinese have taken place so closely together, giving us the opportunity to realize that there is no such thing as a model revolution ("*the* revolution") and to contrast the D-Day concept of revolution with that of protracted struggle. Every revolution is unique, and the concept of revolution must itself change with every revolution. That does not mean that the Russian revolutionary model will not continue to linger in many minds and act as a barrier to the very notion of change. In China they discovered through practice in the twenties that they couldn't make the Russian Revolution in China; they had to make their own revolution. To the average American the word "revolution" still means what the Communist Party has been proclaiming. That doesn't mean that we have to give up the word "revolution." But we must be very clear that we are not talking about the Russian Revolution or the Chinese Revolution—or the first American Revolution. We have to be constantly aware of the different levels on which we are discussing and clarifying, but basically we must use the word "revolution" to emphasize the changes that must take place in the concept and the uniqueness of every revolution, rather than evade the question by avoiding the use of the word.

GETTING PEOPLE TO THINKING

There is a great deal of discussion going on about populism because of George Wallace and George McGovern. There is something in a guy like Truman which is "populist" in the sense of responding to grievances which create a momentum at a particular time. This is very different from giving leadership.

The average person takes it for granted that there are leaders and there is "me"—in fact, a whole lot of little me's whom politicians should please. How do you turn masses of people who are the products of mass production and mass consumption society into reflective individuals? Because, clearly, only reflective individuals can live with a sense of history, can relate to other people as human beings, can rise above their own egos—especially in an age of mass production. Only reflective individuals are genuinely subjects rather than objects. What we are trying to do is to get people to think—not to think certain thoughts but to begin *thinking*.

The first thing we need is the courage to depart from the old categories and to discover new ones. It takes a lot of courage. Obviously we are going to be attacked from every possible angle as soon as we project the idea that there are new distinctions. We have to accept the idea that we begin small, without any illusions that we are going to have a mass party or make the revolution in a few years. We are going to discover whether there are some people who think as we do. We are trying to project new notions of human relations—not abstract ones like "brotherhood" or "sisterhood" but specific ones. We are trying to do it around specific struggles, e.g., crime, young girls. If we don't discover anybody who wants to relate to these new ways of relating to people, maybe we will have to start on a new track, or with different people.

WE ARE NOT HUMPTY DUMPTY

It is not just a question of what is wrong with this country. That is obvious enough. But what is the specific contradiction which creates this state of frustration in the midst of plenty, in all sections of society? Change has been taking place so rapidly in this country that few people feel a part of even the twenties and thirties, let alone of 1776. This country is like a ship which started out from a port and doesn't know from whence it came and where it is going.

What has happened to people that an Arthur Bremer can sell his memoirs for $100,000? How did people create and why are they continuing to create a society which is demolishing them? How does one break through the vicious circle? The only way is by reinforcing the idea that human beings control society, not vice versa. And therefore that people have to begin asking, "What am I? Who am I? And what kind of society do I want to create as an expression of my being?" Otherwise the next bunch of assassins is going to sell their memoirs for $200,000. People have permitted this to happen because the only ones who can stop it haven't done anything to stop it—and this is people themselves.

In the 1950s, Allen Wheelis wrote that the technological revolution and the destruction of rural society was creating faceless masses who would be ripe for a Hitler (*The Quest for Identity*). Now it seems rather that what we will get are more Rabbits and Arthur Bremers: self-focused individuals.

People created this society—not devils, not gods. It was created by people and only people can change it. It is not going to be abstract man/woman who is going to change it, but specific people who see the need to express an enlarged concept of man/woman. Blacks in America lived like animals in terms of their material conditions, but they were not animals. They knew they were not animals, and nobody was going to turn them into animals. Today a lot of people go around saying that the system has turned then into animals, and they are going to behave like animals. The change will begin when people say, "Nobody is going to turn me into an animal. I am going to change the society which tries to turn me into one." That is the fantastic thing about Mao, that he led 700 million people to stand up and say, "If we are not going to be animals, we have to behave like men and women"—that is, according to the most advanced ideas of human nature.

What should human life revolve around? The person who goes to the suburbs is not trying to create a better America; he/she is trying to escape the problems of this world. There are eight million people in Sweden, organized and cared for from the cradle to the grave. Yet many Swedes cut their throats every year because that is a horrible way to live. Maybe to have the second highest standard of living in the world, as they do, isn't the most important goal of human life. Then what is important to human life?

It is fashionable today to talk about people's helplessness, hopelessness, isolation, about their resemblance to Humpty Dumpty. But man/woman is not Humpty Dumpty. People are not the prisoners of objective social forces. They are the ones who have to pick up their own pieces. This general principle can't be stressed too often. It is absolutely crucial to any revolution: "Who is responsible? You are." This doesn't mean that everybody has exactly the same responsibility; but human beings threw themselves off the wall. The notion of man/woman is in pieces. The only ones who can put the notion of man/woman back together again are men and women themselves.

We have to persuade people that "nobody else is going to do this except me. I can't wait on George Wallace or George McGovern to do it. I have to figure out my role in the process of putting myself together again. I have absolutely no right to say 'I am nobody and therefore I play no role.' " We cannot begin any kind of discussion, any kind of confrontation, any kind of struggle, unless we begin with "you have a responsibility; don't blame it on anybody else. You have no right to say 'I am nobody.' "

Note: We are not saying "You are responsible for what is happening to you!" in the sense of blaming people or trying to induce guilt in them. What we are saying is, "Don't just come complaining to me about everything that's going. You have as much responsibility for changing it as I do—and I am ready to work with you when you are ready to do something."

We have to begin seeing how to address ourselves to people, to develop some policies for addressing ourselves to them, in such a way that "people power" or "people responsibility" will begin to mean something to them—not that they think in terms of taking power at this stage but that they internalize the concept of their own powers. At the same time we must never lose sight of the fact that this concept is extremely elusive and that it has to be recreated again and again, because it runs so counter to the economist and determinist dogmas that have prevailed for the past 150 years.

Hence the concrete practice that flows from this concept of man/woman cannot possibly be the same concrete practice that flows from the determinist concept of man/woman, i.e., it cannot possibly be the same kind of militant agitation of the masses which the average radical carries on, in the hope that, once in motion, the masses will be captured by the future, whether or not they know it or like it.

What Democracy Really Is

We must redefine democracy—restructure the whole concept of democracy so that we can struggle over it and for it. This means, among other things, making a serious critique of participatory democracy which is based on the romantic idea that anybody can make decisions because he/she is a living, breathing person. There are a whole lot of illusions contained in participatory democracy. Essentially it is based on the purely quantitative, least common denominator, or biological concept of human beings. It is also tied up with concepts of individual rights.

People are not able to make decisions simply by virtue of being born or of having arrived at a certain age, any more than they are able to do so by virtue of being white or black or by being workers. Maybe this was true in another age, in another society, but we can't talk about democracy abstracted from the people or the society we are living in.

What is democracy? Who participates in what? How? What hierarchies are necessary? Who decides, for example, whether there are going to be automobiles in Russia or in China? The population in Russia has probably said now to Kosygin and Brezhnev, "We want automobiles, and if you want to stay in your jobs, you had better give them to us." Who is thinking about this in Russia and seriously considering the example which the U.S. has provided of the fantastically destructive consequences of unlimited auto production?

NOT RIGHTS

It is impossible to bring about significant changes in this country without increasing the capacities, not the rights, of people to make decisions. This is one of the chief things we should be thinking about. One of the main reasons for making social change is precisely to increase the capacity of the American people to make significant social decisions—or to put it another way, to enable Americans to become aware of themselves as people, of what they can be, and what they want to do.

Does everybody, whether he/she is aware of him/herself as a historically evolved being or not, have the same democratic rights? We are not making a revolution for rights. Every one of these questions is tied up with every other: the notion of democracy, of equality, of revolution, of a person, of past and future history. They are all one whole. Where would humankind be if all the important decisions which have advanced humankind had been reached by a vote?

One of the difficulties in making decisions is absence of information. But the major difficulty is that modern Americans have never had any real experiences in decision-making processes on a small scale. As Tocqueville pointed out nearly 150 years ago, when people have no real practice in decision-making in small matters and are nevertheless expected to make them in major matters, it ends up with their making neither. We have to work out how to develop political persons and political process in such a way that the American people can make meaningful decisions on meaningful matters.

A MEANS OR PROCESS

Beginning with the idea that people are responsible, how do we begin to engage people in discussion with each other? Democracy is not an end, it is a very crucial means by which people engage in discussion on fundamental issues and learn to think about issues in *a* political and socially responsible way so that they can make decisions. It isn't easy for people to understand this, simple as it is, because democracy has come to be associated so much with a single act, voting every few years, and with the myth of the equality or the indistinguishability of every individual. People don't see that democracy is a collective political process for arriving at political decisions.

There are more mental patients in the U.S. than any place in the world. Why? Are we going to encourage people to say that it is because Nixon is in power, or because capitalism is in power, or because this is an imperialistic country? Or are we going to enable people to arrive at the conviction that their frustrations arise from the incapacity of the individual to meet the actualities of his/her own life?

For so many years we thought that the class struggle solved the problems of democracy, that when workers took power, or the blacks, we would automatically have democracy. It is only very recently that we have begun to understand that this is not true at all. What does democracy mean? The American Revolution was the first revolution to have consciously sought democracy—in contradistinction to aristocracy, monarchy. Now two hundred years later, we are realizing that their definitions do not begin to cover our questions now.

Democracy is a historical concept like every other political concept, like socialism, like revolution. There is no democracy in any Platonic heaven to which reality has to conform. Nor does any definition in any dictionary create any absolute meanings. The Greeks coined the word originally to mean "rule by the people" as opposed to aristocracy, or oligarchy or rule by various elites; and generally this has been the distinction between democracy and aristocracy—that one is popular and the other elitist rule.

When the United States was founded, democracy was assigned a very specific historical connotation within this general concept. Essentially U.S. democracy was the promise that everyone would be able to pursue life, liberty and happiness without the restraints of government. It meant that everyone in a sense could go his/her own way, do his/her own thing on the basis of the specific conditions of the U.S. at the time—the immense territory, the absence of feudal restraints—as well as the general philosophy of "private vices, public benefits" which had arisen in Europe to free the rising bourgeoisie from the political restraints of the king and the aristocracy.

Of course, some people already had more property and power than others, although among whites there was far less inequality than in Europe. As time passed, these and others got even more property and began to control the society more and more. This is what most U.S. radicals have dedicated themselves to exposing and correcting. They have pressed essentially for a realization of the original democratic ideals: that everyone should have the same rights, the same conditions.

We should be able to appreciate the idealistic, or non-historical weaknesses of this kind of thinking. Why should we be trying today to realize the original concept of democracy? We should be able to take the historical stage where we are now and define what we mean by democracy. Democracy is the process, the method, by which we increase people's capacities to understand and struggle over issues and to develop their political judgments for making decisions. All this is precisely what we are trying to achieve. Why shouldn't we therefore be able to grasp this basic concept of democracy as means and promote it as such.

Advocators' statement *Crime Among Our People* is an example of democracy. It calls upon people to begin facing the issues of crime, understanding it, doing something about it themselves instead of expecting the system to do something about it. In the final analysis, more than democracy is obviously needed to do something about crime, but to get to "the final analysis," we must first initiate and undertake processes that will get people involved. Moreover, regardless of what may be necessary in the way of centralism and exercise of force at certain crucial points in the political process, democracy must remain the continuing means for developing the responsibility of human beings.

Most radicals can't see this. Essentially, what they are saying is, "There isn't any democracy in the U.S.; therefore the hell with democracy, let's have communism!," as if under communism there would be no problem in encouraging people to advance themselves politically, or as Lenin put it after the Russian Revolution, "culturally."

AMERICANS AND DEMOCRACY

The opposite of U.S. democracy isn't communism—although most Americans think in such terms. The opposite of what we have in the U.S. today is a genuine process of people developing themselves as socially responsible human individuals. When anyone criticizes U.S. democracy, most Americans think you are a "goddamn red." We have to make clear that when we criticize U.S. democracy, we are proposing greater responsibility on the part of people, an enlargement of people's concept of themselves as self-determining.

Every American today, by and large, thinks of democracy as a thing—what Hegel calls a "fixed concept." Our job, having ourselves stopped thinking of it as a thing, is to help others not to think of it that way. We have to shatter the idea that any concept is a thing—whether it be society, the system, socialism, etc. Radicals have got caught up in the trap of abusing or debunking democracy as a thing, or "capitalist trick," just as conservatives have got caught up in the business of debunking socialism as a thing or "communist trick."

Democracy is an aspect of human development. It is not an end result or a "promised land" any more than communism is. Both are stages, aspects of a process of development by which human beings arrive at a better understanding of their relationships and responsibilities.

IN THE AMERICAN TRADITION

Because of China's collectivist traditions (Joseph Needham is very clear on this in *The Past in China's Present*), Mao could talk easily about communism to the Chinese people he was dealing with. We can't take over Mao's method because we are not Chinese; we are not an agrarian country with a communal tradition. Nevertheless we are trying to approach the same end of the "new man/woman" that Mao is. What means can we take to get to the same end? We are a technological society, a bourgeois society; even the working class is bourgeois. We don't have any peasants to speak of; we have a lot of lumpen. How do we begin to move to the same end? We have to do it in American as well as human terms. We have been struggling with both.

It is impossible to move the average American, to bring about self-movement in the average American, if you leave out the notion of democracy. Whether this notion is good or bad doesn't make the slightest difference. One has to cope with it. Therefore we have to redefine democracy in terms of the historical development of the concept; and we also have to encompass within an American concept of democracy the indispensable human ingredients of communism—just as Mao had to incorporate in his concepts of communism the indispensable human ingredients of democracy.

The most illuminating single statement about democracy, in the present period, was written by Mao in "On the Correct Handling of Contradictions Among the People." That is because Mao is not a chauvinist; he recognizes the fact that, like every advance in human history, democracy belongs to everybody globally. Democracy is a global concept, one of the most important means by which human beings relate to one another socially and politically.

By embracing the idea that democracy is a capitalist trick, radicals have boxed themselves in, they have crippled themselves. Thus they say that because the bourgeoisie controls all the means of democratic discussion, the press, the mass media—therefore we can't employ democracy. Then what can we employ? The bourgeoisie also has a monopoly on arms, on skills. The decision as to what means to use in order to advance the struggle can't be made simply on the basis of how much power there is on the side of the bourgeoisie; it has to be made on the basis of what is necessary to the development of human beings. The methods of democratic discussion are precisely the ones which we can begin to use to a considerable extent in the U.S.—if we think less in terms of manipulating the minds of the people, as the bourgeoisie does, and more in terms of how to stimulate, to provoke, and to develop the thinking of the people; if we do not think of ourselves in competition with the bourgeoisie but more in terms of doing something else, having another goal. The idea that you can use arms in the U.S. in the way that you can use them in Guinea-Bissau or Algeria or Guatemala is just bizarre. If the majority of the population lives in the hills, that is one thing. If it lives in the cities where people are so dependent on the infrastructure and on each other, it is something else.

REDEFINING DEMOCRACY

What we should do is seize the concept of democracy boldly and define it ourselves, in terms of human development in general and American development in particular—as a process that people need in order to relate to one another and to develop their humanity, and never as much as at this stage of history.

People are always saying that the U.S. is a democracy. That is not all that the U.S. is; that is not all that any country is. The important thing for us to understand is that there are not too many basic methods for developing human relations between people. In fact, there are very few. Democracy is one of these. Its opposite is authoritarianism. For us to give up this method just because it has been misused, and therefore to imply that we are for its opposite, is not only to give up one of the most powerful means which any society has to develop human relations, political consciousness and social responsibility. It is also to give up one of the most powerful weapons we have to persuade people in the U.S. to make a revolution.

AS AMERICAN AS APPLE PIE

Up to now radicals have been trying to persuade Americans to become communists or socialists, a concept to which they have become less favorable over the years, not more. But democracy is as American as apple pie. Let us advance it as boldly as we can, not halfheartedly, not reluctantly, not grudgingly, as if somebody forced us to, but wholeheartedly, with conviction and confidence in ourselves. Mao, in "Correct Handling of Contradictions Among the People," had no hesitations about embracing democracy as a means. He said that the opposite of democracy is coercion or administrative measures, and "all attempts to use administrative orders or coercive measures to settle ideological questions or questions of right and wrong are not only ineffective but harmful." It can be argued that Mao said this only because the Chinese Communists already had power, but Mao's motives are not what concern us. Is it true or isn't it that democracy is the best means to settle ideological questions at any time, before you have power or after you get power? You cannot settle ideological questions by the whip or by coercion, just as you cannot transform people by the whip or by coercion. True, in any power struggle, you have to use force, but you do so as rarely as possible and only after you have isolated those against whom you must use force. Otherwise you don't have a movement, you have a continuing civil war. You don't have a society, you have a prison.

We are not talking about using the democratic political system. Nor are we saying that the people in the U.S. are democratically inclined in the way that we are defining democracy. In fact, they are just the opposite; they are always evading serious political discussion rather than seeking it. Not only don't they give a damn about whether we smash the Vietnamese people to bits; they don't even want to discuss it.

At the time of the first American Revolution the concept of democracy was within the framework of rights. Later it was used by those with more power and property to deprive others of rights and of equality. It is still being used in this way in Vietnam by the United States. We are not now talking about democracy in terms of rights or equality. We are talking about it in terms of responsibilities, of roles, of relations and as a method, not a thing. To attack democracy as a "thing" which is being used by the capitalist to confuse, to destroy, to deprive, to minimize and reduce people to statistics, is still thinking as a victim thinks, as distinguished from the way a revolutionist (someone who is ready to give revolutionary leadership) thinks. Bold revolutionary leadership involves being able to embrace a political concept like the democratic process and urge people to exercise it in ways that will enlarge themselves.

Today's Search for Human Identity

The certainty that Lenin had in Russia and Mao has in China, that it is possible to unite people around some principle, is what gave them strength. In the case of Lenin it was "Bread, Peace and Land"; in the case of Mao it was "National Unity against Imperialism" in 1937 and the struggle for a "New Man" in 1966. It is possible to do the same thing here if we are not in a hurry and if we have trust in what is fundamental to people as expressed in all their past history, their past revolutions, their past struggles. Essentially, unity will derive from the projection of the idea of the uniqueness of man/woman as human beings—not identical, not homogeneous, not equal in the eyes of Jesus (as Billy Graham tries to unify man/woman) but as capable of continually extending and enlarging him/herself.

We are trying to unify people by appealing to that which is within them already but which they don't know is there—their desire not to be selfish s.o.b.'s, building eight foot walls between them and their neighbors—even though they do these things. Our job, without any sense of hurry, is to project to people—especially to kids—that humanity is not what you have thought it is; it is something else that you are feeling it is, and the reason you are alienated is that you have not broken through to this.

Is the specific thing which unites humankind the desire to live purposefully rather than purposelessly? Purposefulness is something which is part of the American heritage. It comes out in the concept of manifest destiny. Americans have always believed that this country had a reason for existence, and they have always believed therefore that they were not living aimlessly.

When Hurricane Agnes struck, people lived together very closely. In time of disaster, people are afforded a purpose that goes beyond their narrow selves. But apart from disaster, what is purpose? We are not talking about purposefulness in general or just "having a purpose in life." Billy Graham can talk about that as well as we can. It is not a question of the present or the immediate future or the indefinite future. If you want to define who you are, you have to define yourself in relation to the human past and to the future you foresee for humankind, not just for yourself. Shakespeare was a genius at implying this.

Most Americans have a purpose, but the purpose is a small, mean, nasty one. "I am working my head off to get rich or to beat my competitors or to buy a fancy car." They have a purpose, but it isn't the one that is profoundly human enough to satisfy all the characteristics that reside in man/woman, characteristics which he/she doesn't know anything about but which are there just the same. This is why a peasant is an infinitely finer kind of person to work with than a middle-class American. A peasant does know his/her purpose and his/her relationship to other people in relation to it. So a peasant growing rice in Vietnam is much closer to a notion of humankind than an average middle-class American can possibly be or is, at this point.

A NEW WORLD

This nation, unlike other nations, was founded by people who believed that they were founding a new world, making a new beginning. Those who came here on their own later (everyone except the blacks) also came believing that, even while they were pursuing their own survival and happiness, they were participating in the building of a new world. No matter what people have been doing all along, they have been doing it in the belief that, however individualistically-oriented they were and perhaps precisely because of this, their personal performances were a contribution to a new way of doing things. That is why Dvorak called his symphony *New World Symphony.*

What we are discussing is the fact that Americans don't believe any longer that what we are doing for personal purposes has any connection to what the country is doing as part of a larger human purpose. The earlier conviction that what we were doing as individuals was part of a greater human purpose may have been an illusion but it was nevertheless very much a part of our being human. Even "saving the world for democracy" was part of a much wider context in our minds and in our self-concept. That is why participation of the U.S. in World War I and even World War II, Korea and Vietnam has raised very serious doubts. So that twenty-five years after World War II, the average American no longer has a sense of man's/woman's purpose, only of his/her own private purpose. What is the basis for a sense of grand purpose? Is it getting more welfare, or getting rid of the honkies or buying a home in the suburbs?

TOWARDS NEW UNITIES

Mao talks about a national purpose around which the Chinese Communist Party can mobilize the Chinese people—including their history, their passions, their temperaments. What the outcome will be we don't know, and in an important sense it doesn't matter, because when they mobilize this, they have already undertaken to mobilize the forces of the future, at least the future of China. In this country we are still groping. What is it that we are trying to mobilize?

Mao in 1937 took a very, very sharp turn from the old line of class struggle to the new line of national purpose—unite with everybody, including a mass murderer like Chiang Kai-shek, around the national purpose of defeating Japanese imperialism. In one sense his task was much easier than ours since China was being invaded. (Admittedly, making comparisons of greater ease or difficulty when you are dealing with two completely different situations are abstract, intellectual comparisons.) But in the sense that he had to overcome the opposition of all those who insisted on continuing the class struggle in the old form, it wasn't an easy task at all. The first turn he took away from class struggle took a lot of courage.

Then in 1966 Mao broke with the idea of pure national purpose and moved to global purpose—although characteristically, he didn't talk about it as global purpose. He didn't say, "We are going to try and save the world." He talked of creating the "new man/woman," without reference to any national boundaries.

What is very interesting is that although nearly thirty years separate these two major turns, in each case Mao moved to a much wider conception that (a) transcended previous divisions between people, and (b) created new dualities or bases for conflict.

THE NEED FOR ONE-NESS

In the past, immediate necessities forced people to concern themselves about the person next door and about nature. This is no longer the case. Yet people still have the need for interaction—although they don't know it. Those who are poor still think that their main problem is getting some more for themselves; but the main problem of both rich and poor is the loss they have suffered of their feeling of one-ness with other people and with nature. Even the person who says, "All I need is to get me some more money" feels deep down that the problem is "nobody ain't together no more." Even the person who thinks "If I can just get mine" feels the dilemma deep down inside of the loss of togetherness. This is very much the reason for the apathy in the country—the loss of that feeling of one-ness which was near normal in the period of agriculture. In the past even the person who dreamed "if I were a rich man" like Tevye in *Fiddler on the Roof* didn't want to be separated from his/her village.

What are the elements in the U.S. tradition—in the sense of tradition in the prologue to *Fiddler on the Roof*, as a sense of strength and unity that comes from shared meanings? What about the idea that "America is not so much a nation as a world" (Melville)? Individuals went through incredible hardships to come to this country. They had very personal reasons for doing so; survival for oneself and one's family played an important role. But people didn't undergo so many sacrifices only for personal reasons. They did so in the conviction that when they got to these shores, they were joining something that was ongoing. There was an enormous drive within them: they may have been coming to pick up gold in the streets, but they went through a helluva process to get here to do it. It wasn't just a thought in their heads which motivated them; it wasn't some idea of "better relations." It was more a sense that "if you don't live a certain way, you are not a human being!"

What about the statement in the Cleveland speech last April:

> Two strands in the cultural tradition of the American people are now coming into irreconcilable conflict; on the one hand, their materialism and their individualism; on the other, their concept of themselves and their history as a great people, capable of individual creativity, courage, commitment, imbued with hope, ready to make sacrifices and undergo great risks in the pursuit and struggle to achieve great goals, acting as an inspiration and beacon to all Mankind.

What this leaves out is what we might call a "third strand": the search for the basic nature of humanity that has expressed itself for a million years and isn't limited to the American experience or to American people. This is the next stage we in America are trying to get to. But we are not raising it exclusively in relation to the U.S.; it doesn't have anything to do with being American or Scottish or English. The problem of Western man/woman—we don't know how it is going to turn up in Asia or Africa—is to realize that after all he/she has accomplished, he/she has still done it without realizing his/her own human nature. Never before in human history have people had so much—much much more than any kings in the past—and yet felt such a lack of one-ness with themselves and others.

We have to move beyond the past, stop debunking the American past and the past of Western man/woman. Debunking, exposing the past is the thinking of people who feel they have been left out of a dream, and therefore feel betrayed or victimized, or of people who are still striving to realize a dream from the past. The notion that you are trying to "fulfill the American dream" today limits your thinking. The American dream of democracy and equality was a dream that was appropriate to the rebellion against feudalism and monarchy two hundred years ago. It is utterly inadequate now that we have gone through a couple of hundred years of capitalist development and technology.

Without slandering Martin Luther King, we have to recognize that when he said, "I have a dream" of a black and white kid walking down the street, hand in hand, that was an utterly inadequate dream for this country in this period. That was the old American dream of "the melting pot." We have to dream about something else—way beyond this. Only through the projection of a dream which is far beyond this, can we draw out from people as they presently are, regardless of whether they are black or white, their capacities to go beyond where they presently are.

SOCIALISM ISN'T A "THING"

Do we need an idea of how the new society works? All workers who have ever been introduced to the idea of socialism have always wanted to know something about how it works. What they are saying is that, before they support something new, they must have some idea of what it is going to be like. They want some idea from you as to where they are going. But isn't this because they are still seeing themselves as workers who are being taken somewhere by somebody else—so that all they have to do is accept or support or put their shoulders behind the wheel? Isn't this because they still see socialism as a project, a thing, or a task? The people who came to America have been chiefly proletarians, doers, pragmatists. That has been their strength and their weakness.

A powerful element in the American tradition centers around building a new society, with a great deal of thrust and drive, with busy, energetic, resourceful hands. But it is dangerous to talk about building a new society as if it is a project or a thing. A great deal of manifest destiny and U.S. imperialism comes from precisely this kind of thinking—Americans building a new society and then spreading it to the rest of the world. In point of fact, having built a new society, Americans have now discovered that it isn't sufficient to serve their dreams and certainly not to serve the dreams of Cubans and Filipinos and Vietnamese. Having built their new society with great thrust and drive, Americans have discovered that they have not only destroyed their environment but are destroying themselves.

We cannot extend the American dream until we have extended the American's notion of his/her self as a human being. When Americans have enlarged their selves, they will be able to create new forms of social relations. We can't discover what socialism would be like without discovering a much enlarged idea of the kind of man/woman who is going to live in it; the different wants, the different demands he/she will make on him/herself. Socialism is not the person of today thinking about or living under different social relations. Socialism will be an expression of this different kind of man/woman, a man/woman who has enlarged his/her own conception of him/herself. There will be no revolution in the U.S. unless it is an extension of man and woman's concept of themselves as human, not as Americans but as human beings.

ANOTHER WAY

Do we need a visceral image of another way of living? Not a blueprint or a physical structure, but another way. Originally, when people heard "To each according to his needs, from each according to his abilities," they got a very powerful visceral image. They thought it was wonderful. Now, today, if you asked people about this without calling it communism, ninety percent would probably call it a wonderful idea but they wouldn't consider it worth fighting for. It does not meet a powerful human need within themselves. In the same way, although people continue to fight to get to the top for themselves as individuals, nobody in the U.S. would fight for an upwardly mobile society. (Blacks were ready to fight for this until very recently; it was a powerful element in the Civil Rights struggle and the struggle for integration.) We will not arrive at a conception of another way to live until we have done a lot of thinking and imagining, shattering a lot of chains to the past and the idea that people have to live tomorrow the way they lived yesterday.

Mao persuaded millions of Chinese that their relationship to each other *was* their life. Americans don't believe that. Ask an American about that, and he/she will say, "I don't know what you are talking about. All I want is something for me and mine." This is where we must start. How can we persuade Americans that they are demolishing their selves by thinking that way, by thinking only of their own petty selves, by thinking only in the present and of the immediate future? How can we persuade them that it is possible to think another way, that they might find life more satisfactory if they began to think another way, that they would love it? This is why they felt so good about themselves after Hurricane Agnes. This is also why so many people join the church and discover a serenity, not an absence of struggle, but a feeling that they know what they believe for the first time in their bloody lives. But that is also why we have to be much more concrete.

How can we be more concrete? We are not sure at this point, we are still groping. We know that fundamentally what people need is an acknowledgment, a recognition that their relationship to others is necessary to their own sense of selfhood. Then they could begin to untangle what kinds of relationships are necessary.

After the experience of Agnes, people felt emptied of something, of a relationship they had had to others in the wake of the disaster. They had been doing things with one another, pulling people out of canals, feeding and clothing people. Through their relationships with others, they felt that they themselves existed. But does it take a catastrophe from nature to produce this kind of shared activity and shared humanity? Or is it possible to bring about the acknowledgment of this human need in a more consistent way? Obviously people move from activity to thought and learn through particular actions. This is where in a sense one could begin. But is that a sufficient way to begin?

The whole history of man/woman has been the exploration of human grandeur, not nature's but humanity's. The new society is going to be built by people who want to continue to explore, to enlarge their sense, their appreciation, their visceral enjoyment of their own grandeur—not because they want more Cadillacs or more things, but because they want to discover more about their selves. *Only a few people ever had that privilege before.* Everybody else was working for survival. Now practically everybody has that privilege, that need.

This is the problem of America. Americans today feel blank or deprived of something. They don't know what it is, but they feel (because it is true) that they are deprived of something, of thinking about and exploring their own grandeur, the grandeur of humanity, and deriving from it enormous pleasure. This is why Bob Dylan wrote some of his songs, songs of people searching for their own human identity, not American identity or Chinese identity or black identity, but human identity. They are searching, trying to discover what it is to be human. The new society is going to be built by people who are consciously searching for an enlargement of what it means to be human.

Searching for one's human identity, exploring, expanding, enlarging the grandeur of being human—that is a new way of life, in the sense in which we have been using "way." "Way" implies a kind of activity, a quality and not just an amount of human activity. The quality of this new way of life then is a continuing search, a continuing expansion, enlargement, exploration of what it means to be human.

This way is the history of man/woman. Our task today is to reunite man/woman with this historical search, with this search for self, expressed over millennia, in opposition to the search for material domination and for domination over nature, as expressed over the last few centuries.

WHY MAN/WOMAN CREATED THE GODS

People created religion, religion didn't create people. That was a hell of a creation. Why did people create religion? So that they would have a relation to something outside themselves which would still be an expression of themselves. They created religion so that they would have an idea of how great humanity is and still not have to accept responsibility for humanity. That was a fantastically creative, imaginative and contradictory thing to do.

Human beings didn't want to polarize themselves so they created somebody else to do it. They were evading responsibility for doing it themselves. When people begin to get a sense of their own powers, it is hell for them to accept that they have within themselves these powers and the responsibility for these powers. So they create gods and devils to enable them to evade the responsibility for their own powers.

Religion permitted people to put upon the gods the responsibility for all the things they conceived of themselves and to take care of aspects of their nature which at that point they didn't feel capable of handling. Thus religion relieved people of a whole lot of responsibility. (Note: Monotheism or the notion of a single god emerged at the same time as the State in the West. See Erich Fromm, *You Shall Be as Gods*.)

It was not until the French Revolution, only two hundred years ago, that people began to contemplate seriously that men and women could undertake the responsibility for these aspects of their own nature—without dependence on external forces. During these two hundred years, people have drastically increased their capacity to make and manipulate things. But have they really grown in awareness and in their acceptance of their own capacities to shape their destiny, their own greatness? Aren't they still trying to create something outside themselves on which they can place responsibility? Haven't they just transferred to another set of people the powers to shape and determine their destiny that they once invested in the gods? People say that "the only reason I can't do something is that lousy s.o.b. of a capitalist." Even though there has been such a fantastic increase in technology, has there been sufficient progress in people's acceptance of their self-determination, their repudiation of all forms of determinism?

People invented gods to worship and devils to fear or blame. And they are still doing it today—only they blame other people instead of devils.

Marx realized that instead of men and women relating vertically to the gods, they needed to relate horizontally to people. But Marx did not transcend sufficiently the notion of determination by outside forces. Consequently he built much of his theory on the notion that that bunch of people over there are responsible for what is happening to this bunch of people over here. It was true at the time. But now we are coming to the end of that. People are now struggling to discover what they are struggling for and what they are struggling against. The struggle by one bunch of people against another only begins after two sides are defined and people have an opportunity to exercise their responsibility to choose. Man/woman has to be struggling for something, not just against "bad guys." The other kind of struggle, of victims against villains, can go on for the rest of your life, without any development.

FROM NECESSITY TO FREEDOM

In this era of transition what is distinctively human *begins* to transcend objective necessity. Mao isn't asking the Chinese to work their asses off just to grow more rice; he is asking them to do so to become more human. This is a tremendous difference, and we have yet to go into it as thoroughly as is necessary. What is the transition from necessity to freedom? It is from where you do something because you are determined by forces outside your control, to where you have a choice as to what to do. This is freedom, as distinct from emancipation or liberation. Emancipation or liberation is *from* something—out of oppression. Freedom is *toward* doing the things that are human.

For example, the Third World believes rightly that the First World should not monopolize the world's resources. Are we in the First World going to admit the validity of that concept—or do we have to have a war over it? That is the next stage in the development of man/woman—to think in terms of what is human and what is inhuman, not just to react to pressures. Movement from the realm of necessity to the realm of freedom is movement from the realm of reacting to the realm of choice. What we face is a choice between what amounts to two roads, the road of more Cadillacs and more refrigerators versus the road of sharing. What we mean by confrontation is not what takes place between "good guys" and "bad guys," but between two roads, the right road and the wrong one. We don't know who are the "good guys" and who are the bad ones until we know the roads, and until people have been given an opportunity to consider and choose between the two roads. We have to pose the two roads for people to think about, so that they can see that they have only one choice; the human road which advances man/woman in relationship to his/her millennial struggle, as contrasted with the other road which demolishes and sets man/woman back.

One of the most important reasons for understanding democracy as a process or a method is that through discussion, the different roads, the different ways of doing things are clarified, refined, polarized, so that people can see the difference between the ways and make a real choice. The vote that ends the discussion is not the only or even the most important thing; it is only the termination of a process by which people get to understand and struggle over alternatives, begin to enlarge and widen their concept of themselves as human. We have focused so much on the single act of the vote that we have lost sight of the importance of the process, the movement, the struggle for clarification. In thinking about democracy, "Der Tag" (Election Day) thinking dominates just as it does in the thinking about revolution. People have lost sight of the fact that Homo sapiens has lived for fifty thousand years and is probably going to live for another fifty million years, and therefore that we should be thinking of the process and not just in terms of instant achievement. Most radicals think, "I am going to make the revolution tomorrow morning—" or "we are going to have socialism tomorrow." There is no such thing as socialism. There is an idea of socialism, of a way of life towards which humanity strives, rather than "let's make a revolution so that we can get socialism." Socialism is a *way* of living.

IMPORTANCE OF SELF-CONCEPT

People who don't believe that this potentiality exists in humans can't take humanity anywhere. They will just build organizations to manipulate people or to tell others what to do. We are saying that what people discover, think, feel within themselves is the determinant of what they do. You can't persuade people to do anything if they don't feel it within themselves.

All past revolutionary movements have depended upon the belief that the proletariat or the oppressed were all going to feel like doing the same thing, and all you had to do was get them into motion. We have reached the stage now where we cannot interpret an individual's actions as an expression of the objective forces. All that an individual's actions express is either the backwardness or the advance in the development of that individual. So what we are saying to people is, "You don't have to be backward! You don't have to join the Movement, although you may end up by doing that. What you do have to do is recognize your human identity. Your *human* identity is your identity. Your reason for existence is your participation in the human search for identity that has been taking place for fifty thousand years."

To convey this to others, and to persuade others to help create this search in others, is the reason for our existence. It is extremely difficult to hold fast to the philosophy that what people do is determined by what they think and feel about themselves and the potentialities of humanity. What a person does about anything, whether it is about a fire or a bird, let alone what he/she does about work or community, is shaped by what he/she thinks and feels about him/herself as a human being. To realize the importance of one's self-concept—not that it *should* govern one's activities but that it *does* govern one's activities— that is the question. So that if people think of themselves as meaningless, they will engage in meaningless activities; if they think of themselves as base, in base activities; if they think of themselves as victimized, then in victim's activities.

How do people think of themselves? If they have thoughts that develop their self-reliance, their confidence in themselves and in the dynamic role of men and women, they will be able to accomplish wonders. That is why Mao has written a philosophical document every time a great leap forward was to be made in the Chinese Revolution, enlarging our concepts of what humanity is—which is the task of philosophy. That is why the Chinese have been spending so much time reading and discussing the thoughts of Mao, to enlarge their concepts of themselves. Because how you think, feel about yourself, how ready you are to think well of yourself, determines how you are going to act.

A REVIEW

This summer we have discovered that, instead of getting closer to programs, we are getting closer to problems. We need to think even more, to get closer to the attitude that Mao has: that you don't change anything until you change everything. And so you begin with philosophy and theory before you get to policies and programs. We are discovering that this is a very difficult thing to do in the United States. It is hard enough to do in China. How do we do it here? In the past two years we have been getting rid of a lot of the old stuff about freedom, equality, rights, democracy, and so forth. But we still haven't been able to get at *here* what Mao has been able to get at in China.

We started thinking that we were going to proceed systematically and programmatically to deal with work, the family, etc., with particulars and specifics. What we had to say about the particulars is important but only because we constantly went back to the general, making very clear how we are rejecting all forms of historical determinism, economic as well as religious—yesterday's thinking—and that we are really trying to grasp the meaning of human self-determination: that human beings really can determine what they are going to do, that people can only do what they think they can do.

This is a terribly difficult concept, not only to convey to others, but to believe in oneself. We are so used to giving all sorts of reasons why we can't do things. And everything around us, in philosophy as well as in society, the sheer weight of it all, contributes to that feeling of fatalism, of determinism. (All philosophers, except for Nietzsche, have talked about ideas and not about man.)

We have established that we are searching for human identity. To have confidence in human beings and in yourself without being arrogant, like everything in life that's really important, is very dangerous, very risky. There is nothing important that doesn't contain duality and that isn't risky, that isn't dangerous. Nothing that matters is really safe. No artist when he/she sits down to paint or sculpt knows if his/her creation will be a flop or a masterpiece. But he/she has to do it.

To have that same feeling about a revolution in the U.S. is very difficult to achieve, because everyone wants to travel the road that has already been established. Everybody wants to travel what he/she considers the scientific, the proven course. But that has nothing to do with a revolution. A revolution is not what has been done, but what has to be done. A revolution is a new beginning. If human beings are really going to determine their actions, they are not going to be determined by the past. They are going to create something new.

This summer we are beginning to appreciate how important this philosophy is. It is not a matter of caring for poor Indians or Africans or other victims. The question is, "What does it mean to be a caring person in the twentieth century?" It involves caring about your human self, about where you are going in relation to transcending the human past.

From this general conception, we get closer to particulars. For example, this summer we have not been talking only about women in general, about how they are dominated or victimized. We have been discussing how to challenge sixteen-year-old girls whose self-concept is so low that they can only find identity through having a child by a football star or a rock musician. We have been discussing how to take basic yet very advanced ideas of human self-determination and human evolution and make them the property of the most oppressed. We are still looking for how best to convey or illuminate to these young people what is within them, to help them to understand that they don't even know how to answer the question (although it is a good question) of what they want to do with themselves because nobody has given them the opportunity to think grandly about themselves.

It takes a great deal of time, of coming and going, of back and forth. There is an organic development to these conversations, even though we may not be proceeding as rapidly as others might wish. But when you are trying to discover something, it is very different from having some charts with empty spaces to be filled in. *For so long people have believed that there is an automatic answer to every question, that the tendency is to expect quick resolutions. For what we are attempting to do in these conversations, there are no automatic resolutions or quick answers. What we are trying to discover is also ourselves. What we are getting rid of is preconceptions not only in others but in ourselves.*

The example of Darwin is instructive here. Darwin had arrived at his ideas on natural selection as early as 1844, but his *Origin of Species* was not published until 1859, fifteen years later, and then as Huxley explains (*Essays of a Humanist*) only because he was pushed into publication by Alfred Wallace, who had arrived at the same conclusion independently. So great is the power of conventional thinking that it takes a lot of nerve to go against it.

Chardin is another example. Chardin said that man is going to create a Noosphere, an envelope of mind, that would cover the planet. It is a fantastic thought.

We have to learn to think with the same boldness. We have to shatter all the limitations of the past in order to be able to say, "There is another way to evaluate humanity and our relationship to ourselves." That is why the word "socialism" is in a certain sense misleading. It connotes a way that is already determined, when it is actually something that people will be continually creating anew, out of their urge, their need to become more and more grandly human.

We are very much aware of the need for organizations and programs, but we are equally aware of the need for new ideas in a period of great transition. New ideas don't automatically assume programmatic form, nor is it possible to take ideas which are a drastic departure from past traditions and sling them, like hash, into a program. If Darwin had rushed out with his ideas on evolution, he would have been torn to pieces. If we were to go out now and say on public platforms that we don't believe everybody is equal, people would automatically think we were denying the equality of blacks and whites, of women and men. Nobody would recognize that we were talking about the uniqueness of every individual and of every action; that each individual is different, and that the individuality, the differences, the inequalities, the non-reductive quality of people is the motive force for human advancement.

Huxley said that Darwin read Malthus, and suddenly by a process of creative imagination or intuition, it struck him that the answer he was searching for was natural selection. This kind of thinking operates constantly in human society. We don't know the answers. You can't program them into a computer because a computer can only give you the answers you programmed into it. One has to have the almost fanatical belief that answers come from within people, not people in general, but particular people. Nobody knows what the answers are, and nobody knows who among people are going to be the individuals who are going to come up with the answers that matter But all of a sudden, there is a new addition to human thought, to human feeling, to human compassions which didn't come from a computer.

Practically all philosophers (except Nietzsche, which is why he is so important) have conceived of the struggles from classical Greek civilization into the middle ages, then from the theological-religious sense of history or society into the beginnings of humanism and then into the beginnings of industrial capitalism, as a logical pattern: B followed A and C followed B. They haven't realized that we might have to smash the pattern in order to discover the identity behind the pattern. Even Marx and Lenin were still following this train of thought, this inter-relationship between A, B, C.

When Darwin spoke, he completely shattered this train of thought. He said, "Humans didn't develop that way; they developed differently." Everyone prior to Darwin had believed that it was heresy to believe that humans and apes had common ancestors.

Then Chardin comes along. Writing from revolutionary China between 1926 and 1946, Chardin remarked repeatedly on how China was undergoing simultaneously the intellectual, social and political revolution that other countries had undergone successively. He also wrote constantly of the "need to repress useless and sentimental reactions" to the European horror and to search for how "a new Man might rise out of the crisis" (*Letters to Two Friends, 1926–1952*).

Chardin has something Chinese-Japanese about him. He isn't imposing anything. He is just saying, "I wish you would look. The development of humankind has been through the development of mind. So if you want to think indefinitely into the future of the human being, you have to look into the development of his/her mind." He isn't paying any attention to what anybody else in the past has said; he says, "I am saying something new."

Similarly when we talk about revolution, about politics, about socialism, we have to think about something completely new—not unrelated to the past because nothing is unrelated to the past—but not limited by the past. Marx and Lenin were at the end of an epoch, expressed through oppression, class struggle, etc. Their "new man" was both the victim of *that* past and the vanquisher of *that* past. Our "new man/woman" is new in the sense that he/she has transcended *that* past and faces a new future, unforeseeable by Marx and Lenin, demanding that he/she face his/her potentiality (including the irreversible technology) rather than his/her millennial victimization. Mao is trying to create the "new man" but still in relation to the ideas of Marx and Lenin because of where China is. Our "new man/woman" is new—not simply freeing him/herself of old oppression. His/her newness resides within, not in escaping from the old, other guy.

That is why, each summer, we get more enmeshed in thoughts we had not even thought of before. We are not looking for solutions. All previous movements were looking for programs and solutions. We are looking for process. We don't know what the solutions are going to be.

The Conversations in Maine are not carried out under duress or under the pressure of producing solutions. They are themselves a process. Some people want us to give them answers so that they can use their skills to help. Some of these people are very serious—like the ones at Cyrus Eaton's Pugwash Conferences, for example. But they are looking for answers—which is why they never come up with any.

1972

Projections, Not Rejections

We expect to move a little step forward each summer, maybe only a little tiny step. This year we are discussing positives more, and it is pretty hard to grasp positives. It is much easier to reject something—which is what most radicals have been doing up to now.

One of the main questions on our minds is how much we can key in on this country, our country, and at the same time have a global concept. It is important to start this way because so many things we've thought in the past came from Europe and from the concepts Marx derived from his perceptions in the middle of the nineteenth century. We know that you can't discuss the U.S. without discussing the rest of the world, because everything is tied up with everything else; U.S. economics is tied up with world economics. But we have to look at questions from the standpoint of what *we* can do.

For example, the question of welfare has a lot to do with the economy, but it also has a lot to do with how human beings should live and share responsibility for society in all its many manifestations. We have chosen to take it up from the point of view of whether people should be zombies.

One of the reasons why we have to key in on the U.S. is because the U.S. context has so much rejection in it. We recognize that the positives we put forward will not be readily accepted by people, but we are trying to avoid being so liberal that what we say makes everybody happy but at the same time also doesn't challenge anybody to become revolutionary. In doing this, we are testing others as well as ourselves. What we say goes against the grain of what a lot of people think. But that is what a revolutionist should be doing—*going against the grain.* For example, we have a position in regard to political prisoners. We have refused to allow the concept of political prisoners to be distorted to the point where any cat who goes down the street and steals a car becomes a "political prisoner" because he/she lives in the ghetto. Some folks are not going to like our saying that, because a lot of people now believe and are being encouraged to believe that they are political prisoners every time they get arrested for stealing.

Life is not simple: It is agony and it is ecstasy. Without agony there can't be ecstasy, and if you haven't known ecstasy, you don't know what agony is either. You only know sadness or pain.

Rejecting Cynicism

Many young people do not think of themselves as shaping the world. When we ask them why, it appears that they feel like victims, that they are being played with. It is the "Student As Nigger" complex.

We cannot accept everything that young people do as the expression of the new society because most of them are still in the stage of rejection. Look at the Black Panther Party, for example. Those kids tried to be more political than most black militants who just thought in terms of picking up the gun. But right now, you can expect very little from Black Panther youth. They have been wiped out all over the country—like the young Indian braves. The white kids are equally lost. They started out rejecting their parents, as bourgeois s.o.b.'s, who had created all this mess. They took the attitude to their parents: "If you hadn't done what you did, we would have a different relationship with blacks." The white kids played a tremendous role in the black movement in the early days, and they also took the movement beyond the question of blacks. They said their parents had messed up the whole world. Black youth didn't totally reject their parents in the same sense but they were very critical. Then black radicals began to establish symbols that put them in an idealistic realm and separated them off from the rest of their communities, which were facing real problems.

Many young people complain about fragmentation, but fragmentation itself is a product of the difference between people in terms of how they judge what is progress and what is not progress. Fragmentation has to start from the idea that there was at one time a unity—a piece of cheese that wasn't cut up. Then things fell apart. During World War II there was tremendous unity in this country. After the war, fragmentation began when blacks began to struggle against what was. The Vietnam War fragmented the society even more because for the first time people were really divided and clashing head-on over the foreign policy of the country. Now a lot of people think that we can patch up that fragmentation and go back to the past. Nixon represented this patching up to a lot of people.

We have to ask ourselves, "Wasn't that fragmentation a contribution to making more people concerned about the way our society should go?" There are many different views now and a whole lot more thinking about a whole lot more things. Immediately after World War II people were concerned only about whether there would be full employment. Now the simple questions that once kept us unified have become more complex.

Fragmentation is not necessarily a bad thing. It has caused a lot of pain, but it has compelled all of us, more than ever before, to begin to wonder about questions we never thought of in the past, especially about how we would govern this country and what we really mean by self-government—which up to now we have only celebrated as a slogan or as Fourth of July rhetoric.

Having seen the Senate Select Committee hearings on Watergate and the House Judiciary Committee hearings, one can begin to see an alternative to settling controversial questions by violence. We had never seen up to this time the possibility of using the media as a means to focus the attention of people on particular issues and engage them in debate among themselves as well as to witness the kind of debate which is involved in the process of serious decision-making. The House Judiciary Committee hearings gave us an insight into what Hannah Arendt calls "political space" or politics. Up to now Americans have thought of politics mainly as shenanigans, logrolling, and so on; something that individuals did only for their own self-interest, to please their constituents, in order to get re-elected, or to evade issues. Now we have seen something take place here which we can explore. But we can explore it further only if we stop being cynics, about technology and about people: we can see the potential in technology if we know how we want to use it, as a means of bringing people together for debate, discussion, exploration in order to arrive at decisions for an entire country.

We have to be able to take something like the House Judiciary hearings and explain how they are manifestations of the capacity of ordinary people to behave in a socially responsible fashion when faced with the necessity to do so. The House Judiciary hearings are also an illustration of the scarcity of this kind of behavior in the past twenty-five years. The HJC, when faced with a particular problem, responded very well. But it was a very special problem: they were not really facing the problems of how people should live together, as, for example, those who wrote the Constitution did in 1787–1789. That the HJC hearings stand so alone is a demonstration of the fantastic degradation that has been happening in this country. It just proves how far we still are from facing our real problems.

To this a cynic might respond that reaching out to the belief that things can go in a positive direction is "just" another form of trying to achieve emotional security for yourself.

In the first place, what is wrong with seeking emotional security? Why should we look down on a search for security? All living species have sought security. Judgments can be made about the way one searches for security but not about the search itself.

Why should people accept insecurity? To search for security could mean opening one's mind. If you are cynical about people, if you don't believe in their potential to go beyond where they are, then there is no use talking about change. You just let things stay where they are, and whatever happens will happen. Cynicism is much worse than sexism or racism because it denies the human potential in *everyone,* regardless of sex or race.

The Search for Community in Music

Modern popular music in the United States represents an effort by young people to discover communality—not through Bach or Beethoven but through the immediacies of rock and roll, or jazz or country and western. They are searching in this medium to discover a way to express communality. That is why 600,000 went to Watkins Glen. Young people are searching for almost any form in which communality may be expressed, and the forms at this moment are rock and roll or country and western.

For seventy-five years there has been this search for communality in music and through music in the United States. Negro blues was the search among Negroes—it had nothing to do with "rights." It wasn't only the rhythm that was taken over by whites; it was the search. Whites took over a great deal of jazz, not because of its musical quality but because it expressed something that all whites wanted and missed in their lives. "Why should only blacks have it? Why can't we have it?" whites asked. That is what Mezz Mezzrow, the Jewish saxophone player, was searching for in *Really the Blues*. Music is one of the ways in which America expresses its extraordinarily passionate search for communality.

Perhaps it is because Americans have so little in common, in terms of background and a history which they have created together, that they have found this communality in music. At one time, Americans didn't talk the same, they didn't eat the same foods, and in particular, they have never created a political community together. Music was the least antagonistic because it evoked the most basic feelings. So it became one of the few ways through which people could find their communality in a non-antagonistic way.

This music is something of unbelievable importance in the U.S. Someone from China couldn't have the faintest idea of it. This music is rooted both in the agony and the ecstasy of this country. That is why jazz could only have been created in the U.S.—not in Africa or Europe (and that is why the Black Nationalist attempts to disown jazz are nonsense). Western music is much more related to the cowhand, the lonesome cowboy far away from home. It never took on the social meaning or brought people together the way that jazz did. (Neither did hillbilly music.) The music coming up from the South, which united the African and European strands, brought people together because it was a totally innovative creation of this country. Black blues was sad: the guy had lost his woman; "my baby done left me." Hillbilly music was gay. Western music and mountain hillbilly music were regional—not the basis of an enlargement as blues and jazz were.

We should distinguish between Woodstock Nation and Watkins Glen and what happened in blues and jazz. Blues and jazz and country music came out of genuine communities expressing the aspirations of the people in these communities. As a result of the form in which they expressed these aspirations, other people related to their music and therefore some unity was achieved between different types of people within the country.

On the other hand, what we see taking place in Woodstock Nation and Watkins Glen is not an expression of communities. What we witness here is a lot of alienated individuals who are alike in their lostness, coming together from all parts of the country to a particular place, to hear performers brought together by promoters who have seen the possibility of making money from all these alienated individuals, people on the fringe or outskirts of the society, who want to come together. They are reminiscent of Huey Newton's Intercommunalism—which embodied the illusion that somehow or another we are going to create communities by bringing a lot of different types of victims together, together.

In the early days we had music coming out of the aspirations of musicians who were part of a community and who were part of its historical development. This is not what is taking place now. What is taking place now is undoubtedly an important social phenomenon, but in jazz we had the cultural creation of a community which is something very different.

Why do people go to country music, "bluegrass" concerts today? Bluegrass music seems to attract a kind of longhair, youngish type who wants to be close to popular movement and be non-elitist. What various groups like in music at this point (whether this is always true one is not sure) has a great deal to do with the kind of people they want to be with and the kind of people they don't want to be with. When people say they don't like classical music, they often mean that they don't want to be with people who like classical music. They are expressing a social attitude through the form of an opinion about what they like in music. They are not musicians. They are listening to what the people whom they want to be with listen to. The musician listens to music differently. For one thing, he/she knows a lot about it.

Red Women's Detachment and *White Haired Girl* may mean a great deal to the Chinese at this particular point because they relate very intimately to the kind of struggle they are engaged in. Also the music is close enough to the music they know so that they feel at home with it. People who know dance in other countries may be attracted by the highly skillful dancing. On the other hand, *The East Is Red* is very moving to anyone. It is an epic film of the revolution, containing portions which like the *New World Symphony* convey a sense of great masses of people and nature in motion. Some of Mao's poems have this same combination of epic and lyric quality. Written in Chinese characters, they probably mean a great deal more to the Chinese than they can possibly mean to us.

When Beethoven wrote the last movement to the *Ninth Symphony*, he was celebrating the brotherhood and sisterhood of man/woman. Then, for some fantastic reason, Dvorak, who wasn't a particularly great musician, came to the United States and wrote the *New World Symphony* in which he celebrated not the general grandeur of humanity but the potentiality of humanity. He wasn't just creating a piece of classical music. In the *New World Symphony* you feel the historical movement of man/woman. It is like the sound track of a huge drama, an epic.

How do we project the potentiality of man/woman on a grand scale today? Duke Ellington does it in his *Sacred Music Concert*: "In the Beginning, God" is a celebration of "In the Beginning, Man."

Music is a human creation that tells us something about the development of man/woman. The rock and rollers are expressing their frustrations. Rock and roll is a rejection, including amplification to the point where the sound blasts your eardrums. In the music of somebody like Johnny Cash, a lot of people see some immediate relation to their notion of life, especially what they are searching for from the past.

Maybe music, including classical music, can tell us something more than what has been. Is life delicate? Is it exquisite? Is it harsh and demanding? Music is a human instrument that tells us about the development of man/woman—all of it, not just rejection or nostalgia.

FROM YESTERDAY TO TOMORROW

The grandeur of the *New World Symphony* is that it expressed all the ethnic groups of the United States. Jazz was more uniquely a creation of black Americans. Gershwin began to make a unity between black and white in his music. Then, when the blacks began to go toward Black Power, they diffused the American strand. So no one knows where they are going today.

In the U.S. music in its various forms is the expression of a variety of cultures. Why did Stravinsky spend the last forty years of his life in Los Angeles? Stravinsky shattered all kinds of notions of music. Then he came to this country, not in order to be American but because, as he said, "In order to think or to feel, I have to live in America." Why do so many people come here? Because here is a place where you can discover how to move from yesterday to tomorrow. This, oddly enough, is the one place where you can escape the limitations of the past, the limitations of yesterday's cultures, and begin to wonder what tomorrow's culture will be.

We don't know what the outcome will be. The United States is a hotbed of new thought, precisely because it doesn't have a culture, because it isn't a nation, because it isn't white or black, Slavic or Eskimo.

A long time ago Katherine Dunham, the black dancer-anthropologist, said a beautiful thing: "We can't look merely at our past but we can look at our past and bring it into the present. We look towards the future." Does an artist need a philosophy to base his/her artistry on—or do we look to artists to break free and point a way?

When a Sicilian came here in 1910, he/she came because he/she thought that life here would be better than in Sicily. He/she didn't come here with any ideas of culture at all. For the same reason people went West—for land, for beaver skins, gold, or something like that. The early settlers and the later immigrants didn't come here looking for a culture. They came representing a culture. But then they became enmeshed in a whole way of life.

Precisely because American hasn't a culture, we are not only free to discover what music is, what sculpture is. We are also free to discover what new human relationships are. In this country, minus the material pressures on the one hand and the cultural restrictions on the other, we are incredibly free to wonder what would be better material relations and better human relations. We are the freest country in the world—which makes it that much more difficult to discover how we can go about changing this country. Nobody knows what they want to overthrow. The same thing goes for culture. In light of the fact that we don't have a culture, we are free to wonder what a culture would be. What is music, what is choreography? Why is Jerome Robbins the kind of guy he is? When he went to Russia, he scared the devil out of them, because dancers in Russia dance in the classical tradition. Then Jerome Robbins goes there and says there are countless different ways to dance—ways to use dance to express your thoughts.

This country is tearing the world apart, not only technologically but in every other way. All sculptors, all painters, most of the writers who amount to anything all over the world, come to America because we don't have a culture. But also, because we are human beings, we are searching for something which unites us and which in the end becomes a culture.

OUR UNIQUE FREEDOM TO INVENT

The creation of any new art form is always a tremendous rupture from a previous form. When there is virtually no form to break with, you can invent freely. This is as true in politics as in art. Our freedom to invent new politics is unparalleled in the history of the world. But we have to invent this new politics.

All sorts of people come from all over the world to America to escape the limitations of cultures. Whether, having come from elsewhere they will all be able to be creative here is questionable. Those who do create do belong to a culture in the sense that they developed out of the culture. They are prophets who go beyond—not expatriates, who are very different from prophets. The prophet, through all kinds of struggles in relation to his/her culture, is able to leap out of it.

In a revolutionary period you have changes of form in art. (That is the way we have to think about politics also. It must move outside of what has previously been considered political to include many other aspects of life.)

For example, why should people expect great new music to emerge as jazz? Jazz, which burst forth on the American scene, has already taken us all a huge step forward. So why should we expect jazz to develop further any more than we would expect classical music to develop further. Both were created in a particular period by particular people. The music which at one time was a great transcendence of limitations by a particular people (Malraux says that "all art is a revolt against man's fate—all great art transfigures the meaning of the world") can't possibly be created at this time by any other people. It was created under very unique conditions. Reverent epic music—which is very political in the sense that Leonard Bernstein's *Mass* and Ellington's *Sacred Concert* are political—transcends jazz. They are not attempts to extend jazz, to make it more sophisticated or more versatile like, for example, progressive jazz. *Mass* and *Sacred Concert* burst out of the new historical environment of the early 1970s, following upon the explosions and revelations of the 1960s. As a result, they expand our entire social horizon, bringing us so much more of the human spirit, its infinite variety, its conflicts and contradictions, its aspirations and its shortcomings. They bring to mind the Greek drama of Periclean Athens. Previously the main form of Greek art had been sculpture, but then it moved into the new form of drama which brought us individuals in social conflict with one another on a huge stage, struggling for new relations in a period of transition.

We are trying to get away from the idea that the more you look at each individual man/woman, the more you understand man/woman. We are inclined to think that the more you look at the individual, the less you understand the species.

In *Manas* (June 12, 1974) Henry Geiger quotes W. Norman Brown writing about Indian art: "Sculpture was not meant to be a reminder of a human being or of an apotheosis of man, but of something abstract, spiritual in its reality beyond apprehension by the sense, an ocular reference to universal knowledge that might somehow become comprehensible to humanity."

He then quotes Laurence Binyon in *The Flight of the Dragon*: "Some of the finest Buddhist art is to be found in portraiture, both painted and sculptured. But it is to be noted that the portraiture of the kind so prevalent in Europe scarcely seems to exist. Most of these portraits were made after death, and partook of an ideal character, and only great personalities of saints, sages, heroes seem to have been thought worthy of portrayal. It was the ideal embodied in the man, rather than his external features, which it sought to represent. These Buddhist portraits are remarkable for contained intensity of expression; in them, too, the aim of rhythmical vitality is once again manifested."

Like the Buddhists we have to have a concept of the ideal. It may be an American ideal or a Chinese ideal, but you can't judge man/woman by looking at each individual. One has to confront each individual with a more or less ideal notion of what a human being could be—not "is" or "was" but "could be." In America, we are free to think about what a human being could be. We are not controlled by any ideology or any culture. That is both why we are free and why we have so incredibly much responsibility to the world to demonstrate how all the past limitations can be shattered. And this is also why we are so lost. Because when you are free, you are also floundering until you find your direction.

Rock and roll is a strange phenomenon in which disappointment with their parents and with American society has led a whole generation into pure subjectivity. That is what rock and roll is, even though it has a background for its subjectivity.

Is there any music in this period that enables us to look as man/woman in an enlarged sense? When there are revolutionary or truly new thoughts, not just rephrases of old thoughts, there will be new music. It is absolutely fantastic that in the 1930s "Solidarity Forever" was the song that everybody sang. And then in the 1960s, "We Shall Overcome" became the song that everybody sang. Neither was composed by musicians. Both sprang out of a new set of relations. We believe that there will be a new music when a few of us have advanced a new set of thoughts about human relations or a new set of human relations. We are going to write the preamble to which someone will write a new song.

What Is the Human Spirit?

Many young people are looking for something spiritual. We are finding it terribly difficult to talk about this for fear that if we did, we would be talking like Jesus. Mao talks about the human spirit very easily because the notion of human spirit, if you are Chinese, is associated with the way people have been relating among themselves for thousands of years and also how they have related themselves to philosophy or to ideas. In the United States there is a total absence of that sense of relationship to a historical past and the development of the human species. To relate to a person suggests going up to the person and giving him/her a kiss or a Freedom Now handshake.

How do we concretize the search for a sense of the human spirit so that a kid can look for it or understand what is being talked about and so that the word "spirit" does not bring to mind the Holy Ghost or Jesus Christ?

Ho Chi Minh had to give peasants who had no sense of national identity a concept of a national identity. Each peasant knew about his/her little village, his/her own ancestry. (In that sense he/she knew much more than the average American.) But what he/she knew was extremely limited, narrow: some rituals, some rice paddies, some symbols. Ho recognized that the first thing to overcome was the lack of a sense of national identity on the part of the peasants. He saw that the Vietnamese peasants lacked a sense of national identity not only because they had been deprived of it by French and American imperialism but because they themselves had never developed to that stage. But recognizing where they were in relation to where they still had to go, he could project to them where they had to go.

Americans also lack that sense of national identity or history. On the one hand, each of us is different, and on the other, each of us lacks the same thing.

The difference between ourselves and Ho is that the Vietnamese had an external antagonist against the background of which they had to discover their national identity or selfhood. But in the United States, although we have fought wars, we have never really been in one. Our antagonist is ourselves, our own limitations. What we are searching for is the way to get at the antagonist. Ho had a visible tangible enemy. Our main enemy is an internal one. That means developing a trend of thought very different from the thought of the past. It has taken us so long to free ourselves from the European notions of external enemies—the French versus the Germans. In the thirties or even the early sixties, you could still mobilize people against the obvious external class or race enemy, but since then too many workers and too many blacks have become a part of the system.

Mao had the courage to launch the "Great Proletarian Cultural Revolution" in order to let the peasants know that they had to smash the limitations which had been imposed upon them and to discover what limitations they wanted to impose upon themselves. How do you do that in the United States where there are no immediate practical projects over which to struggle in order to make these discoveries? At this point we can't start great leaps forward—except in the heads of a few people.

LITERATURE, HISTORY, POLITICS

One way is by helping Americans to recognize what is distinctively American about themselves. They can recognize this (1) through the distinctive character of America as exemplified in its great literature; (2) through the historical development or lack of historical development in this country; and (3) through drastic proposals with regard to very concrete issues like work, schools, etc.

American literature reveals the American character. And Melville is really the crucial writer. There are four characters of Melville's who are more important than Ahab in relating to young people: Ishmael, the guy who runs away from routinism; Billy Budd, the guy who is full of values but is extremely inarticulate; Bartleby the Scrivener, the guy who says he prefers not to (the abstainer); and Pierre who contemplates his navel. The worst part about Billy Budd is that he doesn't seek to find the words by which he can develop and express his feelings and turn them into thoughts. He remains content to be inarticulate; he prefers, like so many Americans, to remain an innocent. In the same way that Bartleby the Scrivener abstains from the act, Billy Budd abstains from the search for the words which will enable him to turn his feelings into thoughts and thus discover his human identity. These characters are very meaningful as representative types of American youth. Melville discovered them.

The second thing is to discover our history. Our history is that, for the most part, we have no history. Except for a few people who descended from the early settlers, everybody else came recently or was forced to come here The overwhelming majority of Americans have no sense of having participated as a people in the humanizing political struggle to create a nation. The discovery of our differences, the struggle over these differences in a political way—rather than on an ethnic basis—is something that we still have to do. The discovery of our political identity, who we are as American people, is an enterprise, an adventure which lies before us. We are still in the process of creating the American nation.

Only a very few people participated in the initial creation of the American nation, in numbers as well as in terms of ancestry. The rest of us who came as immigrants, or as slaves who were excluded by force, still have that great socializing, humanizing, individualizing experience before us. We must want to make that experience, feel that it is necessary to the development of ourselves as human. We must want to make this country a distinctive nation, standing for something important among nations. A nation is something that a people have to create; they can't inherit it and become somebody worthwhile, any more than a rich man's son can become somebody by inheriting his father's wealth. We have to create this nation through a discovery of its past history and a concept of the future we want. We can't just be complainers or abstainers or holier-than-thou innocents. We have to want to do more than return to nature and to "grand unity" as the Taoists did at the beginning of the Chinese nation 2500 years ago. We have to want a concept of what is right and what is wrong and to want to be creators of those concepts. We have to want to establish our own equivalent of "the mandate of heaven" which a government loses when it no longer advances the humanity of the people. We have to want to make definitions of national boundaries which the Chinese also had to do 2500 years ago. We have to want to do all these things—and find the people who want also to do these things. We have to explain why it is necessary and then find the people who want to pioneer, to take the leadership in creating a new nation.

What is the role of the human spirit in all this? One may want to discover oneself or one's role in the creation of that nation which gives one pride and integrity. But nationhood is more than pride and integrity. Nationhood involves politics, assuming the responsibility for decisions, and struggling for the power necessary to decide where your country is going in relation to crucial issues.

What could persuade young people that this is elemental to their search for brotherhood and sisterhood? Well, first of all, not all young people are alike. Some of them have concepts of development. So when you talk to them about human evolution or development from membership in a family to membership in a clan, to membership in a nation, it means something to them; they have some feeling for the struggles that are necessary for great numbers of people to move from one stage to the next.

The third step is very important: making the drastic proposals that open political controversy and political struggle; for example, closing down schools, freezing mobility and so on.

When we begin to break down concretely what we mean by a spiritual revolution, when we make clear that human spirit is essentially the courage to grapple with difficult concepts and questions in a revolutionary way—then we stop thinking about spirit as something like the Holy Ghost.

In China Mao says that if you have spirit, there are different ways to exemplify it. There are very particular things that have to be done, very concrete problems that have to be grappled with, like terracing a mountain or growing apples in a tropical climate. We don't have the same forms, the same problems in the United States. So to talk about "spirit" seems general and without application. That is what bothers so many young people. They feel the urge to concentrate all their passions, aspirations and feelings together in something worthwhile. Then all of a sudden, they run into a vacuum because they don't know what to do. Do they create the vacuum themselves—by believing that they can put it all together in an instant, without recognizing all the labor, patience and suffering of the negative, all the struggles in theory and method that they have to go through? In a sense they want signals instead of symbols. "We have all these passions; tell us what to do."

In China and Russia there were concrete struggles in which spirit could be visibly demonstrated. But we can't find in the U.S. the kinds of demonstrations within experience that the Chinese found. So Americans have to be ready to perform without the experiences; or to find various ways to make experience meaningful. They can't say, "I don't have the practical experiences; therefore I can't grasp the theory." They have to recognize that there is no simple answer just because they want simple answers. But we do need the kind of answers that give them some place to begin. There is intense pressure to transfer some experiences from China to the U.S., because if we could do that, it would be infinitely simpler.

THE MYTH OF EQUALITY

Thinking zoologically, if insects are 300 million years older than man/ woman, then maybe we should begin wondering what time means. Chardin says that the average zoological species (technically speaking, phylum) lives 88 million years. Humankind has lived only a few. We have another 55–60 million years ahead of us. We are not trying here to solve the problems of humankind for all time. We are merely trying to make a small advance. We are not trying to establish the ultimate. We are just trying to persuade people to wonder what would be better tomorrow than it is today. What would be better? What do you have to do to make it better?

When young people first begin to do some serious thinking about themselves, for example, in adolescence, they begin to argue the question, "Is it society which determines or is it the individual who determines?" This question recurs again and again. The kids who begin to argue the question in college bull sessions think that they are arguing it scientifically or as abstract knowledge. But we know that when we argue the question today, we are concerned with the answer in terms of how it enables us, as revolutionists, to persuade men and women that they can change their society. What philosophical presuppositions do we need, in terms of *our* very fundamental goal and purpose to make society into a better place for people to live?

Until now progressives (since Rousseau) have believed, and believed very fundamentally—even though in their practice they may not have followed this presupposition—that we all began as equal, and then society distorted, or perverted us into differences. Therefore what we must do is change society so that we can revert to our original stage of angelic equality.

Now we are saying that if we accept the idea that people are born different rather than equal, we will be able to create a society in which there will be greater justice, greater potentiality for the development of individuals, greater equality, greater order. In other words, starting from this presupposition, we could develop a qualitatively better society.

By keeping this process clear, we can purify or purge ourselves of a notion or assumption which has been held for a great many years and which we have all shared (because we were thinking within a particular framework) that everything began as equal, and then difference was introduced by an evil influence (society). We have all been prisoners of this idea of natural equality. We see through our eyes, not with them, i.e., *what we see is shaped by what we believe.*

The philosophy of the Chinese Communists doesn't have within it the idea of equality as we have it because the Chinese didn't go through the period of Christianity which asserted that everybody is equal in the sight of God; nor did they go through the period of Rousseau and the democratic revolution which advanced the idea that "all men are created equal." We must never forget that by the time the Chinese embraced Marxism, they had behind them thousands of years of history of many different ideas. When they became Marxists, they did not wipe out all the wisdom which had been accumulated over the centuries. The Chinese expect differences among people to exist and to be constantly emerging. Therefore they have found it relatively easy to avoid the trap of ultra-democracy.

All people are born unequal, mentally and physically. Everybody is born different. Diversity characterizes every grain of sand on the beach; how much more then must it be true of human beings? The idea that everybody is the same is an idea that was created by the human mind at a particular time in order to struggle against a stratified society.

The ancients, and religious people in general, think that special people are born special because of some gift from the gods or from God: for example, the mother mated with a god. Thus Jesus' specialness was explained by a myth of God's entering somehow into Mary's womb. In the past it has been considered necessary that we find special reasons (myths) for special people. Now we are beginning to see that it is not necessary to have special reasons for special people. Specialness is not something which has to be explained. It is something which we should expect. What would require very special explanation (or a myth) would be everybody's being the same.

But there comes a time when you have to realize that an idea which was created to advance the struggle for a more just society, and which has enabled us to advance to where we are today, not only does not advance the struggle for a more just society but actually acts as a barrier to creating a more just society. That is where we are now. Today we are handicapped by the myth of equality because, for example, if everybody is equal, then leadership isn't necessary, nor is it necessary for people to accept the demand upon themselves to develop beyond where they are.

So what we are talking about here, which might evolve into a philosophy adopted by many, may one hundred or two hundred or even fifty years from now be re-evaluated, just as we are now reevaluating the idea of equality.

Up to now, for the last one hundred years, it has been generally assumed that Marx and Rousseau were totally right and everybody else was totally wrong. We are now saying that they were right for their time but not for now; and also that they were never totally right—nor is it possible ever to develop a philosophy that is totally right.

Rousseau and Marx were part of the historical process, emerging as very special people at a very early stage of capitalism. It is not a question of whether they were right any more than it is a question of whether capitalism was right. Capitalism happened, and they developed ideas to struggle against its dehumanization of people. Now, just as we have to establish that capitalism isn't the final society, we have to establish that Rousseau and Marx didn't say the last word. We have to think of historical process, not in terms of huge abstractions like "the sovereignty of the people" or "the general will" or "class is the locomotive of history" but in terms of people using their minds. The next revolution in America is going to be made by people who use their minds and who do not just react out of animosity. The next stage of human development will be made by the advanced use of that most human thing called the mind. Up to now, we have used our minds creatively in relation to technical problems. Now we have to use our minds creatively in relation to human problems.

In *Earthwalk* Philip Slater says, "The search for social justice over the past century has rested in large part on principles of consistency, objectivity, fairness, equality, and so on. In the fight against exploitation and oppression a major weapon has been to expose the fact that two individuals from different social backgrounds are not treated the same before the law, or that they have unequal opportunities, or that they receive different responses for certain behavior." In other words, in the past it has been necessary to emphasize the concept of equality because the main effort has been against the unequal treatment of people in society. Obviously we are against an unfair society. But there is a huge difference between a society aspiring only to give everybody "a fair shake" and a society that "grasps both ends to pull forth the middle" because it recognizes that both ends do exist but doesn't reward those already gifted with additional privileges.

Why do we talk so much about what we can do from within ourselves and developing our own potential and not so much about others oppressing us? Because people who think chiefly of oppression carry a monkey on their backs which cripples them. For example, a black student can be bright and study hard but still find it impossible to learn because all the time he/she is sitting in class he/she is thinking, "The only reason that guy is getting seventy-five dollars an hour and I have to sit here listening to him is because he's white and I'm black." So he/she works and studies but all he/she is seeing before him/her all the time is the oppressor. We know a lot of young people who carry this monkey on their backs.

The immediate response of most people, not only because of their oppressed position in society but because of the prevailing ideas of equality, is to react against oppression, to see themselves as victims, to be afraid of the concept of inequality as implying hierarchy and privilege for some people as opposed to themselves. That is a natural response of oppressed people that they do not seem to be able to move beyond, not because they are stupid or want to mislead themselves but because we have not struggled sufficiently to develop positive ideas of inequality so that we can see relations between unequals as enriching and expanding oneself and one's relations with others. So that intellectuals, for example, who have the opportunity to live and work with workers and vice versa, see themselves as expanded and enriched by this relationship and by the contradictions inherent in it, instead of each trying to become like the other.

CLASS AND COMMUNITY

If you think that everybody is equal, then it is impossible to think in terms of communities that are made up of diverse people.

The concept of belonging to a class is based on belonging to something that is defined by antagonism to an enemy class, so that those within a class are not seen in terms of their differences but rather as equals by virtue of how their groups are defined. Communities are very different from classes. People have belonged to communities much longer than they have belonged to classes.

It is only with the European Middle Ages, building on the Christian notion that everybody is born equal, that we get the basis of the notion of class. This notion comes very late in the development of humankind. After this came the notion that nobody could be thrown out of the community. All previous people have always thrown somebody out, e.g., the aged. The aged accepted this because communities make distinctions between who is valuable and who isn't.

Equality is a reductive concept that leads one to think of least common denominators and therefore of stagnant pools where we need to see springs, of faceless masses where we need to see a rich variety of individuals. We need many metaphors to help us understand how an idea that was once a peak has now become a plateau. Most people are not thinking at all, but what is so sad is that those who call themselves radicals are still thinking in terms of these plateaus. What is more, radicals will fight harder to defend outmoded levels of thinking than the average person. So that if you want to think on a higher level, you practically have to engage in a crusade because radicals fight so hard to defend these old ideas. In other words, they are more conservative than ordinary people.

When we are ready to say positively that all men and women are created unequal, and see within that the potential for creating a more just social order, then we can begin making divisions among the unequal, discovering the ways in which inequality expresses itself, for example, in the fact that some oppressed people become thugs while others who are equally oppressed seek revolutionary ways to go beyond the present situation.

The notion of being special is more than just believing that everyone is born different from everyone else. It also means that some people, because they feel more or know more or express ideas in a way that others can't, have more to contribute to the advancement of humanity at certain times than others have, for example, Leonardo or Buddha or Malcolm X.

It isn't possible to make a revolution in the U.S. without recognizing that there are special people. But it isn't a matter of picking out the people first and then saying that their ideas are special. That is always the danger in any recognition of special people. What is necessary is the exact opposite. First you pick out the special ideas, and then you wonder which people express or embrace them.

Psychic Hunger

We are trying to discover how to get people to understand why they are miserable. One way we will *not* achieve this is by telling people how miserable they are. Somehow or other, we must begin to help people understand that they are capable of envisaging another way to live. Not that we are able to give them this other way. But to show them that they are capable of envisaging another way to live—if only as a feeling of lack—and that is the main reason why they are so miserable. Animals are not miserable because they don't experience this contradiction between the lives they are living and the sense of another way to live, which expresses itself in human beings as psychic hunger.

A new book has come out, called *Russ and Tom: Two American Tragedies*, which tells the story of Ross Lockridge, who wrote *Raintree County*, and Tom Heggen, who wrote *Mr. Roberts*. Both these guys achieved phenomenal success almost overnight; yet both shot themselves a few years later. Why did two apparently bright guys discover that making a million dollars, achieving instant international success, destroyed rather than enlarged them? These guys didn't really have a notion of what their true psychic hunger was, or they wouldn't have committed suicide.

What does your psyche want? What would satisfy the hungers of your psyche? To be thought of as generous or as kind? Or as the grandfather of all the kids on the block? Or perhaps to be thought of as wise? We know that Nixon wanted to go down in the history books as a great man but did he ever wonder or try to define what makes a man great?

How do we help Americans to understand what they are missing and don't even know that they are missing? (One way is by playing them Ellington's *Sacred Concert.*) The House Judiciary Committee proceedings enlarged and elevated everybody who participated in them and thereby everybody who viewed them. If we can begin to grasp this, we may be able to find the words to express it. It is very different from seeing people only as mean, brutish, utilitarian creatures—which, of course, they also are. The Constitutional Convention of 1787 was probably one of the greatest convocations that has taken place in human history—even if they did arrive at the decision that the slave was only three-fifths of a person. The gravity of what they were doing elevated all who participated.

REDEFINING REVOLUTION

It isn't a luxury to wonder about these questions that the average guy or gal never bothers to think about. You cannot begin to have revolutionary thoughts if you start by wondering what other people are going to think, especially other radicals. Revolutionists have to think that what they think is worth thinking about and not worry about what their grandchildren will think of them. Because what their grandchildren will think tomorrow depends a lot upon what they themselves think and do today.

The word "revolution" is so tainted, so surcharged with past meanings that people respond automatically. Everybody thinks he/she understands what a revolution is. Yet we continue to use the word because one of the major responsibilities of a revolutionist is to redefine revolution, just as it is to redefine socialism. If somebody asks you if you are a revolutionist, you can't just say "yes" because in a way that capitulates to his or her definition of what a revolutionist is. A lot of radicals say "yes" the same way that they would check the box on a questionnaire on race, sex, or religion. You don't help the person who asked the question by just checking the box. If you are on a platform and somebody asks you this question, you say, "I am glad you asked me that question. Let me explain why I say I am a revolutionist."

We must boldly redefine revolution. Our job as people who are advancing the American revolution is to persuade people that their psychic hunger can be satisfied by doing things that are elevated. A revolutionist is a person who is daring enough to believe that people can live differently. You have to believe that you are capable of explaining the concepts you believe in, knowing that other people have other and contradictory ideas about these same things. Just as you can explain the difference between the Russian view of socialism and the Chinese view, and the limitations and narrowness of the former. A lot of people to this day believe that capitalism, socialism, etc. are "things." They see relationships as things. Seeing relationships as things (reification) paralyzes them in their capacity to envisage new relationships which they can participate in creating.

When people in their search for how to live better are ready to make evolutionary changes by choice, then we will be able to have revolution.

When people lived in tribes, they weren't lonely. But in all the advanced countries of the world, we have arrived at a point where practically everybody is lonely because they have been deprived of community. Much more in America than anywhere else—as illustrated in the murderous and extremely important cartoons of William Hamilton in the *New Yorker*—people feel dehumanized. But how do we move from non-humanity to humanity?

Without the sense of the need for community, why should anyone have a sense of the need for revolution, except abstractly? We have to arrive at revolution, not begin with it. The only reason one would ever want a revolution in this country is because one wanted to be one again with one's fellow human beings. When people want to live differently from the way they are living now, then they will make revolution and not before. Part of our job is to indicate that the passion and the dedication which Guevara put into Bolivia was misplaced—and we are trying to discover the new place to put it.

We have to decide what we think in order to change what others think. To make a revolution it is necessary to persuade some people who have some powers, some beliefs that they would like to see extended. If they feel that way, they will make a change. Yet some people still think that if you raise a red flag and support an ideology which nobody but your followers understand, you will make a revolution.

WHEN ARE PEOPLE FREE?

When is a human being free? Up to now the individualistic concept of freedom has dominated the world. It has now led to the concept of "doing your own thing." Therefore it is necessary to create a new concept of freedom on another, deeper level.

An individual is free when he/she is able to do what you think a human being ought to do in a given set of circumstances. So if you want to live a life that you enjoy, if you want to live a life that your kids can respect (rather than run off to Haight-Ashbury), you have to think about things that you haven't been thinking about before. This new radicalism is going to be based on a new notion of humanity and therefore a new notion of freedom. Until you arrive at that, you are going to keep running around in circles.

You are unhappy because you are a prisoner of your life. The only way to become happy is to become free. To become free you have to incorporate a whole lot of things into your thoughts that you are not including now. For example, if you are going to talk about pollution, you may have to incorporate into your thoughts the reduction of your standard of living. If you don't want Third World peoples to insist upon their freedom to pollute the planet by rapid industrialization, you may have to accept some responsibility for having gotten there first and therefore you may have to stop something so that they may begin something. If you can't think that way, then you are not free.

PSYCHES DON'T LIVE ON BREAD

In *The Social Contract* Ardrey says, correctly, that the hunger for psychic security is as important to human beings as belly-hunger. If people begin to feel psychically secure, having experienced the absolutely catastrophic emotions of psychic insecurity, then they can take the next step.

How do you persuade people that they are psychically hungry? You might say to a person, "You are psychically hungry, but you don't know it because you have never looked at it." In a sense that is the kind of thing we have been saying to workers in the shop to whom we sell *But What about the Workers?* We say, "You have been fighting for higher wages and better working conditions in the plant. But you can't go two blocks from the plant gate without worrying about having your head blown off. What good are better working conditions and higher wages if you can't get home in one piece?" To which many reply essentially, "It is better than not getting home with bad wages and bad working conditions." This is also true but not true enough. How does one persuade people that one does not live by bread alone? The average gal or guy says, "First give me some bread and then I will worry about the other things." In China they are just getting the bread and having gotten it, their aspirations have been raised. So it is possible to spur them on. But here are people who are eating as well as Rockefeller—and some even better—but they are still envious of Rockefeller.

How does one take this beyond confrontation? Because at the moment of confrontation, a guy or gal will say, "that's right." But the moment you stop confronting them, they deliberately go back to their old way of not thinking about the contradiction. They want to "just live and enjoy myself"—even though they are not really enjoying themselves.

When we say that we have to revise Marxism, we mean it in the most profound sense. Marx was the end of a historical epoch, not the beginning of a new one. In essence, he was thinking that if you could satisfy the material needs of people, then you would discover how beautiful people can be. The course of the U.S., especially since the end of World War II, has proved that this is simply not true. Therefore we find this contradiction between belly fullness and psychic hunger. Everybody is subject to belly hunger but most people don't have the slightest idea of psychic hunger because that requires a sensitivity and awareness of a thousand things which most people have never bothered to investigate.

The problem of the American revolutionist is not to persuade people to struggle just against the obvious oppressor when the oppressor is inside oneself. That is why we are beginning all over again on another level which Marx didn't have to grapple with—because up to only a few years ago the struggle *was* for survival and material security. But now the struggle isn't for material security; it is for psychic security, internal security. That is the problem we have to look at. How does one accept responsibility for this problem? It isn't by going to Columbus Circle and making militant speeches, saying, "To hell with the boss." Duke Ellington says it his way in his *Sacred Concert*. We have to discover how to do that in terms of politics or political struggle. We don't have to teach people how to struggle against something. We have to project to them that, "you have to decide what you are struggling for." Mao didn't have to face that question in China because the Chinese knew what they were struggling for. It isn't difficult to know this when you are starving or when your kid is working fourteen hours a day in a coal mine.

We are not probing for answers so much as we are trying to find the right questions. What is it that John D. Rockefeller III (who wrote "The Second American Revolution") and Joe Doakes who drives a bus *both* need? Suppose that instead of using a phrase like "psychic security," we used one like "living purposefully." But that implies that you have already gone through the process of comparing values so that you have decided for what purpose you are living. Whereas psychic insecurity is living without the faintest idea of why you are living.

Psyches don't live on bread. It is not a question of physical well-being. We are talking about the need of people for spiritual relationships with themselves, with others, with their surroundings. You can't tackle this by writing a *Das Kapital*. We need something else—but what it is we don't know. It is not likely to be a book at all—because books don't mobilize forces. At most a book or manifesto can move only a few people.

How do we begin? One way is to try to persuade people to think about community. How does one go about inspiring or persuading people to think about community? We are beginning—even though it may be twenty years before people can look back and say that we made a beginning. Also the beginning never has an end. It has climaxes which lead to new beginnings. A lot of people who follow Marx think that there is an end. We believed that for years. Now we realize that one year, two years, twenty years from now, we or others may discover another thought that it was impossible for us to think about this summer. We accept the fact that there are mysteries which we have to incorporate into what we know now, always looking for further illumination. We recognize that whatever concept we could possibly evolve about a community, having looked back and tried to sum up all that has been true of communities, would nevertheless only be a beginning of the struggle to form something which has never existed before. We would be scared of a blueprint if we came up with one.

Community

THE LIMITS OF THE CITY

In a recent *Manas*, Geiger says that after Murray Bookchin's *Limits of the City*, nobody needs to write another book about the city. *The Limits of the City* deals with cities not as a city planner does but as a place where people live and with a recognition that there are limits to what people can take in their lives. Tokyo with 11 million people (or New York or London) isn't even a city any more, let alone a community. It is a megalopolis, an agglomeration. It isn't something that anybody is proud of in a nationalistic sense. So a guy or gal living in that city can feel, "I am just going to f— this up." We are not saying that they ought to, but it is no wonder that people living in New York act that way. They have no relationship to anything in particular. Everybody pays attention to urban planners who say that if we would just plan a city properly, we would solve the problems of the city—which is absolutely ridiculous. It is impossible to plan a city of eight million properly. It should be smashed. Eight million people can't be a community. So urban planning and city planning studies are worthless—except from an engineering point of view. "How do you run an expressway through Manhattan?" is a legitimate question, but it has nothing to do with city planning.

The only way to solve these problems is to start with the hunger of the psyche. How would people like to live? You build a city around the way people would like to live. You can't compel people to live in a city you would like to build.

There are a tremendous number of people who would like to leave New York and go to the suburbs. They are really running away because they feel that their lives are a constant misery to them. The poor would like to leave also but they know they can't, so they call the others s.o.b.s for running away. Those who go to the suburbs are leaving a horror behind. Yet we know that as long as they just see themselves as escaping, eventually the suburbs come to the same end. Crime is now rising in the suburbs.

At the same time we have to recognize that what they do reflects a serious situation. There is a desire to break up the cities by most people in them, except the thugs and thieves who can ply their trade best in the most crowded surroundings. Most city dwellers feel trapped and would like to escape. The people who run to the suburbs are running for negative reasons. If they left the cities for positive reasons, they wouldn't go to the suburbs.

Why are state capitals in the United States not the biggest cities? In Europe the spiritual, cultural and political center was the capital. So you were a citizen in the sense that you belonged to and felt a part of "public space."

After the Depression, American cities became administrative centers for people on welfare in one form or another, and the chance of their developing into a political center was lost. One of the real problems is the Welfare State. The Welfare State is not a government of the people. In the concept of "government by, of and for the people" there is a lot of ambiguity, but there is a clear difference between government by and government for the people. In the concept of government by the people, there is some sense of the people having responsibility for the government. When the Depression came in the 1930s, in the wake of mechanization of agriculture and the displacement of people from the land, the chances of the city becoming something of a real political center for acquiring "grandeur" were lost.

When FDR started the Welfare State, he made a bunch of decisions which have altered the face of America ever since. By and large, up to now, we have thought that the development of the Welfare State was associated with the development of socialism and the rise of socialist consciousness—which is exactly what has not happened.

The city can become a city in the sense of a "public space" only after one has created a sense of social grandeur, so that the city is representative of the highest possible level of social relationships and human achievements. Until people begin to think in terms of striving for the highest possible level of social relationships and human achievement, it is impossible to rebuild the cities.

The word city is associated in its origins with *civitas,* with civilization, the place where civilization came together. Mumford gives his concept of the city in *The City in History.* The city emerged after man/woman moved from nomadic society into more or less stable agricultural society. The cities became the nuclei where people got together on market day or where artists met to discuss art. In its origins it was both the center of civilization and, almost immediately, a walled city to fight off the barbarians, including your own barbarians, e.g., starving farmers who wanted the grain that had been stored in the city. The city became the embodiment of the highest aspects of civilization and also of the conflicts within civilization—which is why all early cities were walled cities. Roosevelt turned this around and made the city the dispenser of grains to displaced farmers.

Americans have traditionally run away from the city as they became more affluent. They have run away from the responsibilities of the city. Beacon Hill in Boston was the last European manifestation of the center of the city as the center of civilization. Perhaps up to the early days of the Civil War, maybe only up to the time of Jackson, there was some idea that the most cultivated people had responsibility to govern. There was some idea of noblesse oblige, or the responsibilities of the aristocracy, with regard to governing. This disappeared completely after the Civil War. After that, those who became politicians were those who dispensed the spoils. They were the servants of the industrial bourgeoisie or of certain sectional interests.

A very different concept of politics goes along with the very different concept of the city in the U.S.

The city grew because it represented certain forces which were centripetal, tending to come together rather than fly apart. It didn't grow on the basis of any theory. No city in America, except Boston or perhaps Philadelphia, ever grew on the basis of an idea. Boston and Philadelphia represented the end of the concept of the city as the center of cultural achievement, social responsibility and political action. Philadelphia, city of Love. Nashville, Tennessee, New Orleans, you might say were proto-cities. The courthouse in Nashville is a pseudo-Greek temple. It is not by accident that so many courthouses in cities around the U.S. were pseudo-Greek temples. The Greek cities symbolized the kinds of cities the people who built the courthouses would have liked to create. But as the U.S. became industrialized and all values except profit were destroyed, the Greek notion of the city went out the window. The city lost its value as a center of civilization. It was just a center where one made money by land speculation, by finance or by starting industry.

Every European city for centuries was the center of civilization for that country. Stockholm, Amsterdam. To this day there isn't a Dutch who wouldn't die to save Amsterdam. Do you think any New Yorker today would die for New York, or a Detroiter for Detroit?

Most American radicals derive their idea of a city from New York, i.e., the city as an agglomeration of cultures—Jews, Sicilians, Chinese, etc. But all the immigrants from Europe and Asia and the American countryside who came to New York didn't make it a city. They destroyed it as a city. Not that it was their fault; there was no countervailing force which prevented them from destroying it. LaGuardia, who was Mayor during the thirties, talked about the city as an international world and did a great deal to make that kind of a city out of New York. He made clear that you couldn't build New York into a city which just included WASPS; it had to include everybody. But is a conglomeration of minorities an ideal city?

One of the greatest weaknesses of Frank Lloyd Wright was that he was a populist, an agrarian romantic. He had an absolute passion for living in a close relationship with Nature. He didn't believe in putting together a whole lot of people in one spot. The idea of a city being the very center of a society was foreign to him. He saw civilization as permeating the whole society, the whole nation. Why shouldn't every place be civilized? Why shouldn't every place have a relationship to a tree or a cow or a neighbor? It is terribly easy to get romantic and think, "Wouldn't it be wonderful if everybody lived not in a city but in a glorified, civilized, rural communal environment?" But that is contrary to the historical tendency of people to get together. Some will be living in communes and some in cities. In a civilized society there will be subways. Not that working underground is civilized— but we are going to live with cities for a long time. Our challenge isn't to destroy the concept of cities but to recreate the notion of what a city is for—besides just an enormous accumulation of people all trying to get enough to eat. A city is an idea, a symbol.

Mumford, as contrasted with Wright, was very concerned with the accumulation of tradition which is possible in a city and very difficult in the country. In the U.S. it is difficult to accumulate any traditions at all because the society has been expanding so rapidly and there is so much space. We are just coming to the situation where we can think about tradition, because tradition comes from reflection. Reflection depends upon not being able to escape the necessity to reflect, as well as having the time to reflect, and being in the company of other reflectors—which is what a city makes possible. This is where Americans are today for the first time.

Originally the concept of the city was that of a self-governing polity. It was not only the center of tradition or of whatever industry there was but the center of the politics of the area.

The city is a historical concept. For people in China, over the last hundred years, the city was a place like Shanghai, ruled by the imperialists and the center of vice and corruption.

It is terribly difficult to discuss anything today without referring to China—but we must never forget that Mao is discussing human relationships with people who already have a communal relationship. Apart from a few cities like Canton and Shanghai, China is still communal in the sense that it is made up of innumerable agricultural villages. The Chinese appear determined to maintain a balance between town and country and to avoid the kind of urban migration which has ended up destroying the American city.

HOW DO COMMUNITIES START?

In the past socialists have assumed that bringing the means of production under social control would bring them under human control. But today we can see that only those means of production and only those communities which are on a scale capable of human control can be controlled by human beings. How do you persuade people who are used to production on a mass scale to accept things on a human scale?

We started with the idea of international socialism: We were striving for the international party which would lead the human race—put in its crassest form. At this point we would say that it is individual communities that we are striving for. We don't mean communes—but rather people who are willing to think communally in their communities. Because if you begin to think in one community communally, you have respect for what another community which also thinks communally is striving for. For example, you don't decide to build a road going this way while another community is building it that way—so that the two couldn't possibly meet: The two communities have to put themselves into some contact. And you can extend this indefinitely up to the limit of human experience.

The main thing is to start with the understanding that people have to think in terms of an immediacy of relationship, not in terms of general wants or general needs, or in terms of modern technology permitting everybody to be given everything they want, without anybody having to work and with everything being decided by computers.

It is impossible to build socialism on a national scale or from the top down. After certain minimal needs are guaranteed, each community must become responsible for what it does. This is a frightfully complicated thing. For example, no one little community can put up the $300 million needed for an oil refinery. But they can struggle to get other communities to cooperate with them to build one.

How do communities start? Do they start at all? Most people think that communities begin by bringing people together, whereas it is not so much a question of starting communities from scratch but rather of attempting to get people who are *already together physically* to struggle to transform themselves and their relationships into something more than a physical togetherness—into communities. We cannot go back to Genesis, and like God, take matter, give it form and then rest on the seventh day—or like Noah start all over again with a male and a female from each species.

People on a block in Detroit can discover that they are in agreement about something which is sufficiently important so that each one is ready to accept the diversity of others. You can't force the result. All you can do is put forward the idea that it is possible to have such ideas on which people can come together in a new relationship. It is possible to go to people who are simply together geographically and point out that they are not a community but that they can become one. If they don't become one, they will continue only to be enemies to one another, as they are today.

Under certain circumstances people are forced to act like a community temporarily, e.g., after a tornado or hurricane. We have witnessed many times the sense of community temporarily evolving out of emergency situations. But we have also seen the dissolution as soon as the emergency passed. We also know that it is possible under certain types of leadership for communities to be developed out of people who are together geographically, even though the crisis is not a dramatic one. For example, when people begin to sense that their problems are mounting, a few people can take the initiative of proposing some type of organization or action which will resolve some of the problems or make it possible to avoid certain very undesirable alternatives.

It is important to recognize that everybody doesn't wake up one morning and say, "We have to do something." That spontaneous reaction only comes in cases of natural disasters.

Based upon past experiences, when the few initiators put forward the idea of organizing, about half the people will not want to do anything, while about twenty percent will probably be willing to undertake the responsibility of persuading others. What characterizes that twenty percent? One thing appears to be clear. They must feel that they have a stake in the actual place. They can't just be transients.

NETWORKS AND COMMUNITIES

Can communities be made up of people who don't live together but feel similarly? An important distinction should be made between networks and communities. Networks are made up of people who have a common interest which involves part of their lives—whereas communities are associations of people who by virtue of the totality of their lives being involved are unable to function outside the community. Those who came together at Woodstock really form a network. They share something in common for a particular time but only one aspect of their lives. A community consists of people who are interdependent for an extended period of time.

How does one begin to project the idea of interdependence? For example, the Bucharest Population Conference began today. Nine-tenths of the people from the developing nations are undoubtedly saying, "Don't chatter to us about birth control. Begin by giving up some of your wealth." They are talking about the community of people on the planet. But isn't it premature to talk about people on the planet as a community?

In *The Summer before the Dark* Doris Lessing has some marvelous passages on the kinds of people who attend these conferences from all over the world—some in turbans, some in derbies. But whatever their garb, they are the same kind of people who come from all over the world to talk sometimes in Cairo, sometimes in Geneva, sometimes in Bucharest. They are the kind of people who can't talk meaningfully about interdependence because they are all the same types—the bureaucrats or social planners of the world, a sociological category like "workers of the world."

We can't talk about the world community until we find out more about what the local community is.

What distinguishes a community from the sociological category of "workers" or "bureaucrats"? The community has to be conceived on the model of the family in the sense that there is diversity and genuine interdependence in a family. The family is based on opposite sexes, different ages, different abilities, different responsibilities. The relations of the members to one another are essential to the being of each. None exists apart from his/her relations to the other. They are not all strong or all weak. Those who are strong give of their strength to the weak and the weak require the strong. They learn from each other, depend on each other. These characteristics also exist in an ecosystem—and on another level within a community. Without these characteristics you don't have a community. These qualities are not sufficient but they are necessary.

It is as if we have gone back some five thousand years in rethinking certain fundamentals. We are not talking about a theological community or a feudal community. But we are saying that today there are no communities, and that we have to start all over again to create communities because they are essential to the development of human beings.

One example of the kind of problem we face is what is happening in New England where the states are yelling their heads off about paying too much for heating oil. Yet when somebody says, "Let me build you a refinery to make some heating oil," not a single place in New England will accept a refinery. We are not saying that one of them should. But if everybody says, "No, not me," how can you tackle such questions?

What about the concept of the town zoning plan which places

the responsibility upon towns to choose between alternatives? So that if you want gas at the rate equal to other places and don't want to burn wood, then you have to come up with a proposal which makes it possible for you to have it. Then you have the responsibility to mobilize your people to accept this proposal, but you can't keep passing the buck.

The House Judiciary Committee members were faced with the responsibility to decide what they thought was right and not just what their constituents thought. These people transcended their constituents. You can't have communities until people are ready to transcend personal interests on behalf of the community and are ready to make decisions based on what they think is right and not on taking a poll of what their neighbors or their constituents think.

For the first time in history, by means of TV, individuals made decisions for which they were ready to take responsibility before the eyes of the world, now and in the future, and not just in accordance with their constituents' views. People have been arguing for the last 200 years whether those elected represent their constituents or are themselves individuals with judgment. It has been a dilemma of representative government for 200 years. In the House Judiciary Committee hearings, this dilemma was resolved—with the help of modern technology. For the first time we began to see what might be involved in individuals acting as community people. Up to now we have only seen technology destroying communities. Here we got a glimpse of how technology might help the individual to act as a community person.

WHY COMMUNITY IS A REVOLUTIONARY IDEA

There is a great difference between an organic community and a community formed by virtue of political actions. A family is like an organic community. To transform a bunch of people in a particular area into a community, there must be actual interdependence, i.e., dependence upon each other for continued existence which includes material security, security of life and limb, psychological security. If people can get these things elsewhere, if regardless of their relations to one another in their geographical area, they can be secure in life and limb, be satisfied emotionally and able to subsist materially, you don't have community.

In the U.S., especially with the tremendous mobility of the last fifty years, people have thought that they were getting, and actually have been getting, these things outside their geographical area. Which is why community is such a revolutionary idea at this time. Today some people will take anything which resembles a community, e.g., communes or Jehovah's Witnesses or the Muslims, because the need for community is so great. Their turf is in their heads, they are idealistic, whereas a community has to have real turf.

Real communities have to accept real people with all their defects and deformities. You can't throw out of the community those who are blind, dumb, old or who don't agree with you. Communes tried to be too precious. If you associate only with likeminded people and you are a human being, not a school of fish, you end up like Brook Farm or the Spanish Inquisition. Or like Fruitlands, where after a while people said, "Since we are trying to grow upwards, not downwards, we should only eat upwards-growing vegetables!"

There are certain things on which communities have to agree. But after a decision has been reached on any issue, you can't throw out those who don't agree with the majority decision or tell them, "If you don't agree, go some place else." Those who don't agree have to go along with the majority, which raises the very complex question of whether those who were against the Vietnam War should have gone to Canada or should have stayed here and struggled against the war and eventually gone to prison.

You can't build a community until you have sufficient agreement, to begin with, on certain questions on which there are neither majorities or minorities. Otherwise there isn't a community. If the majority says, "We want an oil refinery," you can't blow it up because you don't agree. You accept the idea of majority rule with regard to ongoing decisions.

There has to be some structure which enables everybody to participate and requires everybody to assume responsibility. Some people want to be *in* the community but not *of* it. When those embattled farmers fired the shot heard round the world and went home to their wives, some of them undoubtedly said, "Why did you do that? Now we're going to be evicted." Which ones represented the community? Those who fired the shots? Or those who were afraid of being evicted? One of the things we should expect in a modern community, as compared with those in the past, is that there will be constant change and therefore constant struggles. There will be times, many times, when the future will be struggling against the present within the community. Allowances must be made in the consensus which creates the community for these struggles *for* change and *against* change. If you don't, you may have a community in the sense of the past or an "eco-system," but you won't have a community for the modern world. Into our thinking about the community must go the concepts of continuing change, continuing struggles, friction and development.

We all have two pictures in our mind. One is that of a country where everything started small. The other is New York City. When you get to New York, you have this big hodgepodge. Do you have to take one area in New York and say "the hell with the rest of it" and try to create a community there? Or do you have to have a struggle in New York first to break up into communities because there are other things which must be done before you can decentralize? You just can't say to people, "You have to leave New York and go to some place else to live so that we can break up New York into some kind of manageable communities." First you have to generate a force of people who believe this is necessary. And those people must have already started in a direction and accomplished certain objectives together so that they can believe that to make this major move is going to mean some further benefit to them. There must have been some advancement significant enough to make them think that this colossal change is worth it. It is like the Chinese people saying in the 1950s, "At least we are eating regularly now and there haven't been any disastrous floods. Why should we upset the applecart? We better keep on advancing the way we have been." But the advancement doesn't have to be in terms of satisfying a belly need as in China.

We have to avoid simplistic analyses. It appears that at one stage the tribal community abandoned the old people because the survival of the community depended on the best use of a very limited number of resources. There was not enough to share with the old who were assumed to have played their role in the perpetuation of the species. At another stage the tribal community began to realize that the one thing you cannot be born with is wisdom, that wisdom can only be acquired through living (and therefore through age), and that wisdom is a very important resource for the survival and advancement of the community. So they began to value the old, and to spend a great deal of their resources in caring for them, as for example, the Chinese and the American Indians.

The person with very unusual and advanced ideas has often in the past been forced out of the community because he/she appears as a threat. Communities tend to be quite conservative in the sense of believing that their preservation and perpetuation depend upon maintaining the existing relationships rather than creating new ones. That's why Savonarola was burned at the stake; Galileo was not only because he decided to retract. (Was Galileo wrong when he said, "Maybe I serve a greater purpose alive than dead"? Should he have been a martyr in order to prove his point that the earth went around the sun rather than vice versa? Or should he have stayed alive?)

Some people argue that the individual who first puts forward a new and exotic idea is purged from the community but that later the new ideas are received back without the individual and that this is a better way to accept the ideas. But maybe if a person lives and remains in the community, the new ideas have to stand a greater test, and the individual also.

In the past, communities have been small enough and change has been slow enough so that there has been more time to arrive at decisions. A community has differences within it, but it also has limits.

CAN EVERYBODY HAVE EVERYTHING?

In Russia the Stakhanovites go to the Black Sea resorts where the aristocracy used to go. Cape Cod used to be one of the most beautiful stretches of country in the world. Likewise Martha's Vineyard. But if you provide that everybody can go to a place, you are destroying the only reason why people want to go there. By a process of natural selection in the old days, people with wealth were able to live on the Cranberry Islands. Next came those with relatively good jobs and long vacations—professorial types in general, a privileged middle class. Now if you say that everybody should enjoy something of which there is a scarcity—which is always going to be the case with natural resources—then you have to establish some other criterion by which you choose who can enjoy what. If it is not money, then it tends to be the favorites of those who have the power. So you establish another process of selection which one can hardly regard as more advanced than the previous one.

Up to this time China hasn't had this problem because the idea of enjoying yourself more than on a Sunday afternoon scarcely exists. Some people who have enjoyed certain privileges in the past are still allowed these privileges because they will die away soon. We know of a man, for example, who still lives in the very nice house he lived in before the revolution. He is now seventy years old, and when he dies they will probably turn his house into something like a school. The new people who occupy top positions are being re-educated to believe that if they have a vacation, they should spend it shoveling manure at the May 7th Cadre School. It is not a society where you must spend a lot of your time figuring out how to distribute enjoyment.

This is important, not in the abstract sense of how you provide justice but from the point of view of revolutionary philosophy. The answer isn't just a question of equality for the masses. We have to think not only of what it means today but tomorrow, when there will be twice as many masses. This is why the concept of the "new man/woman" is so important. How long it will take to create the "new man/woman" we don't know. Mao says eight to ten generations. We can merely wonder about the parameters within which one makes these judgments. Should everybody have everything? When Marx evolved the concept of "from each according to their ability, to each according to their needs," people's wants were very simple. But now there is universal TV. Why shouldn't everybody want everything?

The Chinese make clear that higher education is a scarce resource, and they make clear to the country as a whole that this resource has been created by the labor of a great many people, dead and living. It is the result of the accumulated labors of past as well as present generations. Therefore they explain to people that if one person is able to go to college, it is because other people are doing other kinds of work to make it possible. The person who enjoys higher education has to look upon it as a privilege and repay society for the privilege after he or she has enjoyed it. Few people in this country look on anything in this way. But in China they try to get kids to understand this from very early; for example, there are trees to enjoy only because "uncle" workers did a lot of planting and cultivating in the remote as well as recent past, and therefore others should not despoil the results of their labors.

The distinction between a privilege and a right is so important, but very difficult to recognize except in a situation where there is scarcity. In this country university education has come to be looked upon as a right which entails no responsibilities—so out of proportion has the concept of rights become. Unless we accept that a lot of things we have taken for granted can be taken away (not in a crude sense), it is hard to think of anything being worked out in this country at all. When you have more or less inculcated the idea of rights in people's minds and there is so much stuff lying around, it is difficult to convey to people the truth that what is, is the result of human effort.

Once things are considered a privilege and a resource, it is necessary for people to earn the privilege by making some contribution. In Russia enjoying such privileges as going to the Black Sea is probably based upon party membership—which is also considered a privilege. In China at the present time the party member has a lot of work to do in terms of political responsibility, manual work, continuing self-criticism, and the other responsibilities that go along with leadership, which are much greater than those of the average person. Only very few people, proportionately, are party members.

What the Chinese have done during these last few years has done so much to clarify the concrete meaning of socialism. For example, they guarantee certain minimal necessities—enough to eat, a certain amount of education, health services, housing. But after that, people have to make choices. They are paid for their labor so that they have the wherewithal to decide, e.g., to use their money for a sewing machine or a radio or a bicycle. Some people say that this is only because the Chinese are still at such a low material level, but we think it involves a much deeper understanding of human nature and the need for human beings to be constantly making choices in order to develop their selfhood and self-reliance.

PUTTING DOWN ROOTS

Take the question of scenic sections of states like Maine or Oregon. Should these be open to everyone? Probably the first step would be to recognize that this is a community question. So a lot of communities in Maine or Oregon may have a right to decide what they would like their community to be like. They cannot assume the responsibility for satisfying the hunger of four million people from Brooklyn for fresh air.

When you take the responsibility for decision-making, certain other things go along it, such as the responsibility of people to stay and accept the consequences of their decisions. Suppose Swans Islanders said, "We need a lot of money in the community. Therefore we are going to bring in some developers and we don't give a damn what they do, because we will get enough money from selling the land so that we can move some place else and let the people who come afterwards suffer the consequences. We will make a quick buck." Democratic decision-making doesn't mean anything if it doesn't involve responsibility for the future. Correspondingly, people in Maine have to recognize that there are four million people in Brooklyn bursting at the seams to move out some place. Is each community going to say, "You are not going to move here, go some place else"? Or are they also responsible for wondering about those four million people? They can't just shut their minds to the needs of people in cities.

If you are only talking about a few people coming for a short vacation, that is one thing. When you begin to talk about people coming in numbers, you have to think about what an area can support. Maine has about a million people. On Swan's Island there are about 350 native or year-round residents. Their houses are not freshly painted or kept up like those on Cranberry where there are a lot of summer people. Does this have to do with money? For example, Poles in Hamtramck don't make any more than the blacks in adjoining neighborhoods, but their homes are all freshly painted. The Poles have lived in Hamtramck for generations and plan to stay there, whereas blacks coming into a neighborhood like ours think they will get out soon—which is a very different attitude.

One of the best-known stories in China is that of the man from a barren mountain village who told Mao that the people in his village, having heard that China was going to have tractors, wanted to move down to the plains where they could use tractors. Mao told him that if everybody who lived in the mountains came down to the plains, the plains would become unlivable. So the man went back and the villagers decided to terrace the land so that tractors could be used on it. The result is Tachai—from which everyone in China is urged to learn.

Should a community in Maine welcome tourists? When you bring money into an area through tourism, you also encourage your kids to think differently about the way they want to live. Will they be baby-sitting for summer folk, trying to capture a summer boyfriend? They will turn into certain types just as the Bermudians have in the wake of U.S. tourism. You have to think of all these things. It is not only a question of not excluding people from the city but also of the kind of diversification in your community that will make your people more self-reliant and less servile. You have to develop some kind of productive resources, some creative autonomy and not just exploit the natural resources of the sunset and the sea. Long before American tourists came to Jamaica, Jamaicans had lived there for hundreds of years. Now they don't want to live that way any longer. They think of how people in advanced countries live and they feel that they have been deprived of that way of life.

People from all over the country, including Los Angeles, come to Maine for vacations. What is the basis for selecting who can come, which is another way of excluding some people? This is not only a question of who can come to the country but also who can go to the city. In China most of the people are still in the country. Here we have the problem of whether city kids from Brookline, Brooklyn, etc. should come and flood Maine. Could we carry on meaningful education in this country around the question of abolishing the division of labor between town and country, between manual and mental labor, such as is being carried on in China? They carry on this education by sending city kids to the country for at least a couple of years. They have the power to do it. But they also had some ideas behind the power—otherwise they would have had to cut off a lot of heads. Maybe rather than bus for racial integration, it would be good to see a lot of city kids go to school in the country and vice-versa.

Fundamentally don't we want to persuade people that you can be just as civilized in the country as you can be in the city? Proletarians are going to be the hardest to convince of this. That is why it has taken us so many years to shatter the easy formulations. Those who have been most oppressed are often still on the "rights" level. They still think that everybody else has been enjoying these things all these years—now it's our turn. We recognize now that the masses are not just Rousseau's "fallen angels," as, like other Marxists, we thought for so long. But at the same time we know that the ones we have to persuade to think more broadly are the masses—because if the masses haven't grasped advanced ideas, any society has nothing but a mess on its hands. If all you do is persuade some Harvard professionals, you have only skimmed the surface. You may get their agreement easily but that doesn't signify any real changes in society.

What is necessary to a community—and what does community provide? Only through community can we begin to eliminate these poisons in a systemic, concrete and serious way. If we agree on this, we can begin to see what are some of the essentials of a community.

You don't work towards a revolution or socialism in general. Creating the community is perhaps the best place to start. Even to create it is a hell of a task. Many young people believe in community, but that doesn't mean that they will create communities. They may create communes. But they are all too much alike, in age and background. They are usually extremely mobile; they have not developed enough responsibility to a particular place so that they can understand other people who have a responsibility to particular places as more than "squares." They are more likely to set themselves up in antagonism to an existing community, like a foreign body. Communes often think the community should adopt their way of thinking rather than accepting that a community which has been some place for two hundred years has its own ideas and its own dynamics.

The editor of the *Maine Times* is always asking, "How do we protect the Maine communities that now exist from being demolished by McDonald or Kentucky Fried Chicken franchises? How do you permit them to remain themselves when every force is arrayed against them, and the force inside themselves has been dribbling away for a hundred years? How do we enlarge the sense of community in these communities and also help others to understand what they mean, how valuable they are, and how fragile?"

It can't be done defensively. These communities are defenseless in the face of the anti-community forces. They have to become propagandists for communities, not just for themselves, and try to help others understand what they stand for—and ask other Americans what *they* stand for. If they don't stand for communities, what do they stand for—a McDonald's next door?

Let us assume that in the few communities which do exist in this country today, the sense of community is already there. Do we start there or do we start where there is no sense of community at all? Most of the time the material basis of these communities is dying out. A farm is mechanized and people go to the city.

The logging industry in Maine isn't dying out but the communities from which the loggers come no longer think of themselves as communities. They are not dying out because the loggers go to the city but because of something inside a logger's head or heart. Loggers think the school isn't good enough for their kids because it doesn't have a physics laboratory. The opposite side is the little island in the Atlantic which had a volcanic explosion a few years ago. The British who own the island said it was too dangerous for the people to stay there, so they took five thousand or so of them to Britain. Then, when things cooled down, they offered the native people a choice, "now that you have seen London" sort of thing. Something like eighty percent chose to go back. Even though they don't have much but sheep and fish on the island, they have a close community and the people said, "It doesn't matter what we have in material things, if we have that." How does one persuade a Maine logger of that?

We are in Maine on the Cranberry Islands. Summer folk are really the only industry up here. Before the summer folk came seventy-five or so years ago, people lived by fishing, some dairying, some stone work, and some hauling. They don't depend on these now. Years ago the old folks had difficulties keeping the young people on the islands. Now the young folk are staying or coming back from the city. They resent the fact that their folks have sold their land to summer people. In their fashion they are searching for a sense of community. Some blacks are also going back South.

But we have to avoid drawing conclusions too quickly. Many of these people don't give a damn about what is happening in Washington, except insofar as it affects them immediately. They don't give a damn about people elsewhere in the world or in the city, except insofar as these folks in the city might come to the island or might buy up the land and drive them off.

The spirit at this juncture may be more important than the material basis. Some of the young people coming back have chosen the community over the material things in the city. Maybe they will want the community so much they will decide to build boats again. Maybe if the schools aren't good enough, they will make them better instead of moving to the city because they have discovered that fancy schools don't necessarily turn out good people. Having been to the city, they are also less conservative than their folks.

We have said that before you can have a community, people have to have a stake in the area. If people just drift in and out, you have mobile people, gas station nomads. One of the real weaknesses of the city is that people don't have a stake in a particular area.

Should we start out with people who already have a sense of community? Do we look for them, and when we find them, what do we do? Study them, encourage them, protect them like a form of endangered species?

The *Maine Times* has carried stories recently which deal with the question of community. There was a lawyer who retired, planning to play golf. Meanwhile he heard that the Common Council leased some city land for a high-rise. He didn't like the idea (among other things, it would mess up his golf) so he started investigating and discovered that there had been an undercover deal. Knowing what to do as a lawyer, he got a petition campaign started, which created a sharp controversy in the community with people on both sides. After a bitter struggle, in which neighbors were polarized on both sides, the high-rise projects were defeated, and the community had to become reconciled again. In another case, community people had leased some land from the city on which there were growing vegetable gardens, partly to combat the high cost of living, partly to involve their kids in growing things. Here again a sharp controversy arose when the city wanted to sell the land for some industrial or commercial purpose.

These controversies did not only involve economics. In the first case the behind-the-scenes character of the deal figured in the struggle. In the second case there was the question of educating the kids. The chief point is that today's issues cannot be settled on the basis of economics. As long as we look for the solution in economics, it is utterly impossible to arrive at a resolution. If the question is not economics, what is it? It has to be something which deals with spiritual values or community values.

We have been thinking that the struggle will provide the answers. Maybe you don't get answers without struggle, but struggle itself does not provide answers. It all depends on what you are struggling about.

HOW DOES ONE STRUGGLE?

By what means does one struggle? If you are going to live together after the struggle is resolved, if you are still going to be neighbors, you have to carry on the struggle in a certain way. It is much easier to polarize than it is to arrive at unity through struggle, so that you can divide again and come together again on the next issue. A community involves living together despite differences, but not an unprincipled living together where you don't stand for anything, so you fall for *everything.*

We can't throw economics out the window, because people have to have certain material things in order to live. But when you create structures by means of which people can live together, they must embody certain values. To build the foundation of a community you can't start with economics. You can't begin with a factory and expect a sense of community from the people who come to town looking for a job. If everybody is coming only for economic reasons, then what you end up with is a Lordstown, Ohio.

The hunger today in the U.S. is of the psyche, not the belly. In India the hunger is primarily of the belly. Not that they lack psyche, but that a bowl of rice is a matter of life and death. In the U.S. the question is whether we should build more cars. Suddenly one realizes that the crying of one's psyche is at the heart of one's misery. And therefore one has to wonder how does one satisfy the crying of the psyche which can't be done by economic means.

This is crucial to the understanding of community. Because a community is a group of people who feel so related that they will give up economic advantages in order to protect their psychic community.

First one creates the community and then the community decides. If it didn't decide, it wouldn't be a community. But it can't split down the middle over economics or it will have destroyed itself as a community. For example, different people will differ about whether this piece of land should be zoned for this or that. They can differ all they like, but when they agree, they agree for a common reason. There may be rich and poor in the community, and the rich may tend to have different interests from the poor. But the community must pose issues in terms of reasons, goals and values which go beyond economics and beyond the differences between rich and poor, or it destroys itself. When the Chinese talk about class struggle, they are not talking about struggle between rich and poor. They are talking about those who have the interests of the community at heart versus those who have only their selfish individualistic interests at heart. That is the big step Mao took beyond the Marxists. He came to this very early, in his realization that workers in themselves are limited and must overcome their limitations.

ON PRACTICE

What does one say to a young man or woman who is satisfied to live on welfare, satisfied to be nothing? There are millions of people doing just that. How can we motivate them to want something more than that? People who have really accepted welfare can't be motivated by more money because only a great deal of money, tens of thousands of dollars, would motivate them. They are not going to take a factory job for only a few dollars more than they are getting on welfare. If it isn't money, what is it? And if one finds it possible to answer that extraordinarily difficult question, then how does one go about persuading people that they want this thing which is other than money?

In the 1930s the work ethic was enough. People would have responded to the question, "Wouldn't you like a real job?" Today there are people on ADC who join Jehovah's Witnesses or the Muslims and they will work because these groups, their new community, insist that they work. One way to define a community is to say it is an aggregate of people who enable others to respond that way: If you are going to join them, you are going to carry your own weight. Otherwise you are not in that community.

What happened between 1945 and 1960 to change this? Did something of value disappear during these years, some pride that people had which made them prefer to work rather than be on welfare? Was there a fragmentation of the community during that period? Was it the after-effects of the war? Those who had been on WPA went into the defense plants or the armed services during the war. After the war people in the community stopped judging one another.

During the 1930s families began to break up because there wasn't enough food in the house for young people to stay, so they hit the road. CCC camps were started. With the Second World War almost everybody had jobs. During the war most people thought they were working for a social purpose. There was a tremendous unity in the country, so that after World War II, individual incentives were no longer enough.

Almost all communities in the U.S., except for a few religious communities, have been shattered in the last hundred years by people moving North or West. That which held the community together got lost. People moved to San Francisco or Chicago without thinking, "I have lost something that once existed and that my parents or grandparents thought was precious." The average guy and gal in America may wish they had a home or a base or a community. They may wish they could discover what was the glue, so to speak, which held people together in the past, but they do nothing about it.

Before the war or in the 1930s nobody thought about community at all. The radicals viewed small town communities as bourgeois (Sinclair Lewis's *Main Street*), and thought of themselves as standing for a new community of the working class which had altogether different parameters. There was a point in the thirties when every union was to some degree a community. Now they are business organizations whose function is to get more money. Welfare also helped to destroy the community because it had to be administered impartially on a non-specific, national scale without any judgments or value distinctions: "We can't let people starve, can we?" If one was human, the answer was obviously no, so a system was set up.

The radicals didn't think it was necessary to think of communities because they were working for the community of the human race or the community of generalized citizens. Everybody was going to search more or less together for the same things. In other words, the class was going to be a community. The idea was murderous then, even though we agreed with it. And it is murderous now, since it still hangs on in the back of our minds.

As a result, we have neither a community nor the feelings and thoughts and values which make a community possible. We have to recreate the sense of the validity of the community. Maybe even in the smallest sense of growing our own vegetable gardens together, instead of going to the A&P. And from there extending it to a whole lot of other things; not through "free schools" because most free schools have little relation to a community, but perhaps by participation in the community discussing, "What do we mean by education?" in which one community doesn't have to agree with another one at all.

PAST STEPS IN SEARCH OF COMMUNITY

We are beginning to realize that the need for community is as deep in the human species as in any animal species—in all organic things.

Since the end of World War II Western man/woman has been seeking to replace what was destroyed by World War I and the Depression with some form of community. During the 1930s they sought to replace it in the limited form of the class community, in the union. Stemming from the Russian Revolution and the thoughts of Karl Marx, the thinking was that the bourgeoisie having created nothing but unending crisis, what we must do is create a community of the working class on the basis of economic man and woman and the workers in the plant. But that idea didn't create communities. All it did was create interest groups.

In the 1960s, the rebellions and the Vietnam War having again revealed the bankruptcy of bourgeois society, people tried again to establish communities. But now the communal criteria were based on race, sex, age. Again they were thinking in limited terms about the nature of communities.

Still we have to recognize that there is a very profound need for community which has up to now been expressing itself in limited ways. Recognizing this, we want to understand the meaning of community in a deeper sense. Hopefully we understand things about human beings, communities, and the relationships between people that 19th century thinkers didn't and couldn't understand. We know that unless we think in terms of much more complex relationships between people and have a deeper understanding of the complexities of human nature, what we will do is not build but destroy communities. We will frustrate this need for community which exists so profoundly within the human species.

THE NEED FOR CONTINUITY

One of the greatest needs of human beings is for continuity. Sometimes privileged people can contribute more continuity to a community than people who are plebeian—although people who are plebeian contribute something else unique. In the same way age contributes something to a community which youth cannot, and vice versa. (Note the inclusion in the new Chinese Constitution of the provision that the leading body of every organ of state "must be a three-in-one combination of the old, the middle-aged and the young.") This way of thinking which is so terribly necessary to the building of a community has been lacking up to now. A community has to be willing to accept the good with the bad—otherwise it isn't a community. For example, why do we live in Detroit where we are shoveling snow from November to April? Because if we just left Detroit and went some place where we didn't have to shovel snow, we could never build a community. As long as people are always moving to where things are better, or as long as people are always trying to expel from a community those elements who don't "fit" a particular standard at a particular time, we will never create communities.

Bateson says in *Steps to an Ecology of Mind* that up to now man/womankind has thought in terms of a single species and the survival of that species. He says that we will not be thinking in terms of the unit necessary for survival until we think of man/womankind and the environment together as part of a single unit. We have to think of units in larger and more complex terms than we have thought up to now, both spatially and temporally.

THE NEED FOR VALUES

To go back, why is it that so many people accept welfare as a norm and as a way of life? Some of the old glues that held people together were church, courtesies, a sense that you belonged to a particular area, a particular family. You word meant something. You were mincemeat in the community if you didn't keep your word. You knew all the thugs and whores in the community. Now the development of transportation has made solving crime practically impossible. Somebody steals something in Detroit and is in Chicago within an hour.

Today we are trying to make schools play the role of the church, the family and the community, plus teaching the three Rs. All these glues are gone. Because the community has disappeared, the school doesn't mean anything, the church doesn't mean anything.

We must never forget that during this period when the bonds that held us together were disintegrating, the bourgeoisie was also losing its legitimacy. It still wanted to keep its power, so it was ready to make all kinds of economic concessions to the masses in the form of various pacification programs. For example, they said we will expand welfare because we don't want any trouble.

It is strange that despite the enormous mobility in the 1930s and 1940s many of the old values continued in the relationships between people. There was a great deal of trust among people during the

Depression, a respect and readiness to sacrifice and assist others. This was also true during the war despite the tremendous physical mobility. But then after the war bourgeois expediency began to dominate and everybody began to look for what he/she could get from everybody else. The bourgeoisie said, "If we don't give the returning GIs the GI Bill, they will disrupt the society. If we don't give blacks certain things, they will make a mess." Everybody began capitulating to pressures. And ever since that time a kind of utilitarian manipulative attitude towards others has become more and more the norm in the U.S., becoming even more prevalent since the rebellions of the sixties.

This behavior in terms of expediency was not created so much by technological and physical changes as by a political situation that developed in the relationships between the ruling class and the masses. Therefore there are no principles in the country today governing anything, including the question of whether people should go on welfare. All we have are, on the one side, Republicans who are trying to save on taxes, who say that welfare is too expensive. That is an economic argument, to which somebody on the other side replies with another economic argument: that the money has come from exploitation of a whole lot of people anyway. As long as you deal with fundamental questions of how a human being should live in *that* way, everybody screws everybody else, and you can't have a community.

Human beings need community in the same way that all organic things need inter-relationships of a very intensive character, as the barnacle needs the wood on which it can fasten or the mussel needs the rocks and the mud. We must not get lost by concentrating too much on the complexities of these inter-relationships. Ardrey says all kinds of communities of all kinds of species have discovered ways not to grow too big, not to overextend themselves. In animals these are programmed instincts. They operate that way for whatever reason. We have to think it out.

We have to recreate a desire for the values which enable a community to exist. If people don't want these values, you simply can't create a community no matter how hard you try or how many federal dollars you pour in.

When we talk about values, we must be careful not to become romantic and idealistic the way the Cultural Nationalists are, with their idea of Ujamaa or togetherness. They are saying that there are certain values which blacks represent, values which come out of their past in the African village. Therefore, because they are an African people living in a white society which doesn't have these values, blacks must recognize these values in themselves and organize a social reality for themselves based upon these values: they are hoping that you can resurrect something from two hundred years ago. But the notion that you can transfer the values of an African village to Nairobi or New York is absurd.

The reason why some of these groups have been able to mobilize people around them was not because of the *past*—which provided the mystique—but because there is in blacks in the *present* a desire for these values, as there is in others also. But these values can only be realized by struggling against those with other values—on the strength of your values versus theirs—not on the basis of race. The romanticism and idealism of the Cultural Nationalists stem from their assumption that blacks don't have to struggle against themselves and other blacks to create these values. They spread the myth that somehow in their genes blacks have the ability to work together, while whites, because of something in their genes, don't. You can go to all sorts of people, white or black, and they will agree that what we need is more trust, more cooperation, more community. It isn't difficult for people to agree to that. But where do we go from there? Billy Graham says this all the time.

Even though everybody is saying that the main problem is the economy, the thing that people worry about most of the time—including the poor—is not so much how they are going to make ends meet as their relationships with their kids and their neighbors and why they don't dare to walk outdoors on the streets at night. Most of the time people are worrying about the lack of respect between people, the lack of values, not the lack of money.

WAS THE U.S. EVER A COMMUNITY?

Is it correct to say that up to World War II the U.S. was a community in a certain sense? There were a great many shared values, across the board, up and down, within the society. We are not saying that we should go back to that community. It is not possible; it is not desirable. But we have to recognize that, despite the enormous size of the country, there were some values which were shared by everybody.

A lot of older people are longing for that past. Among whites and older blacks there is a great deal of nostalgia. The enormous popularity of the movie *Walking Tall* is an expression of this. When older people say, "we don't understand these young people, they have so many opportunities that we didn't have," they are saying that if *they* had these opportunities, they would know what to do with them. The older generation sweat blood because they believed in something, even though they may have wished that they didn't have to sweat so much blood for it.

Young people look at a community as the peer group with whom one must conform, whom one must not challenge. That is one kind of togetherness which is destructive and has become even more destructive in the last period. It is difficult to get a judgment from a young person of anyone else in his/her group. They are always worried about what somebody in their own group will say about them. It is a kind of gang mentality.

In older communities people recognized their dependence on one another. You didn't get bread unless there was a baker and you didn't get blessed unless there was a rabbi or a priest. Today nobody knows that the bread is baked by a baker. You just go to the store and buy it with money, without any idea of who made it or how they made it. You don't feel dependent upon any persons. You only depend upon the stability of the system so that your check arrives in the mail and the value of the money doesn't fall too fast and the supermarket is there. We don't recognize that we are murdering ourselves by this kind of living.

The U.S. before World War II wasn't really a community. It was hardly a nation. It was a conglomeration of people united by certain ideas—the Declaration of Independence, the Constitution, free enterprise, the opportunity for mobility geographically, and up and down the social scale. The U.S. was nationally independent, like France or Sweden, but national independence doesn't create a community. It only provides the arena for individuals and classes to struggle to advance themselves.

Europe before World War I was absolutely confident that it was the repository of all Western civilization, that its continuity since ancient Greece and the Roman Empire represented the continuity of civilization. They didn't pay much attention to Chinese, African or any other civilization, they were very confident of their own. They still believed in the church, in art, that they were creating advanced political and social forms and advancing parliamentary democracy. World War I they conceived of as the war to end all wars. They really did think it was possible for the European community to end all wars, even though the war was fought between members of the European community. They thought they epitomized something. Their confidence in a sense gave them a feeling of community.

That European community—the community which had seen itself as the product of centuries of progress—got totally demolished in 1918. The U.S. never saw itself that way. We were merely the exemplification of a document called the Declaration of Independence, another called the Constitution, and of the idea that anybody, except "obviously" slaves, could come to this country and become anything. This was something completely different from the European sense of community. The American sense was an opportunistic one. The Europeans felt that they were the product of centuries of common struggle within their communities; for example, the people in Rheims who took a hundred years to build the cathedral. The only people in the U.S. who had anything like this sense of community were some in New England.

In the U.S. confidence was more that of the frontiersman, and the railroad baron. The majority of the population considered that they were having a relatively fine time, as compared to their uncles, aunts and cousins in Sicily or Yugoslavia or Ireland. But the U.S. didn't perceive itself as a community in the sense of Europe.

When we talk about the U.S. not being culture-bound and therefore free to create something new, we use "culture" in the sense of something which has come from centuries of continuous development, which everybody feels part of from top to bottom, and which gives the intellectuals and leaders of society a kind of moral authority, so that they don't have to rest only on wealth or on force. The U.S. has no culture in that sense. On the other hand, we can use the word "culture" in the sense that the U.S. has a materialistic culture.

The Declaration of Independence and the Constitution are not things that the ordinary American feels proud of, as even cockneys in England feel proud of Shakespeare's plays—feeling that they have been part of their creation. That is why it is dangerous to start from the idea that the U.S. was ever a community—at least not in the sense that we are now trying to define community.

INSTITUTIONS ARE THE DEATH OF COMMUNITIES

We would be delighted to see this whole country start proliferating with people trying to form communities of every kind. The more these are formed, the greater our opportunity to point out what a wonderful idea it is to strive for community, as well as to point to the limitations of particular striving. For example, are blacks really going to create communities by huddling together in "black nations"? We are glad that they are at least thinking about starting something and then discovering that they are not striving deeply enough.

Take education. We all know that years ago the community thought that people who went on in school were better people. We know today that people who have a "good education" are just another interest group. We don't think much of anyone who went on to get a Ph.D. because in the process education has become so money-and-job oriented. When you hear people say, "We want our children to get a better education, we want better schools," they don't mean that they want their kids to get an education to be better people who are able to relate to other people in a better way so that we can reach a higher level of humanity. The end of education is already preconceived as an economic one. That is why it is so necessary to examine what a struggle is for.

A few years ago everybody who was "progressive" was in favor of busing. It was impossible, they said, for young blacks to understand the ramifications of living in a white society unless they went to school with white kids and vice versa. We are inclined to think that the time has come to shatter this approach. One cannot solve questions of this depth in this way. And when you try to solve profound questions in a superficial way, you only create more obstacles.

It is possible to say that this country is made up of institutions: educational institutions, welfare institutions, and so forth, rather than that it is a nation of communities. Maybe if we were to counterpose communities to institutions, we could get somewhere. A community has limits, it is enclosed, it has a circumference, whereas an institution expands without limit. (Prison institutions are expanding without limit although they are certainly enclosed.) A community consists of people in their infinite variety, with a variety of different inter-relationships; institutions consist of individuals in a limited aspect of themselves, as teachers, as bureaucrats or as workers. Institutions are the death of communities.

If you talk to someone who is struggling for a "better education," and you say, "What you should be thinking about is serving the community instead of just getting a better education," he/she will reply, "I am going to school to become a dentist or a social worker, and a dentist or social worker serves the community. What is wrong with that?"

Must education be the means to discover what is within oneself rather than for service in the community? Serving the community comes out of the further development of oneself: the self has to continue the search for a oneness with other people—which may make you unequal with other people, but at the same time puts you in continuity with the advancement of the human race.

The average guy or gal who decides that he/she will serve the community usually thinks of taking sociology—which is exactly the way not to serve the community but to become part of an institution. Yet we cannot return to the concept of the humanities or liberal arts concept of education which still prevailed before World War II. Before World War II higher education was still for the purpose of creating cultivated persons. Now we have the idea of higher education to get a better job in institutions, which has nothing to do with becoming a better human being.

We look at education in the future as being for humanity in the sense that from the beginning, and not just in higher education, the individual will be thinking of and practicing how to serve humanity. Schools will not only develop people intellectually, but ethically, socially and productively; you can't teach a kid only ABCs until the twelfth grade and then start talking to him or her about responsibilities to humanity and the human value of work.

In older communities people were given some sense of the humanities outside of school. "Don't kick the dog." "Don't kill every bird you see." There was a relatively practical process of education in values within the community. In the old days, if you kicked a dog, the neighbor would whip your butt. Today if a neighbor whips a kid's butt for kicking the dog, the kid's mother may whip the neighbor's butt. Today we are at the stage where we don't have the church and the family and the community to teach these values.

We refuse to believe that in a more comfortable seat, or in that white school which is programmed to advance kids only in functional institutional roles, kids will learn what it is necessary for them to learn. How do we cut across the gimmickry of class struggle, of busing, of black and white kids sitting side by side understanding each other better? How do we get back to something more fundamental?

Enlarging the Concept of the Family

We are trying to find out what a community is and we are trying to find ways by which we can convey to people the importance of communities. One of the things we should not do is try and make institutions fill human needs that only communities can fill and which institutions cannot fulfill by virtue of their very nature. One of the errors of the Marxists is to think that you can have a community within the shop. We should also not try to make the school a community. This is one of the errors of those people who set up progressive schools, thinking that a school can fill the role of the community.

Sociologists write about the family as an institution, but the family and the home are more like communities than they are like institutions. Even in the worst of homes (and we are *not* saying certain homes should be maintained), you do have face-to-face relations between people with all their good and bad qualities and therefore the beginnings of the struggle towards community.

Maybe the first thing one should do is get rid of the rules that make it necessary for the father to get out so that the children can get on ADC. It is terribly necessary that we maintain the general principle of the home and the family. We are not saying that we don't believe in divorce or that we believe in the nuclear family; what we are trying to do is enlarge the concept of the family. At this stage, through the family, we can try to illustrate to people what community is. A family is the original community, and every aspect of the community—or almost every aspect—is in the family: the bright child and the slow child, the chores, the need for trust, the differences, and cooperation. The home used to be the place where each person had a role. We may have to start from that elementary level to make clear what a community is. Otherwise the generalizations become too abstract.

For years the black community blamed the schools for what was happening to black kids. Today only the least thoughtful do this. Those who are beginning to wonder a bit and beginning to realize how profound our problems are, are beginning to ask questions about the home and the community: "We can't only blame the schools," they say. "We have to look at the home, the community, and all the things that go into the community." There are also the economic problems. How can one have a home if the father has to move a thousand miles away for a job: Which doesn't mean that we should focus on the economic situation—although you can't leave it out.

Historically, in the development of the U.S., families came first, then communities, and then the institutions set up by the community. Many of the values in the community were interchangeable with those in the home.

The community set up certain institutions, schools, churches. But not until the last period, say, the last fifty years, in this country, have we begun to think about institutions as independent entities. The whole field of sociology is relatively new.

The church under feudalism was an institution, but not in the sense that it is today. Under feudalism people exchanged goods and services with one another. There were face-to-face relations. The Gothic cathedral is a fantastic example of the intimate relation between community and institutions under feudalism. Institutions hadn't established the antagonistic relations to life that they have today. Today an institution is something which has absolutely nothing to do with the life of the average person. It is like the Internal Revenue Service. It's there and it has its own logic.

The church in this country used to be part of the community. You went to the preacher to get advice on moral questions. Often it was where you got your first schooling through reading the Bible and where you got some soup when you had nothing to eat. Particularly as you went westward, the only way you brought civility to a community was through the church.

In the same way the community set up a town council to serve its needs. Thus both church and town council were agencies of the community; they didn't have their own logic. The grange wasn't an institution. It was the getting together of people who had a common interest in their problems of agriculture.

SOCIAL RELATIONSHIPS ARE HUMAN RELATIONSHIPS

We have arrived at the incredible point where we believe we can use the family as a way to illustrate human relationships to the average American. We don't know any radicals in the U.S. who would say this. It is puzzling to have reached this point, and almost frightening to have gone so far back in the evolution of human history. You can't go further back than the family unless you go back to biology. Yet revolutionists have to deal with dangerous concepts. If there are no risks involved, it is probably not worth dealing with. When Hitler was dealing with the phenomenon of alienated Germans seeking "escape from freedom," he talked about Kinder, Kirche and Kuchen. It isn't accidental that he had to deal with these—because they are the fundamentals. It is also interesting that the one place where you do not have a feminist movement today is China: the struggle of women for equality in China is not a feminist movement. Is this because Mao and the Chinese believe in the family? They do not believe in the patriarchal family of Confucius in which the woman is subordinate to the man, and they mobilize the people to struggle against this tradition. They do not believe that young people should simply listen to their parents. They believe that there should be struggle between old and new ideas in the family as well as in the whole society. At the same time they believe in the respect of the young for the old and in using the past to advance the present. They do not just throw out the family with the abandon of the average Western radical.

In China the children are taught to think in terms of family, for example, to call older people uncles and aunts, related or not. It is a country where you have three to four generations living together under one roof, where grandparents are not put into institutions. An institution is a place where people are isolated according to a single aspect of their personalities—age, or expertise in engineering, or graduate degrees in social work, or particular handicaps.

We are willing to accept the family almost as a kind of species unit. A lot of birds and animals don't have families except during the hatching season. Elephants, who have a very long gestation period, longer than people, have a terrific sense of family. Families, to get back to this elemental unit, enable us to discover—maybe for the first time in 200 years—what the more complex unit should represent. Not the complexity of getting to the moon. But the complexity of creating new human relationships. We think that, using the idea of the family, we may be able to project something about community and human relations which won't be so abstract.

In the traditional family you had to work. You were instructed in how to work in the family on a very elementary level, how to cut wood, how to let a neighbor have some wood in exchange for corn and molasses. Social relationships in the community came out of the wisdom of the family.

In a community when you do something for somebody, you feel that in time they will do something for you. You don't have to put an exchange value on your services or goods immediately; you don't have to turn them into commodities. When you have the perspective of settling in a community, how you decide questions of money and costs are shaped by the expectations of the human relationship you are going to be having with others in the community. So the social relationships determine the economic.

ECONOMICS SHOULD BE A BRANCH OF WISDOM

Schumacher in *Small Is Beautiful* says that "economics should be a branch of wisdom." In other words, economics should be a creation of the people who have learned certain values within their elementary relations within the family and the community. This is completely different from the traditional Marxist approach that social relationships are dependent upon economic relationships—which is why it has taken us so long to get here. We are saying that the economic relationships into which men and women enter are only one aspect of their human being; and should not govern their human relationships.

Marx (for whatever reasons) gave priority to economic man/woman at a very early stage of capitalism. Probably because he was so convinced that workers in the process of capitalist production would become a community of "socialized labor," he actually helped advance the domination of our lives by economics because he conceptualized what capitalism was actually doing. Economics under feudalism was a big plantation thing. Queen Elizabeth still owns six villages! Just when feudalism was breaking up, Marx elaborated a concept which separated the process of production from the rest of the community. Even though he posed it as a way to help people become socialists, in a certain sense he acted as a catalyst for capitalism. Capitalism created economic man/woman, reduced man/woman to a very fragmented aspect of his/her total nature. And Marx conceptualized this direction of capitalism into a philosophy, so that since that time Marxists have said to the masses, "You want to become free? Then smash capitalism. You don't have to think about changing yourself at all."

This separating out or isolating a single aspect of human nature and interpreting it as the totality was very much a characteristic of nineteenth century thinking. Marx did it with economics, Freud with sex. Freud interpreted all social relationships in terms of sexual relationships within the family. That is why Jung was so much greater than Freud. If Jung were sitting here, he might say, "I think you people are on the right track. You are trying to look at what is indigenous to the human species. This is the first time I have heard some people begin to wonder about what to do tomorrow in relation to what I, Jung, label the archetypal, i.e., something which is indigenous to the human species, coming from a million years out of the past of the species."

What we are beginning to appreciate more and more is that Marx was a product of his generation, of his history, and also a very beautiful man, especially as a young man. We shouldn't expect him to be other than a product of his time. Now all of a sudden we discover ourselves a product of our time, which experienced all the passions of Marxism and all the struggles of Marxist revolutionists, but suddenly, because we are still passionate about changing society, discover that Marx's ideas are not enough. We are amazed to find that we hadn't really been looking at social relationships. We had been assuming the Marxist attitude to social relationships as determined by economic relationships. "All" we had to do, we thought, was get rid of capitalist relations in economics, and humanity would blossom. Now we have to wonder what kind of human beings would want to get rid of capitalism. They would have to be more than economic men and women. Marx couldn't have said, "economics is a branch of wisdom," but we have to believe that in order to alter the economics. We cannot wait to discover the wisdom only after we alter the economics.

Another very helpful formulation of Schumacher's is "the market is the institutionalization of irresponsibility." If we begin with who people are, not what class they belong to or their relations to the means of production, then we will be able to create a different kind of economic relationships. We have to start with people who think people should be different in order to have a different kind of economics. Men and woman didn't alienate themselves; but they permitted themselves to be alienated. It is important to see this, because today we are asking people to take the responsibility for wondering who is presently doing the alienating. You begin to see that it is self-defeating to blame your situation on somebody else.

In 1974 in the U.S. one can take responsibilities which in 1934 one couldn't possibly have accepted: "But now I think I can." This is an evolution of the self through experience and reflection, as you begin to realize that to get bogged down in blaming people for what happened in the past is to cripple yourself.

At the stage when Marx wrote *Capital,* what else could European workers do except struggle against their oppressors? Their task was entirely different from what American workers have to do now. At that time a European worker couldn't have said, "I have to change myself as well as get you off my back."

Marx thought in terms of economic man/woman as fundamental, while capitalism was creating him/her as fragmented man/woman. In a certain sense Marx was a prisoner of his time. As a young man, he was struggling against the young Hegelian intellectuals who saw everything in terms of ideas and had no relationship to the masses or to production. So Marx put the emphasis on production. Generally speaking, Marx thought of rural people as idiots and of city people as the bearers of progress. We also thought that for a long time, and it is only now that we have lived in the middle of the urban crisis that we can begin to see the virtues of rural life. We can hardly expect Marx to have seen that, especially since he inherited both the concept of the Greek city-state and the tradition of the town, which had emerged under feudalism as the center of ideas, skills, trade, art. He saw and was intrigued by the scientific thought and technologies which were developing in the cities in such contrast to the superstitions and the sickle and scythe which were all the peasants had.

Mao appreciated the countryside because the city in China had been either the imperial city or the imperialist city, and because of everything that the world had learned in the past twenty years about the depth of the urban crisis. If the Chinese Revolution had taken place before the Russian Revolution, it too might have fallen into the trap of vulgar materialism and urbanization.

Marx was very conscious of what he called "the fetishism of commodities," namely, that *things* would begin to intrude between human beings and therefore that people would begin to interpret their human relationships or relationships to other people in terms of things. One of the reasons why he looked to the plant and the workers as the bearers of progress was that he thought that in the plant there at least would be face-to-face relations between workers, a community. This community of socialized labor was his community of the future. He didn't have any idea of how individualistic the workers in the plant would become.

The average radical has as much difficulty seeing Marx as a product of his age as the average Christian has in seeing Jesus as a product of his age. In a recent biography (by McLellan), Marx is quoted as saying in 1850 that without a proletarian revolution Europe is going to lag way behind the U.S. as is, for example, southern Europe to northern Europe. So that Marx was talking about a particular revolution, the European revolution, and it was as a European patriot, and not as a "citizen of the world" that Marx advocated the European socialist revolution. Yet since that time everybody has talked about Marx as if he were an abstract internationalist ("workers of the world, unite") when he was, in fact, a European, very much concerned with Europe and European workers.

In the same way Trotskyists have argued all these years about Trotsky's notion of Russia as a worker's state without recognizing that Trotsky was talking as a Russian patriot. He wasn't just arguing abstractions, even though his followers were. He was arguing about the Russia he had been brought up in, in which he had led a revolution, which he loved and wanted to shape into something he could be proud of.

What do we mean by *human* relationships? The family is the beginning of human relations from which we can extend our concepts. We don't know what the next stage is. That doesn't bother us. What would bother us is if we could explain too quickly what we mean by human relationships. Talking about capitalism versus socialism encourages you to put a lid on your mind, to think that you have answers before you have even begun to develop the questions that are necessary and to think that there is a *thing* such as economics apart from human beings. On the other hand, counterposing a socialist to a capitalist outlook forces you to examine your own mind, your own thoughts.

In the notion of the family we have found something that almost all people have experienced and therefore something concrete upon which people can reflect as a basis for gaining some real insight into the concept of human relationships and their search for community. Up to now we have said that not until people begin to think in a different way can they begin to create something different. Through using the notion of family we can try to help them begin thinking differently.

Not until people have lived in a community will they really be able to think of the unit of survival in terms of the human species within the context of the environment.

FREEING OUR MINDS

We have to free our minds, our imaginations, from the limitations of the past. After more than a hundred years *of* using certain ideas and trying to get somewhere with them, we discover that Western women/men have stultified our imaginations and our capacity to conceive of new human relationships. By breaking through the rigidities of the past period, by going back maybe a million years to the elemental social unit, by wondering how we can use the concept of this unit rather than just repeat what Darwin, Freud or Marx said, we are freeing our minds to think differently about human relationships. It takes a lot of imagination to free yourself from all the things you and your forebears have been taught for a hundred years.

Watergate hasn't changed the way that millions of people think, but it has created a situation in which it is possible to change the way that people think. There are two tendencies now: to go back to normal and forget everything about Watergate, *or* wonder what Watergate can mean in helping us to overcome the morass of our daily lives. There is a great desire to get back to normal. We are the same and yet we are not the same. In New York recently, some kids stole the regents exams and sold them for huge sums of money. Other kids felt sorry for them because they were caught, and the prosecutor decided not to prosecute because with Watergate going on, he said the kids couldn't be held responsible for their actions. We find that absolutely hair-raising. If Watergate is seen in terms of Nixon, and not as a question of what is happening in America, then Watergate has changed nothing. Watergate is an extraordinary example of what happens when you don't look at the totality. It has persuaded a whole lot of Americans that we can't look at things the way we used to. They may not know how to look at things differently, but their minds are more open than before. The whole world is caught up in the same dilemma. We are being forced to think in much more general terms than we have ever thought before. Watergate makes it necessary for us to think *and talk* much more generally about morality. If we are silent about values, then they can't possibly exist for us.

Despite the enormous leap of the Chinese Revolution with its tremendously advanced political leadership, the Chinese masses still began sinking back to immediate self-interest, consumerism, utilitarianism, individualism. If it had been only a question of Liu Shao-chi and a few of his cronies, it wouldn't have been necessary to launch the Cultural Revolution. If this can happen to masses of people after the Chinese Revolution, surely an event like the resignation of Nixon (along with all the other things that took place: the role of the press, the judiciary, the House Judiciary Committee) isn't going to change things, in the sense that everything is now going to move forward in a positive direction. When something like Watergate occurs, we must think of introducing ideas and questions which produce further changes in the direction we think things should go. We can't talk about "things" changing.

We should avoid getting into Aristotelian, undialectical, either-or dilemmas about who changes what, the people or the situation. A situation, first of all, is a social event involving people and relationships between people. Certain people changed the situation from one in which Nixon was in the White House carrying on, to the situation that we are in today, where Nixon is out of the White House. Some people say, "The people changed the situation" as if the American people brought about this change. But most people didn't bring about that change; they were only spectators. We can't talk about the American people that way. It is a form of flattery or demagogy. A lot of people didn't do a damn thing. Nevertheless even they are more susceptible to changing themselves now than they were prior to the change which was brought about by other people.

NOT CLASS-ANGLERS

One reason why we are making such a big leap forward in our discussion of the family is that we are no longer thinking of the family as Marx and Engels did, only as an agency of exploitation, as in *Origin of the State, Private Property, and the Family*. Thus many radicals think that "we" will eliminate exploitation and the family at the same time. Thinking of everything in terms of relations between oppressed and oppressor and of the history of humanity as the history of class struggle, class-angling everything, the tendency has been to ignore everything else that human beings have created over the centuries. The history of humanity is seen as an uninterrupted series of October Revolutions.

We have also tended to see the family, state, politics, leadership, within these parameters—that they are all the products of exploitation. A large number of radicals still think this way. They use the word "exploitation" as if everybody understands what it means. For anybody to use anybody else for any purpose has been regarded as exploitation. Is all division of labor exploitative?

The implication has been that if "you" could get rid of exploitation, everybody else would know exactly how to live in relation to everybody else. It is like saying that if you got rid of capitalism, you get rid of capital. But you have capital under socialism too. It is a different kind of capital, social capital, but it is still capital in the sense that it is withheld—by the choice of the creators of the capital. Otherwise there wouldn't be the wherewithal to build dams or battleships.

Human Needs Go beyond Material Needs

Was it only because of the economic factor that people stuck together in families? Might we say that survival factors were involved, including survival of the human mind and the human spirit? Human needs include much more than economic needs.

Long before the Chinese Revolution became part of our theoretical framework, radicals based themselves on what Engels said in *Origin of the Family*. They were not just talking about the nuclear family of which people had little conception in Engels' time. But hasn't the human species always needed a framework, a cadre, within which the young could be developed and trained? That is not the way Marx looked at the family, but Marx comes very late on the scene of human thought, even though for most radicals in the U.S. human thinking practically begins with Marx. Is that because the U.S. itself begins as a nation so late? Americans don't have a whole history of ideas prior to Marx, as the Chinese do, so that it is difficult for Americans to develop a sense of proportion in relation to Marx's ideas.

Marx talked about capitalism destroying the family ("the bourgeoisie destroys all patriarchal and idyllic relations"), but even as radicals were denouncing capitalism for its destruction of the family, the ideas of *Origin of the Family* were encouraging radicals to reject the family—just as Marx wrote about labor within the exploitative relationship of capital, and in the end a lot of people began rejecting work altogether on the basis of Marxism. Capitalism destroyed the dignity of work, but what Marx was saying also helped to destroy the desire on the part of the worker to do any work.

Now just as we are trying to go back to why men and women work, we are also asking why the family is necessary to the development of human beings. In what sense is it an embodiment of the need of the human species for community on an intimate scale and for experiences which contribute to the advancement of human beings? Not any particular family or particular kind of family, such as the nuclear family or the extended family, but the family as such.

Looking at the family from that point of view, we might say that the family is a place where you can talk about what your grandmother and grandfather and your uncles and aunts did, and thus very early get a sense of continuity and of history—all of which are very important to human development. A family is a place where you can, through some immediate personal experiences, develop an appreciation of the need for cooperation and at the same time a certain division of labor, e.g., men can't have babies, people of different ages give and take different things. If we begin looking at the family this way, in terms of human development and not immediately in terms of class struggle or exploitation, we begin to understand better what human needs are.

Often, when American Jews look at the Israeli kibbutz, they may see only the day-care centers and forget that the kibbutz was originally a family which replaced the nuclear family, especially in the agricultural areas.

In a family you have to deal with a whole lot of difficult questions in a very personal way, e.g., your aging grandmother or your brutal brother. What do we do about them? In a family you learn that there are some things you can't have until you get older.

So if we go back to the fundamentals of the human species instead of seeing the family through the spectacles of the class struggle, we begin to get a different concept of the family's contribution to the values that we believe are necessary for human beings to live together, and in the course of doing this we begin to get another definition of what the class struggle should be about.

We have been thinking of the family in terms of private property all these years, and as the women's movement has developed and influenced all of us, the tendency has been even more to think of the family only in terms of exploitative relations. There are all kinds of risks involved in trying to change our thinking about these questions. For example, the post–World War II generation of college-educated parents said, "We are not going to try and change society; we are going to raise our kids within the family to be new people." So they moved to the suburbs and raised their kids—who then seceded from the family because they saw it in very narrow terms, as not only the beginning but the end. On the other hand, we are trying to discover the elementary contributions made by the family relationships.

The Loud family shown on the TV series wasn't a family at all. Why not? Each individual was doing his/her own thing. The fact that it was called "The American Family" is almost an exact illustration of how few people understand what a family really is. These were people with enough money: they didn't fight over grocery bills or rip somebody off to buy a bike. They had the same name and lived in the same house; yet they weren't a family. Their relations were so murderously contemporary, so white suburban America. This is the reality we face—that the American family does not embody the kinds of relationships that we think the family can and should contribute to the development of the individual and the community.

Why did Americans demolish the family so much more rapidly than the English or French? Why did the black community disintegrate practically overnight? Americans have never had traditions in the sense that Europeans or Asians did. So that even though this country evolved in continuity with European tradition, we were not really rooted in any tradition. Many Italians talk about family traditions in the old country. *Southern blacks in the north talk about "down home," but in this country nobody is ever home. We are always somewhere else.* The American family broke up faster than any others because the immigrants broke up their families to come here or had them broken up. Then, in coming here, they discovered all kinds of substitutes for the family. Not the least of these was mobility: in the early years there was plenty of space; in the later years, plenty of cars. The notion of the family in the U.S. is a memory.

How can you call something a family which does not live up to the idea of a family? What is a family? In the past, under less complex conditions, family relations didn't have to be developed as consciously and systematically as they have to be today. External necessities compelled people to develop solid relationships. Today, given the enormous abundance—the vast number of things people actually own—the mobility, the human relationships of the kind we are talking about have to be very consciously created.

The average white Protestant American family looking at the Loud family said, "That is a family." Whereas the average Jewish or Italian Americans might have said, "Shit, that isn't a family." Even though Italians and Jewish, Chinese and other foreign families in America are becoming more like the average white U.S. family all the time.

We are not saying that the family has to be recreated before we can talk about struggle for a socialist society. We are saying that in the attempt to visualize what a socialist society would look like, we find the concept of family very helpful. We are saying that we have to rethink our notions of the family because our notions about the family have been so affected by the capitalist destruction of the family and by Marx's ideas of the origin of the family. We are affirming the values that the family can contribute to the growth of the individual.

THE FAMILY AND POLITICS

At the same time we have to look beyond the family to the conflicts that develop in relation to wider loyalties.

In every period of great transition there is a crisis like that immortalized by Sophocles in the Greek drama about Antigone, the girl who wanted her brother to be buried suitably and goes to great lengths to defy the king, her uncle, who is determined to deny her brother such a burial because he had rebelled against the state. Antigone affirms the ties of the family and insists that they have priority over and beyond any political loyalties. Aristotle thought a great deal about this question, as did Hegel (see the section on human and divine law in the *Phenomenology*).

This question of relationship between the family (as community) and the political community is involved in the controversy over unconditional amnesty. Many parents, sisters, wives want unconditional amnesty for their sons, brothers, husbands who fled to Canada or Sweden to avoid the draft, or who went AWOL, or who got undesirable discharges for any reason whatever—including the rape of a Vietnamese girl. Some of these men were opposed to the Vietnam War in principle. Some wanted to save their own skins. Some cut out because they didn't like the food. But many people—including those who saw the war as a crime and those who were not at all opposed to the war but whose loved ones were soldiers—don't want to discuss the question of who should get amnesty and who should not. They just want to forget the whole thing and start life afresh. They don't want to learn any political lessons from this controversy over amnesty, and they don't want to teach any lessons. For them it is enough to say that the Vietnam War was a crime and a mistake. The radicals are going along with all this confusion, just as they've gone along with the cry about freeing political prisoners, because they don't want to challenge the masses. They want to encourage them to think like victims.

We have to ask ourselves, and others, some more difficult questions. Doesn't every nation have a right to demand the allegiance of its citizens? And if a citizen is convinced that what his/her government is doing is wrong, doesn't that citizen have not only a right but a duty to struggle politically against that government, to change its policy or to overthrow it—and accept the consequences of this, including going to jail? Doesn't a citizen have a right to take it upon him/herself to decide the policy of a country only insofar as he/she is willing to struggle politically and not just cop out? Isn't that the difference between being part of a mob and being a citizen in a political community? How do you object to what your government does?

We will be the constitution-framers of the 1980s and/or 1990s. The positions we take with regard to this question, the clarification we search for, the courage we have to challenge those who see their loved ones only as victims and not as creators of the political community, will help us enormously to write the new constitution.

Traditionally, among people with some property, funerals used to raise questions such as the distribution and redistribution of property. What most family members were interested in was the will: who was going to get what? American blacks and other poor folks used the funeral as an opportunity for a family reunion and to review the past. You achieved a sense of continuity. Today when you go to a funeral, it is difficult to get beyond contemporary questions—crime, race. What should be our response under such circumstances? Should we raise questions of how human beings should live?

In the ancient family there were some values which have gotten lost in the scramble for individual advancement. What is the purpose of the class struggle? To get more of the pie for the poor? Or to reconstitute some of the values that need to exist in the family? The concept of class struggle as a struggle of the poor versus the rich used to be a more or less legitimate summation of mass struggle up to the time of Marx. But since that time social concerns have evolved beyond that.

One of the virtues of the ancient family was that you were bound together by necessity. You had to share, to survive materially. But in the course of human development we are discovering that there is another kind of necessity. We completely overlooked the psychic hunger which was also being satisfied in the family. We are using the family as an illustration of that psychic necessity.

BRINGING SOCIETY INTO THE FAMILY

There are millions of kids in this country today who have broken with their families and are strangers wandering in the land because they haven't found any substitute to give them a sense of belonging. What is there in the American family they rejected that made it impossible to satisfy their basic need for belonging within their families? Many of these families were just blood relations who lived together in a house. They were not a family because they had developed any relationships other than blood or economic relationships. Maybe there was something missing in the family and in the connections between the family and the rest of society.

Rebel without a Cause, the first of the major contemporary films about youth in revolt against the family, showed the father unable to answer the questions which the youngster was asking about society. Society was supportive of the family, but the parents, despite their economic and physical authority, lacked the moral authority which comes from knowing where you are going. The history of the last twenty years shows that the revolt of youth against the family is not simply the traditional revolt of young people but an expression of the search by young people for positions on social questions. When Kennedy said, "Ask not what your country can do for you but what you can do for your country," practically every radical thought he was just an s.o.b. asking people to support him. They didn't see what many young people saw or felt, that he was asking people to think about the totality of the society in which we live.

Why should kids get so angry at their parents for not having social values when nobody has been talking about social values? Why shouldn't the kids stay home and struggle with their parents over these questions? Maybe the family unit of the future should encourage, as well as permit, controversy and struggle and thought within it. Who is responsible for creating relationships that will permit this kind of struggle within the family? Only the parents or also the kids? Maybe we need relationships within the family which enable society to come into the family in a different way than it has traditionally come. The family could be an arena in which the questions of society are explored and argued. This is not one of the roles that people have always ascribed to the family.

In *The American Condition* Richard Goodwin discusses politics from his own personal experience of having gone into government in response to Kennedy's appeal to do what you can for your country. He argues that the best people tend to go into government thinking they can change the government, whereas in fact unless a movement has been developed within the society you can't change government and are only extracting the best people from the social movement.

Each person has to ask: "Who am I? Do I have any ideas except antagonistic ones or complaints about what society has denied me? What do I have to do in order to change things?" Goodwin points out that changes only took place in regard to civil rights when a movement was mobilized within the society to struggle for those rights. According to Goodwin, in a period of transition such as ours people have a choice: to mobilize forces within society or to go into government.

How does one change society? The important thing at this point is to persuade people that each individual has his/her own responsibility which has nothing to do with what society does to him/her. As a person, you are a participant in the process of making change. If you just accept society or just complain about it, then you are not a participant in making change. The only way to express your belief in the equality of women or blacks or young people is to make demands on each of them as great as you make on everybody else and to refuse to allow them to get bogged down in their grievances.

We have been saying that if we want to change society, one of the things we have to change is our concept of the role of the family and what it stood for. Again, we are not suggesting that we reconstitute the family structure. We are talking about reconstituting in some form—and we're not sure what that form is—the values for which the family has stood. And we are saying to everyone, black or white, women or men, young or old, you can't wait for society to do that for you or for the family.

WHAT SHALL WE TELL OUR CHILDREN?

Few parents are telling their children anything. Most of them are afraid of their children. It isn't that they wouldn't like to talk to their kids but that they haven't anything to tell them, because they have been so typically American—trying to get things and rise above what they were—trying to give them "the things I didn't have." So most of the kids are just out there. What most parents would like to tell their kids is that Rome wasn't built in a day and that you have to work and struggle for things, but they are hesitant to do this for a number of reasons. Middle Americans are breaking with the kids as much over the question of work as over the question of economics.

We don't blame the kids as much as we do the parents. Perhaps blame is the wrong word. Parents wish the schools would pick up the slack, or they wish the church would revive. You can't blame a kid for being born and raised in a family whose only urge was to get things.

One of the best ways for a child to get an idea of the past is through kinfolk. Children should know grandmothers and uncles and aunts. Black city kids should know something about life down south, how blacks used to live, how they have changed their lives through struggles, that the U.S. has a past which wasn't always the asphalt jungle—

that prior to industry there was agriculture, and prior to TV, radio. They need a sense of tradition in relation to the historical development of this country—the productive apparatus, the family, the music and dancing of the past.

For young people, this sense of continuity with the past in the form of living individuals is invaluable. It gives them the feeling that they came from something, that they came from a specific background. The most awful feeling that anyone can have is the feeling that you just came up from the ground, like a mushroom.

The radical movement went through a period of thinking that all you had to do was throw out the s.o.b.s who oppressed you and automatically that would tell you how to live. Because that idea is so erroneous, we are trying to start over again, not to try to make a kid into a revolutionist, but into a person. To do that we would have to project to him/her a lot of the great things that man/woman has done: the invention of language or the building of the pyramids, the discovery of irrigation and agriculture; man/woman did all these things. Don't give up now. You have to work just as hard as those guys and gals did. You have to think, to imagine, to invent, to care. Just sharing the wealth that the rich presumably have piled up doesn't mean that you acquire knowledge and sensitivity.

The problem of the revolutionary movement is that the only way to create socialism is to create some socialists. How do you go about creating socialists? The development of man/woman is not a class phenomenon, it is a human phenomenon. And if you would like something better than what is, you first have to make up your mind what it is that would be better—not just a bigger Cadillac.

What happens to a society when its young people believe that there isn't much to wonder about? That all the material things that need to be invented have been invented? So little of what is produced and advertised is necessary and so much of what you see all around you and on TV is gimmicks. How do we create a human being— somebody who wonders and creates—out of someone growing up in this situation?

"What is the role of history and of the past?" A kid looks at a submarine and says, "Isn't it wonderful?" without ever wondering what the process was which permitted its creation, how it was that Leonardo 500 years ago imagined this and made drawings of it and said, "I think this is possible." We have to get back to the incredible creativity of man/woman. This is what Bronowski is trying to say in *The Ascent of Man*, that man/woman has acted incredibly in the past and it isn't over. We have to continue thinking the same way. Our job is to enable you to do so—and you can't do it by picking up the gun and shooting the plantation owner.

Parents don't want their kids to work as hard as they did—or to do menial work. They want their kids to have more status. Most working class and middle class Americans have only given their children the wherewithal and the impetus to better themselves—without ever defining what it meant to better oneself or to have ambition.

Where parents have given more to their children, they have given them a sense of the continuing development of humanity—a philosophic attitude toward themselves as part of the evolving human species. This is probably what those born into the upper classes at the turn of the century received. Those were the very rare parents. Or they may have given them a particular ethnic or religious tradition, as with the Jews and perhaps the Chinese and to a certain extent blacks in the south. Black parents imparted something very precious to their children. They in effect said, "We suffered but we survived; we never gave up." They gave their children the sense that they were perpetuators of a people who had managed under intolerable circumstances to survive and even improve themselves not only physically but spiritually. That is real black history, not the black history in books. That is historical identity.

What should an American father tell his kids today? Can he merely behave like Archie Bunker—with nothing to offer to the kids but his own prejudices? The beauty of the program is the forthrightness of his stupidities.

Do we have to be far more specific about what parents should give their kids? What does it mean to be more specific? The philosophic attitude we have to instill in ourselves so as to transmit it to others has to be social. In the U.S. you can't give people a tradition in relation to a community because in a society as mobile as this, there is no such thing. Many communities were built up only yesterday. We have to develop some sense of national identity in the U.S., some sense of the historical development.

Kids are intrigued that we have endured, that we have continued and persisted in doing certain things that we regard as important, that we have lived in a certain place for a certain length of time, that our furniture is old and was put together from bits and pieces rather than bought in a store. We represent something stable and enduring. When we talk about environment, they must see that it is not as if it just occurred to us. That is where the new thought can begin.

We say to the kid, "Why don't you act like a human being?" Yet, nobody demonstrates to the kid what it means to be human.

Look at the cathedral of Rheims. They built it without power tools, they worked at night by candlelight or torchlight, and it took them a hundred years to do it. They invented Gothic architecture out of sheer aspiration. Nobody wrote a treatise on it. Why did they do it? The Gothic cathedral represented the aspirations of communities that had been together long and profoundly enough to build them. Popes or archbishops had nothing to do with it. Does that tell you something about the quality of man/woman? And does it give you pause to wonder how you fit into that quality? They filled gigantic spaces with the most incredible stained glass windows in the world, but they never signed any of them. Nobody knows who made or designed a single one of them. Fundamentally they were peasants, farmers, tenants, serfs, virtually exuding their humanity even under the so-called horror of feudal conditions. They were doing it because they felt the need of doing it. We should say to a kid, "What do *you* feel like doing?"

In Search of American Identity

In the U.S. we have very little tradition to build on. Italians can always look around them and see, for example, the Colosseum. What can we show Americans—except crossing the Mississippi? Yet we do have to find what was in a way great. The things that blacks cherished in the south they preserved until the second migration to the north. They had built up certain values—like telling the truth, making something out of nothing, believing in your own humanity. Then we came north into this melting pot, and our second generation broke with all those traditions. Coming north, we wanted certain things that we thought we could not achieve down south. And we also figured that there were some different people up north that would allow us to do those things. But when the bondage which had held us together and made us preserve values was no longer there, we began to break up. A lot of things broke up. The family structure, the things that an older brother or sister could tell you, were gone: "Ain't no old s.o.b. going to tell me nothing." This was one of the traditions that was broken. Young people didn't think older people had anything to tell them, and older people didn't have any power to tell young people anything. You couldn't spank a kid in the neighborhood for kicking a dog any more. These things had held people together and given them a certain collective strength. All this is now fragmented.

We have to start with the limited things we can refer to. This generation has had the luxury of breaking completely with the past, and therefore of being completely lost. John Brown, Wendell Phillips don't mean anything to young white kids. In England a kid relates to the year 1066. We have nothing of that significance, but we have to take the meager number of things we do have and make the links, imperfect though these maybe. Why should we expect perfection from the past? If the past had been perfect, there wouldn't be anything for us to create. The Civil Rights movement had something because it was based in the south. But the moment the movement came north, it went to Africa and got lost; it broke the link with its own past in the U.S. You can't think about making a contribution to this country if you have already left it in your mind—you can't think because you have removed yourself from your actual history and your actual present.

A USABLE PAST

We have to find a usable past in the U.S., a past with which Americans today can identify. Americans are not going to find themselves only in relation to the future or to the twelfth century in Europe or the fifth century before Christ in Greece. What we must help kids to understand is how the Declaration of Independence came to be written—not just out of the genius of Thomas Jefferson but out of the debates and controversies between all kinds of people searching for a new human identity between 1764 and 1776 as the rupture with their British identity became increasingly inevitable. Not only in relation to the Declaration of Independence but the Constitution, the Abolitionists, the labor movement, the Civil Rights movement, the railroads, even in relation to the Rockefellers. It isn't flag-waving the way it was used to assimilate the immigrants. It is what we who are determined to create a new nation, a new social order in America, do to combat the lostness of today. We use the past to serve the present and the future, making clear as the Chinese do, that if the emperor or the empress commissioned the building of the palace, it was the craftsmen and craftswomen who actually built it, and therefore the palace and its wonders belong to us.

We are seeking more than a material basis for human beings to be human. We do not see everybody in the U.S. as just a materialist. Some kids started with the idea of rejecting the materialism of their parents; and some were rebelling to get more of the material things. The labor movement rebelled for "more" in a period of scarcity; the rebellions of the sixties took place in a period of abundance!

When the Civil Rights movement started out in the South, it was not materialist. It was only when it came North that it grew materialistic and looked outside the country to Africa at the same time. Young whites rebelled against materialism but also against tradition. In the North young blacks called old blacks "Old Moses." White kids said that their parents were "pigs."

When we ask ourselves "What do we tell our kids?" we have to look very hard to find the things in this country that have enough continuity and tradition to pull some people together.

It is going to be very important to focus in on the U.S. and combat the temptation to find our identity with the Vietnamese or the Arabs. When kids ask us about the Constitution, we can't start by telling them what they ought to do now. We have to tell them that the Constitution represented a tremendous leap forward, giving the sense of nationhood that had been created in a military struggle a structure by which to develop. "If it hadn't been for that, you wouldn't be here today talking about the new things you want to do. Unless you understand that, whatever you do that is new is only going to be reactive and not a continuation and transcendence of the past." The American Revolution, with all that we now know of its limitations, is an integral part of the development of humanity. Without it there wouldn't have been the French Revolution or the Mexican Revolution or the Russian Revolution or the Gold Coast Revolution or the Chinese Revolution.

We are revolutionists here in the U.S.; that is, we are continuators and transcenders of what was achieved here. When we refer to

China or Bolivia or Vietnam, it is only to make a point. But to make an American Revolution, we have to discover the resources in the historical development of the United States to give us reason to wonder and go beyond.

For the last few years LeRoi Jones (Amiri Baraka) has been one of the most romantic "Fuck America" nationalists in this country, with one of the strongest mass followings in the country. Then came the concrete situation in Newark where a black Democrat, Gibson, was elected mayor, and Jones came into conflict with him over local issues. Baraka was faced with a lot of young people who had been rejecting everything in this country—and going to pieces. At the same time African liberation leaders began to criticize black nationalists for their biological and non-socialist thinking. So Baraka now says that blacks have to recognize their history in this country as well as in Africa and reject the idea of separatism. If you become a separatist in the U.S., you almost literally go crazy. It is something that happens to you and your brothers and sisters—not in books. So you must begin to struggle for some concept of yourself in relation to this country— which you can do only in relation to its historical development.

We have to start with the philosophic concept of universal human identity, but we have to develop it in relation to the national identity of Americans. Is a nation a nation of communities? And does the U.S. already have an advantage because of its division into states? The work that we have done over the years, on Melville, the Abolitionists, the labor movement, even our very composition—white, black, Chinese, Jew—gives us a feeling for the world that is inside America.

The American tradition can't start with America. The tradition of America derives from the tradition of Europe. In other words, there is much more involved than just going back to your grandfather or grandmother. American history can't be divorced from European history, although you have to decide where to draw the line if you are going to try to establish the distinctiveness of the American Revolution. American history is different from all European history because the Europeans came to a continent which was virtually unpopulated except for a relatively few Indians, and therefore it had to be populated from scratch. Everything about America that is so different from Europe is really what baffles the hell out of us. We are all like gypsies, and young people are more like gypsies than anyone else.

WHAT DO YOU MISS IN LIFE?

Maybe instead of using the phrase "psychic hunger," we should begin asking ourselves and other people, "What do we miss in life?" rather than "What is wrong?" When we talk about what is wrong, it sounds like we are talking about an "it" over there, something outside ourselves. The moment we say, "What is wrong is that we have to lock our doors at night," we are in a sense putting the responsibility on someone else to fix up the situation. We are seeing ourselves as victims and seeing the class struggle not as struggle against our own limitations but in terms of somebody else limiting us. Once a person gets into that frame of mind, it is almost impossible to get out of it.

On the other hand, when I say, "What I am missing in my life is people I can trust, a sense of belonging somewhere," it has a more personal quality. These are concepts in a certain sense and yet they are things people feel very deeply.

If we are thinking about people changing *themselves,* then we have to stick to the needs that people can feel, can think about wanting to satisfy because they are so deeply and personally felt. People have to become conscious of these needs today before they can create communities. In the past one could search for community without the requirement of knowing whether one was materialistic or not materialistic. Today in America you have to be a lot more conscious of the kind of human identity you want to discover.

In *The Social Contract* Ardrey says that animals have three needs: identity, security, and challenge.

It is ridiculous to think that a black man or woman in America today is going to find his/her identity in Africa. He/she has a relationship to Africa, of course, in the sense that an Anglo-Saxon looks back to England rather than Sicily. But identity at this time comes down to what you really miss in life. Your identity is determined by what you miss now, not what your great-great-grandparents in Nigeria or Sweden missed. Your identity lies in yourself, in what you miss. You create your own identity. Until you understand that, you are looking for a will-of-the-wisp. This is where we begin. We talk about identity first and then we talk about security. We are talking about Americans, not people starving to death in Chad or Bombay. They have the greatest material security in the world but they don't feel secure. So one has to wonder, what does security mean, and to what degree does security flow from one's sense of identity and not from how much money you have in the bank? It is not possible to make such a sharp separation between Ardrey's three needs: identity, security, challenge.

People do miss a sense of security even though we now have "Social Security." We thought security could be achieved in the material realm, only to discover that the more material things you have, the less secure you are. People thought that if they only had what Rockefeller has, they would have security, not realizing that he doesn't have security. Psychologically we are very insecure because psychic security comes from a certain confidence in yourself, from trust in other people, a sense of belonging somewhere, from comradeship. Psychic security can go along with being challenged and stimulated and wanting to go beyond where you are; it doesn't mean stasis or inertia. In fact, challenge is probably a necessary ingredient of psychic security, at least it is in the U.S. Maybe someone who is psychically secure is automatically challenged: to wonder and to search is an expression of his/her psychic security or vice versa. (This probably is not true of all peoples; people in other cultures might feel secure only if they were not challenged.)

A lot of the examples Ardrey selects to demonstrate the need for challenge in animals come from the fact that he is an American. Maybe if he had spent more time among South Sea Islanders or East Indians, he might not have recognized the same need for challenge in the animals he observed. He might have selected other animals to observe who are not challenged. Maybe some worms.

The American psyche is very different from every other psyche in the world. In this country, precisely because we have reached a certain point in material development, we feel our psychic needs infinitely more than any other people in the world, without having perhaps the slightest idea why this is so. When we ask, "What do you miss?" we are trying to bring about awareness of these needs.

One of the psychic needs of Americans is to create their own identity, to create themselves. This probably goes back to the way in which this country was created, practically from scratch. Identity isn't looking back at one's grandparents. In America we can't look elsewhere except within ourselves to discover our identity, which is why the American search for identity is quite different from that of the Welsh or the Chinese.

Should we speak of creating our identity rather than discovering it? Americans have an utterly greater freedom than people in other countries; we don't have the same cultural boundaries. Therefore the need is practically to invent oneself. The word "discover" suggests that the identity is already there, lying like a diamond or a snake in the grass. But you don't know that something is a diamond unless you know other things, i.e., that there is a difference between a diamond and a rock. Let us not make too sharp a distinction between "discovering" and "creating." Maybe one does both. What we need to do is bring the pioneering tradition of Americans into the search for identity. Americans miss on a very profound level that necessity to create one's identity.

FOR YOUR OWN SAKE

If you asked someone, "What is your sense of identity?" and she said, "I identify with the poor like St. Theresa," or "I identify with the absolutely helpless," she would be defining a rather limited identity. On the other hand, the person who replies, "I have my identity. I live in Westchester County, have three Cadillacs and three gardeners," is not going to care about other people unless he/she discovers that for the sake of his/her own human identity he/she ought to be thinking of somebody beyond him/herself. In the same way, Americans are not going to care for somebody else until they realize that to discover their own identity they should care for somebody else. One of the things Americans miss today is the opportunity to define themselves, to define who *I am*. Because of our particular historical past, becoming someone new, starting afresh, is part of what we miss.

There is no use urging Americans to care about others. If, on the other hand, an American thinks that for the sake of his/her identity, he/she should care about others, he/she will begin to care about others. In other words, not for the sake of others but for the sake of his/her identity. It has a lot to do with self. We are not trying to demean Americans by saying this. We are recognizing an American characteristic that is deeply rooted in the history of our country, and at the same time challenging Americans to recognize that we have not defined ourselves. Instead we have allowed ourselves to be defined by what others think of us. We want to advance beyond conformity to majority opinion—something that Tocqueville recognized as an American weakness 150 years ago. We are suggesting to Americans that for the sake of how we think about ourselves, for the sake of our own self-concept, we must recognize the necessity of defining ourselves.

SELF-CONCEPT

There is a crucial difference between self-concept and self-interest. It is necessary to recognize the contradiction in Americans: that, on the one hand, we are always affirming our individuality, and on the other hand, in crucial situations, we actually behave more like a mob than like individuals who think for ourselves and have opinions which we respect in ourselves. If you talk to Americans individually, what they say is often of value. But the moment they get with their peers, they begin to exemplify the mass mind. We have to break them of this by accepting and affirming the idea of self-concept as an advanced concept rather than just a selfish concept. We are not trying to promote "selflessness." There is a difference between interest in self and self-interest. Interest in self is inquiring into one's own psyche, one's psychic and human needs, whereas self-interest is catering to one's selfishness.

The tendency of radicals has been to think of society as a mass rather than as comprised of creative individuals who are the only ones who can create a positive society. We are coming closer to this. Even the phrase "socially responsible individual" is inadequate because it suggests that we can take the individual as he/she is and plaster some social responsibility on him/her, when he/she hasn't redefined his/her self.

If we agree that psychic hunger exists, we can also agree that it does not exist, in the sense that people are not aware of it. They are not driven by it consciously as they are driven by belly hunger. Some people are obviously much more aware of psychic hunger than others. Young people in particular are driven to try to satisfy it in various ways, by drugs, by sex, by music, by forming collectives. In most people it is overshadowed by belly hungers.

What are the barriers to recognizing psychic hunger? Is it ignorance of the satisfactions that the recognition and fulfillment of this hunger might bring? If so, perhaps we could tell people about looking at this hunger and how satisfying it would make their lives more meaningful. Are the material things around us a barrier? In earlier less advanced societies people have tried to satisfy their material and spiritual needs, but they have never satisfied their material needs so abundantly that these overshadowed their spiritual needs.

COMPLAINING

Maybe the main thing that keeps people from recognizing their psychic hunger is the act of complaining. People complain so much about all the things that are so terrible in our society: crime, distrust, atrocity after atrocity, how youth treat their parents and parents treat their kids, how men treat women, how whites treat blacks. The very act of complaining puts people into the framework of expecting somebody else to do something about the situation—the framework of seeing themselves as exploited and dependent on others, hence deprived of their own will. This is the most detrimental consequence of thinking constantly in terms of exploitation and victimization. As long as people complain, their psychic hunger cannot become a driving force. They cannot become involved as "I" or "we"—only as "me" or "us."

Should we counterpose psychic needs to material needs? There are many examples of human beings who have chosen to satisfy their spiritual or psychic needs over and above their need for bread. When people used to say, "I want to settle down," they meant they wanted to stop wandering, they wanted a "place." Nobody would have called that "satisfying psychic hunger." But that was what it was. The average person hasn't put a name to this need. People don't say, "I want to satisfy my psychic hunger," any more than they say, "I want socialism rather than capitalism." It is usually somebody from the outside (someone used to conceptualizing) who puts a tag on what people do. When people say, "I wish I could go out on the streets at night without worrying," or, "I wish we could all get together on Thanksgiving the way we used to," they are expressing their psychic hunger.

In India the average guy or gal might be ready to kill you if you talked about psychic hunger versus belly hunger. They have belly hunger, that is what they believe should be satisfied, and correctly so. The development of man/woman is the development of doing something about human needs, not the emancipation of "fallen angels." You are not aware of psychic hunger when you are desperately trying to satisfy belly hunger. Therefore psychic hunger is a luxury in India. But in the Western world now that we can have two chickens in every pot, we are still unsatisfied. We haven't begun to approach a basic psychic need within the human species which has never up to now had the opportunity to express itself so powerfully in the average person because we were too busy collecting bananas or going to work. But now we recognize that this is an enormous need, which in a certain sense was recognized by Marx when he said in effect, let's get rid of capitalism and free man to develop new social relationships. In this country we are free to develop these relationships.

Mao is trying to bring about this tremendous leap in China. He doesn't want to wait five hundred years until the Chinese have satisfied or oversatisfied their material needs so that they can begin to see inside themselves another need. The Chinese have been lucky because they could see what has occurred in other countries, and particularly the U.S. Mao also talks about belly hunger. But he is saying, "If we learn how to build satisfactory internal social relationships, we will also discover how to satisfy belly hunger—rather than the other way around," That is why in the three struggles: class struggle, struggle for production, and struggle for scientific experiment, class struggle is always given priority. In other words, struggling for the appropriate social relationships comes first.

IT STARTS WITH WHAT "I" MISS

What do people mean by the expression "man does not live by bread alone," except that we have spiritual needs, emotional needs that go beyond belly needs? We have to get people talking in a completely different way about what is wrong: that is, in terms of what they miss in life. This is much more important than, for example, listing the benefits that socialism might bring to people. Actually the material things we own point up rather than conceal the things we miss in our lives—as proven by the kids who flee from the suburbs. So we don't say, "Get rid of those material things," although people might want to do this when they begin to think in a different way. The individual him/herself begins to see the contradiction.

We are trying to establish some communication with this psychic hunger in people. If a person says, "I do miss something," we can ask what. Unless people miss something in their lives, they are not going to do anything. It starts with "I"—"I miss comradeship on this block" or "I miss love." You can ask, "What do you mean by love?" or "What do you expect from love?" There are a whole lot of questions which we can pursue from this concept of "missing." What we are trying to do is persuade each person that he/she is a participant in the change from the way things are. We are trying to get people away from the "contemplative" attitude that Marx denounces in the Ninth Thesis on Feuerbach when he said, "Philosophers have only contemplated the world, the thing is to change it." But we are not talking about rushing into practice either, which is the interpretation radicals have given to this thesis. The main thing is to get away from this attitude of objectivity, that what is wrong is over there, that somebody else is doing things to us, and we are only victims.

Most people today do miss the sense of trust, the sense of belonging to a community, the comradeship they used to feel in the community. Youth in the same community miss the sense of guidance from their parents, they miss the feeling that their parents have things to tell them that they don't know. They miss contact with older people with whom they can communicate. Willie and Joe in Bill Mauldin's World War II cartoons had a deep comradeship because they suffered exactly the same things together although one was a coalminer's son and the other a rich man's son. They shared two goals, to stay alive and to kill Germans—not as instruments of foreign policy but to stay alive. Then there was the Resistance Movement in which again people were united by a commonality of goals. That is what the youth miss today. They don't have a commonality of goals. They have only the commonality of rejection. When people talk nostalgically about the 1960s, they are referring (for example) to the Freedom Movement in the South which had a clear common goal.

A lot of people say, "When we didn't have anything, we were together more than now." Most of us thought that what we have today would satisfy our human needs because we thought our human needs were only material ones. What we are discovering is that our human needs involve much more.

A lot of people, not all of them young, have been looking to the East because they think they can discover in Buddhism or Taoism the things that they miss in the West. The search to discover the answers to one's psychic needs in the West by going to the Orient is an escape, posing the solution of psychic needs in the next life or nirvana instead of in society. Our problem is how to answer the questions, Do psychic needs exist? How do you recognize them? How do you satisfy them? without encouraging people to hole themselves up and wait until the resurrection. Many young people recognize these needs but don't relate them to the actual life of men and women here and now. They recognize that their minds are hungry and they try to fill their minds by contemplating the infinite. We have been talking about general needs, which can be made quite concrete—comradeship, for example, is something you can conceptualize in terms that are both historical and concrete. A person can identify with a need like this emotionally, which is very important. It is more important to recognize a need before talking about how to satisfy it. The doing must follow, but it depends upon the recognition of the need in the first place.

WHAT DOES IT MEAN TO CARE?

In *Love and Will* Rollo May says there are four kinds of love in the Western tradition: "One is *sex,* or what we call lust, libido. The second is *eros,* the drive of love to procreate or create—the urge, as the Greeks put it, towards higher forms of being and relationship. A third is *philia,* or friendship, brotherly love. The fourth is agape or *caritas,* as the Latins called it, the love which is devoted to the welfare of the other, the prototype of which is the love of God for man. Every human experience of authentic love is a blending, in varying proportions, of these four."

All four are relationships. People who talk about sexual freedom are rarely talking about relationships to other people; they are usually talking about their own freedom, about orgasms rather than the multiple facets of the human personality which are involved in all human relationships. Because a whole lot of people have looked at relationships between men and women purely in terms of sexual freedom, it becomes possible for some people to produce *Deep Throat,* which makes a lot of money because this attitude already exists in our society towards the relationship of men and women.

When Han Suyin was asked about the Chinese attitude toward sex, she said that in China if a man beats his wife, it is considered a social relationship and the community should interfere. But when it comes to sexual relations between individuals, the Chinese consider these private, not public matters, not matters for public titillation, public celebration or public intervention. That is a very important distinction. It is a shame that we have reached the point in this country that we talk so much about these questions and involve the courts in so much argument about them, trying to decide what is obscenity. Why do we have so much obscenity in this society that we have to spend so much time deciding what it is? There is something wrong with us and with this society. There is no point in dealing with legalities until we deal with ourselves.

As revolutionists we start with the idea that there isn't any such "thing" as obscenity: that there are all kinds of obscenities which each of us is capable of and which have nothing whatsoever to do with sex. Obscenity is a flagrant contravention of what should be social relationships. We can't expect the Supreme Court to issue an edict on that but we should be able to. People spend so much time talking about and seeing *Deep Throat* because we are not spending our time thinking about more important things, because nobody knows what is really more important. People who say that sex is one of the primal urges in life are not saying anything very important because that has been true of every non-hermaphroditic organism that has ever lived on this earth. It doesn't tell us anything about a man or a woman. What is important about human sexuality is the attitude to it, the human acceptance of it as the creation and expression of our selves.

When we begin to think how we should live like human beings, we have to try to put it together with the fact that for 50,000 years, millions of human beings have lived quite differently from the way we do. What makes us think we are so right? Therefore our answer has to embody a lot more than almost anybody in the U.S. is capable of embodying. At the same time we recognize that for the last 5000 years since the rise of the state, there has been a subjugation of women by men in the sense that the governing bodies have been exclusively male. We are coming out of this situation for the first time, so that we are able to look at the relationships between men and women differently.

For there to be really new relationships, men have to be involved in their determination as well as women. In this area, as in others where there has been oppression, it can't only be the oppressed who make all the decisions. Otherwise we are still thinking in terms of victims and victors, rather than all of us moving to a new and higher level. All we do is change the sex of the victims. We also have to challenge women to participate fully in the creation of new relationships for the entire society and not see themselves only as victims, urging them to hold up their half of the sky. Otherwise we continue to confine them to "kitchen politics."

These relationships in the past had a certain validity in the objective circumstances. Now we are moving to a stage of development where they have no validity. So we really are in trouble now.

Take the question of marriage. Obviously it was men who in the past said that women should not have relationships with other men outside of marriage, even as the men were having these relationships. Obviously it was one-sided. But more than onesidedness is involved. Should two people having come together be faithful to one another? What does illegitimate mean? It is illegitimate when people just screw and don't give a damn whether they see one another again. All kinds of soldiers have this illegitimate attitude, for example. In *Whatever Became of Sin?*, Menninger says that we have defined legitimacy only in terms of the law, so that illegitimacy must be proved in a court of law, requiring judges, lawyers, juries, etc., and must also be proved beyond a shadow of a doubt, which means the possibility of acquittal for many who have actually committed crimes. We have left the judgment of what is right and wrong to the courts; therefore we are in a lot of trouble. If something hasn't been proved by the courts to be illegitimate, we can't judge it to be wrong.

There are all kinds of ways to think and to feel, and there are all kinds of ways in which men and woman have lived, including monogamy and polygamy. And none of them is right just because it existed. Our question now is what do *we* think is the way people should live. What do we consider the right way to try to relate to one another here in America? At the same time that we talk about how to live here in America, we must have an idea of what it means in terms of global society and the human species. We can't make a revolution here in America unless somehow or other we can persuade Americans that there are more people on this planet that matter, and more thoughts, more history, more tradition, more concepts than those that grew up here in America. There is a thin line between thinking globally, which we must do, and thinking that on the shoulders of Americans rests the leadership of the world. We have to understand the danger of slipping over this line.

The Middle Kingdom idea that the Chinese have had of themselves for so many centuries has given them a self-centeredness which in this world of global interconnections is very valuable because they don't feel driven to involve themselves in the affairs of other people. It is also a danger because they don't feel the same need to wonder about countries as Americans do.

How is it that in the British Isles, the Irish who hate everybody else, the Scots and Welsh who hate everybody but Scots and Welsh, and the English who don't hate anybody because they just feel superior, have managed to maintain their incredible relationship? Maybe they all had the same background of intense individualism—but apparently also an ability to understand and respect a comparable background of intense individualism in others. That doesn't exist anywhere else in the world. It is this notion of respect that permits them to live together. It is connected to the fact that the British have retained their aristocracy and that there was a peculiar relationship of the capitalist to the landed aristocracy that expressed itself in the educational system, language, and so on. Now that this is gone, we don't know what is going to happen to the United Kingdom in the next hundred years.

No one country is going to determine the direction of the globe absolutely. The American revolution has to project ideas that the whole world will take serious note of, but this doesn't mean the American revolution will project ideas which the whole world will adopt.

There have been many ideas of the proper relationship between men and women. We have to consider these before we rush to a concept of what we would consider the best relationship. It is a must that to advance the human species, we must develop new relationships between men and women. Should men have the rights to lovers and women not have these rights? We think not. These are questions which touch people very deeply. The relationship between men and women—how crucial is it to revolutionary thinking? We don't say that better relations between people will be determined by better relations between men and women, but that better relations between men and women will spring from an idea of better relationships between people, so both men and women will say, "The relations between the sexes up to now have been a ridiculous expression of subjective idiocy."

Better relationships between men and women will develop when men and women together envisage and attempt to create a better relationship between people. When men and women discover that the relationships between people, men and men, men and women, women and women, are barbaric and well beneath the standards which human beings should be striving for, then we will begin to have better relationships between men and women. But the discovery has to be made by men and women, or we will never advance to the next stage. Unless women hold up their half of the sky in making these discoveries, the whole sky will collapse and all of us with it. Women must play a positive and total role. Until individuals irrespective of sex begin to wonder why we maintain our present relations with one another, not only between the sexes but between races and religious groups, as in Northern Ireland, we are not going to solve any questions at all.

WHAT IS PROMISCUITY?

How does one apply the notion of social responsibility to sex? The Puritans believed that you shouldn't have sex with anyone until you got married. The Pope says exactly the same thing. When we talk about social responsibility, we are talking about a total sense of responsibility, not just in relation to sex but to how you drive a car, take care of the dog, relate to your brothers and sisters. What are you willing to give up of your own for the social good? This is the crucial question. As long as you think that nothing is greater than your own good, you can't have a sense of responsibility.

At certain times responsibility within one aspect of life becomes such a crucial issue that through discussing it we are able to illuminate what social responsibility means, e.g., the relation between men and women, welfare, work.

How does one persuade somebody that communication isn't consummated by screwing one another—which is where we are today? Why do so many people think that sex is the first and last form of communication? How does one shift the role of sex in social relationships so that it isn't considered the ultimate form of communication? One has to have a notion of other forms of community. We have to start with thoughts about human relationships, to view relationships between people in a more human way so that we can view sexual relationships more humanly. If someone says that to overcome our present fragmentation, we should all sit down and smoke pot, we can't propose the illegalization of pot. We have to have a positive approach to new relationships and not just talk about what chemicals will do to your body. We have to make clear that a person who relies upon chemicals today is not asking him/herself the necessary and difficult questions.

When the Pope said that people shouldn't have sex except for the purpose of parenthood, he invested the sex act with responsibility, whatever you may think of what he said. It made people think. Today we have found a way to have sex without thinking and therefore a way for people to have sex without thinking of consequences.

What should one think about sex? First of all, you should think that sex is a relationship which does have consequences, as all relationships do, and therefore you should enter into sexual relationships in a socially responsible way. The unit of responsibility at the very minimum must be the two parties involved. A lot of things happen today in regard to sex which are based upon a completely unilateral approach. "I don't give a damn if I give someone VD. My pleasure is all that is involved." Caring is a form of social responsibility. It is a vague but very important concept. One isn't going to solve the sex question by caring just about the sex question but by caring about every other question. It isn't possible to talk about caring in the sex relationship without talking about caring in every other relationship.

In order to be against sexual promiscuity, one has to be against promiscuity in all relationships. To know what you want and to make choices is the opposite of promiscuity. Promiscuity is acting without choice, whether sexual, or intellectual or in the use of violence. If somebody says, "Why the hell should I care who I knock up?" we shouldn't answer, "Because of the population explosion," but rather that if you encourage this promiscuous approach to sex, you are also encouraging a promiscuous approach to everything else. We are not saying that young people shouldn't have sex, but that they should have sex with some consciousness rather than because "everybody is doing it and it's the thing to do when you're out with your peers, and if you don't, you're a square or not communicating."

Promiscuity means essentially a complete absence of discrimination, of choice, of putting a human value on yourself and what you are doing. In that sense the promiscuity so prevalent in sex today is clearly an expression of the complete devaluation that people have made of themselves, of one another, and of all human relationships. Promiscuity in the past has been much less pervasive, much less a constantly increasing phenomenon. That is why it is so important to look at promiscuity as much more than a sexual phenomenon. Once we begin to look at it in this light, what we now call freedom of sexual expression might then begin to assume completely different forms. What we call freedom of sexual expression today has in it the same lack of values that is in everything else. That is why it takes the form of hard-core pornography. We don't even really know what the free human expression of sex might be, once we were freed of the pervasive devaluation of human beings. One of the reasons why we object to the word "duty" or "ought" and instead use the word "is" or the phrase "essentially is" is that it is so easy to slip into moralisms, pure exhortations. Our aim is to challenge constantly and consciously people to wonder *themselves* about what would be a more human attitude to themselves and to other people.

OPPENHEIMER AND THE BOMB

An old tale describes Confucius as living in a cave in a valley where fundamentally nothing had been changed for 2000 years. So, precisely because nothing had changed economically or materially, Confucius was freed to think about man/woman. Since then human beings have been wondering what you should change and how should you go about it. In a sense this has all culminated in the story of *Lawrence and Oppenheimer* (by Nuel Pharr Davis), a piece of superb writing.

We are at a new place, different from anywhere anyone has ever been before. All of a sudden we realize the unity of the planet, the unity of man/womankind. We can make a cinder out of the whole planet, wipe everybody out equally. Suddenly everything has become one: We realize the oneness of humanity, the humanness of the human mind, the responsibility that devolves on the human mind. We can't fool around any more.

Nothing is impossible any more, it just hasn't been done. The question that faces us all from now on is, "Should something be done because it can be done?" Most of those on the Los Alamos project said, "We are trying the impossible" but they all tried it. Oppenheimer was a remarkable choice to head the project. Most of the others on it didn't have thoughts like his.

They were faced with the fact that Germany was working on the same bomb—who was going to get it first? They were faced with a crucial decision. "The bomb is a murderous thing, the world shouldn't have it. That is what we think, but not what the Germans think." Under what compulsions does one do horrible things? It will probably never happen again in the same way that people work on this kind of thing.

That experience was the last we needed to recognize that we can't make decisions that way. Now decisions affect everybody. Physically we can do everything, but morally we have to make choices as to what we do, precisely because we can do everything. Should one contemplate destroying the world which is all we have—on the pretext of saving the world? That is the dilemma posed by the bomb.

We have a long history of men and women destroying other men and women in the name of ideals. For the first time, with the aim of trying to develop a weapon to defend ourselves against others who are likewise concerned with this, we have arrived at the ultimate weapon, the weapon that can destroy man/womankind.

LEARNING FROM THE PAST

We must learn how not to be metaphysical with regard to the past—not to make moral judgments about the past like Monday morning quarterbacks. Radicals and Trotskyites in particular spend a lot of time judging people in the past with a "holier than thou" attitude. We have to learn a quality of generosity in regard to the past, not for the sake of those in the past but for our own sakes.

What can we learn from Los Alamos? One thing is the difference between Lawrence and Oppenheimer. Lawrence could never have mobilized the human and imaginative qualities necessary to produce the bomb the *first* time. To produce the bomb the first time required more than an experimental physicist working with equipment. It required a person with a tradition in the humanities, a speculative theoretical mind, an individual able to elicit cooperation from people. It was this combination which enabled Oppenheimer to bring out the best in his team of workers.

The next thing is the enormous dilemma in which the bomb placed this imaginative creative human being: that he had been able to create this thing but had not really thought through the consequences. Therefore we should learn from this, not to judge him but that we must never again create things of such vast planetary consequences without bringing in other judgments which are essentially ethical.

How do we answer Oppenheimer's dilemma, not in terms of what he should have done but what we should do, learning from him and seeing also that it is ridiculous to believe that somehow one can go back and play that game again?

In 1945 most atomic scientists were thinking, "Suppose the Germans get the bomb ahead of us." That is what they meant by "consequences." When the bomb went off, Oppenheimer wept because he knew we had moved into another stage of responsibility. We can now destroy man/womankind. For the first time we are compelled to wonder what responsibilities we are ready to undertake.

We learn a lot by looking at political people like Martin Luther King, Nkrumah, Malcolm. We have also to learn from looking at people like Oppenheimer who was in a political dilemma even though he was not a political person. We should see his tragedy as our legacy. If a black man can say, "I am not going to look at the past simply in terms of slavery," then we should be able to look at Oppenheimer's dilemma and learn from it.

For ourselves we must be absolutely clear and project to others the absolute necessity to make technological decisions that have planetary consequences with the deepest consideration for the ethical parameters. That may not sound new but we must use every opportunity to deepen our understanding of what it means.

This book is so moving because it describes a world-historical event after which everybody's thinking, consciously or unconsciously, is altered. After Los Alamos war is no longer the same. People can now do what the gods could never do—kill everyone.

It is not only a question of issues, e.g., ban the bomb or don't bomb Vietnam. When a really great historical event takes place, the way that people think, their attitudes toward important questions—their outlook on life—are all altered. When Galileo said, "I am sorry but the sun doesn't go around the earth" and was unwilling to get burned at the stake, that affected a few hundred thousand people. But the dilemma created by the bomb forces everybody on the planet to think. The Chinese may say they want the bomb for different reasons but they are thinking.

Einstein said, "When man split the atom, he changed everything but the human mind." Man/woman has made everything technologically possible, but our capacities, our human capacities have not been altered. Therefore what is necessary now is to develop our human capacities to correspond to our extraordinary technological capacities. Los Alamos compels us to look at the way we have to change.

This change is only possible when some particular people begin to persuade others to change their minds. Two ways in which our minds have changed in order to correspond with revolutionary change in technological capacities: *The Bulletin of Atomic Scientists* which expresses the determination of atomic scientists no longer to separate technological questions from political questions; and we ourselves. We are attempting to transform politics completely, refusing to continue in the value-free tradition of Machiavelli, insisting that the main contradiction in the U.S. is between technological overdevelopment and moral underdevelopment. Ruskin, William Morris, Marx (and especially the young Marx) all recognized that the Industrial Revolution would bring contradictions. But the *Bulletin of Atomic Scientists* expresses the recognition of such contradictions by those who are themselves the most extreme embodiment of technological development. They are saying, "*We* have to begin thinking differently." That is different than people from outside looking in.

What is the difference between those who made the bomb and those who put the first man on the moon? The guys who went up to the moon don't seem to be thinking about it as a dilemma. A lot of people discuss the pros and cons of going to the moon but chiefly in terms of money. Should one spend the money on inner space or outer space? Whereas when the bomb was created, the people involved became conscious of their human responsibilities in a new way. And it caused an important internal split. In relation to outer space, scientists talk about measuring the effects of non-gravity, whether spider webs weave in space, and so on. It all sounds so hygienic, but you can't talk about the bomb that way.

In the course of human development there come cataclysmic moments when humankind is faced with things on a larger scale than ever before. Los Alamos was one of those moments in history, compelling man/woman to wonder about our humanity, not about technology. The bomb going off made it necessary perhaps for the first time in history for people to think of themselves not as Americans or French or Sicilians but as human beings making crucial decisions. The bomb created that milestone.

We can now look at ourselves in a different way, as the only ones who can save the world—or destroy it.

If Lawrence had invented the bomb rather than Oppenheimer, it would have been that much more difficult to recognize the consequences of its invention. That is why Oppenheimer was so attacked. The politicians understood Lawrence because they were like him. But because it was Oppenheimer, men/women were given a fantastic opportunity to discover something about ourselves. This is the first time in history that men/women have been faced with our fate on a planetary scale.

THE SPIRITUAL ATOM BOMB

Instead of the physical atom bomb, we must use the spiritual atom bomb of ideas. That is what the Vietnamese did in appealing to the world against the U.S. counter-revolution in Vietnam. They won the hearts and minds of the people of the world to their cause. In making available to the rest of the world what they are learning about the concrete building of socialism, the Chinese are also using a spiritual atom bomb. From 1940 to the present day, beginning with the European Resistance and the people's anti-Japanese war in China, we have seen the developments of wars based upon ideas. The principal factor has been ideology, not weapons.

A great nation can't be controlled by fear. Russians were afraid they were going to be attacked by everybody else, so they did things like over-run the Baltic countries. Because we have not started to think differently in this country, the U.S. still thinks of protecting copper mines in Chile. *We* say, "Let the ideas fight themselves out."

Resistance to invasion is the only legitimate use of military weapons, whether by a small or large nation. If we came to power, we would dissolve SAC immediately, precisely in order to demonstrate our conviction that we must be thinking differently about global interests if we are going to have a decent world. McGovern retreated on the question of global interests because he was afraid of antagonizing people. But a leadership which is ready to lead people must be ready to take positions which may antagonize the majority of people, or may even get you thrown out. In fact, maybe you ought to say or try things which would get you thrown out—in order to confront people with their need to change.

Differences between nations must be settled by ideological (rather than physical) struggle. That is what we are going to struggle for and try to persuade people to accept, knowing how difficult it will be for them to do and knowing the enormous past which bogs us down. That is what *putting politics in command of the military means today in international relations.* For the advanced nations Los Alamos posed this question for the first time.

WHAT IS SELF-DEFENSE?

If we had power, we would state some general principles in regard to the relationships between nations which we believe are correct in a universal sense, and then we would implement them unilaterally.

For example, we believe in self-defense. But what does self-defense mean? At one time the oceans were considered adequate means of self-defense. Only in the last few years have we discovered the technology which makes us wonder what are defensive and what are offensive weapons. You can't have 400 Polaris missiles for self-defense and then say that we wouldn't dream of having 450 because that would be offensive weaponry.

The character of the modern world has made it ridiculous to think that you can defend yourself through developed technological apparatus, e.g., Polaris submarines. When we say a nation has the right to defend itself, what we are saying is that we believe in national boundaries, and that if you are invaded, you have the right to defend yourself. That is a political, not a military position. We believe in nations—in areas for which people assume responsibility: Any weapons that could be seriously effective outside your own boundaries are weapons of offense.

The important point is to establish principles and then apply those principles within your sphere of responsibility which is your own nation. To attempt, first, to persuade other nations of this leads one into the type of negotiations and power relations which at this stage do not advance these principles but rather provide the arena within which all the old power relations are perpetuated.

It is impossible to solve any problems in America without thinking of the rest of the world. We have not only the technology but produce almost all the food. Do we say to the American farmers, "Cut your production in half because we don't want to sell food to the rest of the world and keep them dependent on us"? Then what is the American taxpayer going to do to support the American farmer? In producing 60 percent of the food of the world, the American farmer has not only been keeping millions from starving to death but has also increased the dependence of these millions on the U.S. and at the same time expanded American production, American profits and the American standard of living. We tend to think of victimization as a static situation, whereas it is a relationship which is self-perpetuating. When you help somebody, you may also help them to become a victim. What then does one do? Just say, "We have been victimizing you all this time; now starve so that you can face your own responsibilities." Or can we ask Americans to do something different because what we have done is make others more dependent?

If the Americans don't have a 200 mile fishing limit, they won't starve to death, even though they may have to reduce their standard of living. But if the Peruvians don't have a 200 mile fishing limit, they will starve to death. Can't we say to Americans, "Doesn't that mean anything to you—or don't you give a damn?" That question can't be answered economically. The only way to answer is to think in terms of human beings. What do you want Peruvians to live on if Americans fish up all the fish? That means facing Americans with their responsibilities to make some choices. Why can't we accept a twelve mile fishing limit for ourselves and a 200 mile fishing limit for Peruvians?

We must all begin to *do,* even if with less efficiency and with a lower standard of living.

TODAY'S LION'S DENS

This summer we are beginning anew, not with what we are *against* but what we are *for,* not rejections but projections. We are searching for the fundamentals, the elements of the new. We have been searching in unexplored territory, and some of it has seemed hit and miss.

We have stressed what the founding fathers were doing in 1787–89 more than in 1776, that is, seeking a better way for people to live together. But they were doing it for *their* world, the world of the 1780s, expressing this as profoundly as they were able to do at that time, while we have to do it for *our* world, the world of the 1980s.

We have stressed the need for a certain kind of people, those interested in ideas, capable of passionate conviction, and concerned to persuade others to examine their own ideas and explore other ideas. We believe that this kind of person is to be found in the community as much, if not more, than among intellectuals who have a careerist interest in ideas.

How do we persuade others to become participants in this search, to become aware of their psychic hunger? We have suggested that this might be done by asking people what do you miss in life? rather than by asking them what is wrong?—which leads to complaints and blaming others or just trying to get others off your back.

We have been going back to the basic social groupings in which people have lived together and learned how to live together—families, communities, nations, looking at these not in terms of Marx's concepts of history as class struggle or of exploited versus exploiters but in terms of man/woman's search for community—better ways to live together.

Some people think of "we" as just my immediate family. For others it means their community, race, or sex—or only those who agree with them. Most people who think of human beings as "we" still think of human beings on one side and the environment on the other. When we look at the pictures of Earth taken from outer space, we should be able to see that we and our environment are inseparable. We belong to a common unit of survival. We have to see ourselves in an alienated relationship with nature rather than as part of nature. They talk of a battle with nature, forgetting that even if we win that battle, we would find ourselves on the losing side. If we are not going to lose that battle, we have to change a lot of ideas about ourselves.

Freud in the nineteenth century was trying to make man/woman realize that their biology and their psychology were much more interrelated than we realized. He focused on sex as a manifestation of our biological nature.

In a sense what Freud did for sex, Marx did for the belly. Against the young Hegelian idealists who lived in the realm of ideas, he tried to relate man/woman to our biological nature. But when, in the *Communist Manifesto*, he said that as a result of capitalism, "all that is holy is profaned and man must face with sober senses his conditions of life and his relations with his kind," he was not talking about the belly at all.

We are beginning to discover that maybe the ancients or the

American Indians knew a lot of things that were sacred which had nothing to do with the belly. In fact they were willing to starve to death for these because they were qualities or relationships that had developed within man/woman when we crossed the threshold of reflection. How do we persuade people of the importance of these? How do we get back to these without saying that "I can't eat steak unless everybody in the world is eating steak?" which is a quantitative notion? How does one think "I can't go to bed happy at night unless I am at peace with the things that are sacred to me."

Maybe it is necessary to go backward materialistically. Maybe it is our job to persuade people that this is not going backwards at all but that in a spiritual way it is going forwards—in terms of things that human beings have always held most sacred. Maybe people can realize that mobility isn't what I am looking for. I am looking for place. How do we project to people that if we want some of the things we miss in life, like community and comradeship, we have to accept a diminution in material things?

We have to arrive at the point where we can be very free without being afraid of being called Jesus freaks or reactionaries. If a bourgeois like John Gardner comments on the environment, we don't have to say that he can't possibly mean it or that he can't do anything about it because he is a reactionary, but rather that what he is saying we will have to face eventually.

How do we persuade ourselves first of all that "man/woman does not live by bread alone"? And if not by bread alone, what is it other than bread that man/woman lives by?

HISTORY AS STRUGGLE

One of the things we have been trying to say this summer is that instead of seeing history as class struggle, we must see it as a continuing struggle to create human social relationships, and that the struggle for those has been as important, most of the time more important, than the struggle for material things. If we don't see this throughout the history of humanity, we will think that it is only yesterday that man/woman got rid of the belly hunger and caught on to psychic hunger, and we will not understand this psychic hunger deeply enough. Insofar as we have accomplished anything, it is because we have recognized that the very family unit has been an expression of the human need for community and that human needs cannot be compartmentalized into material needs on the one side and spiritual needs on the other. We look at the family unit not in terms of exploitation but of the positive human need for community because we look at history and the basic struggles of society in a different way.

We have to be careful not to idealize existing families or former families or existing or former communities. We are talking about the need for community which has been manifested in human development. The idea of community is not just something we pulled out of our hats. But you can't just create a family or a community from your idea or your ideal of a family or community. We have to start from what *is*, from the communities within which we live and from the contradictions which are either destroying them or can possibly lead to a transformation of these communities.

We have stressed the difference between networks and communities. Networks are the criss-crossings created by and between individuals with common interests from various already existing communities. Communities tend to be conservative but they also contain prophetic elements which try to transform them—who are not to be confused with the "community agent."

Suburban communities tend to center around the raising of children. It is always easy to get a community together around the question of a light on the corner or a block party, but today we have to challenge people to create communities around issues and questions on a higher level.

Our discussions show how free we must make ourselves in order not to be limited by previous concepts. All previous revolutionaries have judged themselves by their perseverance and dedication in fighting *against* capitalism, and by how single-minded they were in their rejection of capitalism and being on the right side (that of the workers). We will judge ourselves rather by our perseverance and dedication in fighting *for* something, and if in the process of fighting for something, people discover how much they are against capitalism, then they will make a revolution against capitalism.

We have been discovering what we are fighting for on four levels: as individuals defining themselves anew, as families making new sets of values, as communities extending the human values discovered in the family, and as nations. The family, the community and the nation are all human social units which human beings have created in their struggles to create more appropriate relations among themselves.

Radicals are constantly trying to reach the human being from the economic standpoint. We are convinced that you can only arrive at the human by beginning with the human.

"SOUL"

If you have only so much territory and you have run as far as you can go until you reach the ocean and folks are crowding behind you, then you begin to realize that it may be necessary to restructure your relationships. That doesn't mean you are running backwards. The sheer quantity of people and the advances of technology have put us in this strange dilemma where we have to think of human relationships in different terms than the relatively simplistic answers of Karl Marx. Because we are the most technologically advanced people in the world and have enjoyed the highest standard of living, we are the first to discover through experience that "more" isn't "better." As of now in this country there is no concept of limit, no concept of enough, only the idea of "more." Somewhere along the line we have to introduce the concept of limit. The solution is not in science, it is how we look at "we."

Do we believe that there is an unlimited supply of energy for our knickknacks and gadgets? Do we believe that science is going to solve all our problems? Do we accept science as our God? What did Einstein really mean when he said that when man split the atom, he expanded everything but the human mind?

We could say that Einstein was absolutely correct, and then a man like Billy Graham comes along and says, "I agree with that; the reason we haven't discovered our minds is because we haven't discovered Jesus." How *does* one go about discovering what is in man/woman's mind or what this mind is? It isn't that we don't recognize Jesus who, according to Billy Graham, understood everything that is in man/woman's mind and in fact put everything there. Our problem is to persuade people that they have minds and that the most important thing human beings have done down through history was to use their minds. However, during the last couple of hundred years, we have been using our minds only scientifically and technologically, leaving out every other aspect of the human mind altogether. Now we have to rediscover our minds or our hearts or souls—*we should not be scared of the word "soul."* And after we discover that, we will have the courage to say to a Bolivian, "Don't be in such a rush to build an oil refinery or an eight-lane highway to Brasilia, that hair-raising manifestation of the misuse of the human mind."

How does one go about persuading each person that "you are a helluva lot nicer person than you think you are, than you believe is possible. You just don't know much about yourself." That is what the communes and the youth movement were trying to discover in their way, and we are trying to discover in another way.

We have to do it in a political framework, rather than just in a rebellious framework. We are trying to discover how to liberate people to think about their minds or their hearts or their souls, so that out of that liberation will come all kinds of forms of which we know nothing as yet. We may call these forms "socialism" or "communism" but we will never get them until people discover that they have to look inside themselves for what they miss in life and not outside themselves.

Up to now philosophers have understood that the human mind, in addition to functioning analytically and scientifically, functions in two other ways. We exercise moral judgment—which enables us to relate to our fellow human beings. This is the realm of social relationships, and morality essentially involves the creation of appropriate relationships with one's kind, putting a value judgment on one's relationships with one's kind. You have to have a certain concept of your humanity and of the history of humanity in order to establish these values.

Then there is aesthetic judgment which is essentially the recognition of the sacred or of the totality which is greater than man/woman. Because art expresses and appeals to such deep and as yet uncategorized feelings in people, it tells us more about the grandeur of which human beings are capable than any other use of the human mind.

Kant recognized these three aspects of mind: scientific reason, moral judgment and aesthetic judgment. Could we say that there is also a fourth capacity which is the capacity for politics, which on the basis of these three other aspects of mind, engages in discussion, debate and struggle in order to arrive at appropriate decisions in regard to social relations?

We have to begin by recognizing these capacities of the mind and that most human beings don't begin to exercise these capacities, which is why we must struggle to get people to utilize them.

If you asked a guy or gal on your block, "What does joy mean to you?" he/she would probably translate joy in terms of possessions. "I have my two beautiful children" or "I have a nice house, car." Not "I feel joy" or "I like looking at a plant growing." Our political job is to persuade people that the search for joy is, as it were, the aim of man/woman, and that if you constantly search for it in the wrong way, you will never get there. In order to get there, you have to look differently at practically everything you have ever looked at in your life. You can't look for it in material things, although, of course, you have to have bread and butter and shoes. But you have to look at things differently than you have looked at them up to now.

One of the great horrors of the socialist movement is that it has presupposed, in accordance with the "fallen angel" theory, that workers really understand all this and are only prevented from arriving at it because of the capitalist monkey on their backs. And for nearly 200 years everybody in the Western world—and by osmosis most of the rest of the people in the world—has been persuaded of this. So that we have barricaded ourselves against an investigation or a search for the basis of joy by assuming that it has something to do with the method of production or with what is produced. This is the watershed we have arrived at. So we (now) sound as if we were talking like the apostles, Matthew, Mark, Luke and John—but we are not. We are advancing the very latest scientific approach to man/woman, scientific in that we recognize that we have a mind and a heart and a soul. That is scientific.

We are confronting the *way* that we have been thinking, not confronting our minds as things. Mind is minding; it is a way of knowing, a way of thinking, a way of appreciating, and a capacity for thinking a million different ways. Most people don't utilize their minds for anything more than reacting. When man/woman crossed the threshold of reflection, we became the heirs and heiresses to a fantastic accumulation of values and forms none of which we really know anything about as yet. When we do beautiful things, it is because it is in our human nature to do these things, and when we don't, we are being false to our human nature. We are false to our human nature maybe 98 percent of the time.

When you get to the point of believing, as we do, that you have to confront people with the way that they have been thinking, particularly if they have been thinking that "all men are equal" or that everybody is entitled to anything he or she wants to do, you are bordering on impeachable offenses. You are not only confronting people, you are affronting them. We have to tell people in New York, for example, that there is a limit to our material expectations and that from now on it is not so much a choice between different forms of more as it is between different forms of less: And that in the process of making these choices, and only in such a process, will we have the opportunity to discover or re-establish those links with others that have been missing in our lives, because up to now we have chosen ways of life which preclude making these links even though our psyches cry for them.

How do we concretize this? What do we actually say to our friends and in our communities? Why shouldn't it be possible for us to talk to people with the same kind of passion and conviction that was in "the Sermon on the Mount?" We are not saying that we should go around like Jesus freaks. But we are at a period in history like that when Jesus was preaching that the rich person can't enter the kingdom of heaven: And he was appealing to people's psychic hunger. It was never so true as today that people can experience in their own lives that you can have three Cadillacs and ten fur coats and still be miserable because you lack that which is most essential for your humanity. We are not talking about going around the streets, saying "the end is at hand" or that everybody should love one another, as the flower children did essentially.

What does one say? Could we ask people "What are your values?" as a beginning—and if they answer: "whatever puts me ahead of everybody else" then we could say "your values stink."

Let's say the president makes a speech on TV and says, "We have to husband all our resources." Maybe five percent take him seriously and the rest say, 'f— it.' " He has all this power, the exposure on TV, and he gets a five percent response. Let's say one of us goes on TV. Would we say, "We have to husband our resources?" That is much too abstract. We would explain more exactly what it means to husband, why we have to do so, and why it is absolutely impossible for every single one listening to be richer tomorrow or have more goods or more energy at his/her disposal. The response would still be only five percent, but it might be a different five percent and they might have learned something different. We would also say that we don't just want agreement from individuals, even though there has to be agreement before we can move. "We want you to have a block meeting or church meeting to talk to others about this." There never is any effort to get people into this kind of political motion in the U.S. Instead what we always get next is legislation, and legislation doesn't influence people to think and practice what they think. What we should say is, "If you agree, don't write your Senator. To hell with your Senator. First of all, you have to internalize and believe what I have said so passionately that you want to go out and tell it to somebody else. That is what we call political action." We are saying, "this is the situation. We have to change our course completely; we are not going to get richer and richer. Now let's start a movement to face everybody with this situation. Every one of us is participant in this. You can't delegate it to somebody else, and you can't blame somebody else."

Somebody has to say these things rather than just cheer people up because the GI Bill ran out or a project wasn't refunded. What we *don't* want to do is commiserate with people. We want to tell them, "You are only looking for your own private satisfactions and asking me to help you get your private satisfactions."

There have to be people in the community who can back up this kind of talk, people who have confidence in the capacity of other people to change. One has to say more than "you're not going to get richer"; one has to be quite specific—to say, for example, "Every community in the U.S. is not going to get new housing. You are going to have to keep up those you have, paint the house you are living in, and you are not going to be able to move into another community and benefit from what they have done to keep their community up and run away from what you have done to put your community down. It is time you put your roots down and re-made your own community." Maine citizens can't say, "We don't want an oil refinery here but we need more heating oil, so let's put one in the state of Delaware." That is an impermissible thought. You have to make up your own mind that if you want to use oil, the oil refinery has to go up in Maine. You have to pay the price of what you want.

We have to know that what we are saying goes beyond generalization. It isn't enough to say that we are destroying the planet. Everybody can say that. We have to be so specific that the average guy or gal can understand that he/she plays a role in it, including the guy in the ghetto who wants to go to college. So one asks him, "Why do you want to go to college? To get a job at $18,000 a year?"

Husband your resources, don't destroy the planet, are so abstract that anybody can agree. The first thing to tell people is that what you are going to tell them is not what they want to hear. "But it is about time we started listening to things that we don't want to hear because we are going to have to face them anyway. We have to begin looking at ourselves as a community which is going to disagree about many questions before we can arrive at some kind of decisions. Questions of this kind are being faced all over the country in one form or other. Essentially it is the same question but each community, and each individual, has to begin looking at the world and what we have been doing differently."

From there we can begin dealing with specifics, e.g., the oil refinery. They either are willing to have the oil refinery in their own backyard or they are willing to live on less oil. All sorts of changes are coming in our lives. Eventually we will have to face all these questions in their totality but it is fortunate that this issue now allows us to look at concrete problems in a new way.

If we could do a lot of this kind of talking all over the place, we could begin to answer the question, How does one persuade people? The opportunities are enormous for this kind of confrontation. If we take the issues as they arise, then all the general questions we have been raising take on life and meaning.

What do we say to the teachers' union? "It is about time everybody stopped thinking that they are going to get theirs, that they can complain about inflation but think that *their* wages and *their* demands for more don't play a role in inflation." We really have to say the impeachable things. Twenty years ago, if somebody got up and made a speech like this at a union, you were a reactionary Birchite s.o.b. We have to confront the idea of unions as fundamentally an agglomeration of people with vested interests who don't give a goddamn about anybody else, particularly those who don't belong to unions, like housewives or old people or kids or the community. For maybe a hundred years the notion of the struggle to create unions was an enormously progressive struggle. Now we have to create something else. A direction can be progressive for a certain period of time and then become reactionary. To go forward today we have to go against some things that were progressive at one time. We have to do things which some people will think are backwards in order to go forward.

WALKING INTO THE LION'S DEN

We can't make a distinction between what we would say on TV and what one of us would say in the community or to our friends and co-workers. We should all be saying the same thing. It is so easy to think that when you are talking one-to-one with a friend or relative, you are dealing with personal or individual problems. But on the one-to-one level, we should be saying that if you want to solve your personal or individual problems, maybe you ought to start with the problems that are not personal and in that way solve your personal problem. The president should be saying this also. At this juncture we need to be clear enough in our own heads to be able to say this kind of thing, to a friend or at a teachers convention or a Teamsters convention. Raising big controversies is exactly what we need to do.

When we ask a worker whether he/she would take a cut in wages in order to lower prices, he/she is going to say, "They are not going to cut prices." It is always a question of "they"—and this is what we have to deal with.

We have to be willing to walk into the lion's den as well as talk one-to-one. Twenty and thirty years ago a lot of us walked into all kinds of lion's dens. Thirty-five years ago it was walking into the lion's den to say to the guys working at Ford, "We need a union." People got their heads knocked off for that. What is so difficult to realize is that the lion's den has to be a different kind of den at each stage of development. So that what we have to say now is entirely different from what we said thirty, forty years ago. This is part of the historical process. It was one thing for Marx in 1848 Europe still trying to evaluate the French Revolution, to have said that all history is the history of class struggle. To say the same thing today, at the end of the twentieth century, is like saying that history stops once you have socialism or communism. History goes on continuously; we are trying to discover the next stage of radical or philosophical or human history here in the U.S.—realizing also that we are surrounded by a world which is becoming more and more Americanized, Westernized.

One doesn't keep making the same speech in the same den. We are trying to discover what are the lion's dens today. Maybe it isn't the Rockefeller family or the Ford Motor Co. whose workers we are trying to organize against them. Maybe it is the workers themselves on the line or in the oilfields. So the speech is an entirely different one from the one we would have made twenty-five years ago. We are still searching for that speech, sure that fifty years from now someone will make a still different speech. We are not trying to guess what kind of speech they will make, because to some degree that speech depends upon the speeches we make today.

PROJECTIONS, NOT REJECTIONS

What we have been saying about the family and the community is still much too abstract. Up to this time, we, like most radicals, have believed that in order to establish a better society, all we have to do is smash up the present society.

We are not trying to reconstitute the family. It is bullshit to say that. We are saying that maybe in order to build a new society, in order to talk about new social relations concretely and not abstractly, in order not to be talking like evangelists or giving the impression that the human spirit is ephemeral like the holy ghost, we can use a molecular beginning like the family as an illustration of the kind of human relations that people have been seeking to establish over millions of years.

The difference between the Chinese and the Russian Revolutions is that in the Chinese Revolution the concept of building up the people, mobilizing them to develop and transform themselves, anticipates and precedes any questions of power and confrontation. The Chinese Revolution was successful because the party did not try to attribute to the masses its own abstractions.

When a radical asks us, "Which do you mean, the capitalist community or the socialist community?" we have to be able to reply confidently, "We are trying to build communities now, under capitalism, not because we accept capitalism but because unless we try to build something with people where we are, we and they can't discover what is wrong with capitalism except abstractly."

We are not saying that we don't give a damn what the Marxists think. What they think is not just what some screwy individuals think—the thinking of Marxists is not some crackpot thinking, but a thinking which has developed over the last 200 years in response to the French Revolution. It permeates the society and therefore it is unlikely that it doesn't influence us. It permeates those who are oppressed—it is the victim thinking.

We have to take the stand that if we cannot persuade people to think in this society about another way to live, if we can't, in this society, develop drives in people to want to live another way, then we will never be able to get rid of the inhuman relations within this society. We will always be prisoners of this society.

Richard Cloward and Frances Piven are perhaps the best examples of people who believe that you can get a new society by fucking up or smashing capitalism. Their strategy has been to get more and more people on welfare on the assumption that this will mess up the mechanisms of the capitalist system. We are absolutely opposed to that kind of thinking. As long as you do that kind of thinking, you increase the victim mentality of people, mess them up, and make it impossible for them to do anything to build a new society.

We are not trying to mess up capitalism. We are trying to get people to create communities—new relations which in the end will make it necessary for people to go beyond capitalism. We are not going to be deterred, for example, by those who say that trying to get people off welfare rather than on welfare means that we are supporting capitalism.

The first need is to get people moving in their minds, to believe that it is possible to live better—not that something or somebody else is the obstacle in the way of our living better. We are not trying to *raise* the political consciousness of the masses, as Lenin was trying to do and as most radicals in the U.S. are still trying to do, to recognize capitalism as the obstacle in the road to their getting the "Bread, Peace and Land" they want and need. We are trying to *change* the consciousness of the American people to recognize that what they have been wanting and still want is the greatest obstacle to their satisfying their deep human need for community and for new social relations.

Why is it so important to make this break in our thinking? Because for the last 200 years the French Revolution has been the model of revolution. Basically that model is based on the concept of the unity of opposites whereby the masses and the bourgeoisie overthrow feudalism, which then leads to the emergence of the antagonism between the masses and the bourgeoisie. This was the French scenario from 1789 to 1795 which was the background of Marx's thinking. That is why he put so much emphasis on the sans culottes. That is why C. L. R. James did so much work on the French Revolution. Basically it was the material wants of the oppressed masses and their demands which intensified the class struggle during the French Revolution and this has been the general model of revolutionary thinking.

We are saying that this model of class struggle represents only rebellion and not revolution—only the anger of the masses against those who have oppressed them and not the vision of a new society which motivates revolutionary struggle. Revolution only begins when people begin to think about how they can create a better set of human relations and begin to try to create them.

In the American Revolution, for example, the colonists struggled to redefine themselves *before* they arrived at the Declaration of Independence and the military struggle for freedom against Britain. You had the attempt to set up new political relations involved in the writing of state constitutions which culminated in the Constitutional Convention of 1787 and the Federalist papers which debated the new structures and the new relations before the whole people.

Which model is more important to us—not in India but in the U.S.—the model of the French Revolution or that of the American Revolution, the model based upon the militancy of oppressed, impoverished masses—or the model based on people blessed with material plenty but struggling to define their identity and develop a structure for their social relationships and their political relations? Obviously we will not try to structure relations as they structured them in 1787 any more than we are struggling for liberty and equality as they were in 1776. But it is how we think about the *sequence* of struggle which is important—the understanding that in the U.S where we have not had to worry about material necessities in the way that they have had to do elsewhere, physical struggle cannot begin until there has developed clarity about the human identity for which one is struggling.

We are trying to set up a process in motion in a certain direction. Then, if people want to continue in that direction, they have to struggle. Advance takes place through conceiving the positive concretely. Creating a new sense of society, a new sense of humanity, a new set of human relations in this country, will depend not upon the extent of one's antagonism to the capitalist system. It will flow from what we arrive at in terms of a positive vision. Bombs are not going to destroy capitalism. People who want to live differently are the only ones who can create something different from capitalism.

ONE SMALL STEP FORWARD

While we were in Maine, we read in the paper that James P. Cannon had died. When the Trotskyites split from the U.S. Communist Party in 1928, James P. Cannon was one of the leaders of the split. He had the courage to say, "I think that Trotsky is right." So they split or got thrown out. Trotsky got thrown out of Russia shortly thereafter. Cannon believed almost explicitly in everything Trotsky said, including Trotsky's almost mechanical notion of the role of the proletariat in the class struggle which he had taken from the October Revolution. Cannon was an utterly forthright and courageous man. But Cannon knew almost nothing about blacks or about minorities in this country. He didn't know anything about complexities.

He represented a proletarian quality which we could never have absorbed through, for example, someone like William Z. Foster. Because, although Cannon was a proletarian type, he was the kind of proletarian who could co-exist with a Max Shachtman or an intellectual like James Burnham as long as these intellectuals did not become too flighty. Cannon was not a small or a mean man; he had a basic faith in the proletariat, but he sensed that there was much more to life, to history, to politics and to revolution than just the proletariat. He welcomed intellectuals as long as they did not go off in all directions. C. L. R. James used to say of Cannon that he was not the kind of man who would trample on a minority. He would not line up his majority against you unless you got too far out of line and forced him to do it. Everybody who has a political party has to do that at a certain point. You can't let it be torn apart from whim. So Cannon was a man who had a great deal to teach about how to live within a party. He was the kind of chairman who could sit back and not have to interfere with everything going on. He was not an insecure person.

Between 1938 and 1940 there were all kinds of struggles inside the Trotskyite movement inside the U.S. In 1938 there was not only the battle about what the Red Army was doing in Finland but about the role of the black man in America. Cannon didn't give a damn about the Negro struggle—all he cared about was the class struggle. Not that he was prejudiced; he just took the old socialist position. C. L. R. James came over in 1938 and while he didn't know what Cannon knew, he knew a lot of things Cannon didn't know. James knew a lot about history for a thousand years back. He was a West Indian who went to Europe from Trinidad, that peculiar crossroads of Europe, the Western Hemisphere and Africa, and then through the Trotskyite movement came to the U.S.

By 1936 C. L. R. James had thought about all the important things in European civilization and then he wrote *World Revolution*. Having written it, it crystallized in him the idea that the ideas in that book were permanent. So he became a preacher of world revolution, something like Trotsky. But he was a man of extreme breadth. He knew European history, he knew literature, he knew music, he wrote plays. Without C. L. R. James none of us would be talking the way we are talking today. It has nothing to do with his being right or wrong. We were able to go beyond the proletarian-ness of Cannon because of C. L. R. James.

C. L. R. began to realize, the moment he came to this country, that you can't make a revolution thinking as categorically and inflexibly as Cannon thought.

So the struggle got hotter and hotter between him and the categorical abstractions of Cannon and his boys. Cannon was perfectly willing to use a whole lot of people who didn't know anything except how to defend Cannon and the party—much like Nixon's boys. They didn't care whom they slaughtered—which is one of the reasons why polemics in those days were really so murderous. Shachtman was a genius at this kind of slaughter because he was bright as hell—he could demolish you with a crack—and he had no moral standards at all. It isn't a question of whether an individual has morals. It is a question of whether individuals think that morals matter. And in those days no radicals thought that morals mattered. That is why Trotsky wrote "Their Morals and Ours"—which most of us thought marvelous at the time.

C. L. R. James said that morals did matter, civilization mattered, what had been happening to blacks mattered. The whole concept of class struggle had to be enlarged, enriched by the values which had been created by civilization over the years. You don't just plow ahead and make the revolution by setting up barricades at factory gates—which is what a lot of radicals still think. So C. L. R. and Cannon drew further apart, fundamentally on the question of whether the class struggle was as clear-cut as Cannon thought.

It was on this basis that the split took place between Cannon and ourselves in 1940, leading to the formation of the Workers Party in 1940 under the leadership of Shachtman, C. L. R. and Marty Abern. Cannon was left with the legitimate Trotskyite movement and we began looking for new ideas.

Muste was part of this search, even though he had split before then. In 1939 Muste went to Europe and saw the clouds of war piling up. He had been a minister, a very religious man. When he came back in the fall of 1939, he said, "I am splitting with you." He provided a kind of spiritual basis for the split because he gave us an idea of the things that were happening in and to Europe and which he realized couldn't be solved by hanging on to the old classical notion of the working class, coming out of the October Revolution and making the revolution on "Bread, Peace and Land."

Muste went back to God, very beautifully, much the same way that Duke did in his *Sacred Concert,* without getting on his knees. But his leaving the Trotskyites had been a kind of shock. So that when the Workers party was formed, it was with the idea of injecting a greater sense of civilization and of history into the Movement and a sense that things were different in the U.S. than in Russia in 1917. C. L. R. was crucial to this because in a sense he embodied the idea that it had been all right to be a Wobbly back in 1912 but that didn't mean that Wobblies could run the world in 1940, which is where many radicals still are.

C.L.R. became a leader of the Workers Party only two or three years after he came to this country, which was something of an achievement. Shachtman was the one who held the party together—by his rhetoric, but C. L. R. held it together by ideas. Then this broke up because C. L. R. couldn't see eye-to-eye with McKinney, a black man who was a continuator of the trade union tradition. McKinney really believed that there was no "Negro Question"; that it was only a question of the workers versus the bosses. It should be noted, however, that the last thing C. L. R. said about the "Negro Question" was back in 1948, and today he (or Bewick Press) is still saying the same thing, even though three decades have passed, and the whole world has changed.

So there wasn't a nice straight line in the Trotskyist movement in the U.S. Because the Communist Party was so tied up with the zig-zags of the Kremlin, their experiences were not as meaningful to the development of the struggle around the American Revolution as those in the Trotskyite movement where we were grappling with the new developments that were taking place and splitting over them. In many respects Cannon, who was thirty-eight at the time of the split between Stalin and Trotsky and who had been shaped by the experiences of the First World War, remained at the standpoint of the solidarity of the workers. But at the same time he understood his limitations as a proletarian and therefore welcomed intellectuals into the party. He was very happy that he had Trotsky to line up with on a world scale, so that the proletarian movement in the U.S. had this kind of cultural depth and internationalism which Trotsky represented. During this whole period you could feel a kind of psychic hunger on the part of proletarians who came to the radical movement, e.g., from the American Workers Party or the Conference of Progressive Labor Action, for politics, ideas, greater breadth. They would get a certain amount from the party, and then events themselves would get too complicated and there would be a split. The ideas from Trotsky were too narrow, because although he was a very developed individual, he still thought in terms of the October Revolution and couldn't respond to what was taking place in Germany except in the 1917 concepts of the class struggle. Trotsky had very little sensitivity to what was happening to European civilization in the post–World War I years. In 1934 Trotsky-ism had represented a broadening of the horizons of those coming from the American Workers Party but no longer by 1939.

Although he was an organizer, Marty Abern also understood his limitations. He was hungry for the sort of thing which he thought C. L. R. offered. He was a great respecter of Muste; he regretted very much that he had to break with Burnham; he couldn't stand Shacht-man whom he saw as a smart aleck from the Bronx. There was some-thing about Cannon's boys which offended him. They were Nixon people like Ehrlichman and Haldeman, while he had come from the old socialist movement.

In the years after the split from Cannon, the Johnson-Forrest tendency was actually an intellectual faction within the Workers Party. Throughout the World War II years we made an intensive effort to understand Marx in the light of European history and civilization, German Classical Philosophy, English Political Economy, and French politics in and after the French Revolution. We carried on studies that were fantastic: Adam Smith, Ricardo, and *Capital* in light of the development of German Classical Philosophy and English Political Economy, dialectics, Shakespeare, Beethoven, Melville, the Abolitionists, Negro history, Marcus Garvey. We did a huge intellectual work during these years because we thought it was necessary to the American Revolution and because we saw the American working class as heirs to all this. Raya Dunayevskaya is still living on that work today. Only C. L. R. could have given us the leadership in this.

Inside the Workers Party, from 1943, we took a position versus McKinney on the "Negro Question," versus Shachtman and Gates on the Russia question, versus Ernie Lund on the American question, versus the retrogressionists on the question of the national liberation struggles in Europe, which we saw as containing the potential for the European socialist revolution.

In 1946 or 1947 Cannon made a speech entitled the Coming American Revolution and C. L. R. said, "There is no use having two groups who both believe in the coming American Revolution," so we went back to the SWP. We foresaw the workers striking after World War II; black proletarians in Detroit looking for a revolutionary movement that would take them beyond where the union was going to the SWP. So after an interim period of several months, during which we published the *American Workers* pamphlet, the *Invading Socialist Society*, etc., we went back into the SWP. Cannon was glad for us to come in and permitted us a great deal of freedom, including trusting one of our members to put the paper to bed each week. C. L. R. thought we could now give a greater breadth and meaning to revolution in the U.S. because of what World War II had meant in the U.S. and the world. Cannon knew we had ideas and it was understood that we could continue developing them, but we would also do our daily party work in a disciplined way, which we did, selling the *Militant*, getting election petitions signed, etc.

Among us the habit of the investigation of the philosophy that lay behind past history, present movements, etc., had been established. We were extremely conscious that without a notion of the philosophical and historical basis of what you are doing, you don't understand anything. Some of us were philosophically trained but the workers among us had also developed this habit. In the other tendencies this was not true. Raya was the confident expositor of what had happened in Russia. Lyman represented a significant strand in the American Revolution. C. L. R. was always trying to understand the American Revolution, and pressing forward the work on Melville and the Abolitionists.

It was fascinating that this pressure came from someone from outside the U.S. C. L. R. was always trying to reconcile the two strands of the French and American Revolutions, seeing the French Revolution as a prototype as Marx had, but at the same time sensing the unique quality of the American Revolution. Since the Russian Revolution there has been this struggle inside the U.S. radical movement, arguments and splits over the question again and again as to the "exceptional" character of the American Revolution. It remains a critical question to this day.

While he was here, C. L. R. had a real feeling for the American Revolution. If he hadn't left the U.S. in 1953, would he have been able to do what we are doing now? Some day someone is going to ask this "if" about us, and we will be turning in our graves, realizing that we hadn't anticipated, hadn't evolved in relation to reality. It is ridiculous to say that if Caesar had been a different kind of man, the Roman Empire might have been different. But there are times when a book, a person, a discussion can change a person. With C. L. R. we came within a hairsbreadth of this. He was fantastically desirous.

C. L. R. stopped at a certain point. We (here) are trying to go beyond where he was and where we were with him. Today he is living on his laurels. He isn't trying to open up his mind any further. An auto accident in 1960 had something to do with this.

But the decline began taking place even before the 1960 accident.

When C. L. R. left this country in 1953, he left behind his base and became a cosmopolite. In the U.S., although he had been to some extent underground, he had an organization of Americans of very different types, blacks, women, middle class professionals, intellectuals, youth, workers, who were passionately concerned with the American

Revolution, even though we had some idealistic views about American workers derived from reading Marx. But in 1953 C. L. R. was already becoming a Marxist egocentric, something which, strangely enough, Cannon never became. Cannon never tried to ballyhoo Cannon. C. L. R. chose to write chapter 7 of *Mariners, Renegades and Castaways*. Up to that point the book was beautiful. Then suddenly it began to focus on the suffering of a particular guy on Ellis Island. What compelled C. L. R. to think of himself as a political prisoner? He wasn't one, he was completely free as soon as he left the borders of the U.S. That chapter is a fantastic illustration of the role of subjectivity. True, C. L. R used to hold forth, lying on the couch, but he had never been subjective to the degree that he was in chapter 7 of *Mariners*. It was almost as if he was thinking about making the revolution in order to prove that he was the leader of the revolution rather than to advance the revolution.

After 1953 C. L. R. didn't have the challenge of the United States which had never failed to excite him. He went to Trinidad, formed a group and then left. It seemed as if he was experimenting because he was never really passionately concerned with the Trinidad Revolution as he had been with the American Revolution. His intervention in Trinidad was based on class struggle being the answer to everything: "I am on the side of the oil workers." Period. He lectured about the West Indian Federation, brilliant lectures, but they lacked the feeling he had had for the American Revolution, which was fed by the passions of those of us in the organization who were very much a part of his life and of whose life he was also very much a part.

We broke from Cannon in 1951 and from C. L. R. in 1962. Now we are trying to make clear the need to advance beyond the idea that all radicals have held—that in order to advance socialism, you must first smash capitalism. We have to advance towards the new society by projecting an entirely different way to live and by building new social ties.

One of the reason why we are so alive and so vibrant and so important is that we still believe that we are at the beginning. We believe that when Duke Ellington says in his concert of *Sacred Music*, "In the beginning, God" he is saying, "In the beginning, Humankind." He is saying, "Hey, man or woman, I am trying to project to you that there are mysteries you don't know anything about at all. But they are there or you wouldn't be here." He recites the books of the Old and the New Testament: "These were forms of which there may be a million others. The very fact that I am putting these to jazz is another form. So when I say 'God,' I don't mean a person with a white beard. I am saying that there are mysteries in each of us which we have to solve in ourselves." That is why he ends with that fantastic dance by Bunny Briggs. Everybody can praise what he/she thinks is God by doing what he/she thinks would praise his/her God. And if you don't do what you think praises your God, then you have demeaned yourself.

This year we are beginning anew, going into unexplored territory, starting at the bottom in the basics of human needs, before they were categorized and rigidified into compartments by sociologists and then institutionalized. We can do this only because we came from somewhere. We couldn't begin anew if we weren't also a continuation. We are continuing lifelong struggles that we realize did not start with us but started back a million years ago and have no end. The day we give up we will have ceased to be what a human being ought to be.

1974

Final Thoughts

When we started these conversations ten years ago, we were not thinking about publication. What we were trying to do was reexamine for ourselves the ideas that had motivated us for the greater part of our adult lives as they had motivated other dedicated persons for over a hundred years. It has never been our intention to take anything away from their dedication—or from ours.

In the course of our explorations, we concluded that, whether we liked it or not, the epoch had come to an end when it was progressive to think of the history of humanity as the history of class struggle. The process of questioning our previous thoughts has been painful, but it has also been joyous because we have been searching for another way to view the history of humanity that could inspire as much commitment from ourselves and others as Marx's ideas have done. Through our explorations we have arrived at the conviction that the American Revolution two hundred years ago is the key to this other view of history because it was made not to create a system or an "ism" but a new kind of person: a citizen.

Why did the Conversations start when they did? To ask that is a little like asking why the American Revolution took place when it did. Like anything important, our conversations were begun for a variety of very particular reasons, coincidences, personalities, and efforts. Our experiences and interrelationships over the past thirty or more years had provided us with the opportunity to ask questions that others had hesitated to ask because they didn't want to be considered anti-Marxist. We had gone through the Marxist experience for more than thirty years, as the American colonists had gone through the experience of settling the new continent for 150 years. Suddenly we (it could have been somebody else, but it wasn't) said, "There are some questions to be asked here." This is exactly the kind of thing that happened to Thomas Jefferson, Ben Franklin, the Adamses, and others when they began to make the American Revolution. After 150 years in which hundreds of thousands of people had undergone a wide range of new experiences, a few individuals began to wonder how their ideas differed from those they had been accepting from European philosophers.

The analogy isn't far-fetched. Since the Russian Revolution those Americans most passionately committed to economic and social justice in this country have been attracted to the Marxist movement. Then a few of us for some reason said, "It is time to ask some questions." That is the dynamics of the human process. A philosophy is not some sort of abstraction that one discovers like a crocodile as one is going up the Nile. It is the culmination of experiences and thoughts about those experiences.

We came together because of the coincidence of our private and political lives and the situation in which we found ourselves. In 1968, finding ourselves on a little island in Maine where we could relax and reflect away from the immediate pressures of daily existence, we decided that our questions mattered. *We* decided that. Objective social forces didn't make the decision because objective social forces don't decide what a person thinks. The four of us, with similar political experiences but otherwise as dissimilar as four individuals could possibly be, decided that what we were thinking so coincided that we wanted to talk about it. That was the beginning.

In 1968 the United States was coming to the end of a decade of unprecedented demonstrations and rebellions. In addition, the many revolutions taking place world-wide, especially the revolution in China, were making it evident that the Russian Revolution had not been the final revolution. The coincidence of what was taking place in the United States with what was taking place in the world gave focus to the questions that had been at the back of our minds for many years. So we could ask ourselves whether the class struggle or the rebellions of oppressed masses against their oppressors was, in fact, the basis for a revolution in the United States.

This kind of radicalism was experiencing a revival among movement activists in the United States precisely because the rebellions of the oppressed and Third World revolutions had played such a key role in the movements of the 1960s. Meanwhile, because we had already dedicated so much of our lives to building organizations on this kind of thinking, we had arrived at the point of wondering whether our country—the technologically most advanced country in the world—could make a revolution based on theories drawn from the European experience. Even then, it took us two summers before we were able in 1970 to draw a clear distinction between rebellions and revolutions.

Today we can say unhesitatingly that revolutionary change in this country will be brought about not because of people's class but because great numbers of Americans, regardless of class, have begun to demand more of themselves as persons and as citizens. In other words, we have finally freed ourselves of Marxist or European theories of class and faceless masses.

All revolutions are changes but not all changes are alike. The American Revolution was such a profound revolution because it changed people's concepts of what it means to be a human being. The Russian Revolution wasn't trying to change human beings. It aimed to change the relationships of social forces and to develop the productive forces.

The uniqueness of the American Revolution was that it was based on a redefinition of human beings. Our Declaration of Independence wasn't anything like Rhodesia a few years ago telling Britain that it was cutting off all ties. Ours was a declaration of aspirations for humankind. The motion for independence had actually been passed on July 2, 1776. So what we celebrate on July Fourth is not a declaration of independence but a declaration of principles. The fact that Americans today do not behave in accordance with principles is precisely our challenge. What we have to do is use the American Revolution as history is always used: to make clear to Americans our unique and elemental strength as a people and why our nation matters to the human race.

The American Revolution was the result of a fantastic coincidence of circumstances. We are not trying to reproduce it two hundred years later. Americans in the eighteenth century were capable of understanding that they would like to be independent, to be free, to be democratic. Because of their circumstances they comprehended these ideas in a way that no Englishmen or Frenchmen could have. It took them a long time to arrive at these ideas—but in 1776 they signed the Declaration of Independence.

The average American today hasn't the slightest idea of what we mean by aspirations for the whole human race or that the distinction between the American Revolution and all others was that our revolution was based on principles for humankind and not on animosity or class struggle. If Americans today do not think about principles in this way, how do we reproduce this attitude? That is the question uppermost in our minds. It is precisely because Americans don't think this way that we need an organization of people who do and who are ready to dedicate themselves to persuading others that this, the American tradition, is the only way to begin resolving our problems.

In building a core of people who are ready to assume this challenge, we have to go beyond not only the notions that Marx projected but the forms in which Marx's notions have been carried out. (At this stage we have to think about the form as well as the content because otherwise somebody is going to get the form mixed up with the content, insisting, for instance, that we should build little revolutionary cells.) What the new form will be we don't know, except that we have to be careful that it doesn't emulate the old form just as the content does not emulate the old content.

We believe that if we can discover how to persuade the American people to explore the opportunities we now have to intervene consciously in advancing the evolution of the human race, we can change the United States and thereby the whole world.

This is a philosophical question, not a material or economic one. The American Revolution was not made for subjective reasons, except in the sense that its proponents were subjective individuals who cared. It was a historical coincidence that this phenomenon happened in North America. But it did happen. We are saying to every American, "We have one hair-raising responsibility because we created one hair-raising new kind of nation. Don't keep talking about your grievances. You as an American, without even knowing it, did something that up to now no one else in history has done. What do you think about *that*?"

What would happen if everybody thought and talked that way? How can we get people to understand what we mean when we say that a revolution must be made on a declaration of aspirations and not on bitterness?

Every nation has ideas in its past, achievements in its past, that remain with its people so that if you address them in terms of these ideas and achievements you evoke a resonance. For example, if you talk to the Chinese in homilies (as Mao understood very well), they will respond because of what they have been raised to appreciate as their national identity. We believe that despite all the cynicism, opportunism, and reductive thinking in the United States today, the American people can begin to think differently about themselves and the future of humanity if we challenge them in terms of principles and aspirations for the whole human race. They may relapse into sociological jargon and victim thinking, but our job is to keep posing to them this other kind of thinking and evoke this resonance. Not everybody is going to talk this way to the American people. It must begin with those few individuals whose thought-processes are no longer paralyzed by the leftist notion that workers are going to change society just because they are workers.

We hope that those of you who read these Conversations will get from them some insight into the process by which we have arrived at this point and that they will stimulate you to begin reexamining your own thinking so that you can go beyond what we have done. Perhaps in the future we can find the form through which together we can advance our thinking and the thinking of the American people.

Sutton Island, Maine
September 3, 1977

Left to right: Matt Birkhold, Soh Suzuki, Marcia Lee, and Amaka Okechukwu at the Sutton Island boat house during the commemoration of Grace Lee Boggs's life, summer 2016. Photograph courtesy of Matt Birkhold.

Reflections, 2018

MICHAEL DOAN, EDITOR

In September 2017, a call was sent to friends and comrades of Grace, Jimmy, and the Boggs Center. Some fifty years following the initial *Conversations in Maine,* and in the spirit of loving and struggling over ideas, we hoped to spark a fresh series of conversations *about conversations.*

The following questions were posed:

> Why do conversations matter?
> Which conversations have been most important to you in your work?
> How and why have conversations in Maine, among other conversations with Grace, Jim, and other comrades, mattered to you?
> How and why has *Conversations in Maine* been important to you?
> Why are conversations particularly important at this time on the "clock of the world"?
> What questions do we need to struggle with as we look fifty years into the future?

The reflections gathered here are the fruits of our collective efforts. You will find commentary on what it is that keeps bringing us together, continually shapes and strengthens our relationships, and holds us fast to one another, even in those moments when we may wish to drift apart.

Some reflections focus on conversations with, about, or inspired by Jimmy and Grace. Others trace the legacy of conversations long past into the present and future.

Each is a gesture of togetherness and hope, rooted in remembrance and relation.

As we listen in on conversations first sparked in 1967, let us all find our own Maines—our own hope together, today.

Conversations in the Living Room at 3061 Field Street

FRANK JOYCE

It started a long time ago. Me climbing the steps at 3061 Field Street, the two-family flat on Detroit's east side where Jimmy and Grace lived beginning in 1962. Usually just Jimmy and Grace were there, but sometimes others too.

Detroit really is different. There are deep historical reasons for that. (I highly recommend Tiya Miles's *The Dawn of Detroit* for an understanding of how it all began more than three hundred years ago.) The quality of political engagement and dialogue during the 1960s in Detroit and since was not like what took place elsewhere in the United States. Jimmy and Grace were a very big reason.

If we reverse engineer from where things are now we can see how it worked. The fertile minds and intense disagreements between Jimmy and Grace turned into dialogue, curiosity, and exploration.

People were steadily attracted to a vision of who we can become. Old people. Young people. Black people. White people. Asian people. Native people. Hispanic people. Any sexual identity or ability. Musicians, scholars, artists, factory workers, poor people, affluent people, famous people, soon-to-be famous people, never to be famous people . . . all kinds of people.

This diversity came naturally. Not because boxes were being checked off, but because all who came knew they would be accepted and respected, enlightened and energized. At 3061 Field Street people are free to talk and—even more rare—listen deeply to one another.

This decades-long conversation-like-no-other has produced so many beacons. From Save Our Sons and Daughters (SOSAD), the survivors of homicide support group, to Peace Zones for Life. From Detroit City of Hope to Reimagining Work. From columns in the *Michigan Citizen* newspaper to *Riverwise* magazine, a new communication platform launched in 2017. And so much more.

As much as I still have to learn, if I know anything at all about what it means to *be the change*, I have three people especially to thank. One is the late Vincent Harding. The other two are Jimmy and

Grace. Because I knew Grace and Jimmy for a very long time and interacted with them over many decades, I learned the most from them. I even cotaught a class on revolution with Jimmy and Grace back in the 1970s.

Yes, there were arguments. Sometimes, to be honest, they scared me. They were too loud. The ratio of heat to light was off. I struggle with getting that right to this day. But figuring out how to have constructive and productive conflict is one of the great challenges bestowed upon us by the weight of five hundred years of the white way of thinking.

Once Jimmy died, Grace had to become the living embodiment of being the change by herself. She did. *She* changed. All the time.

She moved relentlessly past old doctrine and ideology. The older she got, the more her ravenous curiosity brought her to new understandings, new vision, and new approaches. Want to make Grace happy? Give her a new book or a new article or a new idea. It could be about neuroscience, politics, economics, history, psychology, what we have to learn from animals, or damn near anything.

Of course, within the changes there were constants. Her ascetic lifestyle. And 3061 Field Street, where she continued to live until the day she died. I often quote Grace saying, "The most revolutionary thing I ever did was stay put."

And there was her capacity to listen. Her belief that women have so much to teach. Her insistence that *thinking* about what we are doing is just as important as the doing itself.

Grace let *us* nourish *her*. That was another of her gifts. If we are to be the change we want to see in the world, we will have to nourish each other just as *Conversations in Maine* still nourishes us today.

Frank Joyce is a lifelong Detroit-based activist and writer. He is coeditor with Karin Aguilar–San Juan of *The People Make the Peace: Lessons from the Vietnam Antiwar Movement.*

Remembering Jimmy: On the Passing of James Boggs, African American Revolutionary

GLORIA "ANEB" HOUSE

I was a young SNCC worker when I met Jimmy and Grace in their warm, expansive home on Field Street in Detroit. That was in 1966 or '67. It was good to be with them from the very first time. They were excited about movement work—ours and theirs—and ready to discuss it at length. Though it didn't occur to me then why I loved Grace and Jimmy in the special way one loves comrades, I know now the bond came from our sense of celebrating each other's lives and political commitment. We were truly glad for our dialogue from one generation to another, thankful for each other's being there.

Over the years this quality of camaraderie persisted in the affirmation that each of us was working to realize a vision of the future that we shared. *Affirmation* is the word that comes when I see Jimmy's face in my mind's eye. He said "yes" to life in so many ways—from the simplest smile, to his courageous political fighting, and even in his bout with cancer during the last years. I fully trusted that when he asked, "How you been doin', Glory?" he really was concerned about how this particular soldier in the movement was faring, and I knew for certain that he wished me well.

What was it about Jimmy that made it possible for him to give such inspiration to fellow fighters? It was his deeply rooted belief in himself and the kind of life he had chosen that enabled Jimmy to support others who made revolutionary choices. Fully centered in the integrity of his own cultural heritage, his political direction, his personality and character, Jimmy was free to be intensely involved with social problems, emerging ideas, and proposed actions. He seemed to be striving always to understand, respond to, and be a part of social change that moved us closer to fulfilling our humanity. Vulnerable and questioning, he would admit when he didn't have an answer and encourage everybody present to risk engaging in the search.

Gloria "Aneb" House is a Detroit-based educator, human rights activist, poet, and cultural worker.

An Asian American Icon?

ROB YANAGIDA

Four decades after the publication of *Conversations in Maine,* Grace Lee Boggs appeared before an overflow auditorium at U.C. Berkeley alongside Angela Davis, also an activist and philosopher. The event was called "On Revolution: A Conversation." In their exchange on violence and nonviolence, Grace stressed that nonviolence is "an important philosophy because it respects the capacity of human beings to grow . . . and we owe that to each other." It was a view, she added, that took her a long time to learn. She interrupted the appreciative audience, with a gleam in her eyes: "All of you who are clapping— I suggest you do some more thinking!"[1] Captured in *American Revolutionary,* the Peabody Award–winning film by Grace Lee, the scene is illustrative. Grace appreciated ideas that evolved.

Reading these four veteran activists today as they reexamine their own evolving ideas allows us to reexamine our own. Their exchanges about Marxism in China and one's responsibility as an activist have impacted my own perspective. The rest of this essay sketches my observations as I have, over several decades, connected and reconnected with the Boggses and their views.

I heard Grace address what was her first large audience of Asian American activists at a 1970 conference in New York City. She spoke about mistakes in movements, and of her own. She critiqued Americans for our tendency to think quantitatively and individualistically. She encouraged us to draw from Asian culture "that sense of a continuing history which helps you to think dialectically."[2] I am still struggling with what she meant for my own view of history.

In 1974 I led a campaign in New York City against racially discriminatory hiring practices in the construction industry and for the hiring of Asian American construction workers. Multigenerational picket lines encircled Confucius Plaza, a forty-story apartment tower rising in the heart of the Chinatown enclave, with youth alongside immigrant Chinese women garment workers and the elderly. Tensions escalated with the arrest of fifty-seven protesters. I wrote then: "Once the idea of fighting against racial oppression was grasped by the community, sweeping changes and powerful forces were set in motion."[3] Quoting me in her 2016 social history, *Serve the People: Making Asian America in the Long Sixties,* Karen L. Ishizuka noted how this characterized a period of what has been recognized as the Asian American Movement.

The following year, I met James Boggs and Grace at their home in Detroit with members of my political collective. In our study of their writings and our discussions, we had completely missed the vision they had developed in *Conversations* and articulated in *Revolution and Evolution* of a uniquely American revolution—the first revolution to require the people to make material sacrifices.[4] We left going our separate ways. My own path eventually led to years of disillusionment and cynicism with activism.

It took thirty more years for me to reunite with Grace. This was when I first learned about *Conversations.* Reading it, I could in retrospect sense the questioning yet great attention given by them to the Chinese people and Mao. Ideas change reality, and reality changes ideas. Their discussion called "Chiding" foreshadows the 2012 audience interactions in Berkeley: using discomfort to awaken people to their own potential, showing people that "their struggle is infinitely richer than they think it is, infinitely larger than their present selves."[5]

The audiences for *Conversations* have changed and broadened since. Grace has come to be regarded as a public intellectual and, especially for Asian Americans, an icon. New generations of Asian American writers, intellectuals, activists, and media makers have fostered this acclaim by directly attributing their ideas and work to her inspiration. As Scott Kurashige notes in *American Revolutionary,* Grace represents the uniting of people from different races and backgrounds in a way that is now defining America. Grace Lee, now a member of the Academy of Motion Pictures Arts and Sciences and a Korean American, toured the United States with Grace Lee Boggs and their biographical film, which connected thousands in person and a great many thousands more through major network broadcasts. Another telling scene in the film is when Grace, commenting on her celebrity, protested with a laugh, "But I am *not* an Asian American icon."[6]

Both apart from and due to this strange status, Grace continued to expound that Asian Americans have a distinct responsibility. She wrote that "because Asian civilizations are so ancient and because the global role of the East is growing so fast, Asian Americans have a unique contribution to make to the next American Revolution, although only time will tell what that role will be."[7]

Movements in today's global capitalism differ from the period in which *Conversations* was published. Rather than a single class driving democratic change, we consider the multitude through the lens of intersectionality. The racist legacy from the enslavement of African Americans in the United States remains, but is now disrupted by new liberatory movements expressing a new humanity. We seek visionary organizing, not just protest organizing.

Grace Lee Boggs personified the activist-philosopher over generations. As an Asian American woman, neither black nor white, she created new ideas and lessons to pass on. The vision and challenge she and James Boggs shared remain for those who propose to transform institutions, participating in "the continuing reflection and transformation that . . . all revolutionaries need to undergo as reality changes."[8]

Their examples in life are part of what propels me to grapple with new social realities in my life. I take to heart Grace's suggestion that we "do some more thinking."

NOTES

1. See *American Revolutionary: The Evolution of Grace Lee Boggs,* directed and produced by Grace Lee; producers, Caroline Libresco and Austin Wilkin, LeeLee Films, 2013.
2. Grace Lee Boggs, *Asian-Americans & the U.S. Movement* (Detroit: Asian Political Alliance, n.d.).
3. Karen L. Ishizuka, *Serve the People: Making Asian America in the Long Sixties* (London: Verso, 2016), 180.
4. James and Grace Lee Boggs, *Revolution and Evolution in the Twentieth Century* (New York: Monthly Review Press, 1974), 140
5. For a discussion of chiding, see this volume, the chapter titled "New Questions for an American Revolution."
6. *American Revolutionary: The Evolution of Grace Lee Boggs.*
7. Grace Lee Boggs, with Scott Kurashige, *The Next American Revolution: Sustainable Activism for the Twenty-First Century* (Berkeley: University of California Press, 2011), xix.
8. Ibid., 80.

Rob Yanagida is an activist, lawyer, and founder of Asian Americans for Equality. He develops worker co-ops and democratic community enterprises and works with law collaboratives in Oakland, California.

The Humanity of Conversation:
Walking the Talk Together

BILL WYLIE-KELLERMANN

Let me exercise the prerogative of a movement pastor and go somewhat theological in this reflection.

To begin with, during the years of these conversations in Maine, I was a seminarian in New York City just beginning my own conversations—biblical, political, communitarian—with three mentors who would become lifelong friends. Indeed, I was joining their conversation. They were Daniel Berrigan, the poet and priest just then released from federal prison for liturgically burning Vietnam draft files in Catonsville, Maryland; William Stringfellow, Harvard-trained street lawyer who broke open the New Testament language of "principalities and powers"; and Walter Wink, activist-scholar who, following Stringfellow's lead, developed a new and renewed theology of nonviolence, with a magisterial trilogy to explicate it.[1] By coincidence, many of those conversations transpired on an island off the coast, where Berrigan had a hermitage on the bluff. (Could it be the wind and the waters are somehow themselves sacred conversation partners?)

Let it be said that a question mark is the most prominent form of punctuation in the collectively written *Conversations in Maine*. Questions provoke the conversation and are multiplied by it. So, no surprise that connecting these two conversations (my mentors' and Maine) is an underlying and recurring question: What does it mean to be human—in this present moment? Notice that another question, "What time is it?," is fused and allied, inseparably, making humanity a dynamic, rooted in place and time, not fixed and universally answerable. Even in this short period of years it is striking to see the conversation transform the language itself: "Man," "the new man," "man/womankind," "Human Spirit," "human beings."

Stringfellow, in his formulation, made this very question key to theological ethics: What does it mean to live humanly in the midst of death? He also framed reflection within the location of history. Recalling resistance to Nazism as small, fragile, audacious, even extemporaneous action that could seem hard, hapless, and exceedingly risky in the moment, he wrote:

> Why would human beings take such risks? It is not, I think, because they were heroes or because they besought martyrdom; they were, at the outset, like the Apostles, quite ordinary men and women of various and usual stations and occupations in life. How is their tenacity explained? . . . Why did these human beings have such uncommon hope? The answer to such questions is, I believe, that the act of resistance to the power of death incarnate in Nazism was the only means of retaining sanity and conscience. In the circumstances of the Nazi tyranny, *resistance became the only human way to live.*[2]

This turns out to be a fundamentally biblical question, even if one long obscured. Walter Wink, the scripture scholar who was denied tenure and "blacklisted" for openly criticizing the disengaged objectivism of the biblical academy, was my New Testament professor in the early seventies. His magnum opus, *The Human Being: Jesus and the Enigma of the Son of the Man,* argues that "son of man" (literally "human being" in a Hebraic formulation), as a way in which Jesus refers to himself in the third person, is not some divine title but a fully human, even collective term.[3] Rethink these lines in that way: "Blessed are you when people hate you . . . on account of the human being." Or, "The human being has authority on earth to forgive sins." Being human is basic to Jesus's own ethic and vocation. As Dan Berrigan put, "In Jesus we see God in trouble for being human."

Before his death, while Wink was being taken bit by bit in chronic illness, he compiled an autobiography of his life in activism and scholarship (and the dialogics between the two). His title? *Just Jesus: My Struggle to Become Human.*[4]

These two conversations first joined for me in the early eighties when Grace and Jimmy came to the Detroit Catholic Worker for a "clarification of thought" evening. They were fresh from the struggle against the neighborhood destruction wrought by the General Motors Poletown plant. What struck me in that hospitality house living room circle was how much their critical, communitarian, and hopeful vision of humanity comported so readily with the personalist Christian anarchism of the Worker movement (nonviolence, resistance, community, and service). And somehow, they managed it all in plain language without the benefit of Jesus or even God to speak of.

In Maine, the four were quite explicit about this latter point. They shared a Marxian sense of religion as the obscuring of agency and responsibility. But they also probed the question "How do we concretize the search for a sense of the human spirit so that a kid can look for it or understand what is being talked about and so that the word 'spirit' does not bring to mind the Holy Ghost or Jesus Christ?"[5]

In the late eighties Grace joined a theological course I was teaching, "Discerning the Angel of Detroit," an attempt to get at the spirituality or genius of the city and how awareness of such could figure into urban transformation. We did bible study together. The sessions were substantially a conversation between the participants, her and myself (and over my shoulder, the theological mentors) about scripture and social history. I have written about this elsewhere,[6] but it was the occasion for me to understand again how movement work, at least in part, is spiritual struggle. It was also roughly the point where Grace and Jimmy began to speak of "rebuilding, redefining, and *respiriting* Detroit." I count that a kind of concrete and practical mysticism we are only just beginning to appreciate.

And still the questions abound: How are we to live humanly in the midst of expulsion, gentrification, incarceration? What does community for humans have to do with river and earth, with neighborhood and creaturehood? What risks are we prepared to take for the sake of humanity, not the least of which our own? To these and so many more, we find the answer by walking it.

NOTES

1. See Bill Wylie-Kellermann, *Principalities in Particular: A Practical Theology of the Powers That Be* (Minneapolis: Fortress Press, 2017), where I have written about the theological conversation between the three of them and Martin Luther King Jr.

2. William Stringfellow, *An Ethic for Christians and Other Aliens in a Strange Land* (Waco, Tex.: Word Books, 1973), 119.

3. Walter Wink, *The Human Being: Jesus and the Enigma of the Son of the Man* (Minneapolis: Fortress Press, 2002).

4. Walter Wink, *Just Jesus: My Struggle to Become Human* (New York: Image Books, 2014).

5. See the conversation in this volume titled "Projections, Not Rejections."

6. Bill Wylie-Kellermann, "Discerning the Angel of Detroit," in *Where the Water Goes Around: Beloved Detroit* (Portland, Ore.: Cascade Books, 2017).

Bill Wylie-Kellermann is a pastor, teacher, and writer.

Revolutionary Humanism
LARRY SPARKS

I became a Revolutionary Humanist in the early 1970s. After my brother almost lost his life in Vietnam I began studying the Vietnam War and, after reading *Conversations in Maine* and *Revolution and Evolution in the Twentieth Century,* came to realize that the war was for oil and to sustain the American Dream by exploiting folks all over the world. These books gave me a historical perspective transcending our dehumanizing values. At a very young age I saw myself as nonreligious, trying to figure out how to reject the racism and homophobia of my southern "white indemnity" and heritage, loving my family but hating some of the things they did and believed in. It was through many conversations with my mentors and revolutionaries Grace Lee and James Boggs, and Betty Thomas Mayen, whose son Paul was my best friend, that I eventually rejected my historical past, somehow knowing on a perceptual level that "to just denounce your history is to denounce your own existence." As a Revolutionary Humanist, I refuse to give credit to something other than human beings for what we have created over three thousand generations, rejecting all mysticism, religion, and violence to mind and body.

I'm writing this to encourage my family and friends to join us in beloved community to make a nonviolent revolution in the United States of America—"Loving our Country Enough to Change It"; challenging the violence that is being done in our names all over the world to sustain the American Dream, while most folks live lives of quiet desperation; becoming the checks and balances needed to keep the three branches of representative government from descending further into fascism; taking back the military, which has paved the way for multinational capital to rape, rob, and plunder the planet, damn near bringing us to extinction.

I've learned a lot from Grace and Lyman Paine about dialectical thinking and the Next American Revolution. I usually sent my notes to my friend and mentor, Grace Lee Boggs, who edited them, correcting grammar, etc.; posed questions, challenging me to transcend whatever area I'm locked into or the simplicity of an idea; challenged me to stay at perception (senses) a little longer before moving to conception (understanding); forced me to see the dialectical/historical nature of a process, or person within that process; reminded me that we're all works in progress and of the earth. I'm amazed, after all of these years, how deeply affected I am by the philosophy of Dialectical Humanism, the seeds of which were planted in the early seventies. Ideas flowing out of *Conversations in Maine, Revolution and Evolution,* Grace's auto-biography, *Living for Change,* and, at ninety-six, *The Next American Revolution,* which she coauthored with Scott Kurashige, have shaped my thinking. As a twenty-year-old activist, I received permission to transcend my limitations and to realize that we're all at different levels of development and struggle. They were always emphasizing transformation beyond self to humanity, beyond the narrow dehumanizing values of this society, focusing on the need to create the Next American Revolution for our time, not for all time, in keeping with the Jeffersonian tradition of a revolution every generation.

Today we continue the work of creating a new society in which every human being is free from commodification, creating communities where everyone can move toward their full potential in a more loving, sharing, and caring way. This is a place where Jim (my partner of thirty-two years) and I can continue our lifelong journey together.

Larry Sparks is the publications director of the James and Grace Lee Boggs Center to Nurture Community Leadership.

Teachings from Our Friend, Freddy Paine

JANICE FIALKA

Almost every summer, Rich, Micah, Emma, and I traveled to Sutton Island off the coast of Maine to spend time with our dear teacher and friend, Freddy Paine. The island was magical to us. We took long walks into the pine forest, watched brilliant sunsets, eagerly awaited the deer at dusk, basked in the warm sun, climbed jagged rocks, rested, and talked into the wee hours of the star-lit night. But the main attraction on the island for us was *Freddy Paine.* Her stories, energy, dancing to *Fiddler on the Roof,* her love, and her deep passion to make this world a better place brought us back to the island almost every year. On May 3, 1999, at the young age of eighty-seven, Freddy died. We know that we were very fortunate to have her in our lives.

The following are some thoughts stirred during our visit to Sutton Island three months after Freddy's passing. It was our first time without her. These thoughts are our way to keep her powerful spirit alive.

Since my arrival on Sutton Island, I've been keeping my voice at a softer pitch. I foolishly think my whispering might be a way to try to quiet the wonderful spunk of lots of young children in Freddy's house. As the hours move forward, I'm more aware that my softer voice is really my attempt to stay open to what Freddy might be saying to me during our first visit on the island without her. I so much want to hear her stories one more time.

Earlier today, while walking past an open closet, I saw the small wicker basket she used to carry on her daily walks on the island. I ached for her when I saw the bag. A walk with Freddy was an event. It was then that all the island-stories unraveled as she hiked briskly through the magic of tall pine trees and soft green moss. She'd always take her clippers and the basket. "Pa Paine told me never to go out of the house without your clippers. Wear them around your neck like a necklace. If a branch is in your way, you clip it for your safety and for that of the next person." Pa Paine taught Freddy the island rules of etiquette and Freddy taught all of us.

On those walks she carried her bag on her arm eager to fill it with chanterelle mushrooms. She taught us all the delight of finding one of those rare and edible treats tucked away in the shady nooks of green moss. Each one, and there were never many, was sacred! When we returned from our walk, she'd routinely place the basket and clippers on the hook, and put the few precious mushrooms on the wooden counter where they'd sit, waiting to be carefully added to the right dish that would honor their delicacy.

Freddy hiked and gathered mushrooms for many years, until walks became rare for her body, though her spirit soared with strength and wisdom. Freddy's walks on the island represent how she lived her life everywhere on this earth, not just on the island. She traveled with her clippers (her fiery passion) ready to trim away dangerous obstacles, which would hurt the next traveler. She had this deep sense of responsibility to clear the way for those who followed after her.

Today, when I see the basket hanging in the back of the closet, I yearn for Freddy. Her joyful spunkiness leaps out at me. She is dancing as if she was Tevye in Fiddler on the Roof, her arms are raised, fingers snapping and her tiny body sashays.

At that moment, I hear Freddy. I hear what she'd been trying to say to me. "Carry your clippers. Clear the path for yourself and for those who follow you, even when you know that the branches will grow back later. It's just what you do. And one more thing. Don't forget to look for the few chanterelles along the way. There won't be a lot, but the ones you find will be damn good."

I'm listening, Freddy.

Janice Fialka is a storyteller, author, social worker, and author of *What Matters: Reflections on Disability, Community, and Love.*

Conversations in the Age of Trump

SCOTT KURASHIGE

The 2016 election of Donald Trump has brought a renewed wave of white nationalism, authoritarianism, and kleptocracy. Long before this, Grace Lee Boggs had been telling us we live in a time of great hope and great danger. Grace saw the danger reach a new height with the state takeover of Detroit by an autocratic emergency manager in 2013. This was, in her view, a product of the "counter-revolution. This is how she described the situation in an August 2013 column:

> With growing unemployment, the crisis in the Mideast, and the decline in this country's global dominance, we have come to the end of the American Dream. The situation reminds me of the 1930s when good Germans, demoralized by their defeat in WWI, unemployment and inflation, followed Hitler into the Holocaust.
>
> These days, in our country, a growing number of white people feel that, as they are becoming the minority and a black man has been elected president, the country is no longer theirs. They are becoming increasingly desperate and dangerous.[1]

Grace did not underestimate the threat of the "counter-revolution." "Its defeat," she wrote, "will take a lot of cooperation, courage, and principled struggle." As always, however, Grace rose to the challenge. She was inspired to see the resistance building all around Detroit, the nation, and the world. "We have just begun to fight," she declared.[2]

It is this spirit—one that Grace, Jimmy, Freddy, and Lyman shared with all those they encountered—that has kept so many of their comrades from wallowing in fear and falling into despair through repeated local, national, and international crises. While we can no longer carry on conversations with them in person, we can carry forward the power of their ideas as we move from resistance to revolution.

Sadly, I only talked with Freddy on two occasions, and I never had a chance to meet Jimmy or Lyman. Thus, my understanding of their theory and practice was conveyed to me largely by Grace. With that caveat in mind, what follows is my sense of how they would carry on a conversation today.

Times like these require clear and sober thinking. I have no doubt Grace would recite her favorite quote from Marx and Engels in *The Communist Manifesto* (1848): "All that is solid melts into air, all that is holy is profaned, and man is at last compelled to face with sober senses his real conditions of life, and his relations with his kind."[3]

As Grace says in the film *American Revolutionary*, "You don't choose the times you live in, but you do choose who you want to be, and you do choose how you want to think."

Marx and Engels responded to a period of tremendous change and uncertainty, when the seemingly unstoppable rise of capitalism upended the traditional norms and ways of life. Now that we have our own monumental and world-changing challenges to face, several lessons from the Boggses and Paines jump to the forefront of my mind.

First, in this time of chaos, fear, and confusion, the most important thing is to Think Dialectically. Trump's election is a sign of a system in crisis. Neoliberalism has destabilized the global capitalist order and the revolts of the left and the right, originating in the 1960s, have opened the door to radical alternatives.

As Jimmy and Grace wrote in *Revolution and Evolution in the Twentieth Century*, we should learn from Hegel that

> progress or development never takes place in a straight line
> or just by quantitative increase or decrease. In other words,
> progressive development is never just evolutionary; it requires
> great and sudden leaps, drastic changes in direction. But neither
> does it take place, as Hegel puts it, "like a shot out of a pistol."
> Maturation through the overcoming of one contradiction after
> another, or what Hegel calls "the labor, patience and suffering of
> the negative" is continually necessary.[4]

Second, to understand changing realities, we should read the eminent historical sociologist Immanuel Wallerstein on the collapse of liberal capitalism, "The Decline of American Power" and "The End of the World as We Know It." When a system is running smoothly, it takes a great amount of force to move it slightly in one direction or the other. But when a system is out of equilibrium, small acts can have profound consequences. This heightens the free will factor. Things that seemed wildly impossible (e.g., the first Black president followed by a president endorsed by the KKK) suddenly become realizable. The world of 2050 will be the world we make: we could create a system more democratic and humane than capitalism, but we could also end up with a system that the other side creates that is even worse.[5]

Third, this is an age of uncertainty—or as Wall Street calls it, "volatility." That is in large measure what makes this a time of both great hope and great danger. We know the danger all too well now. We can't underestimate this danger. When you're dealing with far-right authoritarianism, you have to guard against dogmatism, sectarianism, and ultraleftism. The Boggses and Paines broke with many radicals when they said we must "love America enough to change it."

I want to try to break this down a bit further. When we are organizing a national-democratic majority against creeping fascism, white supremacy, misogyny, and domestic terrorism, we need to reinforce whatever democratic institutions and even symbolism can be found within the American tradition. And we cannot dismiss democracy as a bourgeois creation—we must see democracy as a radical concept and push for grassroots and participatory forms of democracy that actualize democracy's most radical potential. We should, for instance, study Michael Hardt's reading of Jeffersonian democracy and the Declaration of Independence. If Third World movement leaders could find a way to put the Declaration into critical service for their revolutions, then surely we can find a way to connect it with our own people and movements.[6]

We will be playing a ton of defense for the foreseeable future, but we have to make physical and mental space to transcend the mode of opposition. Our movements emanate from the recognition of love as a collective political force. This is not about making nice with Trump voters (although we better be prepared to articulate what Gramsci called a "national-popular" discourse that peels away at least that segment of Trump voters who viewed him negatively and Obama favorably). It's about creating both a vision and a working alternative to the cynicism, scapegoating, and divisiveness that gave rise to Trump.

What we are confronting is not just greedy, lying, power-crazed individuals but also a reactionary movement that Boggses and Paines called the "counter-revolution." Instead of conventional thinking about right versus left or race versus class, they gave us an original way of understanding the primary contradiction shaping our world as economic overdevelopment versus political underdevelopment.

It is necessary but not nearly enough to get the people (Grace came to reject the concept of the "masses") to reject the system, and it should now be clear why. Vulgar materialism and commodification have led to the pursuit of quick fixes ranging from the Wall Street casino economy of the neoliberals to the rising wave of right-wing populism, xenophobic scapegoating, and suicidal oil extraction.

So where is there hope? Thinking dialectically means we must "refuse to admit the authority or permanence of an existing state of reality." We must "be confident that within any particular reality there are internal contradictions which are the basis for negating this reality." We must "constantly seek to find and hold fast the new positive or the new and higher unity which can emerge out of the resolution of those contradictions."[7]

The national-democratic mobilization against fascism, white supremacy, misogyny, and domestic terrorism creates a new urgency, new connections, and new possibilities. But we have also shattered the illusion that just changing presidents can solve our problems. We are forced to explore all the ways to change the world while living in fear of state power.

Part of this work of confronting political underdevelopment means getting more people involved in political organizations from the level of the grass roots to the national party. But it also means reorganizing all aspects of life away from atavism and commodification and toward models of collectivity, sustainability, and solidarity. This is how we engage the multitude in the tasks of building self-reliant parallel structures, sowing the seeds of a new social order, and developing the capacities for self-government in the mode of the Zapatistas. It's what activists in Detroit call visionary organizing in response to the devastation, dispossession, and disenfranchisement, and it's why the lessons of Detroit are critical for the future of us all.

As Grace said in her farewell statement, "A revolution that is based on the people exercising their creativity in the midst of devastation is one of the great historical contributions of humankind."

NOTES

1. Grace Lee Boggs, "In Detroit, We Have Just Begun to Fight," *Common Dreams*, August 18, 2013, http://www.commondreams.org/views/2013/08/18 /detroit-we-have-just-begun-fight.

2. Ibid.

3. Karl Marx and Friedrich Engels, *Manifesto of the Communist Party*, in *The Marx-Engels Reader*, ed. Robert C. Tucker (New York: W. W. Norton, 1978), 476.

4. James and Grace Lee Boggs, *Revolution and Evolution in the Twentieth Century*, 128.

5. Immanuel Wallerstein, *The Decline of American Power: The U.S. in a Chaotic World* (New York: New Press, 2003); Immanuel Wallerstein, *The End of the World as We Know It: Social Science for the Twenty-First Century* (Minneapolis: University of Minnesota Press, 1999). For more on this, see the conversation between Wallerstein and Boggs in the afterword to the paperback edition of Grace Lee Boggs, with Scott Kurashige, *The Next American Revolution*.

6. Thomas Jefferson, *The Declaration of Independence*, ed. Michael Hardt (London: Verso, 2007).

7. James and Grace Lee Boggs, *Revolution and Evolution in the Twentieth Century*, 128–29.

Scott Kurashige is professor of history at the University of California, Los Angeles, author of *The Shifting Grounds of Race: Black and Japanese Americans in the Making of Multiethnic Los Angeles,* and coauthor with Grace Lee Boggs of *The Next American Revolution: Sustainable Activism for the Twenty-First Century.*

A Good Time, and a Pretty Good Conversation
PATRICK CROUCH

On a cold gray winter day, I was browsing the stacks and stacks of used books at one of the great used bookstores in the world: Detroit's John K. King Books. King clearly isn't making a lot of money off this operation. As you enter each section a string hangs down from a fluorescent shop light that you switch on as you enter a section, and switch off when you leave. The place is cold, staff huddle by space heaters by their desks. As I switch on one of these overhead lights, one book catches my eye with stripes down the side and names I know: James and Grace Lee Boggs. I knew the names because the first few nights I've spent in Detroit were in some bunk beds shoved in the back bedroom of Grace and Jimmy's home on Field Street. Let's just say Grace wasn't particularly welcoming, and left me waiting on the front steps for the Boggs Center's director to arrive (she made up for it later with plenty of mornings spent talking in her living room).

I looked at the back cover of the strange group of people: Grace lounging with a huge smile on her face; Lyman looking like he could be sitting on the steps of a Kentucky shack; Freddy caught putting her drink down and coolly holding her cigarette; Jimmy with that intense stare looking off into the distance. It's always Jimmy who holds my attention. I wondered what he was thinking about. He looks like a man with the weight of the world on his mind. With their cigarettes in hand, their drinks by their side, they looked like they knew how to have a good time, and a pretty good conversation. The pages smelled faintly of essential oil, rather than the book dust I was accustomed to. It felt warm and called to me. I paid for the book and took it home where it sat and waited and waited for me.

The book finally made it to the top of the stack. I picked it up, began to read, and was captivated by the style. Most of the time when you're reading a book on philosophy or politics the ideas of the author are presented as concrete, defined, and decided. The author appears to have everything figured out. They provide you with finished, well-thought-out ideas. With *Conversations in Maine* I was struck almost immediately by how many more questions than answers are provided. I also was surprised by how often these questions go unanswered, not because they are rhetorical, but because the authors don't have a definitive answer. While *Conversations in Maine* starts as a conversation among the four authors, the reader is not allowed to be lazy and merely witness this conversation. Because of the constant questioning you are quickly forced to be a part of things, thinking of what your answer would be.

I have had more than one occasion to witness groups of students interacting with Grace for the first time. Similar to *Conversations,* she often spent as much time asking questions as she did answering them, and more often than not her answers were questions as well. These students—perhaps not accustomed to Grace—often saw these questions as rhetorical. But I know they were not for her, and she wasn't looking for folks to offer her an answer she agreed with.

If you wanted to be invited back to have another conversation with Grace the worst thing you could do was agree with her. Often when we talked I would say something she clearly disagreed with and she would get this little glimmer in her eye, the beginning of a smile forming in the corner of her mouth and then lay into me about how I was wrong for not understanding in a dialectical manner. Then ten minutes later she would come back and argue for a position that sounded markedly like the one that I had just put forth and that she had opposed. Grace loved to struggle, and it's clear that all the authors loved to struggle though deep, difficult, hairy ideas. Oftentimes we want to just come up with an answer, something workable. But *Conversations* pushes us to push on to struggle through those difficult questions.

Conversations takes place over years, and you can witness growth and change as the authors return to their lives and come back. From time to time they reference their own previous works and point out their own former ignorance and how much they have learned. There is growth, there is maturity, there is pragmatism, there is compromise, contradiction, and acceptance in *Conversations.* The authors also put forth some unpopular ideas, questioning many ideas that I see as accepted truths in activist circles. *Conversations* pushes you to ask the unpopular, speak the unspeakable, and know that this will help you to grow. This isn't just a practice for the sake of questioning, but for growing, testing, and establishing the validity of ideas. To take ideas whole without nurturing a relationship with them is to not truly own the ideas as your own. One of the great lessons I have taken from *Conversations* is the need for growth, for being open to new ideas, to listen to those whose views I oppose, to try to understand and see if there is an underlying value I couldn't see before. Often in conversations I see others coming to conclusions immediately. I find myself saying: "I want to wait and see, I want to learn more, I want to understand, I'd like to hear their view." This can be very unpopular as most folks just want you to agree with them.

Conversations may be dominated by questions, but it is not without some major ideas. The one that I find myself coming back to over and over again—an idea that Grace put forth over and over again—is the idea of growing one's soul—that we can't just change systems or nations, we have to change people. For me this is the most important part about *Conversations,* the focus on people and their growth as a part of systems change. It's not enough to have a political revolution without a revolution of who we are as people.

This, more than anything else about *Conversations,* has shaped me—realizing that my growth is part of revolutionary action and that it's not self-indulgent to focus on one's self and one's growth. It's not just about the physical work that we do, those things that can be outwardly measured, but also those that can't. *Conversations* has made me slow down, be more sensitive, listen a little more deeply, notice that which is subtle. It has grown me as human, and maybe even grown my soul, just a little.

Patrick Crouch farms with Earthworks Urban Farm and serves on the board of the James and Grace Lee Boggs School, both in Detroit.

The Power of Words
TAWANA "HONEYCOMB" PETTY

My dad used to talk to me until I fell asleep at night. He passed away in 1985, but I can still recall many of our conversations. My mother let me spend hours on the phone with him the evening he passed, because I knew in my gut he wouldn't wake up the next morning. I still find myself trying to reconcile how I knew my father would die that evening. I was only nine years old at the time.

I think my father's attentiveness to nearly every detail in my life, no matter how insignificant, is one of the many reasons I consistently fell in love with men who paid attention to what I had to say. Conversations have held a key to my heart for almost as long as I can remember having thoughts. There is something magical about the reciprocity of ideas that sends a spark into my psyche, illuminating my spirit.

I have always been a talker. When I was growing up, my obsession with words served to be both a gift and a curse. I was often teased in elementary school for talking too much, and this baffled me as a child because I always felt I hadn't said enough. I had so many ideas swirling through my head, and what seemed like a shortage of outlets to express them. I believe this is one of the reasons I leaned on poetry at such a young age. Writing poetry afforded me an opportunity to start a conversation with the world. Performing poetry afforded the world an opportunity to respond. I've been having this dialogue with the world since I was seven.

When I was nineteen years old, I found out I was pregnant with my son, Tyree. It was the most beautifully terrifying revelation I had ever experienced. I was a young mother who had no clue what to do next. The only thing I knew for certain was that I needed to let my baby know that he would always have someone to talk to—someone in his life who would listen to what he had to say. I wanted Tyree to know the power of conversation. I never wanted him to feel invisible. So, I immediately began speaking to my belly, and continued conversations with my son for the duration of my pregnancy.

I became Tyree's listening post and nurtured his love for conversation. He would grow up to become a national public debate champion in high school and a college student preparing to graduate and head to law school. Love of conversation can take on many forms.

These days, I consider myself a visionary organizer who teaches poetry as visionary resistance. I teach young people that their words matter—that they need to use their words in ways that leave places better than when they entered them, or at least don't make them worse. I teach young people the importance of teamwork in conversation. For years, we've been taught that "sticks and stones may break my bones, but words will never hurt me." I learned very early on that this idiom was not only false, but negligent. Words hold tremendous power and we have a responsibility to use our power to project a better society.

Grace and Jimmy Boggs knew the importance of words, and the power of conversation. This movement moment requires that we all use our voices to encourage transformation and create the world we wish to live in.

Tawana "Honeycomb" Petty is a social justice organizer, youth advocate, poet, and the author of *Introducing Honeycomb, Coming Out My Box,* and *Petty Propolis Reader: My Personal and Political Evolution.*

Organizing around the Human Desire to Grow
MATTHEW BIRKHOLD

Within hours of the 2007 acquittal of the police officers who murdered Sean Bell I was at a rally in Queens, New York, to "demand justice." Speaker after speaker spoke to the anger we all felt because police were killing black people with impunity. One speaker in particular forever changed my outlook on organizing. Although I could not fully articulate the intellectual transformation and transformation in my practice that would come, every time I read *Conversations in Maine*, I am given a language that articulates the journey I began that afternoon in Queens.

There were probably somewhere near a hundred people at this rally and one of the speakers began to chastise those of us who were in attendance because there were too few of us there. A comrade turned to me and said, "Wouldn't it be helpful if there were some therapists here?" We engaged a few people from the socialist parties and organizations that are at every rally in New York and when people began to march spontaneously down Queens Boulevard, we went back to Brooklyn. Sitting on the F train, I remember thinking, "There has to be a better way of doing this. Despite showing up to a rally, I was just chastised because there were not more people there and saw self-proclaimed revolutionaries try to take advantage of a family's tragedy to recruit new members. This is not the kind of organizing that will create a revolution. This is not even the kind of organizing that will attract people."

I began to imagine what a different kind of organizing might look like. In conversations I began to ask, "What kind of movement are we even capable of building if all we're doing is allowing anger to guide us?" "What kind of healing do we have to do in order to build a movement that feels loving?" "What kind of healing do I have to do to treat the people in my life better?"

These were profound discussions from which I learned a great deal. *Conversations in Maine* then gave me a language and framework to further think through these discussions. There I found the following passage:

We are trying to discover how to get people to understand why they are miserable. One way we will *not* achieve this is by telling people how miserable they are. Somehow or other, we must begin to help people understand that they are capable of envisaging another way to live. Not that we are able to give them this other way. But to show them they are capable of envisaging another way to live—if only as a feeling of lack—and that is the main reason why they are so miserable.[1]

As an organizer who didn't expect police to be found guilty and was continuously frustrated by people who could not imagine anything beyond a cop watch, I found this passage incredibly meaningful because it provided me with a new way to think about what I was doing.

Rather than beat people in the head with arguments that community conflict resolution teams were necessary because police brutality would continue until the conditions that justify the need for police were eliminated, this passage freed me to understand that revolution was about people's insides as much as it was about material reality. Instead of trying to convince people of my point, if I spent more time encouraging people to imagine the most ideal possible future for their neighborhood, and then ask them how we might get there, they would come up with ideas for block-wide assemblies and community conflict resolution teams on their own.

Conversation in Maine also taught me that if I believed people wanted to develop into their full selves and wanted to grow, my job as an organizer was to organize around the human desire to grow; to organize around the human spirit. Revolution was no longer about pitting social forces against one another to sharpen contradictions. Although I still believe this sharpening of contradictions is important, revolutionists must understand that their job is to organize the energy that emerges from that process into a vision and practices for vastly different kinds of communities. The Boggses and Paines demonstrated this task with a question:

What is it that John D. Rockefeller III (who wrote "The Second American Revolution") and Joe Doakes who drives a bus *both* need? Suppose that instead of using a phrase like "psychic security," we used one like "living purposefully."[2]

Then they wrote:

> Psyches don't live on bread. It is not a question of physical
> well-being. We are talking about the need of people for spiritual
> relationships with themselves, with others, with their surround-
> ings. You can't tackle this by writing a *Das Kapital.* We need
> something else—but what it is we don't know.[3]

Rather than using facts to try and convince people that capitalism
is evil, today I often ask people, "What impact do you think living
under an economic system in which you are subject to starvation
and homelessness without a job means for your sense of self and how
much you think you matter?" The answers I get to this question usually demonstrate to me that what John D. Rockefeller and Joe Doakes
have in common is a desire to grow; to become their full selves. The
answers also demonstrate that people have an intuitive understanding
that capitalism is the reason why it is so difficult to be true to one's self
because they have seen the spiritual relationships we need to become
who we really are destroyed by economic relationships.

Today I consider my work a kind of organizing around the
human spirit's desire to grow and develop. I truly believe Martin Luther King's proclamation that if we were to undergo a radical revolution of values we would look at exploitation, declare it unjust, and take
action to remedy the situation. In *Conversations in Maine,* I was given
access to a language that allowed me to explore what connections
might exist between creating a radical revolution of values and the
ways in which people become committed to becoming the full selves
that we have allowed capitalism, racism, and sexism to beat out of us.

NOTES

1. See the chapter in this volume titled "Projections, Not Rejections."
2. Ibid.
3. Ibid.

Matthew Birkhold is a founder of Visionary Organizing Lab in
Brooklyn, New York.

Conversations on, in, and as Education
EMMA FIALKA-FELDMAN

I was fortunate to be raised in a family where conversations about ourselves, the current state of world affairs, and a history of our nation dominated our kitchen table talks. Articles were left on tables and in piles for my brother and me to read—articles that gave context and history to seemingly "random" moments in the world. Asking questions became as natural as breathing. Attending group conversations was as important, if not more important, than protests and rallies. Visiting Grace on Sunday afternoons to get the newest article she had written was commonplace. August family vacations included a weeklong stint on Sutton Island where I was surrounded by a network of activist family members who gathered to talk, eat, laugh, shout (because we all know arguing to be essential to conversations!), and watch sunsets where colors magically transformed blue skies over the Atlantic Ocean with a palette of colors reminding us all that transformation is both political and spiritual.

My family surrounded me with people who would broaden my understanding of what it means to be human and what it means to make the world a better place. People were always giving me hope for a more beautiful, more human world, not just because of conversations but because of the work they immersed themselves in. They never made conversations or the political "work" easy—but they definitely made the journey enticing, engaging, inclusive, and beautiful, building a world where we would all be able to be more human, human beings.

As I started a master's program in elementary education in Boston, I quickly found a community of educators—far from my family in Michigan—who connected to these values of community, justice, reflection, and conversation. I knew I was joining a profession where burnout was high and where "the systems" of education, racism, and capitalism left little opportunity to provide imagination in the classroom. I also knew, gratefully, of many people who were providing imagination to the roles of teachers, schools, and students. As I was starting my teaching career in 2013, the James and Grace Lee Boggs

School was opening up in Detroit with a mission to "nurture creative, critical thinkers who contribute to the well-being of their communities." Allied Media Projects, also inspired by the ideas of Grace and Jimmy Boggs, was continuing to do transformative work in thinking about the ways arts, media, technology, and justice intersect to transform communities.

I was holding both realities: the reality of despair in education, and the reality of hope in education. I knew the only way I'd make it was if I had a community, just as my parents have beautifully raised me to believe. As the master's program came to an end I knew I needed to continue our work professionally and politically together. So, on a whim in the midst of final course work, teaching lessons, and exhaustion from student teaching in the "system" of public education, where I felt despair suffocating any hope I had for teaching, I sent an email inviting this new group of educators to spend a few days on Sutton Island in August before we jumped into teaching in the Boston Public Schools as first-year teachers. I shared a bit about Grace, Jimmy, and the history of "Conversations in Maine." I asked if they'd be open to reading some articles about education—articles that would continue to ground us in feeling hopeful; articles that would stretch our imaginations, as we became teachers. Thankfully, they agreed.

Before our first year of teaching in 2013, we drove to Sutton Island with two packed cars of groceries, a hefty packet of reading materials (including sections from *Conversations in Maine*; Jimmy Boggs's speech "The Next Development in Education"; Julia Putnam's article "Another Education Is Happening"; and many others), and the growing anxiety of starting out. For four days, we talked, we ate, we laughed, we hiked around the island, we shared our anxieties, and we grounded ourselves in the history, recognizing how much had and had not changed since *Conversations in Maine* was published in 1978. *Conversations* honors the importance of a variety of voices, perspectives, and personal histories as Freddy, Grace, Jimmy, and Lyman each bring their whole selves into the fold.

Since that first trip, our conversations have grown. We continue to drive to Sutton Island each year—this past summer (2017) was the fifth summer of *our* "Conversations in Maine." Over these years we have evolved professionally, politically, spiritually, and personally. Our readings and conversations have changed as our understanding of our country has changed. We've read about mindfulness in teaching as we try to better understand how to take care of ourselves in this work. We've read about climate change, disability justice, inclusive education, the Black Lives Matter movement, the Moral Mondays movement with William Barber, and New Work and emerging economies as we deepened our understanding of how schools intersect with all facets of our communities. Slowly our conversations have also moved away from being directly about the classroom, and are now more about how we evolve and grow to build a more just world.

Conversations in Maine—both the book, and the practice that my educator-friends engage in—remind me that conversations are essential to transformation. Our ideas must evolve for our world to change. Direct action, protests, policy changes, and marches are part of creating a new world. Unless our ideas evolve, however, we are left with much of the same. Conversations must continue. Talking at the dinner table, passing literature and new articles to our neighbors, expanding our circles so that our ideas are challenged, and making time to sift over, argue, and question with our friends are essential to making a world that makes us more human, human beings.

Emma Fialka-Feldman is a Boston public school elementary teacher.

A Spot in the River
ADRIENNE MAREE BROWN

It had to be Hendrix, the gin. When five o'clock rolled around and we gathered in the living room, the gin and tonics were central. Grace was central. Not like a planet we were orbiting around, more like a spot in the river we were all flowing through, being reshaped by.

Grace taught me so many things, but I keep coming back to the experience of sitting in Detroit and Maine in conversations that opened my mind, examined what I believed and wondered, weaving myself with other selves. And Maine was so special.

Being on that tiny magical island was not all about being in conversation—it was about resting deeply, disconnecting from the busy world, going on long walks through fairy-infested forests, jumping in bracing water and drying off in the sun, taking empty buckets down to the water's edge and returning with buckets full of mussels for dinner. It was about deepening relationships with people I work with and love but rarely got to breathe and play with.

And then, inside all of that unwinding and slowing down, there was room for profound depth and being vulnerable, speaking in questions and touching the edges of what we feel certain about. And it was not an exceptional time! It was a practice Grace was in for so much of her life, an iteration she was in with her beloved Jimmy, with her best friends and comrades and students. She kept going back. They, we, kept and keep going back.

We learned that a different understanding was possible when we put ourselves in closer relationship with nature, with beauty, with breath and space and time. We learned that we need such spaces in order to compost the world into solutions we can experiment with and practice.

Maine is part of the pathway for me understanding Emergent Strategy as something our movements could practice. On that island, we were putting our attention on our relationships with earth, with ourselves, and with each other—building relationships that can withstand the pressure that comes from unveiling the world and seeking liberation, from taking on the responsibility of shaping the present and the future.

I recommend everyone find their version of an island in Maine, a place to find quiet and togetherness, to walk edges together. I recommend everyone find a teacher who is willing to be the shore as you flow toward justice.

adrienne maree brown is a facilitator for social justice and black liberation living in Detroit. She is the author of *Emergent Strategy: Shaping Change, Changing Worlds* and coeditor of *Octavia's Brood: Science Fiction from Social Justice Movements.*

Bibliography

Ardrey, Robert. *The Social Contract.* New York: Atheneum, 1970.

Arendt, Hannah. *The Human Condition.* Chicago: University of Chicago Press, 1958.

Bateson, Gregory. *Steps to an Ecology of Mind.* New York: Ballantine Books, 1972.

Binyon, Lawrence. *Flight from the Dragon.* London: J. Murray, 1911.

Bookchin, Murray. *Limits of the City.* New York: Harper & Row, 1974.

Bronowski, J. *The Ascent of Man.* Boston: Little, Brown, 1973.

Cloward, Richard, and Frances Piven. *Regulating the Poor.* New York: Pantheon Books, 1971.

Darwin, Charles. *The Origin of the Species by Means of Natural Selection.* Introduction by Sir Julian Huxley. New York: New American Library, 1958.

Davis, Nuel P. *Lawrence and Oppenheimer.* New York: Simon & Schuster, 1968.

Ellul, Jacques. *The Political Illusion.* New York: Knopf, 1967.

Engels, Friedrich. *Origin of the Family, Private Property and the State.* New York: International Publishers, 1972.

Farb, Peter. *Man's Rise to Civilization.* New York: Dutton, 1968.

Fromm, Erich. *You Shall Be as Gods.* New York: Holt, Rinehart & Winston, 1966.

Goldberg, Maxwell H., ed. *Needles, Burrs and Bibliographies.* State College: Pennsylvania State University, 1969.

Goodman, Paul. *Growing Up Absurd.* New York: Random House, 1960.

Goodwin, Richard. *The American Condition.* Garden City, N.Y.: Doubleday, 1974.

Gough, Kathleen. *The Decline of the State and the Coming of World Society.* Detroit: Correspondence pamphlet, 1961.

Han Suyin. *Asia Today.* Montreal: McGill-Queen's University Press, 1969.

Hegel, Georg W. F. *Phenomenology of Mind.* New York: Macmillan, 1931.

Heggen, Thomas. *Mister Roberts.* New York: Random House, 1948.

Huxley, Sir Julian. *Essays of a Humanist.* New York: Harper & Row, 1964.

James, C. L. R. *Mariners, Renegades and Castaways.* New York, 1953.

———. *World Revolution, 1917–1936.* New York: Pioneer, 1937.

Jung, Carl. *Man and His Symbols.* Garden City, N.Y.: Doubleday, 1964.

Lee, Grace C., Pierre Chaulieu, and J. R. Johnson. *Facing Reality.* Detroit: Correspondence, 1958.

Leggett, John. *Ross and Tom: Two American Tragedies.* New York: Simon & Schuster, 1974.

Lessing, Doris. *Summer Before the Dark.* New York: Knopf, 1973.

Lewis, John Wilson. *Leadership in Communist China.* Ithaca, N.Y.: Cornell University Press, 1963.

Lewis, Sinclair. *Main Street.* New York: Harcourt Press, 1950.

Lockridge, Ross. *Raintree County.* Boston: Houghton Mifflin, 1948.

Malraux, Andre. *Voices of Silence.* London: Secker & Warburg, 1958.

Mao Tsetung. *Selected Readings.* Peking: Foreign Language Press, 1971.

Marx, Karl. *Capital.* Chicago: Charles Kerr, 1912.

———. *Economic and Philosophic Manuscripts of 1844.* Moscow: Foreign Language Publishing House, 1961.

Marx, Karl, and Friedrich Engels. *The German Ideology.* New York: International Publishers, 1939.

May, Rollo. *Love and Will.* New York: W. W. Norton, 1969.

McLellan, David. *Karl Marx.* New York: Viking Press, 1975.

Menninger, Karl Augustus. *Whatever Became of Sin?* New York: Hawthorn Books, 1973.

Mezzrow, Milton. *Really the Blues.* New York: Random House, 1946.

Mumford, Lewis. *The City in History.* New York: Harcourt Brace and World, 1961.

———. *The Myth of the Machine.* New York: Harcourt Brace and World, 1970.

Myrdal, Jan. *Confessions of a Disloyal European.* New York: Pantheon Books, 1968.

Needham, Joseph. *The Past in China's Present.* New York: Far East Reporter pamphlet.

Nelson, Truman. *The Sin of the Prophet.* Boston: Little, Brown, 1952.

Revel, Jean-François. *Without Marx or Jesus: The New American Revolution Has Begun.* Garden City, N.Y.: Doubleday, 1971.

Richman, Barry. *Industrial Society in Communist China.* New York: Random House, 1969.

Riencourt, Amaury de. *The Soul of China.* New York: Coward-McCann, 1958.

Rockefeller, John D., III. *The Second American Revolution: Some Personal Observations.* New York: Harper & Row, 1973.

Schumacher, E. F. *Small Is Beautiful.* New York: Harper & Row, 1973.

Slater, Philip. *Earthwalk.* Garden City, N.Y.: Anchor Press, 1974.

Teilhard de Chardin, Pierre. *Letter to Two Friends, 1926–1952.* New York: New American Library, 1968.

———. *The Phenomenon of Man.* New York: Harper, 1959.

Tocqueville, Alexis de. *Democracy in America.* New York: Knopf, 1945.

Tressell, Robert. *The Ragged Trousered Philanthropists.* London: Lawrence & Wishart, 1971.

Updike, John. *Rabbit Run.* New York: Knopf, 1945.

Wheelis, Allen. *The Quest for Identity.* New York: W. W. Norton, 1958.

Whyte, Lancelot Law. *Focus and Diversions.* London: Cresset Press, 1963.

———. *The Next Development in Man.* New York: Henry Holt, 1948.

Willison, George F. *Saints and Strangers.* New York: Reynal & Hitchcock, 1945.

James Boggs (1919–1993) was an American political activist, autoworker, and the author of numerous books, including *The American Revolution: Pages from a Negro Worker's Notebook.*

Grace Lee Boggs (1915–2015) was a first-generation Chinese American author, philosopher, and social activist. She wrote *Living for Change: An Autobiography* (Minnesota, 1998 and 2016) and was the subject of the film *American Revolutionary: The Evolution of Grace Lee Boggs.*

Lyman Paine (1901–1978) was an architect and activist.

Freddy Paine (1912–1999) was an activist.

Michael Doan is assistant professor of philosophy at Eastern Michigan University.

Richard Feldman is a community and labor activist, board member of the James and Grace Lee Boggs Center to Nurture Community Leadership, and coeditor of *End of the Line: Autoworkers and the American Dream.*

Shea Howell is professor in the Department of Communication and Journalism at Oakland University.

Stephen Ward is associate professor of Afroamerican and African studies at the University of Michigan and editor of *The Next American Revolution: A James Boggs Reader.*